Living Banaras

SUNY Series in Hindu Studies

Wendy Doniger, Editor

Living Banaras

Hindu Religion in Cultural Context

Edited by
Bradley R. Hertel
and Cynthia Ann Humes

State University of New York Press

Published by
State University of New York Press, Albany

© 1993 State University of New York

For information, address State University of New York Press,
State University Plaza, Albany, N.Y. 12246

Production by M. R. Mulholland
Marketing by Fran Keneston

Library of Congress Cataloging-in-Publication Data

Living Banaras : Hindu religion in cultural context / edited by
    Bradley R. Hertel and Cynthia Ann Humes.
        p.   cm. — (SUNY series in Hindu studies)
    Includes bibliographical references and index.
    ISBN 0-7914-1331-4 (alk. paper). — ISBN 0-7914-1332-2 (pbk. :
alk. paper)
        1. Hinduism—India—Vārānasi.   2. Vārānasi (India)—Religious life
and customs.   I. Hertel, Bradley R., 1943–   . II. Humes, Cynthia
Ann, 1958–   . III. Series.
BL1153.7.V36L58   1993
294.5′3′09542—dc20   92-10803
                                                                         CIP

10 9 8 7 6 5 4 3 2 1

Contents

Illustrations   vii

Acknowledgments   xi

Introduction   1
Bradley R. Hertel and Cynthia Ann Humes

1. Crossing the Water: Pilgrimage, Movement, and
Environmental Scenography of the *Ramlila* of Ramnagar   19
Richard Schechner

2. Staring at Frames Till They Turn into Loops: An Excursion
through Some Worlds of Tulsidas   73
Linda Hess

3. What's Taking Place: Neighborhood *Ramlilas* in Banaras   103
Thomas Parkhill

4. Hanuman and the Moral Physique of the Banarsi Wrestler   127
Joseph S. Alter

5. Religious Division and the Mythology of the Past   145
Mary Searle-Chatterjee

6. The Monastic Structure of Banarsi Dandi Sadhus   159
Dana W. Sawyer

7. The Goddess of the Vindhyas in Banaras   181
Cynthia Ann Humes

8. Lolark Kund: Sun and Shiva Worship in the City of Light   205
Ratnesh K. Pathak and Cynthia Ann Humes

9. Language Choice, Religion, and Identity in the Banarsi
Community   245
Beth Simon

Appendices   269
Cynthia Ann Humes

    A. The Thirty-One-Day Program of the Ramnagar *Ramlila*   269

    B. An Encapsulation of the *Ramcharitmanas* by Tulsidas   272

    C. Major Characters of the *Ramayana*   278

    D. General Glossary   283

Bibliography   297

Contributors   309

Index   313

Illustrations

1.1.   Linear representation of the main events portrayed during the month-long cycle of the Ramnagar *Ramlila.*   25

1.2.   Circular representation of the main events portrayed during the month-long cycle of the Ramnagar *Ramlila.*   26

1.3.   Scale map of Ramnagar showing *Ramlila* centers and connecting roads and paths as they were in 1978.   27

1.4.   1946 program-map of the "Sri Ram Lila Ground" at Ramnagar. The program as map shows how important space, journey, and pilgrimage are to the performance. Photo courtesy of the Maharaja of Banaras.   28

1.5.   Vishnu and Lakshmi watch the drama from a Rambag tower. The same boys who are Ram and Sita are also Vishnu and Lakshmi, the "Originals" of whom Ram and Sita are incarnations. Photo, Richard Schechner, 1978.   30

1.6.   Many in the audience follow Ram, Sita, and Lakshman from town to countryside as they begin their exile. Photo, Richard Schechner, 1978.   31

1.7.   Chitrakut, old photo, c. 1925. Photo courtesy of the Maharaja of Banaras.   33

1.8.   Chirakut, 1978. Note how little the environment has changed over five decades. Photo, Richard Schechner.   34

1.9.   Bad weather. The performance is sometimes postponed because of inclement weather. Photo, Richard Schechner, 1978.   36

1.10.   Crowded Lanka on Dashahara with Ravana's effigy in view. Photo, Richard Schechner, 1978.   38

1.11.   Ravana's effigy ablaze atop his fort on Dashahara night. Photo, Richard Schechner, 1978.   39

1.12.   The Dashahara procession moving through a courtyard in the Fort as the maharaja sets out for Lanka. Photo, Richard Schechner, 1976.   40

1.13.   Dashahara as seen by James Prinsep, 1830. It seems as if there were more demons, more elephants—more theatrical grandeur. Photo courtesy of the Maharaja of Banaras.   42

1.14. The maharaja atop his elephant viewing a *lila* (play) in Ayodhya as it appears early in the cycle before Ram's exile. Photo, Richard Schechner, 1978.   43

1.15. The Fort—the maharaja's palace in Ramnagar—as seen while rowing across the Ganga. Photo, Richard Schechner, 1978.   45

1.16. A huge crowd waiting to cross the Ganges by public ferry to reach Ramnagar. Photo, Martin Karcher, 1978.   54

1.17. A son carrying his mother in a basket so that she can visit holy pilgrimage places throughout India. Photo, Richard Schechner, 1978.   56

1.18. Bharat Milap—literally the "meeting with Bharat," but which depicts the reunion of Ram and Lakshman with their brothers Bharat and Shatrughna—performed on a brightly lit square stage erected at the intersection of Ramnagar's two main streets. Photo, Richard Schechner, 1978.   58

1.19. The *jhanki* (frozen moment) pose of *arati* (light ceremony) that closes each *lila*. Photo, Richard Schechner, 1978.   60

1.20. A sadhu said to be 150 years old in 1978. He died in the mid-1980s. Photo, Richard Schechner.   62

1.21. Chitrakut-Rambag in winter: cows grazing, Ram's world resting. Photo, Richard Schechner.   68

2.1.   The four *Ramcharitmanas* dialogues with the *Manas* lake as the center. (Lutgendorf, 1991:25)   76

2.2.   The four *Ramcharitmanas* dialogues with the *Manas* lake as the largest container.   77

3.1.   The *svarup* (human representation of the diety) of Ram during bow *lila* (play) at the Lallapur neighborhood *Ramlila* of Varanasi.   105

3.2.   *Svarups* of Ram and Sita at the Lallapur *Ramlila*.   106

4.1.   A group of wrestlers at the Akhara Bara Ganesha in Banaras.   130

4.2.   *Jor* (sparring) at Kedarnath Akhara in Banaras District.   133

6.1.   Swami Shri Ram Ashrama at Pushkara Math with *danda* (staff) covered to protect it from pollution.   160

6.2.   Swami Shivananda Saraswati at Dharma Sangh, the largest Karpati *math* (monastery) in Banaras.   161

6.3.   Five Dandi *swamis* (religious preceptors) at Ananta Vijna Math.   168

6.4.   Four Dandis at Bhuma Adhyatma Pith. Note that three hold their *dandas* (staffs) uncovered.   169

8.1.   The enormous crowds of devotees at Lolark Kund during
        Lolark Chath Mela.   213
8.2.   A view of Lolark Kund on a normal day without any
        pilgrims. The waters of the *kund* are connected to the
        adjacent well via the long split in the wall of the *kund* on
        the right side. This photo also provides an aerial view of
        the small temple to Surya and Ganesh which is inside
        the square building pictured on the lower left-hand side. 214
8.3.   The temple to Surya and Ganesh from water level. This
        temple often serves as a platform on which the *panda*
        (pilgrimage priest) or *Karinda* (assistant) sits.   216
8.4.   A couple offering *karahiya* (cooked food) to Lord Shiva
        at the Lolarkeshvara Temple with the help of a *panda*
        (priest).   218
8.5.   *Karindas* (assistants) Madan Dube and Vijay Kumar Mishra
        waiting for customers on a normal day beneath the pipal
        tree. In the background, devotees prepare *karahiya*
        (cooked food).   222
8.6.   Fruit and vegetable offerings being removed from Lolark
        Kund by the *Mallah* (boatperson) after the festival.   224
8.7.   Women breaking each other's bangles at Lolark Kund in
        preparation for their marriage to Lolarkeshvara.   227
8.8.   *Mundan* (ritual tonsure) being performed by a *Nau* (barber)
        at Lolark Kund.   229
8.9.   The brass bust of Shiva placed over a *lingam* (phallic
        symbol) on top of the well adjacent to Lolark Kund.   236
8.10.   Image of Lolark Mayee on the pipal tree several feet from
        the Lolarkeshvara Temple surrounded by crowds of
        devotees.   237

Acknowledgments

We are grateful to all of the many people who contributed in a wide variety of ways to make this book possible. We are especially grateful to the people of Banaras who generously shared their experiences and insights. Without their trust, sincerity, patience, and cooperation, the essays of this volume could not have been written. The staff at SUNY Press have been immensely helpful at all stages of this lengthy project. William Eastman provided steadfast support and encouragement from the time of the inception of the project through completion of the first draft. Rosalie Robertson provided great support in working closely with us while the manuscript was being reviewed and revised. More recently, Megeen Mulholland has overseen the many details of the final preparation of the manuscript. We want to express our gratitude to these individuals and to Susan Zorn, the copy editor, for their conscientious effort and close attention to detail. We want to thank the staffs of both Virginia Polytechnic Institute and State University and Claremont McKenna College for helping with seemingly insolvable computer problems, frequent faxing, preparation of the photographs, and—most importantly—coping with the many rounds of revising the manuscript. Special thanks are due Phyllis Light, secretary of the VPI sociology department, for her considerable effort especially during the early rounds of manuscript preparation. We also want to thank James Chriss and Ruan Hoe, graduate students in sociology at VPI, for their help with later revisions. Pam Hawkes of Claremont McKenna provided consistent assistance with computer problems with boundless humor and cheer. Eureka Easterly, a Claremont McKenna College student, generated elegant computer maps of the geography of Ramlila and its representations from Richard Schechner's line drawings. We also would like to thank our spouses and other family members for their constant support and understanding. Finally, to end at the beginning, we wish to thank our mentors Joseph W. Elder and Sheldon Pollock for pointing us down the paths that fortuitously resulted in this project.

Introduction

Bradley R. Hertel and Cynthia Ann Humes

"If any Hindu were asked offhand which city he regarded as the holiest in India, he would probably hesitate no less in naming Varanasi than the Muslim would in naming Mecca."

—Agehananda Bharati (1970:107)

Banaras is said to be such a great pilgrimage place that all 330 million Hindu deities have chosen to dwell there. The steady stream of pilgrims underscores its preeminence for Hinduism and makes clear that every day is a special day in Banaras. Its centrality, however, rests on neither its pilgrims nor its deities but instead is of a primordial nature predating even the gods themselves. The place itself is what renders the city sacred; the temples and illustrious inhabitants serve merely to mark the sanctity of the place. Known also as Varanasi, as Kashi ("The City of Light"), and as Avimukta ("The Never Forsaken"),[1] Banaras holds many special meanings to residents and visitors alike. As Kashi, the city is believed to glow with a divine brilliance that rivals the sun; beautiful and holy, it is often personified as a lovely shimmering goddess. The city is Avimukta, for emotional and devotional attachment to it is "never abandoned" by either its divine or human devotees. It is commonplace for Hindus throughout India to identify with the village or town of their birth even decades after moving away. Displaced Banarsis are especially inclined to see themselves as permanent residents of their former community. The special bonding power of Banaras can be so strong that even after a single visit a pilgrim may identify with the city and never feel fully settled anywhere else.

In recent years a number of India's sacred cities have been the focus of studies by scholars interested in pilgrimage and, more generally, sacred space. Illustrative of this by now large body of literature are the studies of Bhubaneswar (Seymour, 1980), Gaya (Vidyarthi, 1961), Vrindavan (Brooks, 1989), and three sites in West Bengal (Morinis, 1984). Reflecting the great geographic range, the diversity of goals, and the respect shown this city by her pilgrims, Banaras has attracted the attention of many scholars, including Eck (1982), who has provided an in-depth historical overview of Hinduism in Kashi; Saraswati (1975), who briefly summarized the city's diversity of religious traditions and overseers of religious practices; and Vidyarthi, Saraswati, and Jha (1979), who enumerated the great numbers of individual sacred sites in Banaras and who also reported on the caste and regional backgrounds of priests and pilgrims. Other scholars, while taking a pan-Indian approach in their studies of pilgrimage sites, have acknowledged Varanasi as having special importance (Bharati, 1970; Bhardwaj, 1973). Still others have focused on a prominent aspect of Hindu practice in Banaras; for example, Sinha and Saraswati (1978) reported on the ascetics of Varanasi, and Parry (1980, 1981) detailed the death rituals performed at the sacred burning *ghats* (riverbanks), for which Varanasi is well known even among Western laymen with only a few mental images of India. More recently, the contributors to Freitag's (1989a) edited volume have provided insightful glimpses into many of the innumerable facets of Hindu worship and its relation to power in Varanasi.

Banaras has attracted so much attention among scholars in part because Hindus consider the city to be a microcosm of all of Hindu Bharat, sacred "India." Banaras is believed to contain within its boundaries not only each of the four *dhams*, or principal sacred sites of the cardinal directions, but in principle every major sacred site of the Hindu landscape; shrines and temples named for the distant sites which they represent have been built in the architectural style of those regions. In addition to seeking out revered sites of pan-Indian importance, pilgrims from many parts of the country enjoy the opportunity of visiting temples maintained by priests from their home state and linguistic community (Vidyarthi, Saraswati, and Jha, 1979:38). These regional attachments to Banaras are reciprocated by references to Banaras in temples throughout India; Bharati (1970:107) illustrates these ties with the example of a temple in Kanchipuram, Tamil Nadu, in which worshipers crawl through a very narrow passage to symbolically represent the effort required to acquire the merit earned from visiting Banaras. In West Bengal several Shaivite pilgrimage sites are claimed to be "mythically identical with Benares" by pilgrims who "seek to validate the reputation of greatness of their places of pilgrimage by associating their sacred centres with the greatest of the *jyotirliṅgas* ["lingas of light"] and *svayambhuvalingas* [lingas believed to have appeared by themselves in the primordial past]" (Morinis, 1984: 31–32). Banaras is respected as central to, and as the archetypical representative of, Hindu Place. It is isomorphic with the Hindu world; it contains and represents all that is "Hindu." By visiting Banaras pilgrims may have *darshan* (a sacred glimpse) of all sites sacred to Hindus.

Hindus come to Banaras for the full range of rituals associated with the daily, annual, and life cycles. Death rituals in particular are prominent in the city. Its cremation ghats, the Manikarnika and Harishchandra, are required stops for pilgrims and tourists alike. Many elderly Hindus flock to the city in order to die at special hospices where it is believed they will receive the blessing conferred by Lord Shiva on the souls of all who die within the sacred boundaries of his city. Indeed, Banaras is often described as an expansive cremation ground overseen by the great ascetic god Shiva.

But Banaras is much more than a preferred place for Hindus to die. With its profusion of *kunds* (sacred ponds) and three rivers, Banaras is permeated by holy, life-giving waters. It is a special place for the living who pour into the city to live life in the most sacred setting and manner possible. The day begins for many Banarsi Hindus at the numerous bathing ghats along the sacred Ganges River, which attract thousands of visiting pilgrims in addition to pious residents even on nonfestival days. Bathing in the Ganges at Varanasi is believed to be especially purifying and auspicious, in part because the waters touch the holy banks of the refulgent city, situated at its unusual juncture where the Ganga winds northward before resuming its easterly course.

Many of the most common religious activities at Banaras, especially Brahminical traditions modeled according to Sanskrit texts, have been discussed elsewhere. Although these traditions are unquestionably important, Hindu religion is much more than what is recorded in Sanskrit texts and overseen by the Brahmin priesthood. Many nonBrahminical, non-Sanskritic traditions have long been and continue to be of considerable importance to their participants without being accorded scholarly recognition as "mainstream." The point is that in Hindu society outward displays of ritual practice vary widely even within a rather narrowly delimited setting; there are many streams of Hinduism, each with its distinctive characteristics and each in its own way a significant part of the whole.

Attempts to arrive at a holistic understanding of Hinduism are therefore doomed to failure if one defines the search in terms of a few rigidly applied criteria. As Chaudhuri (1979:18) has observed, Hinduism is "a way of life" which, as such, provides guidance for daily life as well as for larger cycles—the week, lunar month, year, life cycle, and still other temporal frameworks. This is in marked contrast to the worldviews of many modern Westerners, for whom the distinction between sacred and profane tends to be much sharper and religion is temporally and spatially a largely compartmentalized institution. With the much broader scope of religion in India, activities which for Westerners might be secular are commonly viewed by Hindus as sacred, so that the distinction "has very little relevance in the Hindu context, since these are not antithetical in Hindu belief and ritual" (Das, 1977:114). Thus, the study of Hindu ritual practice necessarily extends well beyond temple visits, prayer, and pilgrimage to include what might strike some outsiders as decidedly extrareligious activities: theater, wrestling, language, and so on.

The continued interest in the ways that religious practices in Banaras reflect and shape practices throughout and beyond India prompted us to bring together a collection of readings focusing on the current cultural practices and living religious traditions of that city. Rather than examine Banaras's place in traditional ideologies, as others have done, or focus on specific contexts of its recent history, such as the politics of power, this volume offers the reader an in-depth view of many facets of current Banarsi culture seldom examined, as well as a thorough treatment of one of the most popular ongoing religious traditions of India as found in the City of Light: the *Ramlila*. The essays here make clear that Hinduism is a complex reality that often integrates the aesthetic, social, economic, political, and "religious" spheres of life.

The diverse themes and fields of the authors of this book are unified in several important ways. Each author provides an understanding of some aspect of Hindu religion as practiced in what is widely regarded as its most sacred center. Together, the individual chapters celebrate the great breadth of religious practice in Banaras. All of the authors have recently conducted fieldwork there and present firsthand observations of its living traditions.

We begin with three explorations of the *Ramlila*, or "play of Ram," an annual reenactment of Ram's epic journey as recorded in the *Ramayana*, literally "journeying of Ram." Although there are many versions of this epic, the *Ramcharitmanas*, composed by the sixteenth century poet-saint Tulsidas, is the regional favorite in Banaras and is the source on which the Ramnagar *Ramlila*—by far the longest and largest of the presentations in Banaras—is based. Richard Schechner and Linda Hess focus on this dramaticization of Ram's struggle with the demon king Ravana. The Ramnagar *Ramlila* requires thirty-one days for its single annual production, whose scenes shift from place to place rather than remain confined to a stage in the conventional sense. On some of the more important days, this play is viewed by upwards of seventy-five thousand spectators, many of whom are so engrossed by the events portrayed that they do not distinguish between current and past time, between the actors and the gods they represent, and between spectators of the "play" and witnesses of the "actual events." Staged across the Ganges from Banaras in Ramnagar—literally "Ramtown," a reference to the play—the Ramnagar *Ramlila* is sponsored by the king of Banaras, whose palace is there rather than in Banaras proper, as Schechner notes, for the military advantages afforded by that location. Although the Ramnagar *Ramlila* is the most famous, there are hundreds of performances of the "play of Ram" in Varanasi: Thomas Parkhill examines the great variety of *Ramlilas* held in numerous neighborhoods throughout the city.

Schechner explores the mythological and contemporary significance behind the performance of the *Ramayana* at Ramnagar, presented annually for the past 150 years. The Ramnagar *Ramlila* is at once epic in scale and breathtaking in theatrical detail, reflecting the scale and cultural significance of the *Ramayana* itself. All of the performances of the *Ramlila*, but especially that of Ramnagar, transform observers into what Schechner calls "participant-pilgrims," who over the course of the play follow Ram's *lila* (play) by journeying to many sacred places represented by this particular microcosm of the Hindu world. For the *nemi*, or devotee, what takes place is not mere theater; it is more real than life itself. In elevating the play to "hyperreality," the actors along with observers become participants in the life of Ram, and ritually construct his divine world and actions anew. While the lila is actually under way, the *svarups* ("true embodiments") portraying Sita and Ram *are* Sita and Ram, and the devotees on hand for the performance *are* the citizens of Ayodhya. As at other *Ramlilas*, the Ramnagar audience actually sees and hears their gods. The *Ramlila* of Ramnagar changes city to theater, and theater to mythic geography, providing the means to bring devotees inside Ram's world to offer them darshan.

In addition to fulfilling communitywide religious functions of the *Ramlila*, the performance at Ramnagar serves a political end for the king of Banaras. Schechner explains that the worldly power of the king of Banaras and the transcendent power of the king of Ayodhya are linked: just as Vishnu-Ram strides through space to reestablish his lawful authority in all the three worlds, so the maharaja of Ramnagar stakes out his territory through the *Ramlila*, proclaiming in effect that the physical landscape and the *Ramlila* belong to him. This occasion for annually reminding his subjects of his authority is neither coincidence nor casual choice. The spatial isomorphism so prominent in the *Ramlila* is paralleled by the temporal match between the celebration of Ram's power and the king's power. That both are kings, and, like other royal castes throughout northern India, hold weapons *puja* (worship) at this time is further basis for royalty in general and the ruling family in particular to reassert their links to the gods who legitimate their worldly authority. What we see here is a kind of play within the play in which family, caste, and broader Hindu community all have shared bases from which to celebrate the *Ramlila*.

The theme of levels of meaning, so evident in Schechner's opening chapter, is even more pronounced in Hess's discussion of her own journey through the many "frames" of the *Ramcharitmanas*. Banaras, the *Ramcharitmanas*, and the lila are inextricably intertwined, she explains. Participants in the *Ramlila* performance, just like the readers of the *Ramcharitmanas*, are encouraged to give up their preconceived notions of space and time and experience for themselves the divine lila and *maya* (illusion). In the *Ramcharitmanas*, Tulsidas has "found a way not just to tell but to show" what he means. The narrators of Ram's story are themselves players within the lila of the *Ramcharitmanas*; the creation of these multiple narrative frames separates orders of reality, thus permitting the order of "reality" to be thrown into question. And so it is with the *Ramlila*. Just as there is no clear separation of the narrators from the story, so there is no clear delineation between the world and the performance; or between audience and actors. The observers not only see the drama unveil itself to them, but through their actions they participate in and help construct reality. During the course of the month-long play, the "mythic world" becomes progressively more vivid and real, while the "ordinary world" fades into an unconvincing imitation of "reality."

To fully appreciate the social significance of the Ramnagar *Ramlila*, we need to go beyond the enormity of its temporal and spatial dimensions and the importance of its many levels of meaning to view it in its broader social context. As with Banaras in the context of India as a whole, the Ramnagar *Ramlila* is important as much or more for being an archetypical representative of the complex whole of which it is a small part as for its centrality within that whole. Thus, the principle of encapsulated layers of meaning which is so vividly made manifest at Ramnagar is replicated, albeit on a much less grand scale, in hundreds of *Ramlila* presentations performed elsewhere in the vicinity and throughout northern India.

The layered organization of meaning and structure in *Ramlila* performances is reflected in innumerable ways in Hindu culture in the

principle that Dumont (1980:239–45) has identified as "encompassment." He explains that a concept may operate at different levels of
meaning, narrower ones being distinct from and yet incorporated into
broader ones. "At the superior level there is unity; at the inferior level
there is distinction, there is. . .complementariness or contradiction"
(Dumont, 1980:242). For example, *religion* in a more limited sense of
such activities as puja and fasting can be seen as distinct from other
social institutions of education, politics, and so on. For most "Hindus"
their religion is more inclusive. For many, Hinduism is a way of life.
Thus, *Hindu religion* in this broader sense encompasses *religion* in the
narrower meaning. Dumont's analytical framework, which is built on
layers of meaning, is employed by Ostor (1980) in his study of Hindu
ritual practices and is evident in many of the essays in the present
volume.

As a microcosm of the whole, Banaras encompasses the Hindu
world. However, in keeping with the salience in Hinduism of inclusiveness over exclusiveness, Banaras is not alone in this respect. In fact,
microcosms of the whole are present in cultural regions throughout
the country (Dimock, 1963:1-5;cf. Morinis, 1984:47), so that even while
perpetually encompassing all other sacred sites, Banaras is itself
encompassed. What then makes this city so special? Banaras is to the
many other sacred pilgrimage sites of India what the Ramnagar *Ramlila*
is to the many other performances of that epic play and what the Ganges
is to other sacred rivers. More than any other *tirtha* (pilgrimage site),
it is looked to as representing the essence of Hindu place, values, and
customs; that is, its claim to supremacy lies not in its uniqueness but
in the fullness with which it embraces and portrays Hindu place, values,
and ways.

The common depiction of Banaras as an embodied being layered
in *koshas*, or sheaths, offers a parallel view of layered reality and
encompassment. The city is conceived by devout pilgrims as an
embodied spirit. As such, like humans, it is layered in five koshas. The
koshas of Banaras demarcate pilgrimage routes around various
representations of the city that differ in the size and intensity of the
sacred power present (Eck, 1982:350–57). In the middle is the Shiva
temple of Madhyameshvara, "Lord of the Center," which is known as
the "navel of Kashi." The innermost of the koshas is Vishvanath,
followed by Antargriha, Avimukta, Varanasi, and finally Kashi. Each
of these serves as a pilgrimage route. The visitor who has only time
to follow one of the smaller routes feels ebullient because the region
encompassed is so very sacred. The pilgrim who makes one of the more
strenuous journeys around the more extensive koshas is pleased to have

been able to encompass the sacred city in a more elaborate manifestation. In the structure of the five koshas, Banaras encompasses itself as well as core ideas of Hinduism. The koshas are five in number, the most sacred number in Hindu cosmology. The length of Kashi, the outermost kosha, is five kroshas (a unit of distance equal to about two miles) and is punctuated by 108 sacred sites, a number sacred in Hindu cosmology as representing the twelve months times the nine *graha* (planets), that is, as representing all of time and space. For this reason, the *Pancha Kroshi tirthayatra* of Kashi or "pilgrimage of the five kroshas," has been a prominent pilgrimage route for many centuries.

Thomas Parkhill shows that just as the Ramnagar *Ramlila* is the means by which the maharaja attempts to "stake out" and sanctify his territory, so the many neighborhood *Ramlilas* are means by which residents ritually claim and maintain their neighborhood in the City of Light as their own Hindu Place. Ordinarily completed over nine nights rather than a full month, the neighborhood lilas, like the even grander Ramnagar lila, are epic dramatizations that emphatically assert the sacredness of Hindu Place — both in general, that is, of Bharat, or India, and in the specific site of that portrayal: individual neighborhoods for most lilas and, in the case of the Ramnagar lila, the whole of Banaras.

Banaras is best known as a center of Hindu culture and tradition, but, significantly, fully one-quarter of its residents are Muslims. Her neighborhoods do not divide neatly into discrete Muslim places and Hindu places. Therefore, as Parkhill has found, when some Hindus in Muslim-dominated areas have performed the *Ramlila* to claim and maintain the neighborhood as Hindu Place, their attempts have met opposition from Muslims who see their own sacred places within that space "desecrated." The martial theme of the play is itself a factor contributing to the tension between these religious communities. This tension is paralleled by long-standing interreligious antagonism that has been known to surface elsewhere at the time of other annual reenactments celebrating military heroes, such as during parades honoring monkey general Hanuman, a key figure in the *Ramlila*.

This capacity of rituals to both unite and divide is also evident in disagreements among Hindus over how *Ramlilas* should be performed, Parkhill contends. For some, any perceived innovations in lighting or amplification, script, or personnel—traditionally all male and all Brahmin—change the *Ramlila* from potent ritual into diluted theater, which in particularly degenerate form is referred to scathingly as "disco lila." Drawing on his observation of numerous neighborhood *Ramlilas*, Parkhill examines the variations in form and the tensions between those who find certain changes repugnant and those who welcome innovation. This division within the Hindu community is paralleled in other celebrations elsewhere in northern India in which efforts to modernize religious traditions are viewed as vulgar and insulting to some orthodox celebrants.

Out of consideration for the complexity of the *Ramlila*, with its many roles, days, and sections, several resources have been provided in the Appendices to help orient the reader. The first of these offers a brief description of the key events portrayed on each of the thirty-one days of the Ramnagar *Ramlila*, and the next summarizes the seven *kands*, or sections, of the *Ramcharitmanas* on which this version of the *Ramlila* is based. The third appendix is a glossary of short biographical sketches of the major characters of the *Ramayana*, and the fourth is a glossary of many of the more common terms in the present volume. Other terms used less frequently are defined within the text of individual chapters.

Joseph Alter explores the daily routine and philosophy of life of the Banarsi wrestlers. The Banarsi wrestler lives an ascetic life of discipline for maintaining his health. Through diligent adherence to all aspects of his daily regimen, the wrestler pursues spiritual and social goals through activities which for Westerners are usually individual and mundane pursuits. No part of his routine is considered unimportant. Diet, exercise, defecation, cleansing one's teeth, hair, and body, leisure activities, and sleep are all governed by a set of guidelines specific to the wrestler's regimen. Adherence to this way of life requires an extraordinarily high level of commitment which is reinforced by wrestlers' frequent contact with each other and common repulsion by what they see as decay in Hindu customs and values.

The wrestling and related dietary and other practices that set these men apart from other Hindus are physical expressions of what in fact remains a spiritual quest. This is so because the men see their wrestling—and all that that activity implies—more as a means to discipline, mastery of the body, and spiritual attainment than as an end in itself. Competition is part of the routine, but defeating one's opponent is not a paramount concern. Macho invidious displays of one's physique have no place in these wrestlers' lives. Instead, the Banarsi wrestler employs physical means toward developing spiritual purity in his own life and, in turn, in broader society. Alter asserts that the idealized culture of Banaras in general and the figure of the Banarsi wrestler in particular are each a "somewhat self-conscious response to rampant, generic modernism that threatens to undermine a prized way of life." As Parkhill explains, tradition-minded Banarsis oppose "disco *Ramlilas*" which make use of electricity for lighting and amplification or which include nonBrahmins and women as players. Like the strong opponents of change in the performance of the *Ramlila,* the Banarsi wrestlers oppose change which could be seen as distractions from a spiritual life; for them degeneracy is found in "Bombay cinema halls" and "disco mentality." These they regard as unwelcome expressions of "crass commercialism and immoral materialism," which make the maintenance of the "idealized Banaras" a greater challenge and all the more significant of a goal. Parkhill relates that when one neighborhood *Ramlila* encountered communal violence, the *Ramlila* organizers spirited away the svarups of the gods on the shoulders of Banarsi wrestlers. Like Hanuman, the epic hero of the *Ramayana* and patron deity of all *akharas* (public gymnasiums for wrestling), Banarsi wrestlers function as self-conscious protectors of the ideal Hindu order against all threats, whether from outside or inside the Hindu fold. The result is that "the moral physique of the Banarsi wrestler takes on the character of an icon juxtaposed to the degenerate world of filmy fashion." In contrast to the degenerate hedonism which they wrestle to oppose, Banarsi wrestlers follow a utopian path of moral physical reform, a path which offers a vision of power, self-control, and devotion for themselves individually but, more importantly, for society as a whole. Theirs is not primarily an individual or physical pursuit; it is a spiritual and overtly nationalistic quest to preserve Hindu customs for the benefit of present and future generations.

Our focus on Hinduism in Banaras is broadened to include the bearing of Hindu and Muslim starting points on the collective memory of relations between these communities. Myth and history are commonly fused in accounts of the deeds of military leaders. The heroes of one side are villains to those on the other. Such divisions are the subject of Mary Searle-Chatterjee's chapter on Hindu and Muslim collective memories of Ghazi Miyan, an eleventh-century Muslim warrior-saint, and Aurangzeb, last of the great Moghul emperors. These figures function as "symbolic archetypes" which are open to interpretation and deliberate manipulation in the writing of history. Accounts vary appreciably even within each religious community as various factions of Hindus and Muslims develop and promote their own particular mythological representations of these figures' histories. As Searle-Chatterjee demonstrates, many of the mythic portrayals of Ghazi Miyan and Aurangzeb by both Hindu and Muslim communities share similar value systems, which ironically leads them to offer conflicting conclusions as to what is historical fact. For instance, Muslim portrayals of Aurangzeb denying his alleged iconoclasm and of Ghazi Miyan described as a protector of Hindu women against Hindu atrocities reveal a pronounced desire to make both Muslim figures acceptable not only in Hindu society but also within the Muslim community, which has internalized assumptions from the larger Hindu community about acceptable and laudatory values and behavior. Incendiary Hindu indictments of Muslim violence, particularly attributed to Aurangzeb, have been used by various political parties to help win large blocs of communal votes by alienating the two religious groups. Because of the historical importance of Ghazi Miyan and Aurangzeb in their own right but, perhaps more significantly, because of the part their myths play in shaping the collective ego of both religious communities, these myths have evoked strong feelings, including fear, among Muslims, and righteous anger among Hindus, who have valorized their own folk heros such as Shivaji.

Dana Sawyer has studied in depth the Dandi ascetics, so named for their habit of carrying the *danda* (bamboo staff). From the time immediately following his initiation, "the Dandi will carry this staff without letting it touch the ground for the rest of his life, at which time he will be buried with it." Dandis are an all-male, all-Brahmin sect founded by Shankara, the ninth-century C.E. *Advaita* (literally, "nondual," that is, monistic) philosopher. They are an important sect and are respected for their commitment to Shankara's philosophy and intense asceticism. All Dandis are Brahmins, and most complete the three earlier stages of life of student, householder, and hermit before entering the fourth, that of the *ramta* (wandering) ascetic. Thus, in addition to their orthodox philosophy and rigorous asceticism, the fact that Dandis are high caste and older and more established in society at the time of initiation all contribute to their high prestige among ascetics. Although these basic facts about Dandis are not in dispute, Sawyer is struck by the wide gap between popular images of Dandi monastic practices rooted in the precepts of Sanskrit texts and their actual way of life.

Banaras boasts the largest population of Dandi *sannyasins* (person who has entered the fourth and final stage of life), sheltering some two to three hundred, who are roughly one-quarter to one-half of the total number of Dandis in India and close to a fifth of all the ascetics in Banaras. The wandering of Dandis makes greater precision difficult to obtain. However, as Sawyer points out, the number of Dandis in any one place is ephemeral and therefore not central to an understanding of the Dandis' presence in Banaras. After close observation of dozens of Dandi *maths*, or monasteries, Sawyer recognized a clear disjunction between the ideal monastic structure enjoined by traditional sources and the actual monastic structure necessitated by what he terms "guruism," or the emphasis of oral transmission as the source of Dandi authority. "Dandi monastic complexes originate and develop around charismatic gurus rising within their brotherhood," with the result that monastic structures are themselves naturally short-lived. Shankara set up principal learning centers headed by Shankaracharyas or "teachers of Shankara," who are always Dandi sannyasins. In principle, Dandis throughout India are to affiliate with and follow the teachings of the Shankaracharyas and be subject to their leadership. However, the actual relation between the maths and these centers is minimal today. In actual practice, maths are only loosely affiliated with Shankaracharyas. The appearance and subsequent rise and decline in the prominence of a Dandi math depend on the charisma and leadership skills of each new guru in charge of the site rather than on leadership exerted at a distant Dandi center. Only rarely are these gurus closely affiliated with the traditional organs set up by Shankara. Dandi maths are established and may rise and soon or eventually fall with the appearance and disappearance of the charisma and leadership skills of the gurus associated with a particular site. Sawyer maintains that Shankara may have been aware of a significant gap between the ideal and the real Dandi monastic structures even during the time of the founding of the sect but that academicians in much more recent times have failed to recognize this distinction. He urges that future scholarship on this sect rely on ethnographic inquiry in addition to textual analysis.

Banaras is known as an ancient site of worship to various deities. However, it is also a living city. Despite the city's great age, very few of her temples are themselves more than several hundred years old. Most of the major temples are reconstructions; others are wholly new structures. Sawyer's observations on the ebb and flow of Dandi maths hold in general for Hindu temples. What begins as a minor worship site of only local interest can develop quickly or evolve more slowly into a site enjoying regional or even pan-Indian prominence. The specific pattern at any one temple reflects changes in the popularity of the principal deity of the site and the popularity of the temple's initial and subsequent priestly overseers. New temples must compete with more established temples for pilgrims' patronage; in order to attract them, religious officiants at the various sites promote their temples as "ancient" or "special." Cynthia Humes examines the traditions of worship dedicated to the increasingly popular goddess Vindhyavasini at six sites in Banaras, paying particular attention to the *mahatmya*, or "glorification," of each place in Kashi believed to be inhabited by this goddess.

Underscoring the principle of inclusiveness in Hindu ritual practice, Humes also points out in her study that a temple constructed near an already prominent temple may benefit from this juxtaposition because visitors to the better-known site may choose to also visit other nearby temples. In fact, throughout the Hindu world and not just in Banaras, the interest shown by visitors in one temple is more likely to heighten than to detract from interest in nearby temples. Newcomers to the study of Hinduism may find this puzzling but need to keep in mind that the Western pattern of nonoverlapping congregations whose members have undivided loyalties does not hold for most Hindus. Instead, the worship sites with which any Hindu identifies are ordinarily many in number and may but need not include a dominant site, may but need not be a well-defined set in the mind and behavior of a given devotee, may but need not remain unchanged over many years, and may but need not match the configuration of loyalties to particular gods and temples that are of special interest to other family members.

The *Kashi Khand,* or "section on Kashi" in the *Skanda Purana,* is one of the most important Sanskrit mahatmyas of Banaras. This purana or "ancient story" describes a temple in Banaras devoted to Durga, known as Vindhyavasini, the Goddess of the Vindhyas. Humes notes that of the six sites where Vindhyavasini is worshiped today in the sacred city, four claim to be the temple mentioned in the *Kashi Khand.* Officiants at the other two temples offer alternate sources of authority to confirm the illustrious origin of their temples in more recent times. These attempts to sanctify particular temples recall the performance of the *Ramlila* not only to honor the gods but also to sanctify worshipers' neighborhoods; both phenomena are ways to establish devotees' sites as sacred Place.

While holding in common the most popular *puranic* myths pertaining to Vindhyavasini, worship of this goddess at her six Banaras temples reveals marked caste and regional variations. One temple in particular, located in the northern part of the city, has become very prominent because of the rising popularity of its "guru," a Khatri woman believed to be blessed with the gifts of divine healing and a special connection to Vindhyavasini. She performs specific Khatri practices at her temple, which have been conducted at the prominent Vindhyavasini temple in the Uttar Pradesh village called Vindhyachal for hundreds of years, and encourages others to do so as well. If her popularity continues, these practices may gain widespread acceptance among devotees of Vindhyavasini belonging to other castes. In another case, economic factors have clearly affected the prominence of a privately owned "ancient" temple opened to the public in the 1970s in order to obtain donations needed for its physical upkeep and land taxes. Thus the history of the Vindhyavasini temples of Banaras demonstrates that text-based and oral claims of a site's special significance blend with charisma, economic considerations, and location within the broader sacred geography of the city to shape the pilgrimage process.

Ratnesh Pathak and Cynthia Humes discuss worship at the well and temple complex of Lolark Kund, the "Pond of the Trembling Sun," through examination of puranic and folk mythology, historical references, and their own fieldwork. Pathak and Humes first describe this prominent Hindu place and then turn to the variety of functionaries who work there, one of the earliest worship sites in all of Banaras (Eck, 1982:177). Determining the history and understanding the present practices at Lolark Kund are elusive goals which are made difficult by the age of the site, by the fact that much of its history is oral, not written, and by the overlapping meanings and interpretations that are plausible for the same act of worship. Lolark Kund, like the *Ramlila* and the mythic portrayals of Muslim military heroes, is best understood in terms of many layers of meaning, no one of which is unambiguously correct to the exclusion of the others.

Contrary to what one might expect at this temple site ostensibly dedicated to the *aditya* (sun deity) Lolark, today his Lord Shiva, "Lolarkeshvara," is more popularly worshiped. The worship of Surya the Sun, and his many forms, such as Lolark, gradually began to decline in the thirteenth century, just as the popularity of Shiva began to rise. Although most devotees no longer perform the pilgrimage to the twelve *adityas* in Banaras, which involved tracing one's way to this and to the other eleven sites in Banaras associated with each of the twelve portions into which the sun god divided himself, many still frequent Lolark Kund. Why this is so is in part explained by the layering of traditions that have built up at this site. Shared associations with light, fire, and heat, and with benevolence and fertility, have led the Sun and Shiva to become fused to some degree at Lolark. These attributes of those gods make Lolark a center for infertile couples who come for the healing power of the fiery water of the kund, where they bathe and leave offerings which include fruit and vegetables symbolizing the fertility they seek. Many of the women who come to Lolark Kund do so to "marry" Shiva in addition to bathing in the fructifying pond, a symbol of sexual union. This interest in achieving conception through sacred water is an ancient one which draws visitors to other sites in Banaras and peaks at Lolark Kund during the Chath Mela, an annual religious fair that attracts tens of thousands of pilgrims. Many visitors come for other reasons: there are daily bathers at the nearby Tulsi Ghat who stop by to pay their respects to Shiva at Lolark Kund, and in smaller numbers parents come with their young children who receive *mundan* (ritual first haircut).

The religious functionaries at Lolark include the Brahmin *panda* (pilgrimage priest), *karinda* (Brahmin servant and substitute of the panda), *bhaddar* (a lower-ranked Brahmin priest), *Nau* (barber), and *Mallah* (boatman). Pathak and Humes analyze the ritual activities of each specialist, the religious goals and rituals of visitors to Lolark, and the distribution of offerings among the various functionaries. They also give attention to claims that there was a mid-nineteenth-century power struggle between factions of pandas seeking control of the site and discuss the establishment of new shrines by pandas who appear to have been motivated by economic self-interests. Increases in the size of pilgrimage priests' families have led to economic pressures which have been resolved through increased vigilance over the collection of funds at the temple complex and by establishing new foci of worship at the site. Lolark is attracting a growing number of visitors, especially urban dwellers who are better able to support the site with their offering. Such increases in pilgrims and donations often result in charges that pandas are corrupt. These charges are neither more common nor more valid for pandas at Lolark Kund than for their counterparts at other major worship sites.

Beth Simon concludes the volume with her treatment of the relationships among language choice, religion, and self-concept in Banaras. Banarsi Boli, the regional dialect of Banaras, reflects longtime Banaras residents' sense of selfhood, their shared culture, and their attachment to Banaras itself. Many Banarsis also maintain ties to other parts of India through their residence in ethnic and linguistic neighborhoods. Through their use and identity with Banarsi Boli, Banarsis are integrated across these regional identities. In addition, Banarsi Boli is a vehicle for integrating Hindus and Muslims into a common community.

Banarsi Boli, however, is commonly regarded as "a kind of Hindi" and consequently is associated with Hindus. This link between language and religion has been both sharpened and obscured by a streamlining of the Census of India categories for recording the mother tongue. Since 1961 the census has merged into "Hindi" eighteen dialects which it previously differentiated. Bhojpuri, of which Banarsi Boli is a variant, is one of those dialects. Also since 1961, the census has distinguished between Urdu and Hindi, which were previously treated as the same. As a result of these changes, the census in recent decades has shown many fewer bilingual and multilingual speakers, and Hindu-Muslim differences in mother tongue are much greater in recent censuses than in earlier ones. This apparent increase in the ties between language and religion in Banaras and elsewhere in India is due in part to the fact that "Banarsi Boli" is no longer recorded for members of either religious community. Further, since Muslims identify more often as Urdu than as Hindi speakers, introducing the distinction between these close variants of the same language resulted in noticeable linguistic differentiation between Hindus and Muslims in 1961. In more recent decades the number of individuals recorded as Urdu speakers has dramatically increased. These changes in census-taking practices have resulted in distributions that differ considerably from one decade to the next, even though the actual languages spoken may not have changed. The sum of these changes in recording procedures and census results provides an important illustration of our recurring theme of levels of meaning. What for some observers is a distinct language may for others be a dialect. In any event, since Hindi encompasses Bhojpuri, which in turn encompasses Banarsi Boli, the existence and importance of the latter can be overlooked if one views language only in terms of very broad levels of organization.

Simon's discussion of the linguistic diversity in Banaras emphasizes the importance of bilingualism in that city and, more specifically, of the phenomenon of code-switching, which Gumperz (1982:59) defines as "the juxtaposition within the same speech exchange of passages of speech belonging to two different grammatical systems or subsystems." Simon differentiates between unmarked code-switching, in which movement between Hindi and Banarsi Boli occurs rapidly and unself-consciously within the same sentence, and marked code-switching, in which the speaker makes an intentional shift in order to achieve a purpose, which may be to be more emphatic or to call attention to one's religious or Banarsi identity. The popular use of marked code-switching in Banaras is evidence of overt efforts by Banarsis to use language to maintain their identity with Place, whether conceived as shared sacred Hindu Place, or as secular and multi-communal. Especially in its unmarked form, code-switching strongly suggests the presence of a "deep cultural knowledge" of Banarsis' unrecognized but strongly felt ties to their city. Shared attachments to Banarsi Boli support common bonds of residents across other lines of cleavage including those of religion, language, and region of origin.

Banarsis are continually reminded of their ties to their sacred city through their daily ritual baths, the prominence of many of her temples and other sacred sites, their participation in the *Ramlila* and other annual festivals, the large number and variety of sect members and religious specialists, the steady stream of pilgrims, and other more subtle means, including their patterns of speech. Each of these themes is the subject of one or more chapters of the present volume. The three opening chapters on the *Ramlila* can most readily be seen as having a related focus. On a more general plane, some of the other chapters are also linked by such recurring themes as the transformation of mundane place into sacred Hindu Place, the fusion between textual and oral traditions, and the tension between those who wish to preserve old ways and those who advocate change. Despite observable differences in ritual practices and even important differences in values, in a very fundamental way, Banarsi Hindus, like Hindus everywhere, display a deeply felt unity amidst diversity within and across their many identities—as individuals, as residents of a neighborhood, as Banarsis, and in still other identities.

Notes

1. Eck (1982) explains other of the numerous epithets of Banaras, an Anglicized version of *Varanasi*. The origin of *Varanasi* is commonly linked to the names of the rivers Varuna and Assi, which together with the Ganges define its limits (Bharati, 1970:107), but Eck (1982:26–27) suggests a slightly different derivation, that the name comes from *Varanasi*, the earlier name for the Varana River.

Crossing the Water: Pilgrimage, Movement, and
Environmental Scenography of the *Ramlila*
of Ramnagar

Richard Schechner

> I will now proclaim the manly powers of Vishnu
> Who measured out earth's broad expanses,
> Propped up the highest place of meeting:
> Three steps he paced, the widely striding!
>
> For [this], his manly power is Vishnu praised.
> Like a dread beast he wanders where he will,
> Haunting the mountains: in his three wide places
> All worlds and beings dwell...
>
> The marks of his three steps are filled with honey;
> Unfailing they rejoice each in its own way.
>
> —Rig Veda 1. 154, R. C. Zaehner, translator (1966:4-5)

One of Varanasi's greatest events—a performance of magnitude,
a pilgrimage, a display of the maharaja of Banaras's splendor—the
Ramlila of Ramnagar takes place not in the city itself, but across the
Ganga, on the "eastern" bank, a few miles upriver. The Ganga swerves
northward at Varanasi so that its southern bank actually is situated to
the east: thus when one crosses the river from north to south one is
moving from west to east. The conflation is, I think, of great importance.
At this sacred bend Kashi was established: where a pilgrim by crossing
the river might move in any of the four cardinal directions.

Directionality, defined spaces, and movement have been essential
to Vishnu from the earliest accounts of his acts (Gonda, 1987). He is
a being who expands or strides through space (Vishnu means

"expander") reestablishing his lawful authority.[1] Following in his steps is, as the Veda tells us, to step in honey. Ram, Vishnu's seventh incarnation,[2] is known for his "goings" or "journeying" (the *yana* of *Ramayana*). Expanding the worship of Ram is the theme and purpose of the Valmiki *Ramayana*, the Tulsidas *Ramcharitmanas*, and the *Ramlila*. Even the evil Ravana, Ram's archenemy, in death comes to worship Ram.[3]

This worship is the orderliness Vishnu-Ram brings (back) to a troubled world. Measurement is a paradigm of order and proportion, and movement toward the sacred is pilgrimage. The Ramnagar *Ramlila* has plenty of both. *Ramlilas* everywhere, but especially Ramnagar's, are celebratory performances tracing the footsteps of Vishnu. The town of Ramnagar contains in one scene or another all the worlds: divine, human, animal, and demonic. Sometimes Ramnagar is India and Lanka; sometimes it is the kingdoms of Koshala and Videha, homes of Ram and Sita. During the closing days of the *Ramlila*, Ramnagar is Ayodhya, Ram's capital city. The shifts in locale and scale occur organically during the course of the thirty-one-day theatrical narrative. The various locations are not represented by ordinary theater sets but in many instances by permanent sites that are part of Ramnagar's townscape. When not in use these are still called by their *Ramlila* names. Some sites are physical structures or walled-in enclosures, and others are open fields, ponds, or known locations with no special quality to them except that during the *Ramlila* they are part of the story. An example is the intersection of Ramnagar's two main streets where, at the end of their exile, Ram and Lakshman are reunited with their brothers Bharat and Shatrughna. Other sites, like the great pool of the Durga temple that serves as the Kshir Sagar ("Ocean of Milk"), where Vishnu sleeps before incarnating himself as Ram, preexist the *Ramlila* by several centuries. Besides the fixed sites, and just as important, are the roads and pathways connecting focal points. Thus the *Ramlila's* movement map is a complicated web consisting of nodal sites and linking pathways. Many *Ramlila* environments were constructed and the connecting routes laid out some 150 years ago when the Ramnagar *Ramlila* took its present shape.

In all versions of the Ram story throughout South Asia, journeying, wandering, pilgrimage, and marching—movements large and small, secular, religious, adventurous, and military—are essential. Virtually every Hindu knows the Ram story; many believe it to be historical fact. In Hindi-speaking northern India especially, Ram is king of kings. There is something deeply Indo-European about the *Ramayana*: the Aryans who may have brought the story with them into India were nomadic, and in other areas of Asia and Europe where they went, Aryans brought similar stories of adventurous travels or expectations.[4] Movement over great distances in the *Ramayana* is made necessary by a war that expresses lust, religion, and politics, a war involving the whole cosmos, from the gods of high heaven and demons of the underworld to the human and animal inhabitants of middle earth. The divine-human heroes admire and collaborate with monkeys and bears.

Moving from site to site is characteristic of the Ramnagar *Ramlila*. *Ramlila* combines the methods of drama, process, and ritual to demonstrate how Vishnu-Ram rid the world of Ravana. Ram prepares India for its golden age, the Ramraj (kingdom of Ram), by "striding": first by going into exile, then by pursuing Ravana south through the spine of India and across the sea to Lanka, and finally by returning to Ayodhya in a triumphant procession. After his coronation (*Durbar*) and public sermon at the very end of the *Ramlila*, Ram continues to move. He mounts the royal elephants for the journey from Ayodhya to the palace of the maharaja of Banaras, a ceremonial visit that takes place in no other *Ramlila* but Ramnagar's. Throughout the *Ramlila* Ram "takes steps" in both senses of the word: he acts, he moves. And thousands of spectators move in his footsteps. He meets Sita by traveling from Ayodhya to Janakpur. He puts the action of ridding the world of Ravana in play by surrendering his claim to the throne and going into exile. He pursues Ravana to Lanka. He displays his authority over his kingdom of Koshala and all of India by riding his royal elephant through the streets of Ramnagar-Ayodhya.

But any summation of the narrative is bare bones. What those attending the *Ramlila* experience is a rich mixture of texts: dramatic, choreographic, ritualistic, religious, popular, musical, spatial, and temporal. The choreographic, spatial, and temporal texts concern us here. The crowds who attend the *Ramlila* join Ram in his journeys through the mythopoetic space of epic India. As they follow, they identify profoundly with Ram: the *Ramlila* is a theater not of make-believe but of hyperreality. Ram's movements are reinforced by the corresponding movements of spectators and the maharaja. Even getting to and going from the *Ramlila* grounds constitutes an important dimension of the performance.

Texts and Narrative Structure

The *Ramlila* incorporates several texts, both literary and performative. The *Ramayana* of Valmiki, never uttered but always present, is the fiber of Ram's story. But what the crowds gathered for the Ramnagar

Ramlila hear is the chanting of Tulsidas's *Ramcharitmanas*, composed in the sixteenth century, and the recitation of *samvads*, poetic texts stitched together in the nineteenth century by scholars under the patronage of the maharaja of Banaras and revised in the 1920s. The *Manas*, as the *Ramcharitmanas* is affectionately abbreviated, is sung by twelve *Ramayanis*, or chanters of the *Ramayana*, who in this case are also household priests of the maharaja. The *Manas* is as familiar to Hindi speakers of northern India as the King James Bible is to English speakers of the West. The samvads render the *Manas* in vernacular Hindi. During each moment of the performance, the chanting of the Ramayanis alternates with characters reciting the samvads, which are not spoken in a naturalistic style as in modern Indian theater, but shouted out slowly, in a singsong way, so that the assembled thousands can catch every word. The Ramayanis always sit close to the maharaja, making him the principal auditor of the *Manas*. But everyone hears the samvads. And when Ram speaks, the crowd roars back *"Bol! Raja Ramchandra ki jai"* ("Speak! Victory to King Ram!"). At emotional or highly dramatic moments people break into *kirtans*, songs whose only text is *"Jai sitaram!"* ("Victory to Sita and Ram!"). People cheer, dance, sing, and worship, animating the *Ramlila* with the rich energy of Hindu practice.

But the *Ramlila* is much more than the proclamation of texts, spectacle, and audience participation. It is the carefully crafted enactment of a narrative transmitting information and values concerning sacred history and geography (closely linked in India by means of a complex pilgrimage system), social hierarchy, ethics, and the personalities of god, heroes, and demons. The *Ramlila* enacts Ram's story, starting with his birth and the birth of his brothers Lakshman, Bharat, and Shatrughna; his education and early adventures; and his winning of Sita by breaking Shiva's bow (symbolically asserting Ram's dominion over Shiva). Then, just before Ram is to be crowned king, Kaikeyi—the youngest of Dasharatha's three queens—insists that the old king grant her two wishes he had promised her. "What do you want?" "That my son Bharat be king and that Ram be sent to the forest in exile for fourteen years!" Forced to grant these wishes (a promise is a promise), Dasharatha dies of grief. But Ram feels no ill will toward his stepmother or half brother. All is part of the cosmic plan, Vishnu's great *lila* (sport, play, theater). Accompanying Ram into exile are Sita and Lakshman.

At Chitrakut Ram establishes a kind of royal residence in exile, where Bharat visits him and begs him to return to Ayodhya. Ram refuses and moves farther into the forest, south to Panchavati. There Shurpanakha, sister of Ravana, seeing Ram and Lakshman, is struck by their beauty. She assumes the form of a comely woman in order

to seduce first Ram and then, when he rejects her, Lakshman.
Lakshman ridicules Shurpanakha and cuts off her nose and ears (a
bloody but comic scene in the Ramnagar *Ramlila*). Resuming her demon
shape, hurt, humiliated, and enraged, Shurpanakha flees across the
sea to Ravana's kingdom in Lanka. Her brother dispatches an army to
avenge her, but Ram and Lakshman promptly slaughter the demons.
Then, using a golden deer as a decoy, Ravana lures Ram and Lakshman
from Sita, kidnaps her, and carries her to Lanka. The divine brothers
gather an army of monkeys and bears—including the great devotee of
Ram, the monkey god Hanuman—to pursue Ravana the length of India
and across the narrow straits to Lanka. Meanwhile, Sita, refusing
Ravana's advances, is imprisoned in a garden, where she awaits her
liberation. After many preparations and adventures—including
Hanuman's foray into Lanka, where he meets with Sita, is captured,
and, when Ravana sets fire to his tail, grows to gigantic size and burns
down the demon king's capital city—Ram's army invades Lanka. A great
war is fought between Ram's forces and Ravana's demon hordes.
Systematically, Ravana's armies and family are defeated and annihilated.
Finally, Ram meets Ravana in single combat and kills him. Sita is rescued
and proves her chastity in a fire ordeal. Then Ram's party climbs onto
Ravana's magic flying chariot, the *pushpaka*, to make their triumphant
journey back to Ayodhya, roughly retracing their outgoing path.
Wherever they go great joyous crowds greet them. As they approach
Ayodhya, Bharat and Shatrughna rush to meet them and the four
brothers are reunited in the famous "Bharat Milap" (reunion with
Bharat). Ram is crowned king in Ayodhya, thus marking the start of
Ramraj, the golden age of his rule. Every Hindu knows this story. And,
again, many believe it to be historical fact.

The three big movements of the epic—birth to marriage, exile to
war, and triumphant return—are divided into five main action groups
in the Ramnagar *Ramlila*: (1) a prelude in which Brahma implores
Vishnu to take on human form and rescue the world which is being
terrorized by Ravana; (2) the birth, education, and initiation of Ram;
(3) the exile, divided between the thirteen years before Sita's kidnaping
and the fourteenth year of war against Ravana (this one year of epic
time takes thirteen days of the *Ramlila*, almost half the entire
performance); (4) the coronation of Ram, his teachings, and the start
of Ramraj; and (5) a postlude performed only at Ramnagar where the
maharaja and his family welcome the *svarups* to the Fort (the maharaja's
palace) and feed them in a ceremony witnessed by a huge audience
of dignitaries and commoners. The next day, in private, the maharaja
pays the performers for their services. These two actions—honoring the

gods and paying the actors—bring the story of Ram into a field controlled by the maharaja, thereby framing the mythos within the political and economic realities of modern India. But not quite, for the noumenon of Ram is not so easily paid off.

The theatrical structure of the Ramnagar *Ramlila* can be represented in linear form (Illus. 1.1). In performance time, the cycle consists of a one-day prelude, seven days of initiations, twenty days of exile, two days of Ramraj, and two days of postlude. This structure can be presented in another, more revealing way (Illus. 1.2). If Queen Kaikeyi had not forced King Dasharatha to stop Ram's coronation, there would be no drama, just a straight line from Ram's birth to his Ramraj. He would not encounter Ravana, and Vishnu's promise to Brahma would go unfulfilled. The heart of the *Ramlila's* drama is Ram's exile, the kidnapping of Sita, and the war against Ravana. In a word, the enacted *Ramlila* makes plausible and theatrically exciting Vishnu's incarnation as Ram, giving flesh to his earthly acts as student, son, warrior, king, husband, protector of *Brahmins*, wandering ascetic, and teacher: all the roles possible for a devout Kshatriya male. The narrative loop of Ram's exile, day 9 through day 28, is where most of the adventures take place, the theatrical core of the *Ramlila's yana*, or journey.

The Theatrical Environments

The shape of the Ramnagar *Ramlila*, with its theatrical environments deployed over approximately fifteen square miles, was defined in the early to middle nineteenth century by religious and ritual specialists, scholars, poets, and theater practitioners assembled and guided by the maharajas of Banaras. The first maharaja of the present royal family was Balwant Singh, who ruled from 1740 to 1770. Balwant constructed the Fort in Ramnagar, and other maharajas have added to it, so that by now it is a conglomeration of buildings and courtyards and by far the largest structure in Ramnagar. The Ramnagar *Ramlila* took much of its present form under the guidance of Maharaja Ishvari Prasad Narain Singh, who ruled from 1835 to 1889. The present maharaja, Vibhuti Narain Singh, has been on the throne since 1935. Of course, since Indian independence in 1947, there has been no kingdom in the actual political sense over which this maharaja reigns. His very identity as a king is dependent to a large degree on his patronage of and participation in the *Ramlila*. Vibhuti, like his predecessors, has a great and personal interest in the *Ramlila* and is active in every aspect of it— from the selection of boys to become the svarups to the careful supervision of the dialogues that constitute the samvads to deciding

1.1

Linear representation of the main events portrayed during the month-long cycle of the Ramnagar *Ramlila*.

	1	2			3A				3B		4	5
	PRELUDE	INITIATIONS	MATURITY		EXILE		CRISIS	WAR		RETURN	RAMRAJ	POSTLUDE
Event	Gods beg Vishnu to incarnate himself as Ram	Ram's boyhood adventures killing demons	Contest for Shiva's bow, courtship of Sita, marriage	Coronation stopped	Exile begins	Journey through the forest to Chitrakut and Panchavati	Shurpanakha appears, Sita kidnaped	Ram pursues Ravana	War in Lanka	Return to Ayodhya, Bharat Milap	Coronation and Teaching	Ceremony, payment at Fort
Day	1	2-5	6-8		9	10-15	16	17-19	20-26	27-28	29-30	31-32

1.2

Circular representation of the main events portrayed during the
month-long cycle of the Ramnagar *Ramlila*.

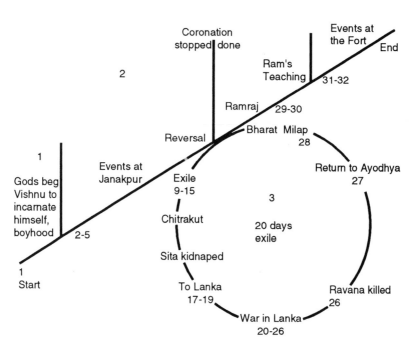

5

4

Coronation   Events at
stopped done   the Fort   End

                              Ram's
2   Teaching   31-32

                    Ramraj   29-30

                          Bharat Milap
         Reversal   28

1
         Events at   Return to Ayodhya
Gods beg Janakpur   Exile   27
Vishnu to   9-15
incarnate   3
himself,
boyhood 2-5   Chitrakut
                                 20 days
                                 exile
                    Sita kidnaped

1
Start   To Lanka   Ravana killed
                    17-19   26
                              War in Lanka
                              20-26

what the spatial arrangements of the *Ramlila* are to be. The *Ramlila*
(literally "Ram's play" or "sport") is performed in Ramnagar ("Ramtown").
All *Ramlilas* are a kind of environmental theater, but none has the scope
of theatrical detail as Ramnagar's. The scale map of the Ramnagar
Ramlila as it was in 1978 (Illus. 1.3) shows five main sites in terms of
fixed environments. This map discloses a different spatial organization
than that seen in a map serving as a program in 1946 (Illus. 1.4). The
discrepancies signal either changes made over the thirty-year gap
between maps (a development I doubt) or the divergence between the
Ramlila space as it is and as its authors mythotheatrically imagine it
to be. The 1946 map conflates the distances separating Ayodhya,

1.3

Scale map of Ramnagar showing *Ramlila* centers and
connecting roads and paths as they were in 1978.

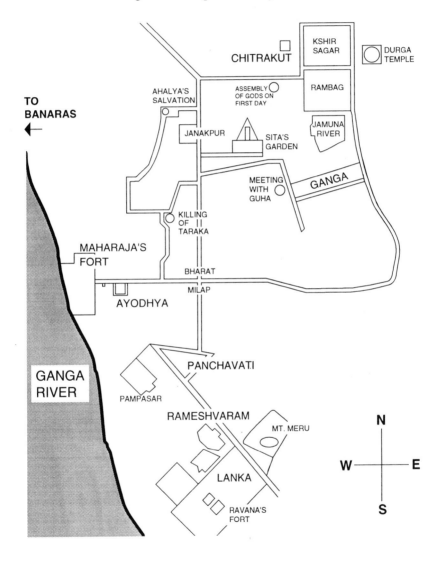

1.4

1946 program-map of the "Sri Ram Lila Ground" at Ramnagar.
The program as map shows how important space, journey,
and pilgrimage are to the performance.
Photo courtesy of the Maharaja of Banaras.

Janakpur, and Rambag; it pushes Panchavati to the east, far away from
Ayodhya and closer to Lanka. Thus it gives the overall impression of
action taking place on a northwest to southeast diagonal axis—from
central India to Rameshvaram to Lanka. This configuration fits the
directionality of the narrative, making the *Ramlila* space an efficient
model of the *Ramcharitmanas*. But the scale map drawn in 1978 shows
a less direct correspondence between narrative and space. Chitrakut
and Rambag are in the northeast, Janakpur in the northwest, Ayodhya,
the Fort, and Panchavati in the west, Bharat Milap in the center, and
Lanka far to the southeast. These centers are linked by roads and paths,
and journeying from place to place is required. Often just as a lila's
first scene begins it abruptly ends, requiring spectators and performers
alike to move to a new setting. Orthodox staging would cluster settings
and keep the crowd assembled in whatever place the lila began, but
in the *Ramlila* frequent moves are intentional: the pilgrimage theme is
integral not only narratively but physically.

The theatrical environment with the most scenes is in and around
Rambag ("Ram's garden"), a 515- by 340-foot walled-in pleasure garden
built in the mid-nineteenth century as a *Ramlila* environment. Rambag
contains several buildings, including at its center a small exquisitely
carved marble gazebo where Ram enunciates his teachings in the next
to final episode of the *Ramlila*. In Rambag there is also a large building
used as a shop for making *Ramlila* effigies and props, a rehearsal hall,
and during the middle of *Ramlila*—from day 9 to day 19—living quarters
for the svarups. The *Ramlila* opens near Rambag's front gate, where
Ravana acquires the powers that he will immediately abuse. But from
atop a Rambag tower Vishnu answers the gods' prayers (Illus. 1.5): "For
your sake I will take on the form of a human. I will rid the earth of
its burden."

That night the scene shifts to the 550-foot-square pool fronting
an old Durga temple just north of Rambag. Reclining on Shesha, the
thousand-headed serpent floating in the middle of the Kshir Sagar,
Vishnu awaits his birth as Ram while Lakshmi, the dutiful Hindu wife,
sits at his feet massaging his legs. On day 9 Ram begins his exile by
traveling nearly three miles from Ayodhya through city streets and alleys
(Illus. 1.6) into the junglelike theatrical environments near Rambag.
Ram, Sita, and Lakshman spend their first night in exile in a forest
hermitage. The next day the tribal chief Guha offers them hospitality,
weeping that all he has to offer are humble bulbs, roots, and fruits.
On day 11 they cross the Jamuna and Ganga rivers, signified by two
small lakes south of Rambag. On day 12 Bharat leaves Ayodhya for
Chitrakut, where Ram has taken up residence.

1.5

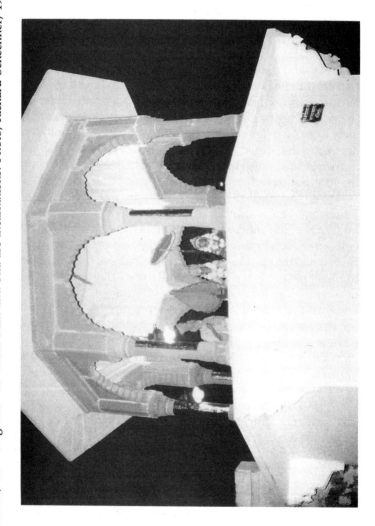

Vishnu and Lakshmi watch the drama from a Rambag tower. The same boys who are Ram and Sita are also Vishnu and Lakshmi, the "Originals" of whom Ram and Sita are incarnations. Photo, Richard Schechner, 1978.

1.6

Many in the audience follow Ram, Sita, and Lakshman from town to countryside as they begin their exile. Photo, Richard Schechner, 1978.

The Rambag site may have been selected because of the large pool of the Durga temple, and to take strength from the *shakti* (divine female power) associated with the temple. Rambag is almost identical in size to the temple pool. The temple dates from around 1700, more than one hundred years before the Ramnagar *Ramlila* began. How Rambag anchors the sense of the *Ramlila's* symmetrical spatial harmony is demonstrated by an anecdote on how physical decay in one site led to the use of a new site and divided loyalties to these settings. The Maharaja Vibhuti Narain Singh's younger brother, C. P. N. Narain Singh, orally reports the following:

> Some years back, but during my lifetime, the wall of Rambag collapsed so the first day's lila [set in Lanka] could not be enacted there. Everything was transferred to Retinbag near to Lanka where there also was a tank and a garden—but in miniature scale. For ten or twelve years the *Ramlila* began in Retinbag—during that time only the real Lanka was used as Lanka. When Rambag was repaired a controversy arose. Some people said, Why not utilize Retinbag? There is a logical justification for continuing there, why bring it back? But other people argued the *Ramlila* should start just outside Rambag. The middle of the cycle, the days at Chitrakut, are also at Rambag, and the end of *Ramlila* is inside Rambag. The cycle begins outside of Rambag in chaos and ends inside Rambag with perfect harmony. So to many people it was less important to have the real Lanka than to experience this rhythmic harmony. So the first lila was brought back from Retinbag.

Chitrakut is situated slightly northwest of Rambag, and, as two photographs taken some fifty years apart show, there has been virtually no change in this environment (Illus. 1.7, 1.8). Chitrakut is near the front of Rambag, close to the pool that was the Kshir Sagar: Ram is still close to Ayodhya, its people, and its concerns. When on day 13 Bharat arrives at Chitrakut to ask Ram to return to Ayodhya and the throne, he is accompanied by hundreds of "Ayodhyans"—spectators who have journeyed with him from the center of Ramnagar. Ram not only rejects Bharat's pleas, but he also decides to move further into the forest to live as a hermit. Thus on day 14 Ram and his party leave for Panchavati deep in the Dandaka forest. The beginning of the three-mile, two-day journey from Chitrakut to Panchavati takes Ram and his party around the Durga pool, where, in front of the temple, they meet Indra, "the god of atmospheric phenomena, wielding the thunderbolt and

1.7

Chitrakut, old photo, c. 1925. Photo courtesy of the Maharaja of Banaras.

1.8

Chitrakut, 1978. Note how little the environment has changed over five decades. Photo, Richard Schechner.

conquering darkness" (Hill, 1952: 512). In 1978, a fierce tempest felicitously struck at the moment of Indra's appearance. After a pause of about an hour, while performers and spectators alike took what cover they could, all resumed the trek to Panchavati. Giving in to the weather is very much part of the *Ramlila* (Illus. 1.9). Nearly every year, several episodes have to be squeezed into days not assigned to them because the weather forces cancellations or sudden endings to a night's performance. Generally, the weather improves as the cycle progresses. By the closing days of the *Ramlila*, the hot, humid rainy season has given way to glorious sunny days and clear brisk cool nights. It is as if even the weather celebrates Ram's triumph.

The events in Janakpur early in the cycle (days 3 to 7) are joyful. This spacious environment, larger than Rambag, straddles one of Ramnagar's main roads. To the east is Sita's pleasure garden, 450 feet by 300 feet. Colorful birds are tethered to tree branches, and in 1978 a real deer grazed the grass next to one made of papier-mâché (by 1988 the live deer was gone). A small Parvati temple completes the bucolic scene. If the forest near Panchavati is wild and dangerous, Sita's garden is domesticity itself. Across the road facing Sita's garden is her father King Janak's palace compound, 200 feet by 325 feet, its main structure a moderately sized temple in which Sita sits. Three other platforms of various heights fill out the environment. One is for the *Dhanushyajna* (bow ritual), the contest of princes to see who can lift and break Shiva's bow and gain Sita as bride. No one can budge the bow except Ram, who not only lifts it but snaps it in three pieces with a flick of his young wrist. Another platform is for Ram, Lakshman, and their chaperon, the sage Vishvamitra. The third is Janak's royal residence, where the wedding of Ram and Sita takes place.[5] Whereas Sita's garden is to some degree naturalistic, Janak's palace compound is pure theatrical convenience. Platforms are set up merely to accommodate the action rather than to represent the way a king's capital might look. This is one of the few *Ramlila* environments that departs wholesale from verisimilitude. The bow contest is extremely decorous, not anything like the rough and deceitful kidnaping of Sita arranged by Ravana at Panchavati. But underneath both scenes is the assumption that Sita is a prize to be won and taken.

Panchavati is deep in the Dandaka forest; it is quite close to Pampasar, a lake in Kishkindha, the monkey kingdom where Ram plans his strategies to regain Sita with the aid of Sugriva. Interestingly, Panchavati and Kishkindha are, as it were, the backyard of Ayodhya. The Panchavati-Kishkindha environments cannot be seen from Ayodhya, but a glance at the scale map shows how close they are to

1.9

Bad weather. The performance is sometimes postponed because of inclement weather.
Photo, Richard Schechner, 1978.

each other. This may be theatrical expediency, or it may indicate an association between Ram's capital and the crisis that precipitates his war against Ravana. On day 16 at Panchavati an intriguing vortex occurs, as if Ravana's seizing of Sita, which precipitates the demon king's downfall and paves the way for Ram's kingship, sucks in the whole story. Thus, midway in the Ramlila's temporal scheme, at the very place where Ram's low point (Panchavati) and high point (Ayodhya) seem to meet, the full narrative is experienced in a flash.

Lanka is a rectangular field about 900 feet by 600 feet, larger than Rambag and the Durga temple pool combined. From Ram's head-quarters on Suvel Hill to Ravana's Fort is 650 feet; from the ashoka garden where Sita is held prisoner to the battlefield halfway between Suvel Hill and Ravana's Fort is 340 feet. Lanka, a lila ground of immense size, is packed full on Dashahara day with seventy-five thousand or more persons (Illus. 1.10). Its huge size gives scope to the epic battles bringing down Meghnad, Kumbhakarna, and finally Ravana himself. It also contains Ravana's fort, 120 feet by 95 feet and his smaller palace, as well as Ram's headquarters and the ashoka garden where Sita is held prisoner. Standing in Lanka, one is swallowed by its immensity. Ram, often framed by small-scale temple architecture, radiates intensity, not size. Ravana, although played by a human actor (except on Dashahara night, when his gigantic effigy—corpse?—true self?—sits atop his fort awaiting cremation [Illus. 1.11]), lives in a world of giants. In the Ramlila large-scale figures appear from time to time: the demoness Taraka is slain on the road to Janakpur on day 3; Shurpanakha shows herself in both her human and demon forms on day 16; later that same day the big vulture battles Ravana; and on day 19 at Rameshvaram the giantess Surasa blocks Hanuman's way to Lanka. In Lanka during the days of battle a number of towering demons enter the war and are defeated.

Lanka is the Ramlila at its biggest. Although distances covered during some of the lilas—journeys of three miles or more—are much larger than Lanka, no single Ramlila "stage" is. Lanka's vast open space is Ravana's kingdom, the Ramlila's ultimate battlefield. On many days the crowds gathered in Lanka exceed ten thousand, and on Dashahara, as already mentioned, seventy-five thousand. On that day Ravana surrenders his life to Ram shortly after the maharaja rides from his Fort through Ramnagar to Lanka in a sumptuous elephant procession (Illus. 1.12). After looping across the battlefield, he retires for the day. "It is not proper for one king to witness the death of another," the maharaja replied when asked why he did not stay for the final battle. Not surprisingly, the biggest mela (fair) of the Ramlila assembles on Lanka's

1.10

Crowded Lanka on Dashahara with Ravana's effigy in view. Photo, Richard Schechner, 1978.

1.11

Ravana's effigy ablaze atop his fort on Dashahara night.
Photo, Richard Schechner, 1978.

1.12

The Dashahara procession moving through a courtyard in the Fort as the maharaja sets out for Lanka. Photo, Richard Schechner, 1976.

fringes, where food, tea and soft drinks, toys, games, dyes, and herbs are all for sale. At Lanka's southern extreme is Ravana's large fort and his smaller palace, both earthen structures. From here emerge the demon king's staunchest allies, his son Meghnad and his brother Kumbhakarna, demons whose bamboo and papier-mâché figures range upwards of thirty feet. These effigies are cleverly built (yet stagehands working the demon can be seen high up in the structure). In battle Ram systematically dismembers Kumbhakarna: first the nose comes off, then the head, and finally the trunk snaps in two.

The immensity of Lanka is a strong way to show the greatness of Ram's victory. The assembly of so many beings of all kinds signifies the universality of Ram's triumph. Yet for ordinary people especially, Ram is god in human form, human sized. His adversaries are beings who have distorted the shape of the world, making it monstrous like themselves. The very bigness of the demons embodies their evil. Studying old drawings and photographs, some from the 1920s, one from about 1830, makes it clear that the battles fought in Lanka now are not of as grand a scale as they used to be (Illus. 1.13). The number of giant effigies and elephants are fewer, a result of reduced budgets, if not changing tastes. In the early 1980s a small road was built across Lanka, and a major highway is planned close by. "Think what that would mean," the maharaja said. "During some of the most delicate scenes—Ram's grieving for wounded Lakshman, Sita's lament as she sits in the ashoka garden—we would hear the roar of trucks, smell the benzene." Intensive lobbying has stalled the highway, but for how long? Pressures are building for further development.

In contrast to Lanka, the stage environments of Panchavati and Kishkindha are small and rustic with few permanent structures, only a small shrine atop a hill, a raised platform or two—for here Ram is in the deep forest, where he meets reclusive sages, demons, and animals. Here magic, deceit, and violence abound. From the forest Ravana kidnaps Sita. Jatayu, the brave vulture who tries to stop Ravana in midair as he carries Sita off, is dismembered and left dying on the ground; Ram, in need of allies for his war against Ravana, kills the monkey king Bali so as to gain the aid of Bali's younger brother, Sugriva. The only unalloyed positive happening in these places is the meeting with the monkey Hanuman, Ram and Sita's chief helper.

The environments of Ayodhya and the Fort—the respective palaces of the *Ramlila*'s two kings, Ram and the maharaja of Banaras—are located at Ramnagar's source where the town meets the Ganga River. Ayodhya is a simple 370- by 285-foot rectangular courtyard with a raised stage at the south end (Illus. 1.14). It is a version of the large interior

1.13

Dashahara as seen by James Prinsep, 1830. It seems as if there were more demons, more elephants—more theatrical grandeur. Photo courtesy of the Maharaja of Banaras.

1.14

The maharaja atop his elephant viewing a *lila* (play) in Ayodhya as it appears early in the cycle before Ram's exile. Photo, Richard Schechner, 1978.

courtyards characteristic of the maharaja's Fort, which is huge and complex (Illus. 1.15); thus Ayodhya is modest possibly so as not to upstage its near neighbor. Ayodhya is the focus of the *Ramlila*'s start and finish: Ram's birth, childhood, and early manhood (days 2 and 3); the return after Ram's marriage to Sita and the crisis leading to Ram's exile (days 7, 8, and 9); Bharat's placing of Ram's sandals on the throne before retiring to Nandigram to live an ascetic life while Ram is in exile (day 14); and Ram's coronation, teaching, and farewell (days 29, 30, and 31). Of these final events, only the coronation takes place wholly in Ayodhya. The other lilas begin there and then move to Rambag or the Fort. By the *Ramlila*'s end Ram is king of all the world, and the whole of Ramnagar is his Ayodhya.

Why Is the Ramnagar *Ramlila* So Big?

Why organize the cycle at Ramnagar on such a vast scale? All other *Ramlilas* are more modest in both space and time. Mansa Ram, founder of the current royal line in the early eighteenth century, rose from the humble position of tax collector. His lineage gained respectability when he arranged his son Balwant Singh's coronation in 1740 as maharaja of Banaras. Balwant ruled until his death in 1770. In part because of their dubious origins, Mansa Ram's descendants faced the difficult task of establishing their line as newly appointed kings. Balwant built the Fort in Ramnagar, establishing there his royal residence. But why would the maharaja of Banaras put his palace on the "bad side"[6] of the Ganga some few kilometers downriver from Banaras? The maharaja wished to firmly establish his power and his tax-collecting abilities, not only in Hindu Banaras but also in the Muslim countryside; therefore he erected the appropriately named Fort as an outpost and barrier between the Nawabs (Muslim rulers) of Avadh and his own Banaras. Later maharajas displayed the exalted position of their family by patronizing, developing, and participating in a *Ramlila* on a grand scale. As Induja Awasthi writes, because "Ramnagar was predominantly a Muslim population, the Maharaja, in the 19th century, in a bid to restore lost glory to the Hindus and to win them over, might have decided to accord state recognition to the *Ramlila*" (n.d.: 2). To this end, the maharajas of the Singh line, wanting to keep hold of the people of Banaras by regularly bringing thousands of them over to the Muslim side of the river, devised a powerful reason for many Hindus to cross the river to Ramnagar, where they were dramatically reminded of the maharaja's splendor, power, and devotion.

1.15

The Fort—the maharaja's palace in Ramnagar—as seen while rowing across the Ganga. Photo, Richard Schechner, 1978.

The motive is forcefully demonstrated on Dashahara, also known as Vijayadashami ("Victory Tenth") which, hardly by accident, is also Durgapuja day, the high point of the nine-day festival of "Durga worship." On this tenth day of the month, Ram slays the demon Ravana, Durga—a militant form of the Great Goddess—destroys the buffalo demon Mahishasura, and the maharaja displays his weapons and royal military authority with spectacular clarity. On Dashahara the narration of the *Ramlila* is interrupted as the maharaja plays out his own story. The festivities begin when the maharaja celebrates a special "weapons puja" (*hathiyar puja*) in one of the large courtyards of the Fort, where a panoply of swords, daggers, guns, and other martial implements, mostly from the late nineteenth and early twentieth centuries, are presented. (We were not allowed to photograph this display, which signaled that in some way it was a very special manifestation, whereas we were allowed to photo almost every other aspect of the *Ramlila*.) After the weapons puja the maharaja leads the Ramnagar *Ramlila*'s largest and most opulent procession: even the elephants have their heads painted and their bodies adorned with silver and silks. The maharaja and his party, great kettledrums booming, issue from the Fort and march down the main street of Ramnagar out to Lanka. The maharaja leads the procession of elephants through cheering crowds into the battleground. Then abruptly the maharaja and his party turn and leave Lanka the way they came, having stayed less than ten minutes, never stopping.

What is the meaning of this strange procession that for the only time in the *Ramlila* violates the performing space? Usually the maharaja remains firmly anchored at the back of the spectators, marking the far end of the "auditorium." The weapons puja is what is left of a very warlike traditional display of kingly might, called *digvijaya*. The digvijaya used to occupy the maharajas on Dashahara, when they marched their armies to the borders of their domain, proclaimed the territory to be theirs, confronted their opposing number across the border, and went home. Thus they showed their ability to make war and also identified themselves with the Vedic horse sacrifice (*ashvamedha yajna*), which Dasharatha himself performs in the *Ramayana* and *Ramcharitmanas*. In this procession the maharaja of Ramnagar stakes out his territory, proclaiming in effect that the *Ramlila* is his. His bold overriding of the performing space clearly shows who is king of the place, both secular and sacred.

William S. Sax digs out the traditional roots of this action. According to Sax, Ram's military campaign is a kind of *digvijaya*, a "conquest of the directions." The term is from Sanskrit *dik*, "direction," plus *vijaya*, meaning "conquest" or "victory"...The *digvijayi* begins with a fire sacrifice, then proceeds in a clockwise direction, travelling east, south, north, and west, conquering his enemies or receiving their submission (much as in the *asvamedha yajna*) until he has conquered or co-opted potential rivals in all directions. He then returns to his point of origin, now transformed into the capital city and center of the earth.

The earliest and most famous account is probably the *Digvijaya* book of the *Mahabharata*, where four of the five Pandava brothers conquer the world simultaneously...After conquering the world by means of a *digvijaya*, ancient Indian kings performed ritual journeys in which they displayed their royal power and commemorated the military campaigns that established their rule. Other annual, royal progresses—the *vijaya-yatra* which had as their objective "the renewal and reconstitution of cosmos, society, and kingdom" [Inden, 1978: 26, 59–60]—occurred annually, after the rainy season...Vijayadasami implies several victories: of Ram over Ravana, of the devotee over his own sins and shortcomings, and of the goddess Durga over the demon Mahisasura in the Durga Puja. According to north Indian tradition, the five Pandava brothers, heroes of the Mahabharata war, took up their previously hidden weapons on this day (at the end of their exile [as Ram approaches the end of his])...Vijayadasami is thus an appropriate day for weapon-worship...Several old-timers in Ramnagar told me that before the British came, the Maharaja would make a procession to the very border of his kingdom that day, in effect challenging his enemies to give battle if they dared. (1982: 15–16)

The maharaja confirmed this, telling us that the Dashahara procession was once an actual display of military might: the reigning maharaja, accompanied by his armed soldiers, would go to the borders of his domain, near Mirzapur some thirty miles east of Ramnagar. In this way, on the day of the final battle between Ram and Ravana, the maharaja publicly marks out, or used to mark out, the extent of his kingdom—as with Vishnu's "expanding," Vamana's striding, and Ram's goings.

Whatever its extrinsic and symbolic purposes, the immensity of the Ramnagar *Ramlila* is consistent with its own internal logic. The intent of the *Ramlila*'s authors was to create a performance that would not be a reduction or parody of the *Ramcharitmanas* but a popular reproduction of it as sacred theater. To this end they integrated temple ritual,

pilgrimage, poetry, and drama. The kernel of the *Ramlila* has remained
constant for more than 150 years, even as diminishing financial
resources, and especially Indian independence and the abolition of
princely states, have meant a scaling back of the numbers of elephants
and effigies. The overall size of the *Ramlila* and its attraction as a
devotional and pilgrimage center are intact. And compared to
Ramnagar's, other *Ramlilas* are small in scale. Some are famous for this
or that scene, such as Varanasi's Nati Imli Bharat Milap, which the
maharaja and a half-million onlookers attend, or Delhi's display of
fireworks as Ravana's effigy explodes on Dashahara. But only Ramnagar
combines spectacularity and devotion: the recitation of the entire
Ramcharitmanas during the action, the focused silence of the *arati*
worship concluding each lila episode, and the many scenes of intense
religious fervor, with pilgrimage both within individual lilas and as a
characteristic of the *Ramlila* taken as a whole. At Ramnagar the
sometimes contradictory combination of magnificence and asceticism
so typical of Hindu tradition is played up. The ascetic tendencies of
the story are played out within the frame of a large-scale theatrical
production. When Ram, Sita, and Lakshman enter the forest, they go
as ascetics, their arms and legs neatly streaked with sandalwood paste
representing the ashes with which renouncers are covered, but they
also continue to wear their fancy royal and godly crowns. The maharaja
says that the crowns ensure the stability of the icon for devoted
spectators. Thus the metamessage of the Ramnagar *Ramlila* even during
the forest scenes is of splendid royal and divine presence. At the same
time, the hundreds of *sadhus* (holy men) at the *Ramlila*, many smeared
in ashes and nearly naked, demonstrate devotion and *tapasya*
(renunciation). Tapasya is also the choice of many spectators walking
barefoot long distances in dust and mud, submitting to rain and other
hardships, and neglecting their businesses and family life for a month.

Transforming Ramnagar into a theater, maintaining environments
of scale, singing the *Ramcharitmanas*, assembling scholars, poets, and
sadhus to compose the samvads, and carefully rehearsing the svarups
so that the samvads are recited with clarity and feeling—all of these
make the Ramnagar *Ramlila* unique. By providing food and lodging for
sadhus, the maharaja guarantees that these holy men from distant
places flock to the *Ramlila*, thereby confirming its authenticity. One
could interpret the provision of food and lodging cynically; one sadhu
told a member of our research team: "Just understand this one thing—
we come for bread. As long as the bread lasts, we'll stay. Do you see
that field there? It's filled with sadhus. But if the maharaja were to stop
feeding them bread, they'd all run." Or one could argue that it is the

dharma (religious duty) of kings to feed holy beggars. In any event, the ambivalences and multiplicities of the *Ramlila* are everywhere visible. The *Ramlila* is not reducible to single meanings or experiences. Rather, it is an extensive cycle of events offering performers and spectators what they are looking for, ranging from bread to devotion, from excitement to meditation, from drama to pilgrimage. The *Ramlila* is felt to be in everyone's interest but for many different reasons.

What haunts the Ramnagar *Ramlila* is India's national dream of Ramraj, the divine rule of Ram in a golden age when the whole nation is united and strong. The vision demands size. Simulating all of India, merging the mythic past with the political present, needs a big field of play. Mahatma Gandhi saw this and used imagery drawn from Ram's story (if not the *Ramlila* itself) to construct the mythos underlying the Indian struggle for independence from Moghul and British rule. Ram's story concerns the emergent sovereignty of a heroic Hindu solar king. This mythos, so much a part of the *Ramlila*, combines religious devotion with nationalist fervor. Each night, rowing back across the Ganga after the lila, those on my boat, led by boatman Ram Das (whose name means "servant of Ram"), sang the following hymn:

> King Ram, leader of the Raghu dynasty,
> Born from Shankara's [Shiva's] drum,
> Born from the waves of the Ganga,
> Husband of pure Sita.

> Born from the mouth of the wise.
> Hail to Sita's Ram,
> And to Hanuman, who carries our burdens
> And grants us favors.

> Hail to Mother Ganga!

This is like Gandhi's rallying song, sung to the same tune:

> King Ram, leader of the Raghu dynasty,
> Husband of pure Sita:
> May we worship this Sita-Ram.
> He is known as Ishvara or Allah.
> May this God bestow good sense on everyone.

Gandhi desired a modern Ramraj that would put an end to Hindu-Muslim hatred and bloodshed. But it is not Gandhi's vision that the *Ramlila* projects. The *Ramlila*'s politics are chauvinist; Allah is not accorded a place equal to Sita-Ram's Ishvara (the Lord). At the *Ramlila* Muslims are present as fireworks technicians, craftsmen, and elephant drivers—all traditional north Indian Muslim work. As spectators, they keep a low profile.

Within India's religious and theatrical tradition there is a strong warrant for the production of large-scale, highly skilled performance representing the widest possible range of emotions, relating sacred and royal stories, and depicting interactions among gods, humans, and demons. The first and most important Sanskrit text on performance is Bharata's *Natyashastra.*[7] This work is both sacred and practical, and begins by narrating the origins, qualities, and functions of drama. The *Natyashastra* explains how in ancient days the "people became addicted to sensual pleasures, were under the sway of desire and greed, became affected with jealousy and anger and found their happiness mixed with sorrow" (1.7–12). The gods wanted an art that would "belong to all the color-groups" (everyone, regardless of caste). Brahma then instructed Bharata in the "fifth Veda,"[8] which was drama, or the

> representation of the way things are in the three worlds [of gods, humans, and demons]. There is [reference to] duty, sometimes to games, sometimes to money, sometimes to peace; and sometimes laughter is found in it, sometimes fighting, sometimes love-making, and sometimes killing. (1.107)

> [Drama] gives diversion to kings, and firmness [of mind] to persons afflicted with sorrow, and [hints of acquiring] money to those who are for earning it, and it brings composure to persons agitated in mind. (1.110)

> The drama as I have devised it, is a mimicry of actions and conducts of people, which is rich in various emotions, and which depicts different situations. This will relate to actions of men good, bad, and indifferent, and will give courage, amusement, and happiness as well as counsel to them all. (1.111–12)

> A mimicry of the exploits of gods, demons, kings as well as house-holders in this world, is called drama. And when human nature with its joys and sorrows, is depicted by means of representation through gestures and the like it is called drama. (1.121)

The occasion for the first theatrical production was Indra's Banner Festival depicting the defeat of demons by the gods with "altercations and tumult and mutual cutting off and piercing [of limbs or bodies]"

(1.55–58). This could have been an accurate description of the *Ramlila's* battle scenes.

The *Natyashastra* is a text of more than eight hundred pages detailing every aspect of theatrical and dance production. It establishes theatrical performance as a recognized kind of celebratory worship. Thus early in the Indian tradition theater is accorded a definite place equal to religious worship: there is no antipathy between the two as there is in Christianity or Islam. The Ramnagar *Ramlila* does not follow the *Natyashastra* in details of production (as some Indian classic dance forms claim to do), but shows its kinship to the text by being a large-scale, didactic, and devotional performance designed for an audience consisting of all castes and classes.

How Much Have the *Ramlila* Environments Changed over Time?

The Lanka environment has suffered encroachment. Is this a trend? Are there other changes taking place? We know next to nothing in detail about the Ramnagar *Ramlila's* first century, from about 1820 to 1920. What we do know after studying writings, drawings, lithographs, and photographs from the late nineteenth and early twentieth centuries, as well as by interviewing many people, is that the *Ramlila* appears to have been surprisingly stable in terms of its physical staging. The samvads recited today were assembled in the 1920s. From the 1920s onward there are photographs showing the physical environments and aspects of the mise-en-scène, which appear to have been more or less the same over the past seventy years except that, as previously noted, the numbers of effigies and elephants have declined. These reductions in scale are confirmed by longtime spectators. A farmer who has attended for fifty-five years said, "The difference is that the maharaja's glory was far greater thirty years ago. He came with one hundred horses, thirty or thirty-five elephants, bullock carts—so much finery that all the people in this field of Lanka could not carry it all. But there's no difference in the lila itself. Absolutely none. Everything is done exactly as it is written in the [*Ramcharit*] manas." Spectators are forgiving concerning sumptuousness as long as what they consider the essence of *Ramlila*—its conformity to the text of Tulsidas—is intact.

The *Ramlila* is changing in some ways, however, because India has radically changed over the past 150 years. Value systems are different, the authority of the maharaja has been reduced if not entirely eliminated, and the population has more than quadrupled since 1850. Processions that in the nineteenth century would actually have moved from city to jungle, from settled areas to wilderness, today are entirely encompassed by houses, farms, factories, or other evidence of human habitation. Bhardwaj's ashram or Guha's village—both supposedly deep in the forest and probably once actually so—are today enclaves wedged into well-farmed areas. What is unchanged is the feeling of movement through various landscapes, the sense of adventure, exile, and danger followed by a triumphant return home. The *Ramlila* narrative is strong and deeply believed, and it is written in the theatrical environments, the paths connecting them, the acting, and even the weather. Regular attenders of the *Ramlila* warmly testify to their experience of being inside Ram's world, as Hess notes in her article:

> In tonight's Lila [day 3] the sage Visvamitra takes Ram and Lakshman on a foray to kill demons in the woods. The use of the world as a stage set goes beyond anything the West might call "verisimilitude." We move from the main street to narrow lanes, a troop of horsemen in front, the Maharaja with his elephants behind, the golden gods in the middle gliding along at shoulder level [borne by devotees—the swarups' feet never touch the ground except when necessary for the drama]. Shopkeepers and laborers stop to watch the gods go by, saluting them with joined palms. The setting becomes steadily more rural. Roads change from pavement to cobblestone to dirt, houses from plaster to brick to mud, on varying levels, with glittering algae-covered ponds, fields of leafy vegetables and corn, moist greenness everywhere. People are at the doorways, in the yards, on the roofs. If Ram really did go to the forest with Visvamitra, would it not have been through lanes like this, past houses, from town to village, while the local people stopped to watch? The sky is brilliant salmon and mauve in the luminous moments before sunset. (Hess, 1983:176–77)

Flow: Pilgrimage, Procession, and Participation

Vishnu expanding creates the cosmos; Vamana's striding recuperates the three worlds; Ram's goings signify India. For several hours each day during a full month Ramnagar is transformed into mythopoetic epic India. The extended space and time of the *Ramlila* puts one inside the action. In Ramnagar, the *Ramlila* is everywhere: in the lilas themselves, in the mela close to whatever lila ground is in use, in the environments not active today but yesterday or tomorrow, in the small shrines where people sing kirtans, and in the dominating presence of the Fort, which signifies the maharaja who sponsors the *Ramlila*. The *Ramlila*'s efficacy is heightened by the way time is experienced. One does not "go to" the *Ramlila* as to a theater. Attending the *Ramlila* on a regular basis throughout a whole month is a different kind of operation. The mind and body are full of the *Ramlila*; it is all-consuming. Yet, for the *nemis* (devoted spectators), who are regular *Ramlila* goers, this total immersion is not exhausting but invigorating. Of course, as the wide variations from lila to lila in crowd size show, relatively few attend all the lilas, but a sizeable proportion see ten or more.

To go to the *Ramlila* as a nemi takes the whole day. Preparations begin with an early morning bath, in the sacred Ganga if possible, with memories of last night's lila still fresh in mind. Routine activities must be completed by noon. Coming from Varanasi means leaving for Ramnagar between 2:00 and 3:00 P.M., since the lila begins at 5:00. You can cross the Ganga by bus at the northern end of Varanasi or from the more southerly *ghats* in one of a fleet of small rowboats or push aboard the always overcrowded public ferry (Illus. 1.16). Once in Ramnagar one easily falls into the stream of pedestrians, bicycles, cycle and scooter rickshaws, and motorcycles. The festive atmosphere takes over. There are snacks and tea and familiar faces. You look forward to the day's story, the next adventures of characters you already know well. The performance usually consists of two parts, one before *sandhya puja* (evening prayers) and one after. The sandhya puja break starts at about 6:00 P.M. and lasts an hour or more. Some people pray; many more snack and socialize. The second part of a day's lila usually ends between 9:00 and 10:00 P.M., though some run later and Ram's coronation is an all-night affair. After the lila most people go directly home. A few stop to sing kirtans or listen to others doing so, or to buy some *pan* (betel) or tea at one of the stalls near the ghat. This mixture of devotion, meditation, celebration, and socializing is typical pilgrimage behavior in India, a happy "time out" from ordinary life, part religious obligation, part vacation. If one crosses the Ganga by rowboat at night (the ferry no longer runs at this hour), one sings hymns, scoops some holy river water onto one's face, and reflects on the lila's events. By the time one retires for the night it is midnight or later, and the next day's lila is not far off. If you are a nemi, for a month the *Ramlila* swallows you.

S. M. Bhardwaj notes, "The number of Hindu sanctuaries in India is so large and the practice of pilgrimage so ubiquitous that the whole of India can be regarded as a vast sacred space organized into a system of pilgrimage centers and their fields" (Bhardwaj, 1973:7). The *Ramlila*'s environmental theater is a model of India as a "vast sacred space." Through the agency of the *Ramlila* environments, spectators can visit the same powerful *tirtha-sthans* or pilgrimage sites that Ram passes through in his epic journeys from Ayodhya to Janakpur to Chitrakut

1.16

A huge crowd waiting to cross the Ganges by public ferry to reach Ramnagar. Photo, Martin Karcher, 1978.

to Panchavati to Lanka and back to Ayodhya. Furthermore, the Ramnager *Ramlila* is itself a pilgrimage attraction. People from all over India come to Banaras during the *Ramlila* season to bathe in the Ganga, visit the Vishvanath temple and other holy sites, and experience the *Ramlila*. In 1978, a man who for two years had been carrying his mother in a basket around India visiting holy places arrived at the *Ramlila* (Illus. 1.17). Their itinerary was very full: they could spare but one morning touring the maharaja's Fort and one night at the *Ramlila* before setting out toward another pilgrimage site.

In a survey conducted in 1978 by William S. Sax, a member of the Schechner-Hess research team, more than 80 percent of the spectators questioned considered the Ramnagar *Ramlila* a pilgrimage center.

Sadhu:	This is certainly a *tirtha*. It is the biggest *Ramlila* in all of India. Everywhere that Ram[a] went on his wanderings is now regarded as a *tirtha-sthan*: Ayodhya, Janakpur, Chitrakut...all of them.
Sax:	But Ram didn't come to Ramnagar.
Sadhu:	If you experience the entire *Ramlila* from start to finish, walk, read the *Ramayana* [*Ramcharitmanas*], and enjoy the *lila*, you have a total pilgrimage experience. The people who do that do go to Ayodhya, Chitrakut, and so on.
Another sadhu:	It's true, completely true. That temple over there is Rameshvaram temple, none other.
Bihari farmer:	I've been to the four *dhams* [primary pilgrimage places], Ayodhya, Chitrakut, Mathura, Brindavan— *lakhs* [hundreds of thousands] of pilgrimage places. I've seen thousands of *lilas* also, but among all those pilgrimage places and *lilas*, I tell you that there was not one place where I got as much peace of mind as here at the Ramnagar *Ramlila*. And there is no place as holy as Kashi [Varanasi].

Even allowing for the respondents' self-congratulatory tone, most people feel that the *Ramlila* environments are sacred and that following the performers from place to place transforms spectators into participant-pilgrims. There is no question that during the *Ramlila* many people travel with Ram, Sita, and other figures.

Paradigmatic of the *Ramlila* is literally following in Ram's footsteps. By means of these daily minipilgrimages spectators participate directly

1.17

A son carrying his mother in a basket so that she can visit holy pilgrimage places throughout India. Photo, Richard Schechner, 1978.

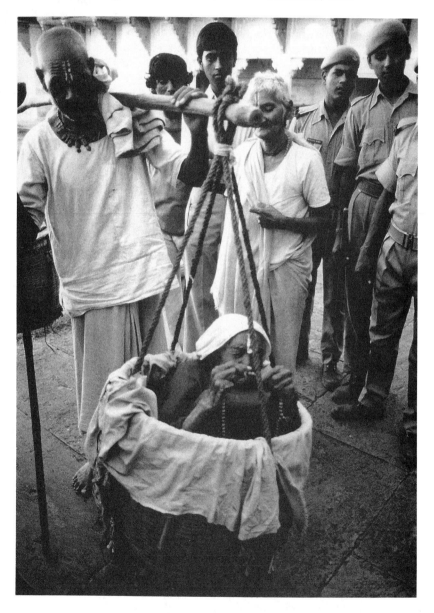

and emotionally in the *Ramlila*. There are the admiring citizens of Ayodhya and Janakpur lining the roads or peering from windows, doorways, or rooftops celebrating the meeting and marriage of Ram and Sita; or the heartbroken citizens of Ayodhya weeping as they follow the royal couple into exile; or hundreds of religious pilgrims joining Bharat as he circumambulates Chitrakut. They follow Ram, Sita, and Lakshman through the forests, where the svarups meet gods, demons, monkeys, and *rishis* (saints and sages). They rush angrily in pursuit of Ravana after he kidnaps Sita; they accompany Ram's army of monkeys and bears when they cross from India into Lanka. When Lakshman is wounded in battle, Ram sends Hanuman to the Himalayas to fetch the only herb that can save him. Some spectators remain close to grief-stricken as Ram laments: "Oh, if I had known I would lose my brother in the forest, I wouldn't have obeyed my father. Wealth, son, wife, home, family come and go repeatedly in this world, but a true brother cannot be found!" Others scamper along with faithful Hanuman, which takes one hour and covers five miles of "real" time and space, one night and thousands of miles of story time. After Ram defeats Ravana and Sita passes her fire ordeal (proving her sexual fidelity to Ram), she takes her place on a huge twenty-foot-high cart next to Ram and Lakshman. Dozens of male spectators tug on the two ropes moving the four-wheeled *pushpaka* out of Lanka and down the long road toward Ayodhya. After a few hundred yards the cart stops at Bhardwaj's ashram, where Ram and his party will spend the night. When the next night the journey home continues, thousands of joyful spectators join in; others line the streets, wave from windows, or salute the heroes from rooftops. The Bharat Milap—the reunion of Ram and Lakshman with Bharat and Shatrughna—occurs where Ramnagar's two main streets intersect (Illus. 1.18). Gradually, over several hours before the meeting, two crowds—one from Bhardwaj's ashram, one coming from Ayodhya—fuse into one.

Many spectators go barefoot at the *Ramlila* because "you don't wear shoes in a temple, and the entire Ram lila ground sanctified by God's presence is like a temple" (Hess, 1983:174). On some nights the spectators' devotion is sorely tested as they walk five miles or more through thunderstorms and mud. This "going along" with the performance is built into the mise-en-scène. If movement itself were not so important, the *Ramlila* could easily be structured in a more theatrically conventional way to reduce or eliminate spectator move-ment. But its creators intended it to be a kind of processional-pilgrimage. Spectators move through various terrains—city, village, farm field, forest. Most of the way is level, but around Panchavati, itself a mountain,

1.18

Bharat Milap—literally the "meeting with Bharat," but which depicts the reunion of Ram and Lakshman with their brothers Bharat and Shatrughna—performed on a brightly lit square stage erected at the intersection of Ramnagar's two main streets. Photo, Richard Schechner, 1978.

there are a few low hills. When the crowd is settled at an environment watching a scene, male and female spectators are generally separated from each other, but during the processions from one location to another everyone mixes.

Stasis: Darshan, Arati, and Jhanki

Some people attend only a few of the thirty-one lilas or come just for the mela. Crowds swell and dwindle not only from one lila to the next but also during each lila. Attendance on any given night is greatest for arati, each lila's closing ceremony when the svarups are honored with the waving of a camphor-flame lamp and a shower of flowers as they are illuminated by flares (Illus. 1.19). During arati it is felt to be particularly beneficial to take *darshan* of the svarups—that is, to get a good clear look at the five boys aged eight to fourteen (or so) who are the gods Ram, Sita, Lakshman, Bharat, and Shatrughna. *Darshan* means "vision" or "seeing." Hindus believe that the sight of a god, a temple icon, a holy person, or a holy site conveys benefit. During arati it is important that the svarups pose perfectly still. This is because the svarups are also *murtis* (literally, material images), the word most commonly used for temple icons. Some temple murtis are extremely powerful, like the orange-red Hanuman enshrined at Sankat Mochan Temple in Varanasi or the black Lord Jagannath of Puri's Krishna temple. Throughout India one finds sacred stones, figures, and *lingams* worn smooth where thousands of hands have stroked them. At nationally renowned sites, as well as locally, people make offerings of incense, sweets, flowers, money, and various other things.

During the dramatic portions of the *Ramlila*, the svarups speak and move, enacting the very events that constitute their godhead, but at arati they attain the focused stillness of murtis. Some *Ramlila* gods, including Brahma, Shiva, Indra, and Hanuman—however convincingly enacted—are recognized as theatrical representations: during the sandhya puja break, for example, Hanuman may take off his mask and chat with spectators. But the five svarups are different. Even with their crowns off (signifying that they are not divine at that moment), the svarups attract the devoted attention of many, who bring them garlands of flowers or touch their feet reverently. During the long night of Ram's coronation, thousands touch and press their feet in a traditional gesture of reverence and respect, so much so that the svarups' feet are squeezed black and blue. The proximate presence of gods acting out mythic events on sacred grounds climaxes at arati. People surge forward for darshan, many having come miles just for the benefit of this moment. They will

1.19

The *jhanki* (frozen moment) pose of *arati* (light ceremony) that closes each *lila*.
Photo, Richard Schechner, 1978.

not tolerate having their view blocked. The svarups fix themselves in distinct poses: Ram smiles slightly, Lakshman alertly guards his brother, Sita is tranquilly resplendent in her bejeweled sari and ornaments. Bharat and Shatrughna, when not there as part of the drama, sometimes appear out of costume dressed in clean white clothes.

The Ramnagar *Ramlila* also offers a kind of "unofficial darshan" as spectators take long looks at the sadhus, Ram-Sita's devotees, and the maharaja, Shiva's representative. The sadhus are keenly appreciated, both as holy persons and as lively individuals who disregard many commonly accepted north Indian social values. Some wear only loincloths; many are smeared with ashes. Vigorously dancing and singing, they tease each other and the public as they celebrate Ram-Sita. They are very highly regarded and believed to be holy; some, like the "150-year-old sadhu" (now dead), are believed to possess "powers" (Illus. 1.20). In terms of the presentation of self, the maharaja is the opposite of the sadhus. He is a model of formal dress, decorum, circumspection, and quiet devotion, displaying himself for the public to admire as he witnesses nearly all the lila episodes. As he rides atop his royal elephant or in his horse-drawn carriage or seated in the back seat of his 1928 Cadillac, his presence helps keep order. When the maharaja appears or departs, he is greeted as the representative of Shiva with shouts of "*Hara, Hara, Mahadev!*" ("Shiva, Shiva, Great God!"), the counterpart to the rolling wave of voices responding to Ram's speeches with, "*Bol! Raja Ramchandra ki jai!*"

The darshans of the *Ramlila* are effective because they are *jhanki*, literally a "glimpse." *Jhanki* is a word some Indian theater experts use to disdain shows emphasizing spectacle over content. But jhanki is much appreciated by ordinary Indians. In the *Ramlila* the tableaux, the frozen iconic moments, are jhanki: Vishnu reclining on the serpent Shesha afloat on the Kshir Sagar, Sita borne into her garden in her silver palanquin, Ram standing gloriously triumphant after breaking Shiva's bow. Each lila's concluding arati is jhanki. For many *Ramlila* spectators jhanki distills from the flow of the action a crystallizing glimpse of a cosmic, eternal divinity.

Ram's Movements, Sita's Stillness

Ram is always on the move. He dynamically fills space as Vishnu-Vamana does. Sita, by contrast, is stillness personified. She sits in her pleasure garden, in Janakpur, in Chitrakut, and for ten long days in Lanka under the ashoka tree where Ravana holds her prisoner. Many women and some men attend Sita, often touching her feet. Even as

1.20

A sadhu said to be 150 years old in 1978. He died in the mid-1980s. Photo, Richard Schechner.

the action surges on the great Lanka battlefield, Sita sits for hours away from it all. There is nothing for her to say, nothing for her to do. Then, in lila 27, the day after Ram's victory, Sita proves that she has been sexually faithful during her captivity when, in her most active scene, she steps through a circle of fire. For most of the *Ramlila*, Sita is passive, the object of males' desires, the victim of their tricks, the prize of their contests and wars. Yet she is celebrated as Ram-Sita, the coequal amalgamated deity. She is always present for the arati ceremony at the end of each night's lila.

Sita's almost absolute stillness counterbalances Ram's extreme activity. Wherever he journeys, she is "home," the place where he stops or to which he returns. His actions are completed by her stillness; his moves to the periphery are answered by her presence at the center. Where she is, he must go. Much could be said from a Western feminist perspective concerning Sita's "position" in the *Ramlila*. She is a model of the orthodox Hindu construction of "wife."

A Double Transformation of Space

At Ramnagar a simultaneous double transformation of place—from city to theater and from theater to mythic geography—occurs. And just as there was a Troy and a Trojan War whose story was reshaped into the *Iliad*, so there may have been historical events underlying the *Ramayana*. According to H. D. Sankalia (1973), these events probably took place in north central India, from today's Ayodhya on the river Sarayu, south to Allahabad (Prayag), west to Chitrakut, and southwest to what was a forested area north of the river Narmada. But as Sanskritization spread the *Ramayana* southward, so the text's geographical field expanded as well. "The gradual spread, first of the *Mahabharata* and then of the *Ramayana* into the Deccan, Karnataka, and Tamil Nadu, shows the slow absorption by society, high and low, of certain ethical values...Simultaneously places all over India came to be associated with episodes in the *Ramayana*" (Sankalia, 1973:55). As the *Ramayana* stories, carried by priests, storytellers, and other kinds of performers, spread south and east, they were identified with local deities and sacred spaces. Indian cultures do not erase their pasts; instead, they remember and reuse. Thus over centuries the subcontinent has become a vast palimpsest of pre-Hindu, Hindu, Muslim, and Western elements. Certainly in the *Ramlila* the Hindu is dominant, but other cultures can also be clearly seen. Specific sites of sacred rivers, crossings, and hilltops are pre-Hindu; the basic narrative, celebratory devotional mood, and pilgrimage pattern is Hindu; and the maharaja's elaborate pageantry and the theatrical style of performing owe much to the Moghuls. Old Western elements are also present. British-era petromax lanterns illuminate most *Ramlila* scenes; the maharaja's brass marching band, his horse and carriage, and his Cadillac all evoke Europe and America. These are just a few examples of the *Ramlila's* multicultural nature.

The geography modeled by the *Ramlila* captures ancient references to rivers and river junctions, hilltops, forests, cities, temples, caves, trees, wells, and paths. Nearly every Hindu knows the story of the *Ramayana*, which has been retold in countless local variations in many Indian languages. Ram's adventures are the subject not only of the *Ramlila* but of many other media, ranging from classic dance and drama to folk theater, modern dramas, movies, and television. In the *Ramcharitmanas*, Ram rules over a great nation larger than modern India but roughly coextensive with it. One might say that Ram's geopoetic domain stretches from Mount Kailash in the Himalayas to Janakpur in Nepal, from Ayodhya and Prayag (Allahabad) on the Gangetic plain across the Ganga, Jamuna, and Godavari rivers to the Dandaka forest of central India, and from the Deccan plateau of peninsular India to Rameshvaram and on to Lanka. Ram's presence as sovereign of this domain is renewed each year by the thousands of *Ramlilas* performed all across north India. Each of these marks out by means of theatrical environments and definite movements a concrete model of the Indian subcontinent. The *Ramlila* ground conflates the historical events underlying the *Ramayana*, the mythic field of Ram's journey, realm, and rule, the modern Indian nation, and the theatrical representation of Ram's story.

Seen this way, the *Ramlila* moves between two poles: <u>Ayodhya</u> = home = Ramnagar = Ram = the maharaja's Fort = rightful authority versus <u>Lanka</u> = away = beyond the city = Ravana = wilderness = tyranny. Between the just order of Ayodhya and the unjust order of Lanka is a disorderly yet adventurous no-man's-land of mountains, rivers, and jungles populated by India's folk villains and heroes—demons and rishis, tribals, monkeys, and bears. In the *Ramlila* there are lands to be visited (Janakpur), explored (Chitrakut to Panchavati), endured (Kishkindha to Rameshvaram), and finally conquered (Lanka). Remarkably, this mythopoetic, dramatically active map of India has remained more or less constant from the time of the Valmiki *Ramayana* (approximately two thousand years ago). It continues to shape the thought, beliefs, and pilgrimage patterns of millions of Indian Hindus.

Ramnagar's Unique Concluding Scenes

During the final episodes of the *Ramlila*, Ram's world merges with the maharaja's in a way unique to Ramnagar. Even before Ram enters Ayodhya to be crowned, a collapse of time and space occurs. From lila 27, the day after Ram's victory over Ravana, and the start of his journey back from Lanka to Ayodhya, Ramnagar first becomes Ram's kingdom and then his capital city. The scale of the action again changes, this time back to human size. In Lanka the scale was grotesquely oversized, demonic. After Ram's victory, Lanka is forgotten as Ramnagar prepares to celebrate Ram's victory, coronation, and reign. Townspeople, royal and common, decorate their homes inside and out. The Fort is festooned with colored lights.

In the *Ramcharitmanas*, during his triumphant return from Lanka, Ram recapitulates the events of the drama, pointing out their sites as the heroes flow home via their aerial cars. The Ram of the *Ramlila* describes and remembers everything, but theatrically the journey home is abbreviated. There is no crossing of rivers, no visits with hermits at Chitrakut. The pushpaka rests the night of lila 26 near a tree sacred to residents of Ramnagar (but not mentioned in the *Ramcharitmanas*) and the night of lila 27 at Bhardwaj's ashram. By the time of Bharat Milap, on the night of lila 28, Ramnagar has become Ayodhya, and Ram and the maharaja share a capital. On day 29 the maharaja, a visiting head of state, sits on a white cloth in Ayodhya (Ram's Fort) as Ram accepts his crown so long deferred. After the coronation, the comrades from the Lanka war bid farewell to the svarups. This scene mixes joy with deeply felt sadness: everyone knows that the *Ramlila* is coming to an end, that a long year must pass before "gods walk the earth for a month." The young monkey Angad, nephew of Sugriva, stumbles slowly down the steps after tearfully saying goodbye to the svarups. Guha reluctantly leaves only after being invited to visit Ayodhya often. The darshan that follows the farewell is the *Ramlila*'s longest, lasting until dawn. First the maharaja, next the royal family, and finally ordinary people each bid farewell to the svarups. At dawn, preceded by his military guard, who splits the surging crowd in two, the maharaja returns for arati.

That evening, *Ramlila*'s thirtieth, the parties of Ram and the maharaja join in a single procession through the streets of Ramnagar to the gazebo at the center of Rambag, where Ram and Lakshman wait with Hanuman sitting behind them holding a royal umbrella. Then come Bharata and Shatrughna with an umbrella held by the Ayodhyan chief minister, Sumantra. Behind them comes the maharaja with one of his men holding the umbrella, and after him his royal family. A large population lines the streets: children jumping up and down in excitement, old and young joining palms and bowing, then rising and cheering. These people are simultaneously residents of ancient Ayodhya, persons celebrating their gods and kings, subjects of a medieval Hindu prince, and people of a modern Indian town enjoying a theatrical spectacle.

The next and final day's events, constituting the Kot Vidai (farewell), further dissolve the boundaries between the worlds of Ram and the maharaja. Although a portion of the *Ramcharitmanas* remains to be chanted, the events of day 31 of the cycle are outside the Ram story and unique to Ramnagar. The five svarups arrive at the Fort late in the afternoon (or at night, as in 1978, when an eclipse of the moon on the *Ramlila*'s second day skewed the whole schedule[9]), riding two magnificent elephants. The maharaja greets the svarups as a devotee of Ram, barefoot, dressed simply. Then they are seated on a low platform while the maharaja washes their feet, applies *tilak* (ornamental marks) to their foreheads, and garlands them. He performs arati to them, and then the svarups are served a sumptuous meal. The Ramayanis-twelve Brahmins led by the maharaja's head priest who, beginning ten days before the *Ramlila* begins and continuing throughout the cycle, chant the entire *Ramcharitmanas*—recite the final portions of Tulsidas's epic. As the svarups eat, the maharaja is handed a one-rupee coin by an attendant. He passes this coin to one of the two priests who act as the stage directors of *Ramlila* and who are known as *vyases*.[10] The vyases give it to Hanuman, who gives it to Ram, Ram gives it to Lakshman, and so on until each of the five svarups is paid. Next the Ramayanis and the other principal performers each get one rupee from the maharaja via the vyas.[11]

I believe this public paying of the performers at the end of the *Ramlila* is an assertion of the "real" order of things, showing who is king in Ramnagar. However, a nemi who has attended the *Ramlila* for many years disagrees: "It is the dharma [duty] of a king to give *dakshina* [an honorarium] to Brahmins." As with so much in the *Ramlila*, the two interpretations do not cancel each other out. After the svarups have eaten—it takes them more than an hour—the maharaja again performs arati. Then each of the svarups takes off his garland and puts it on the maharaja. This gesture is repeated with each member of the royal family, just as at temples the devout give and receive back *prasad* (blessed offerings). Then the royal family retires into the interior of the Fort as elephants arrive to take the svarups back to Ayodhya, where they give darshan to commoners.

The Kot Vidai is trivalent: the maharaja pays his performers even as he and his family welcome visiting royalty, whom they also worship as gods. All three events take place simultaneously, accomplished by the same set of gestures performed within the confines of a palace that is also a theater set. Witnessing the scene are the citizens of Ayodhya-Ramnagar-Varanasi. Meanings radiate outward through three frames: that of Ramnagar, where Vibhuti Narain Singh remains "honorary king"; that of the mythic narrative, where Ram and the others are legendary figures; and that of the cosmic and religious system of Hinduism, where gods are incarnate. Because of the *Ramlila*, the maharaja retains much of his mystique; and despite his real powers having ended with Indian independence in 1947, because of the maharaja, the *Ramlila* is special. Indians call such situations *maya-lila*, the interpenetration of multiple realities and illusions. It is neither possible nor desirable to discover which is more "real" or "basic," maharaja or *Ramlila*, as Linda Hess will show. The largest event cosmically is contained within the mythic event which is contained within the social order of Ramnagar. As with Vishnu-Vamana's three steps, the little encompasses the limitless.

Quiet Time, Waiting Space

In January 1978, and again in January 1983, I visited Ramnagar to survey and photograph the *Ramlila* environments when they were not in use. Not only did I gather "objective data" concerning the size and the architecture of the permanent installations, the distances between stations, and a feel for the overall spatial deployment of the *Ramlila*, but I also wanted to walk undisturbed through Janakpur and Ayodhya, up the little hill of Pampasar, across the grassy field of Panchavati, past the small Shiva temple at Rameshvaram, and into the vast open space of Lanka. I sat where the Chitrakut butterfly-winged tent was raised across from the Durga temple and its deep pool and where now, in winter, cows quietly grazed (Illus. 1.21). I walked the paths that Ram, Sita, and Lakshman walk when, barefoot, they go into exile. Atmaram— the *Ramlila*'s long-time technical director, constructor of the effigies, and keeper of the environments—took me to Agastya's small ashram and to where Ram restored Ahalya to her human form. The *Ramlila* environments, though silent and deserted in chilly January, still released to me their actions. At Chitrakut my mind's eye followed Jayanta, Indra's son, as he took the form of a crow and bit Sita's toe sharply enough for it to bleed a little, in a test of Ram's might and Sita's human "reality." Ram's angry arrow pursued Jayanta through "every

1.21

Chitrakut-Rambag in winter: cows grazing, Ram's world resting. Photo, Richard Schechner.

sphere" until, terrified and remorseful, he fell at Ram's feet crying, "Protect me!" Only half-forgiving, Ram's arrow puts out one of Jayanta's eyes. At Ayodhya I once again saw Dasharatha keel over backwards in a deathly swoon of remorse when he realized that his beloved son Ram must enter the forest for fourteen years of exile. In Lanka I felt the heat and saw the light of the cremation fire consuming Ravana's giant bamboo and papier-mâché body. Standing there in the middle of January's chill and emptiness, I recalled how the maharaja told Linda Hess and me, "We don't look down on Ravana. We don't burn his effigy but cremate him with respect. In Delhi they kill Ravana by burning him. Here we cremate him." Even stranger than evocations of splendid presence was the absence of the *Ramlila*. Bereft of nemis and *chai-walas* (tea sellers), sadhus and Ramayanis, without darshan of the svarups, lacking the maharaja on his elephant, and lacking the crowd's powerful surge at arati—in short, with neither theatrical action nor religious devotion—the *Ramlila* environments, some in need of repair, some simply waiting, some more or less permanently overgrown, lay fallow. In winter the *Ramlila* ground was the world between *yugas*, the cosmic cycles of creation and destruction, awaiting its season of activity.

Notes

1. According to Gonda,

In the age of the *Rig Veda*, India's oldest religious document (c. 1200–1000 BCE), Vishnu must have already been a more important divine figure than it would appear from his comparatively infrequent appearances in the texts...He is celebrated in a few hymns, of which stanzas 1.22.16–21 came to be a sort of confession of faith...These stanzas eulogize the essential feature of the character of the Vedic Vishnu: namely, his taking, from the very place where the gods promote man's interests, three steps, by which he establishes the broad dimensional actuality of the earthly space in which all beings abide...*Viraj*, the idea of extending far and wide the female principle of creation and the hypothesis of the universe conceived as a whole, come to be one of Vishnu's epithets...To the sacrificer, who ritually imitates Vishnu's three strides and so identifies with him, the god imparts the power to conquer the universe and attain "the goal, the safe foundation, the highest light" *Shatapatha Brahmana* 1.9.3.10. Vishnu's pervasiveness also manifests itself in the central cosmic axis, the pillar of the universe, whose lower end is visibly represented by the post erected on the sacrifical ground. This axis reaches the earth in the center or navel of the universe, putting the cosmic levels into communication with each other; it thus provides a means of traveling to heaven as well as a canal through which heavenly blessings reach man. In this navel is located the sacrifice with which Vishnu is constantly identified. (Gonda, 1987:288–89)

2. In one of those paradoxes that tease scholars without troubling practitioners, Vishnu's "seventh incarnation" is not mathematically plausible. King Dasharatha, unhappy because he has no son, performs a sacrifice in the midst of which the fire god Agni appears bearing an offering. "Go, king, divide this offering and distribute the parts in due proportion" (to your three wives). Ram's mother Kaushalya gets half; Kaikeyi, Bharat's mother, gets one-quarter; and Sumitra, mother of Lakshman and Shatrughna, gets two fragments of one-eighth each. All the boys are incarnations of Vishnu, sharing in the divine offering, but Ram alone is considered the incarnation. All the boys are of equal age, but Ram is represented as the eldest, performed in the *Ramlila* by a boy who is several years older than Shatrughna and Bharat and at least one year older than Lakshman. Lakshman and Shatrughna are twins, but in performance Lakshman is several years older than Shatrughna. It sometimes happens that a boy who has played Shatrughna or Bharat later plays Lakshman or Ram. Sita, equal to Ram in holiness, the incarnation of Vishnu's wife Lakshmi, has no human mother. She is born from a furrow her father King Janak ploughs. The question of whether Vishnu's seventh *avatar* (incarnation) is one or four (Sita being of Lakshmi) troubles no one at the *Ramlila*. Of Vishnu's ten avatars, nine have already appeared: Matsya, the fish; Kurma, the tortoise; Varah, the boar; Narasimha, the man-lion; Vamana, the dwarf; Parashuram, Ram with an Ax; Ram; Krishna; Buddha. Each of these avatars is the locus of many stories. Kalki, the tenth avatar, will come to destroy the world at the end of the Kali Yuga, the dark age in which we now live.

3. On day 26 of the Ramnagar *Ramlila*, after the two adversaries have drawn their war chariots up to the battleground and exchanged a few volleys of arrows, the man playing Ravana takes off his ten-headed mask and walks over to Ram. He salutes Ram by folding his hands, bowing before him, and respectfully touching his feet. Then he turns and walks off into the huge Dashahara crowd. After dark Ram shoots an arrow into Ravana's giant effigy, which all day has stood on Ravana's fort. Five hot air balloons are released from behind the effigy, and their tiny yellow flames remain visible for a long time in the night sky. These balloons signify Ravana's spirit rising into Ram's mouth. In the *Ramcharitmanas* the final combat is bloodier but the outcome not any different.

Raghunayak's [Ram's] arrows sped forth like great serpents of doom. One arrow dried up the depths of Ravana's navel; the others furiously smote his heads and arms and carried them away with them. The headless, armless trunk danced upon the ground. The earth sank down, but the trunk rushed violently on. Then the Lord struck it with an arrow and cut it in two. Even as he died, he roared aloud with a great terrible yell,

"Where is Rama, that I may challenge him and slay him in combat?" Earth shook as the Ten-headed fell; the sea, the rivers, the mountains and the elephants of the quarters were troubled. Spreading abroad the two halves of his body, he fell to the ground, crushing beneath him crowds of bears and monkeys. The arrows laid the arms and the heads before Mandodari [Ravana's wife] and returned to the Lord of the world; they all came back and entered his quiver. The gods saw it and beat their drums. His spirit [Ravana's] entered the Lord's mouth; Sambhu [Shiva] and Brahma saw it and were glad. The universe was filled with cries of triumph. (*Ramcharitmanas*, C. 102; Hill, 1952:418–19)

Then the effigy is set ablaze.

4. There are obvious parallels to both the *Iliad* (war fought over an abducted queen) and the *Odyssey* (adventurous travels of a hero). The similarity of these Indian and Greek tales of far-ranging warring travels should not surprise us: their authors were people of the horse, they rode far in several directions— south, west, and east—from their "origins" in the Caucasus region, and they were poets.

5. Actually four weddings take place simultaneously, for not only is Ram married to Sita but his brothers are also married. Only the Ram-Sita marriage is dramatized in the Ramnagar *Ramlila*.

6. At Varanasi the Ganga flows north to south instead of in its general easterly direction. Consequently, the sun rises over the sacred river, making early morning bathing spectacular. Furthermore, Ram is widely celebrated as a solar king, and to some degree it is his radiance that rises over Banaras, the city of Shiva. But Ramnagar is on the eastern bank, the "bad side" of the river, the inauspicious, polluted side. Not wishing to pollute the sacred city, many Varanasi residents journey across the Ganga each morning before dawn to defecate on the far riverbank.

7. All quotations from the *Natyashastra* are from Ghosh (1967).

8. Calling a post-Vedic text a "fifth Veda" is a common way of saying how important a text is. The *Natyashastra* is far from alone in being so represented.

9. The *Ramlila* must start on the fourteenth day of the month—as the moon is waning. Dashahara must be the middle of a waxing moon, on the tenth day of the lunar month. The *Ramlila* must end on a full moon. These requirements can necessitate some peculiar adjustments. In 1982, for example, because of the insertion of an extra half-month in the lunar year, the *Ramlila* had to be calculated backward from the full moon, and so it did not begin on the fourteenth day.

10. One vyas trains the svarups, and the other oversees the rest of the performers. The vyases are present during all lilas, holding big books which contain the samvads and stage directions. Often they whisper dialogue in the ears of the svarups or other performers. They are not shy about making corrections during the performance; the important thing is for everything to be done correctly.

11. This token is supplemented the next day when, in a private audience held in his office at the Fort, the maharaja pays each svarup the traditional sum of Rs. 440. Other *Ramlila* performers are also paid, though less.

2

Staring at Frames Till They Turn into Loops:
An Excursion through Some Worlds of Tulsidas

Linda Hess

> The way Parvati asked questions,
> the way Shiva replied — I will sing it all,
> weaving the narratives strangely.
> If you haven't heard the story before,
> don't be amazed. It's a story beyond
> this world. The wise listen
> without amazement, knowing
> Ram's narrative has no end
> in the universe. They listen with hearts
> of faith. Ram has many kinds of bodies;
> the Ramayana of ten million verses
> is endless. Sages sing in many ways
> for many ages the lovely tale
> of Hari. Give up the doubt
> in your heart, hear the story
> receptively, reverently.[1]

Imagine, as you read these lines of verse, that we are at Tulsighat in Banaras. It is September, the beginning of the *Ramlila* season. The Ganga is at its widest, deepest, swiftest. Climbing steep stairs from the swirling water, we reach a small, cavelike shrine built into the wall of a house that dominates the *ghat* (riverbank). A tiny room protected by bars contains artifacts associated with Tulsidas: a piece of wood from a boat he once rowed; wooden sandals like those often worn by *sadhus* (holy men), like those placed by Bharat on Ram's throne during the exile; a portrait of the poet; a manuscript.

Here, overlooking the river, Tulsidas is believed to have composed much of the *Ramcharitmanas*, the beloved Hindi version of the *Ramayana*,

in the late 1570s. A few steps to the south are sites still used in the Asi
Ramlila, which many local people believe was established by Tulsidas.
Five minutes' walk to the north is the home of Shrinath Mishra, one
of India's foremost Kathavachaks, or oral expounders of the *Ramcharitmanas*.[2] The towering house on Tulsighat itself belongs to Veer Bhadra
Mishra, spiritual head of Sankat Mochan, the city's most popular
Hanuman temple. The large, bright red image of the monkey god there
is also related in local legend to Tulsidas: it originally manifested itself
to him, and he established the temple. Sankat Mochan, like several
other temples and organizations in the city, hosts annual nine-day *Manas*
recitations where dozens of *Brahmins* wrapped in yellow shawls sit in
rows and chant for hours, amidst the rituals of devotion. Across the
river and a bit upstream from Tulsighat, we can see the long walls and
towers of Ramnagar Fort, seat of the maharajas of Banaras since the
mid-eighteenth century. To that fort and to locales within a few miles
of it, tens of thousands of Banarsis will stream every day for a month
in this season to view the celebrated Ramnagar *Ramlila*. There the
Ramcharitmanas springs to life annually on a scale almost unimaginably
large and minute. In fact, the poets, sadhus, and kings who shaped
this *lila* through much of the nineteenth century called it the "living
commentary" on Tulsi's epic poem.

Now, sitting before the tiny Tulsi temple, imagine that we are
having a vision. Instead of the dim shrine, the bars, and the portrait,
we see the poet himself before us, seated on the stone landing over
the water, singing the *Ramcharitmanas*. Following an ancient convention
in Indian literature—as Markandeya did with Vishnu, as the mind of
Yashoda did with Krishna, as the crow Bhushundi did with the child
Ram in the final book of the *Ramcharitmanas*—we enter the saint-poet's
mouth, sliding down the long track of syllables as they emerge from
darkness.[3]

Inside Tulsidas's body is an odd academic figure lecturing on the
Ramcharitmanas. The city, the text, and the performance, she says, are
inextricably intertwined. The text will not stay flat; the lila is not mere
theater. Both use conventions of time and space (the text more obviously
time, the lila more obviously space) to subvert and eventually to
overturn conventional ideas of time and space. The city provides real
time and space in which participants (*bhaktas*)[4] are encouraged to give
up their grip on reality. It is possible, then, to speak of the life of the
city by speaking of the life of the text and its frames, both literary and
performative. This text pervades the city—from the physical settings
of the many neighborhood *Ramlilas* to the minds of citizens, hundreds
of thousands, who know and savor, believe in and identify with, Ram's
story.

Let us begin, the lecturer continues, having established the scope and legitimacy of her purpose, with the narrative structure of the *Manas*, which can be perplexing to an uninitiated reader. It is perplexing because, although we can say that there are four major narrative frames, we never see those frames lined up together. They reveal themselves at odd times and places in the midst of an unwieldy mass of material that overflows the main story line at both ends.

To make things easier, I will first present the frames to you as if they were clear. They take the form of four conversations (*samvad*), in each of which a speaker tells Ram's story to an audience. Here are the four sets of speakers and listeners:

1. Shiva and Parvati (Uma)
2. Kakabhushundi (Bhushundi) and Garuda
3. Yajnavalkya and Bhardwaj
4. Tulsidas and those who hear or read the *Manas*

Although the four narrators never stand up all in a row, they are at one point listed together:

> Shiva made this sweet life-story, graciously
> told it to Uma, and passed it to the crow
> Bhushundi, knowing he had the right
> as Ram's devotee. Yajnavalkya received it
> from the crow and sang it to Bhardwaj,
> both teller and listener equal in virtue
> and vision, knowing God's play.
> Past, present, future — they hold time
> like a plum in the palm of their hands.
> Others, God's wise lovers, listen, tell
> and understand in many ways.
> I heard the story from my guru...
> and shall compose it in common language
> for my own heart's delight. (1.29.3–1.30.2)

The lines indicate a genealogy of telling, though some of the pronouns are ambiguous and the exact order in time has been a matter of debate. There seems to be no disagreement, however, over the proposition that Shiva is the primordial teller. In his book on the text and performance traditions of the *Ramcharitmanas*, Lutgendorf has diagramed the four dialogues as a series of frames surrounding the *Manas* lake (Illus. 2.1). As he points out, the passage suggests a

2.1

The four *Ramcharitmanas* dialogues with the *Manas* lake as the center.
(Lutgendorf, 1991:25)

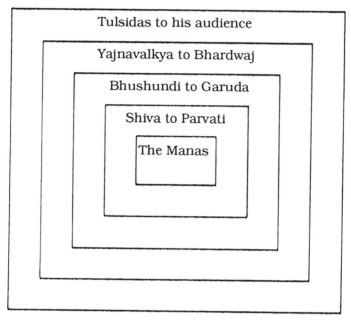

Adapted from Philip Lutgendorf, THE LIFE OF A TEXT: PERFORMING THE RAMCARITMANAS OF TULSIDAS. Copyright © 1991 The Regents of the University of California.

succession of further tellers and listeners.[5] It is also possible to reverse the order of the frames (Illus. 2.2). In the first drawing the *Manas* lake of Ram's deeds is metaphorically the center, and the series of dialogues radiates out in order of spiritual magnitude as well as apparent chronology. In the second, the *Manas* is metaphorically the largest container; in fact, it is infinite, containing everything. Shiva's frame, being the primal telling, is the next largest, Bhushundi's the next, and so on. This reversibility recalls a medieval European definition of God as an intelligible sphere whose center is everywhere and whose circumference is nowhere, beautifully realized in Dante's *Paradiso* when, through a change in level, God's image is transformed from an all-containing radiance which seems at once circular and infinite to an infinitely intense point of light surrounded by swirling angel orders.[6]

2.2

The four *Ramcharitmanas* dialogues with the *Manas* lake as the largest container.

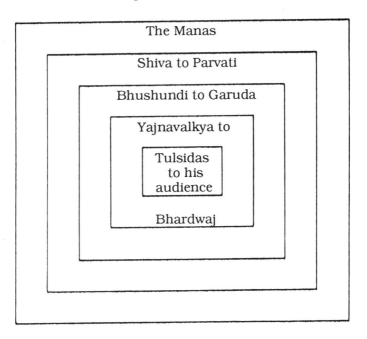

Whichever diagram we use, however, when we actually plunge into the text, our experience of the narrative structure is anything but this clear. The poem begins in Tulsidas's voice with fifteen pages or so of obeisances. After saluting and holding forth on the qualities of gods, gurus, Brahmins, saints, sinners, scriptures, planets, rivers, Ram's name and deeds, and several characters of the *Ramayana*, Tulsidas gives the summary of narrators quoted above and says, "Now I am going to repeat the great dialogue between Shiva and Parvati." But he doesn't. He enters into the most elaborate extended metaphor of the poem, in which the four dialogues become the four ghats or stair-step approaches to the *Manas* pool, with allegorical meanings given to the steps of the ghats, the depths of the water, the ripples on its surface, the lotus leaves, flowers, pollen, juice and fragrance, the swarms of bees, flocks of swans, and so on for several pages.[7]

At last he does enter one of the four dialogues, but it is not that of Shiva and Parvati; rather it is that of Yajnavalkya and Bhardwaj. Bhardwaj lives in Prayag, Tulsidas tells us in the present tense, where all the sages come to bathe in the month of Magh. Once upon a time—

the words *ek bar* signaling an entry into specific past events—at the end
of Magh, when the sages were all leaving for home, Bhardwaj detained
Yajnavalkya and begged him to answer some questions on the relation
between the transcendent and the incarnate Ram. Yajnavalkya replied,
"Bhavani (Parvati) asked a similar question of Shiva, and I will repeat
their conversation to you." Now we have Yajnavalkya telling Bhardwaj
what Shiva told Parvati. In the big chronological picture, Shiva's frame
contains Yajnavalkya's (that is, the god's telling comes first). But in the
narrative as we receive it, the order is reversed, Yajnavalkya's story
containing Shiva's.

To give the so-called frame structure an added fillip, Yajnavalkya
throws in a reference to another telling of Ram's story in which Shiva
is the listener. One day in Tretayuga (the second age), he says, Shiva
and Sati visited the sage Agastya, and the latter related the story of
Ram. After the sage and the god discussed Ram's perfections for a few
days, Shiva and Sati went home. At that point (since it was Tretayuga),
Ram was actually born in Ayodhya. Shiva went to see him and became
enraptured, Sati conceived doubts about the relation between the
transcendent and the incarnate Ram, and Shiva sermonized on that
subject. Her doubts still nagged, and she entered on a series of
misadventures in which she tried unsuccessfully to deceive first Ram,
then Shiva, was rejected by her husband, and ended up immolating
herself at her father's ill-fated sacrifice, eventually to be reborn as Parvati.
All this, we must remind ourselves, is being related by Yajnavalkya to
Bhardwaj. Yajnavalkya goes on to describe Parvati's austerities, Shiva's
incineration of Kama, the marriage of Shiva and Parvati, and much
more.

After thirty pages, Yajnavalkya's narrative has still not come to
Ram's story. "Now," he says, "listen while I tell you of Raghupati's lila"
(1.105). But he doesn't. For the space of several more pages Shiva and
Parvati discuss the *nirguna-saguna* problem, that is, whether God has
form (*saguna*) or lacks form (*nirguna*). Then Shiva says:

Hear, Bhavani, the blessed story, the flawless
Ramcharitmanas, heard by the king of birds, Garuda,
from Bhushundi. Later I'll tell you how that great dialogue
happened. Now hear of Ram's descent, his pure and utterly
beautiful deeds. Boundless are Hari's [Vishnu's] names and
    qualities,
endless, impossible to gauge, his forms and stories.
Now I'll tell you, based on my insight. Listen
reverently. (1.120B–D)

Perhaps no one will be surprised to hear that Shiva does not yet tell the story of Ram's descent. He refers here to the last of the four major dialogues, the one between the crow Bhushundi and Vishnu's avian vehicle, the king of birds, Garuda, promising Parvati that he will tell her more about it later. Much later: about four hundred pages later. At this point Shiva tells a longish tale about Narada's delusion and an even longer one about Ravana's prior birth as King Pratapabhanu, with several other stories laced in. But now we are digging close to the main vein, because most of these stories are about people who will eventually be reborn as Dasharatha, Kaushalya, Ravana, and Kumbhakarna. On page 71 of V. P. Mishra's Kashiraj Trust edition, Shiva, or Yajnavalkya, or Tulsidas, or all three, come(s) to the beginning of the Ram story proper, with the birth of Ravana. From there the narrative moves in fairly straightforward fashion to about the middle of the epic's seventh and last book. The final forty pages are again framing material, featuring the conversation between Bhushundi and Garuda. Like Shiva, I promise to tell you more about that later.

In the body of the epic (from the middle of *Balkand* to the middle of *Uttarkand*) the frames almost disappear. But their traces persist, and two peculiarities about that persistence are especially noteworthy. The first is that small references to the narrators and their listeners are sprinkled throughout the otherwise straightforward telling of the tale. At unpredictable moments, and at many such moments, we get vocatives like "O Bhavani...," "O Uma...," "Listen, Girija," signaling that the speaker is Shiva; or "O Bhardwaj...," "Listen, sage," which means that Yajnavalkya is talking. Or we get Tulsi's signature line, indicating that it is his voice we are hearing. Occasionally the voices crowd close on each other:

> Listen, sage: many poets tell the stories
> of the Lord's descents. Once Narada cursed him,
> furnishing a reason in that age
> for incarnation. Girija was startled
> when she heard those words. But Narada
> was the Lord's devotee, and he had
> great wisdom. Why would such a sage
> curse Lakshmi's Lord? For what offense?
> Tell me that episode, O Shiva.
> Delusion in a sage is most
> amazing. Shiva smiled and said,
> no one's a wise man or a fool.
> Whatever, whenever, however Ram

> wants to make him, at that instant
> he becomes. I'm singing you
> Ram's virtues, Bhardwaj, so listen
> with respect. The breaker
> of worldly bonds—Tulsi,
> drop your drunken pride
> and worship him. (1.124.4–1.124B)

Would it be possible to construct a labyrinthine sketch of the entire text, making clear at any given moment who the foregrounded narrator was? Whether or not clear results are possible, I believe such an effort would be misguided. The mixing of levels seems intended, or taken for granted. It is true that there are explicit priorities among the four main tellers. According to the passage cited previously, Shiva recited the story first, Bhushundi second, Yajnavalkya third, and Tulsidas fourth. But the levels are flattened by the indiscriminate vocatives. In other ways, too, through both form and content, the poem suggests that the telling of the story and the enactment of the story by its principals are going on at the same time. This brings us to the second peculiarity I referred to.

In all three of the mythic dialogues (those prior to Tulsidas's) either the speaker or the listener is also a character in the story. Shiva appears a number of times in the main narrative of the *Ramcharitmanas*—for example, at Ram's wedding and coronation. Bharat visits the ashram of Bhardwaj on his way to meet Ram at Chitrakut. During the war in Lanka, Garuda is called upon to set Ram free from Indrajit's snake net. Some commentators have claimed that Tulsidas has also inserted himself into the narrative. Early in the exile, when Ram, Sita, and Lakshman have just crossed the Jamuna River on their way from Prayag to Chitrakut, a mysterious ascetic suddenly appears before them. Glowing with the energy of austerity, his eyes pouring tears, his body radiating total devotion, he falls prostrate on the ground before his beloved Lord. After a series of prostrations and embraces, this unnamed devotee disappears as mysteriously as he came. According to one prominent literary historian, the suspicion that this is Tulsidas is confirmed by the fact that the encounter occurs near the poet's own place of origin, Rajapur (Shukla, 1968: 128).

In the framing material at either end of the epic, we hear more about how the narrators have been participants in the lila. In telling his own story to Garuda, Bhushundi reveals that for eons he has gone to Ayodhya every time Ram incarnated to enjoy the Lord's child-lila. Shiva and Sati interact with Ram and Sita one Tretayuga. And in a different sort of narrative complication, Shiva shows up several times as a listener to somebody else who is recounting the *Ramcharitmanas*. I have mentioned his hearing Agastya's recitation. He also describes how he heard Bhushundi recite the tale (although Bhushundi is supposed to have originally received the story from Shiva).

As the teeth of our comb become finer, we begin to notice inconsistencies in the information about who told what to whom, and when. Here is one of the most obvious. Shiva and Parvati are often taken to be the original teller and hearer of the tale. But in this text it is only after Sati's misfortunes and rebirth as Parvati that Shiva begins to tell Parvati the tale. So who came first, Sati or Parvati? It may seem impertinent for us to ask this of gods, who are after all eternal and can appear before their births and after their deaths if they want to. But as mortals engaged in our *dharma* of literary analysis, we have a right to press the question: Is this narrative happening in time or isn't it? Don't narratives *have* to happen in time? We will leave the question for the moment.

In *Uttarkand*, after having heard the whole story of Ram's deeds, Parvati poses further questions. How did the crow Bhushundi hear the story? How did you, Shiva, hear the story? Why did such a perfect devotee as Bhushundi wear the body of a crow? When Garuda had a theological problem, why did he go to a crow instead of a sage? What was the conversation between the two birds like?

Shiva tells how he heard the story. While wandering inconsolably after the death of Sati, he arrived at the crow's mountain ashram, which is even farther north than Mount Meru and four *yojanas* (thirty-two miles) beyond the reach of *maya* (illusion). On one of the mountain's four peaks, under one of his ashram's four trees, the crow always told the story of Ram's deeds. Shiva took the form of a swan and listened to the tale, upon which his grief turned to joy.[8]

But wait. Isn't Shiva the primal composer and namer of the *Ramcharitmanas*? This is stated clearly in *Balkand* (29.3, 34.11), and no commentator questions it. Then why does he say he learned it from Bhushundi in the interval between Sati's death and Parvati's birth? We will leave the question for the moment.

The crow tells Garuda that he learned the story of Ram from one Lomash-*rishi* (sage), who learned it from Shiva. Thinking back over his many incarnations, all of which he remembers, Bhushundi reckons that this occurred precisely twenty-seven *kalpas* (a unit of time said to equal one thousand *yugas*) before his present meeting with Garuda, a meeting that takes place after Garuda's encounter with Ram inside the story of the *Ramcharitmanas*.

Who is really the primal teller of the *Manas*? It appears that the matter cannot be unraveled. Even if we insist that it is Shiva, we have an equally knotty problem determining who is the first listener. In a small volume called *Manas Shanka Samadhan* (*Solutions to Doubts in the Manas*), a commentator presents this as one of the great dilemmas of the text and concludes that Shiva first told the tale not to Parvati but to Bhushundi.[9]

The suspicion arises that we could draw from all these imponderable curvings of time what Wendy Doniger O'Flaherty calls a Mobius universe, an entity that seems to have two surfaces (call them time-space, body-soul, inside-outside, or any other duality of grand resonance), but that defies our commonsense observation of its surfaces by curving in such a way as to make surface A and surface B endlessly become each other. O'Flaherty also takes up the term *Strange Loops*, coined by Douglas Hofstadter in his playful study of paradox, *Gödel, Escher, Bach*. Although appreciating Hofstadter's discovery of Western Strange Loops, she concludes that Indian Loops are stranger:

> The ontological rope (or snake) in India is not twisted in on itself merely once, like a simple square knot; it is a very tricky clove hitch, which catches up not only the characters in the story but the author himself—the one who seems to exist on the inviolate level. This is why Indian Strange Loops are even stranger than Western Strange Loops. Our greatest surprise arises not from the discovery that the hierarchy of dreamers is not fixed, as we thought it was, or that we are not at the top of it, as we thought we were, but from the realization that new hierarchies are constantly being created, by our minds and by those who are thinking about us. In India, not even the drawing hand or the author is safe from the entangling ontological coils. No one, not even God, can escape from *maya*.[10]

The Mobius universe in the *Ramcharitmanas* is confirmed in the account of Bhushundi's great vision, the one that liberates him forever from the toils of maya and the rounds of samsara. Telling Garuda his own story, he says that he goes every Tretayuga to Ayodhya on the occasion of Ram's birth and stays for five years, because his chosen form of the deity is the child Ram. During those five years he watches Ram play, fluttering around the divine child and picking up crumbs that drop from his mouth.

But one time (the switch from an eternally recurring present to a particular past event—*ek bar*—recalling the same switch in the

Yajnavalkya-Bhardwaj dialogue) the Lord put on an act that was really too much (*atishay*, excessive). Like an ordinary child he tried to catch the bird, tempting it with cake, laughing when it came close and crying when it flew away, running and jumping and shouting in wild excitement. A moment's doubt arose in the crow. Could this rowdy child be the Lord of perfect consciousness and bliss? As little Ram crawled on hands and knees to grab him, he flew far up in the air. But no matter how far he flew, even to Brahma's heaven, those little arms kept reaching for him, only two fingerbreadths away. Bhushundi got scared. He closed his eyes and reopened them to find himself back in Dasharatha's courtyard, with little Ram looking at him and laughing. Instantly he entered Ram's mouth and beheld innumerable universes—millions of Brahmas and Shivas, suns and moons, gods of death, and so on. He spent one hundred years in each universe, and in each one he saw himself and Ayodhya, Ram, and Dasharatha and all the rest.

Eventually Bhushundi wandered in one of these worlds to his own ashram, where he stayed until he heard of Ram's birth in Ayodhya. He rushed there to witness the Lord's birth. A view of Ram triggered the awareness that he was still in Ram's belly and that all this had occurred in a moment, though it had seemed to take hundreds of eons. Bhushundi was lost in confusion. Seeing his distress the Lord laughed, the crow came out of his mouth, and the child Ram started playing games with him again. This did not soothe him. Dreadfully perplexed and upset, he lost consciousness, fell to the ground, and cried, "Save me, save me, o savior of your troubled devotees!" At this the Lord drew back his maya and Bhushundi was liberated from delusion once and for all.[11]

Here is the familiar theme of entering the mouth of God (see note 3). Tulsidas gives it the mark of his own sort of *bhakti* (devotion): enlightenment comes when the devotee cries out with all his heart for the Lord's refuge, a cry heard repeatedly in the *Ramcharitmanas*. In this vision and others like it, God's body proves to be the ultimate frame, at once the infinite container and the infinitesimal contained. It is his own body bending to become itself again and again that gives the Mobius effect.[12]

Now, back in our world, does a narrative have to happen in time or not? The answer is that a narrative has to have a convention of time, which may be tight or loose. A tight convention makes for a conventional fiction: omniscient narrator and realistic reporting of events in a normal order, with no funny business. A loose convention gives certain signals that things are flowing normally in time but also injects elements that make us doubt the normality of the flow. The result can be the loony digressiveness of *Tristram Shandy,* the morass of memory in *The Good Soldier,* or any of a hundred other possibilities.[13]

Time is a convention for narrative artists to play on, and we have begun to see how Tulsidas plays. He places us in time by recounting sequences of events, creating a hierarchy of narrative frames and a genealogy of narrations. But soon the squares crack open at the corners and proceed to curve. The levels prove to be interpenetrating, indistinguishable. The poet talks now once-upon-a-time, now once-upon-an-eternity, now infinitely-upon-a-time. The vision of countless parallel universes and the packing of eons of experiences into a moment explode conventional sequences, which the narrative structure has been subverting all along. It is a structure which thrusts us into the relativity of time and space, makes us taste lila and maya.

But it is not in Tulsi's interest simply to dismiss time and space as maya. Bhushundi's awakening does not have an Advaitan (belief in the illusory nature of all but the Nondual) flavor. It occurs only when he submits to the embodied Ram, the Ram whose *charit* (action) is the substance of the *Ramcharitmanas,* the Ram of narrative. Tulsidas must have both the narrative Ram and the transcendent Ram. This is the theological core and the motivator for all three of the mythic narratives. In each case the telling is occasioned by someone's inability to comprehend the oneness of the Ram *avatar* (incarnation) and the transcendent Ram. Seeing how incongruously the Ram avatar sometimes behaves, Sati, Parvati, Garuda, Bhushundi, and Bhardwaj all state in one way or another that they can't swallow it.[14] Bhushundi's climactic adventure suggests that the solution is to be swallowed.

The narrative "frames" in the *Ramcharitmanas,* like the bewildering series of layers in many other Indian texts, are a way of demonstrating the meaning of maya or lila. I was once upbraided in an academic conference for seeming to suggest that maya and lila are the same. In fact the ranges of meaning covered by the two terms coincide on almost every point. Both are associated with the fullness of phenomena, creation, form, transformation, magic, illusion. Both are contrasted with something unchanging, pure, or empty. Both are female. The significant difference is simply this: *maya* is more inclined to have a negative connotation, *lila* a positive one. These inclinations are only relative, for both terms are also inclined to remain deeply ambiguous. The key to the difference between the positive and negative charge is theism.

The lila is somebody's lila, and that somebody is God, most often Vishnu. Vaishnavas explain the universe as God's play; the word bears a double meaning, in English as well as in Indian languages, of drama and game, both activities characterized by delight. God performs her or his activity of creating, spinning the universe, weaving the visions, making the magic, being the whole show (many more images are naturally available), with a joy that has no reason. It is suggested that the devotee will share this joy when he or she consummates a relationship of motiveless love with God. The etymology of *lila* is not clear. Edward Dimock brings forth several possibilities at the beginning of his article on Shitala, the Bengali goddess of pustular diseases. Play is central, but there are also interesting associations with fire, licking, hiding, and grace (Dimock, 1982:184–86).[15]

Maya comes from the root *ma*, which some scholars have understood as "to make," others as "to measure"—both obviously related to creation and finitude (O'Flaherty, 1984:117–18). Most of its bad press can be traced to Shankara and later adherents of the Advaita Vedanta school, for whom *maya* is the antithesis of *brahman*, denoting the manyfold veils of illusion that separate us from the nondual truth. It has nothing to do with joy; rather, if understood rightly, it is pure suffering. Since a personal God is not the ultimate reality in Advaita Vedanta, there is no problem of theodicy.

Vaishnava bhakti texts also speak of Vishnu's maya. Sometimes it has a negative charge; often it is presented as God's ultimate mystery, the secret most difficult to penetrate. But when the secret is finally understood, maya becomes lila. A story from the *Matsya Purana* illustrates how the old texts tried to teach about maya and also provides a beautiful example of the Vaishnava tradition of textual layering to which the *Ramcharitmanas* is heir. The following summary is based on a fuller retelling in Zimmer's *Myths and Symbols in Indian Art and Civilization*:

A group of holy men in the forest ashram of Vyasa asked the great sage to reveal the secret of Vishnu's maya. Protesting that no one can understand Vishnu's maya, Vyasa told a story. Once there was a prince named Kamadamana (tamer of desire) whose father urged him to marry, have sons, fulfill his worldly obligations, and partake of the unlimited blessings available to him. The prince refused, describing his myriad incarnations in every mode of existence through countless creations and dissolutions of the cosmos. Having seen through the delusions of samsara, he would no longer get entangled in actions that would bring about rebirth. To bring the point home further to his father, he told a story. In my next-to-last incarnation my name was Sutapas (good austerity). I was such a fervent devotee of Vishnu that he appeared and offered me a boon. I asked to know the secret of his maya. He offered unlimited worldly blessings; I refused. Then he said it was impossible to comprehend his maya, but he would tell a story. Long ago, said Vishnu, the seer Narada, son of Brahma, pleased me with his devotion. I offered him a boon, and he asked to know the secret of my maya. I warned him that it was impossible to understand my maya. When he insisted, I asked him to plunge into a nearby pond. He did so and emerged in the form of a young woman—Sushila, daughter of the king of Banaras. Sushila married the prince of neighboring Vidarbha, experienced the delights of love, became queen of Vidarbha, had many sons and grandsons, and was incomparably happy. But later her husband and father became enemies. In a great battle her husband and father and most of her sons and grandsons were killed. Having ordered that a giant funeral pyre be built and that the bodies of all her relatives be placed upon it, she lit the fire. Crying, "My son! My son!", she threw herself into the roaring flames. Immediately the blaze became cool. Sushila found herself in the form of Narada, being drawn out of the pond by Vishnu. Narada prayed for perfect faith and devotion, the grace always to remember this experience, and the boon that this pool might set free others who plunged into it. Granting these wishes, Vishnu disappeared to his abode, the Milky Ocean. Then Vishnu told Sutapas, "I have told you this tale to teach you that the secret of my maya cannot be understood. If you wish to know why this is so, you can also plunge into the water." He withdrew to the Milky Ocean. Sutapas plunged into the pond and emerged as a young woman.[16]

This tale does not have a Mobius twist (at least in the set of frames that *we* see), but it makes its point well enough: that the stories within stories could go on indefinitely, and there is no way to know what is even relatively real (and further, that understanding of the framing process can come through an experience, but not through a concept). O'Flaherty calls this pattern the receding frame:

The joker in the deck of unreality-testing is the level of the frames: within the dream or vision it is always possible to prove that something is real, but all the author need do is to point out that the whole dream is an unreal part of something else, and all subproofs are then rendered irrelevant. . . Even when scientific principles are applied inside a paradigm, faith encompasses the paradigm on the outermost layer—or rather, on what appears, at any given moment, to be the outermost layer. (1984:197–98)

In the story of Narada (or is it the story of Sutapas? Kamadamana? Vyasa and the holy men? the *Matsya Purana* teller and his listeners? O'Flaherty and us?) we follow an ever more tenuous thread of fictive reality, finally getting most involved at the most remote level, in a vision of an illusion of a transformation. We are left with an image of Sutapas taking the plunge. And will Kamadamana? And will the holy men? And will the *Matsya Purana* listeners? And will we? Or have we? Am I a male sage thinking I am a woman? Who has conjured this audience of academic readers?

Some American and European thinkers, taking an interest in frames in recent decades, have recognized that the activity of framing has much to do with what we consider to be real. A series of frames may suggest an ordering of realities. The order could simply show priority in time. Or it could be a hierarchy of more and less real things, with an assumption, stated or unstated, about what is the measure of realness. People often assume that the sense-based world is the reality we share most indisputably. If we apply that assumption to narrative frames, then the levels become less real as they retreat from the physical world, as they become mere imagination, shadows of shadows. In the *Canterbury Tales*, then, the pardoner who tells a tale is more real than the pardoner about whom a tale is told. The nun's priest is more real than Chaunticleer, and Chaunticleer is more real than the fox and rooster of his dream. The level at which Chaucer addresses us, his audience, is realest of all.

Interestingly, the creation of frames that separate orders of reality also permits the order to be thrown into question. As rules are made to be broken, frames are made to be breached. The fact that boundaries exist (or are imagined to exist) makes it possible to fall over the edge of a frame and experience the shock of changing realities: between dream and waking, art and life, sanity and insanity, sacred and profane, mystical experience and ordinary consciousness, and so on.

Erving Goffman's *Frame Analysis: An Essay on the Organization of Experience* begins with a discussion of how we use frames to focus on what we think is real. According to Goffman, William James wrote insightfully on the subject of frames; but James still insisted on the privileged status of one version of reality—the commonsense world (what is common to all of us, that is, the senses). Goffman (1974:2-3) says:

> I try to follow a tradition established by William James in his famous chapter "The Perception of Reality"...Instead of asking what reality is, he gave matters a subversive phenomenological

twist, italicizing the following question: *Under what circumstances do we think things are real?* The important thing about reality, he implied, is our sense of its realness in contrast to our feeling that some things lack this quality. One can then ask under what conditions such a feeling is generated, and this question speaks to a small, manageable problem having to do with the camera and not what it is the camera takes pictures of.

In his answer, James stressed the factors of selective attention, intimate involvement, and noncontradiction by what is otherwise known. More important, he made a stab at differentiating the several different "worlds" that our attention and interest can make real for us, the possible subuniverses, the "order of existence". . . in each of which an object of a given kind can have its proper being: the world of the senses, the world of scientific objects, the world of abstract philosophical truths, the worlds of myth and super-natural beliefs, the madman's world, etc. Each of these subworlds, according to James, has "its own special and separate style of existence," and "each world, whilst it is attended to, is real after its own fashion; only the reality lapses with the attention." Then, after taking this radical stand, James copped out; he allowed that the world of the senses has a special status, being the one we judge to be the realest reality, the one that retains our liveliest belief, the one before which the other worlds must give way.

Actually Goffman cops out in much the same way, holding himself well back from any radical position on the status of reality. He invokes "common sense" to prevent frames from multiplying madly (p. 11). He finds James guilty of a "scandalous play on the word world (or reality). . .[using] billowy words. . .[that] let in wind as well as light" (p. 3). He insists that the reality of situations does not depend on whether we define them as real: "All the world is not a stage—certainly the theater isn't entirely. (Whether you organize a theater or an aircraft factory, you need to find places for cars to park and coats to be checked, and these had better be real places, which, incidentally, had better carry real insurance against theft.)" (p. 1)

Gregory Bateson, whose essay "A Theory of Play and Fantasy" was germinal for Goffman, pays more attention to the paradoxes, the trouble around the borders, involved in framing. He describes insights that began with his observation of two monkeys in a zoo "playing, i.e., engaged in an interactive sequence of which the unit actions or signals were similar to but not the same as those of combat. It was evident, even to the human observer, that the sequence as a whole was not combat, and...that to the participant monkeys this was not combat" (Bateson, 1972:179). By using fight signals to perform an activity that they understood not to be a fight, the monkeys showed their ability to send and receive a metacommunicative message: *This is play*. Bateson (1972:185) suggests, then, "that play marks a step forward in the evolution of communication—the crucial step in the discovery of map-territory relations. In primary process, map and territory are equated; in secondary process, they can be discriminated. In play, they are both equated and discriminated."

I said about a page ago that frames are made to be breached, that the existence of boundaries allows us to transgress, or to experience the shock of falling over the edge. Bateson (1972:182) cites an interesting example of such transgression from anthropological literature:

> In the Andaman Islands, peace is concluded after each side has been given ceremonial freedom to strike the other. This example, however, also illustrates the labile nature of the frame "This is play," or "This is ritual." The discrimination between map and territory is always liable to break down, and the ritual blows of peace-making are always liable to be mistaken for the "real" blows of combat. In this event, the peace-making ceremony becomes a battle.

Mentioning various activities that are similar to play, including dream, fantasy, ritual, theater, deceit, histrionics, and bluff, Bateson shows how naming or framing them as such gives rise to a paradox. A frame is drawn. The metastatement that defines it is a version of "Everything within this frame is untrue." If the defining statement is within the frame, then it is untrue, and all other messages within the frame will be simultaneously true and untrue. This is logically impossible. If the statement could be outside the frame, there would seem to be no problem. But it cannot be outside the frame, because it is the frame. This status of being neither inside nor outside permits the frame to have its irreducibly ambiguous reality status.[17] The metastatement functions now as if it were inside the frame, now as if it were outside. It flickers. In terms of Bateson's discussion, map and territory are both equated and discriminated.

We return to the Vaishnava ideas of *maya* and *lila*. If we say "Everything in this world is illusion," we run into the problem that the word-concept "illusion" is included in "everything in this world." The framing statement falsifies itself. So Vaishnava storytellers have found a way not just to tell but to show what they mean, to create an experience of coalescing and dissolving realities within a series of frames, each of which appears to be substantial and reliable but subsequently dissolves, caves in, curves into another frame at what once seemed to be another level.

Psychological frames are meant to get things organized, to get jobs done. It is impossible to function in the world without them, as both Goffman and Bateson point out.[18] The job Vaishnava storytellers sometimes want to get done is to make their audiences taste the nature of psychological framing, with no special protectiveness for "common-sense reality" or for the individual ego that needs it.[19] It turns out that this taste is very much like the taste of lila. As Richard Schechner once expressed it to me, "If you don't grant privilege to any particular version of reality, framing *is* play. As long as you define your terms, you can have any 'as if' you want."[20]

In the late 1970s Richard Schechner and I did research together on the *Ramlila* of Ramnagar. The Ramnagar production is remarkable among the many annual *Ramlilas* of north India in several respects, as Schechner makes clear in the previous chapter. Temporally it covers the longest period: thirty or thirty-one days. Spatially it occupies the largest area, ranging over fifteen or twenty square miles of Ramnagar, often involving numerous moves for audience and actors in a single night, moves that may require several miles of walking. This lila has also acquired special grandeur because of the Banaras maharajas' close association with it over nearly two centuries, because of the determination of organizers and audience to preserve its purity and piety, and because of a wide belief in the particular efficacy of its *darshan* (viewing of a deity). The five boys who play the *svarups* (humans representing divine figures)—Ram, Sita, Bharat, Lakshman, and Shatrughna—are treated as, and are believed by many to be, literal embodiments of God during the time of the performance.

I have suggested that the narrative structure of the *Ramcharitmanas* presses audiences toward an experience of what the concept of lila (that is, Vishnu's maya) is about. As we move through that structure, awareness of maya or lila sifts through our pores like mist. In the remainder of this essay I will suggest that the Ramnagar *Ramlila* does the same thing, more dramatically and multidimensionally than the text. It sets up frames and then breaches them, confounding levels of reality, inside and outside, here and there, yesterday and tomorrow.[21]

When I was attending the *Ramlila* every day, typically crossing the Ganga on a rumbling ferry in bright afternoon sun and returning toward midnight in a wooden rowboat to slide and plop up the mud-slicked bank to my dark apartment, I noticed a gradual shift in the locus of my psychological reality. In the early days of the month-long performance, the *Ramlila* was an interruption of my regular life, somebody else's fantasies enacted, the dream of a maharaja's once and future kingdom. Reality was on the other side of the river: in my flat with its familiar objects, the narrow lane with its broad cows, joking neighbors, bumpy cobblestones, the vegetable sellers at the end of the lane, and the paved street with its rickshaws, dust, and shards of broken clay cups.

But as the month went on, the trip across the river began to seem more like a journey into than out of reality. My energies were claimed by the cosmic drama, its physical rigors, emotional intensities, imaginative flights. The mythic world became progressively more vivid, brilliant, and gripping, while the ordinary world paled, like a poorly remembered dream. One night about a third of the way through the month, when most of the regularly attending audience had been deeply drawn into the lila, a thousand of us sat on the ground in a dark forest and listened to Lakshman tell Guha, the tribal chief: "If in a dream the lord of paradise becomes a beggar or a pauper is turned into a king, on waking there is neither loss nor gain. So you should look at this deceiving world" (2.92).[22]

And this the *Ramlila* made us do. While the performance spectacularly opens out the frames of the *Ramcharitmanas*, it remains thoroughly identified with the text and can be seen, finally, to set up and transgress conventions of time, space, and reality in a way familiar to those who have moved consciously through the narrative structure of the *Manas*. The boundaries or frames thus created and transgressed include those between actors and audience; between the staging ground and the world beyond it; between performance time and ordinary time; and between the temporal and the eternal (the Ram who is charit, embodied in movement, and the Ram who is manas, the transcendent, eternal lake of 'mind' itself).

Members of the *Ramlila* audience not only see the drama but act in it. A vast world is created before and around them. In performance after performance, this world is built physically and psychologically. The devotee's days are curved around the necessity of being there. Including transportation, attendance takes six to twelve hours, occasionally more.[23]

The large space of the *Ramlila* is extended to a semblance of infinity by the fact that the "play" is set in the "real world." Our stage embraces town, village, field, forest, and lake. Our floor is the earth and our roof is the sky, often awesome during moments of transition between day and night in this season of transition between the rains and autumn. Unrealistic theater conventions, whether crude or elaborate, are mixed with "real" props and "real" backdrops that can take one's breath away. For example, the Ganga appears in one scene as a brass pot filled with water in the middle of a paved road, in another as a beautiful lake that the gods traverse in a real boat.[24]

The sense of infinity is enhanced by the impossibility of ever seeing the entire lila. Though my privileged status enabled me to pass through police barriers, there was no way I could see every part of the action in three years' attendance. Crowds, transportation failures, getting lost in the dark, being given the wrong directions, falling back from fatigue or illness, becoming caught up in some interesting conversation or observation, all prevented me from staying with the golden gods every moment. Ordinary spectators may take many years to hear all the dialogues once.

Just as there is no clear line between the "play" and the "world," so too there is none between actors and audience. Perhaps the most comprehensive meaning of *bhakti* is participation, and the audience participates in this devotional drama in a marvelous variety of ways. At many points in the performance audience members play specific roles, as the citizens of Ayodhya, the wedding guests at Janakpur, and the townspeople coming out for processions. The audience's cheers and chants are orchestrated into the performance: it would not be right without them. While the audience become actors, many actors mingle with the audience. They may be seen stepping into their costumes just before a scene, hiking from place to place with their masks under their arms, watching the performance, or chatting.

Similarly, the special *Ramlila* time mingles with nonlila time, since every performance is cut by an hour's break while the maharaja goes to perform *sandhya puja*, or evening worship. At that time the sadhus with their *kirtans* (songs of praise) become the star performers, the svarups are available for a kind of free-form darshan, and the lila fades into the *mela*, or fair, which accompanies it (the mela in the midst of the lila seems to play the role of the "profane" world). On the climactic night of Ravana's final defeat the sandhya break lasts three hours, culminating when the huge paper effigy of the demon king is put to the torch. That night, on the far-extending field of Lanka, the interpenetration of divine being and samsara, lila and mela is particularly grand and powerful. The two do not blur or cancel each other, but fade into and out of each other like figure and ground. The gods emerge from the field of the ordinary world, and the ordinary world emerges from the field of cosmic forces.[25]

This elaborate, physically and emotionally consuming, simultaneously limited and unlimited world dissolves on day 31. It simply disappears. The end can come as a rude shock to a devotee, even though he or she has known all along that it was bound to happen. To see a vast world take shape, to become part of it, to accept it as real, and then to have it cease to exist is to be initiated into the dreamlike evanescence of all our "realities."

In addition to the ultimate dissolution with the last performance, there is a dramatic dissolution every night at *arati*. *Arati* is a ceremony done regularly in temples or homes for images of the gods, or in honor of holy places or persons; lights are waved and offerings are made, often to the accompaniment of songs, bells, and other instruments. The *Ramlila* ends every night with a spectacular arati. One of the directors arranges a tableau that includes those of the five svarups who are in that night's lila and other important characters. He places special garlands over the garlands the deities already wear and arranges the figures in perfect iconographic positions: bow and arrow just so, fresh lotus in hand, and so forth. Once Hanuman enters the narrative, he stands behind them in his bright red mask, slowly waving a yak-hair whisk. An outstanding devotee-character at that point of the lila stands before them and waves the tray of burning wicks. The Ramayanis shout out their arati song. Bells, gongs, drums, and conch shells resound. Meanwhile the people, in maximum numbers at this point, are cheering, straining, taken over by a massive fury to see. The climax is reached when a fireworks specialist lights two brilliant flares. The first is red, and it covers the divine tableau with an intense reddish light lasting about thirty seconds. The second glows pink for a moment, then explodes into a shattering white that outlines the gods in a hard dazzle and sends its glare far back over the audience. After another thirty seconds, the white light goes out suddenly; the great tension snaps, and the five-hour drama comes to a decisive close.

Along with the nightly arati there are a number of moments when the *Ramlila* action is arrested to produce a powerful iconographic image. These moments are called *jhanki*—"glimpses." They are accompanied by the same spectacular fireworks as are used for arati. Examples are when Ram holds Shiva's bow aloft, about to break it; when Sita raises the marriage garland over his head; and when the brothers embrace at the end of Ram's fourteen-year exile. An especially beautiful jhanki occurs on the first day: Vishnu reclining on the serpent Shesha—the serpent's hood over the God's head, Lakshmi massaging his legs, Garuda at his feet—floats out under a black starry sky, with a nearly full moon illuminating the huge square pool that serves as the Milky Ocean.

These jhanki—glimpses of a cosmic, eternal divinity—are crystal-lizations of the actions that we see unfolding in space and time. They indicate moments when the contingent and transcendent meet and interpenetrate. To catch the otherwise unseeable transcendent in an image, the producers of the *Ramlila* freeze the action, turn it to iconography, frame it.

One line in the *Ramcharitmanas* was frequently quoted to me as I asked people to speak of how they saw the five boys who put on the guises of the gods. The line occurs in the arena of the Bow Ritual at Janakpur. Many princes have assembled to try to break Shiva's bow and thereby win the hand of Sita. An immense audience watches the spectacle (as an immense audience is watching the *Ramlila* at that moment). When Ram and Lakshman enter, everyone is transfixed by their beauty. But not everyone sees them in the same way. The poet explains: *"Jinha ke rahi bhavna jaisi, prabhu murati tinha dekhi taisi"* ("According to the feeling within him/her, each saw the form of the Lord") (1.241.4). The passage elaborates, saying that to warriors he looks like the embodiment of heroism, to wicked kings he seems terrifying, and to demons he appears as Death itself. Women see him as eros personified; Janak and his queens see him as their child. The learned see his cosmic form with myriad faces, hands, and feet. Yogis see the refulgent absolute. And Ram's devotees see their own beloved personal Lord. Thus, the poet reiterates, each one sees the Prince of Koshala according to his or her feeling.

Similarly, what one sees in the *Ramlila* depends on one's attitude. The devotee who wishes to have a deep experience must come with a great emotional openness, particularly with that perfect openness known as love. The *Ramcharitmanas* and the *Ramlila* based on it teach love, tenderness, selflessness, adoration, all focused on Lord Ram, but tending to become qualities of the devotee's whole personality. They teach this love in an endless fugue of examples, variations, refinements, love surpassing love, love filtered through every type of personality, in rapture and in grief. The Lord and his devotees have in common an emotional liquidity that is continually expressing itself in tears.

I met an old sadhu who seemed to epitomize the simple faith and flowing emotion that the *Manas* recommends. He used to mutter constantly his own incantation of the divine names—*siyajuram jay ram jay jay ram* (*siyaju* is an affectionate form of Sita). I often saw his eyes swimming with tears as he gazed on the svarups or ran after them on the road. Once he said to me, "Today I do not feel much joy, because no tear has come in this noisy crowd." He also said that if we should shed a single tear in listening to the Lord's stories, our debt could never be repaid (meaning that such tears are divine gifts whose value is inestimable).

A seventy-nine-year-old man who had been coming to the *Ramlila* since he was nine interrupted me as I was trying to question him about the truth he experienced. He was breathing fast, his voice trembling: "Enough, enough, enough. What can I say to you? Yesterday I experienced this: I am sitting in Ramji's court and today is the Lord's coronation. Today it is also my experience. I am sitting in the Lord's court. In the whole world there is nothing else. There is only the Lord. I have no curiosity, no wish, no desire."

A few minutes later when I tried to ask him about arati, he interrupted again: "At the time of arati, the Lord himself is present. Whenever and from whatever angle you look, the Lord himself is present. The Lord himself creates this experience, face to face, before these very eyes. Whoever wants to experience it, let him experience it."

Similarly, a postman who had been coming for twenty years interrupted me when I tried to find out about differences among the boys who played Ram.

"Do you feel —," I began.

"I feel beauty," he broke in, "great beauty. There are waves surging in my heart."

"You don't notice any difference?"

"No difference. You shouldn't see any difference, you should keep your mind steady."

I questioned the old sadhu who chanted *siyajuram*, trying to be sensitive in asking about his intimate experience: "I have seen you in the *Ramlila*. You are always in the front. When the Lord moves you move with him, and you stay near him, saying your *japa* (repetition of a mantra) and keeping your eyes on him. When you look at the Lord at the time of arati, what do you feel?"

On hearing the question he withdrew his eyes and began doing his japa. Then he fell silent. After a few moments he looked at me again and said, "It can't be put into words. You try it and see for yourself. You look into those two lotus faces, take darshan with a wish for loving attachment. Then you will know that taste. I can't tell you. *Siyajuram, jay ram jay jay ram, siyajuram jay ram jay jay ram...*"

The much quoted line about *bhavna* "According to the feeling within, each one sees the Lord's form," acknowledges that the *Ramlila* is what you make it. If you come with devotion, you will see God. If you come with cynicism, you will see little boys in threadbare shorts. If you come wanting snacks, you will see refreshment stands. If you come looking for a spectacle, you will see fireworks. This statement thus admits the psychological nature of *Ramlila* darshan. Although some observers might tend to dismiss this experience as "merely psychological," in its largest Indian meaning it accurately reflects the nature of the universe and the human construction of reality. Every witness-participant creates the drama in his or her mind, being at once actor and audience.[26] The *Ramlila* teaches by experience that our realities are mind-made.

I would like to conclude with a *Ramlila* vignette that illustrates the shock of transition from one frame of reality to another.

On the thirty-first day of the lila in 1976, a few minutes before the final arati, I saw an old man who used to ride in the small boat I took going home from the performances. He struck me as pious and childlike; in the boat he sang religious songs that others listened to affectionately. He had two trademarks: a bamboo fan that he always waved, and a cry that he uttered as greeting and comment, as if it said everything. The cry was "*O ram ki maya! O bhagavan ki maya!*" ("Oh, the maya of Ram! Oh, the maya of God!").

Encountering him on the street before the last arati, I smiled to hear the familiar words and to see the fan winnowing the air. But there seemed to be something wrong. He was staggering and his voice was breaking. Then I saw that he was crying. Tears fell down his face as he wailed something that I was gradually able to make out: "It's over, God's lila is over. For a whole year we won't see it. What will we do?"

His legs buckled under him, and a muscular young man helped to hold him up.

"Perhaps he has been drinking," murmured an observer.

"He has not been drinking," said another. "He is absorbed in God."

Spontaneously the young man embraced the old one and lifted him off the ground, shouting the victory cry of the *Ramlila*: "*Bol raja ramchandra ki jay!*" Others echoed it.

"Someone take my hand and lead me away," said the old man piteously. "It's over. God's lila is over."

This essay is about to be over. But first, I want to get you back out of Tulsidas's body. Did you forget that you were in there? Well, that sort of forgetfulness is also well established in Indian literary tradition. Since I am the metateller of the story about the frames that turned into loops, I will achieve closure by bringing you out of Tulsi's mouth, as I sent you in, on some lines of verse. You can imagine them as roller coaster cars bringing you over the last hump of track in our loop-the-loop and gently depositing you back at the ticket booth:

rama ananta ananta gunani, janma karma ananta namani
jala sikara mahi raja gani jai, raghupati carita na barani sirahi (7.52.3–4)

Ram is endless, endless his qualities,
his birth, acts and names endless.
You can count drops in the ocean, specks of dust on the earth,
but you can never finish telling the story of Ram.

Notes

1. *Ramcharitmanas* 1.33.1–8. In this system of referring to the text, the
first number indicated the book or *kand* (here book 1, *Balkand*); the second
indicates the couplet, in either *doha* or *soratha* meter (here *doha* 33); the third
indicated the *chaupai*(s) in the section preceding the couplet (here verses 1–8,
counting each line as one *chaupai*). Translations in this paper are mine.

2. Lutgendorf discusses the role of Kathavachaks in great detail in *The
Life of a Text*, 1991.

3. The myths about Markandeya's and Yashoda's entry into God's mouth,
as well as Arjuna's vision of God in the *Bhagavad Gita*, are discussed by
O'Flaherty in *Dreams, Illusions, and Other Realities* (1984:109–14). See also
O'Flaherty (1980). In these works Wendy Doniger (she no longer uses the name
O'Flaherty) has analyzed in great depth and detail narrative framing and how
it relates to the play of illusion and reality in certain Sanskrit texts. Though
I began the present article before reading <u>Dreams</u>..., I eventually studied
Doniger's book carefully and am much indebted to it.

4. Though *bhakti* is usually translated as devotion, one of its primary
meanings is participation.

5. "Another frame is implied as well: just as Tulsi is relating the story
and commenting on it to his listeners, so they in turn may become tellers of
and commentators on his story through the performance genres that have
developed around its recitation" (Lutgendorf, 1991:26).

6. "[The fifteenth-century theologian Nicholas] Cusanus found this
metaphor in the writings of Meister Eckhart, who in turn refers us to the pseudo-
Hermetic *Liber XXIV philosophorum*, dating back to the twelfth century. Here
we find for the first time the formulation 'God is an infinite sphere, whose
center is everywhere, whose circumference nowhere.' It is in this sense that
the metaphor is used in the first book of [Cusanus's] *De docta ignorantia*. It
appears in the second book, where it describes the being of the cosmos"
(Harries, 1975:7–8). In "The Infinite Sphere: Comments of the History of a
Metaphor," Karsten Harries discusses the emerging importance of *perspective*
between the twelfth and fifteenth centuries, during which period the "infinite
sphere" shifted from being a metaphor for God to being one for the universe.

She also refers to Jorge Luis Borges's (1964) essay on this metaphor: "The Fearful Sphere of Pascal."

See also Dante's *Paradiso*, 28.58ff., and John Ciardi's (Dante, 1961:314) note: "Seen from all lower levels, these spheres are contained in God and surrounded by Him, for God is Allness. Seen in this nonphysical manifestation at the height of heaven, the spheres surround Him, for God is nondimensional essence."

7. For an extended discussion of his metaphor and its meanings, see Lutgendorf (1989a).

8. This episode takes place between 7.56.1 and 7.57.

9. Din, 17–22. The question is discussed under the heading "Who was the first hearer of the *Ramcharitmanas?*"

10. O'Flaherty (1984:259). The discussion of the Mobius universe is on pp. 240–45.

11. This story begins at 7.75.1 and concludes at 7.85.

12. *Hymns for the Drowning: Poems for Visnu by Nammalvar,* trans. A. K. Ramanujan, has wonderful poems expressing Vishnu as the body of the universe, bending to become itself. When the devotee sees this, she or he sees his or her body and the body of God as simultaneously containing and contained by each other.

13. *Shandy* is the eighteenth-century novel by Lawrence Sterne; *Soldier,* the twentieth-century novel by Ford Maddox Ford.

14. For Bhardwaj's question to Yajnavalkya, see 1.46 and the chaupais preceding it. For Sati's question to Shiva, see 1.50 and the chaupais immediately preceding and following it. For Parvati's question to Shiva, see 1.108.1–1.110.4. The story of Garuda's question has its own little frame structure: he takes it successively to Narada, Brahma, and Shiva, each of whom talks of the power of Vishnu's maya and sends him on. Finally when Shiva sends him to Kakabhushundi, his deep doubt is resolved; see 7.58.1–7.63.2. For Bhushundi's doubt, which occurs in the presence of the child Ram, see 7.77–7.78.1.

15. Dimock bases much of his discussion on Coomaraswamy's (1941) "Lila."

16. Zimmer (1946:27–31). O'Flaherty (1984:81–89) discusses several versions of this popular story.

17. When I say that the metastatement is neither inside nor outside, but *is* the frame, I put the matter a little differently from the way Bateson puts it. His dense series of twenty-five numbered steps-in-thought is sometimes difficult to follow. Here is his interesting conclusion:

Our central thesis may be summed up as a statement of the necessity of the paradoxes of abstraction. It is not merely bad natural history to suggest that people might or should obey the Theory of Logical Types in their communications; their failure to do this is not due to mere carelessness or ignorance. Rather, we believe that the paradoxes of abstraction must make their appearance in all communication more complex than that of mood-signals, and that without these paradoxes the evolution of communication would be at an end. Life would then be an endless interchange of stylized messages, a game with rigid rules, unrelieved by change or humor. (Bateson, 1972:193)

18. Schizophrenics, for example, do not function well in the world because they don't frame things:

It seems that the 'word salad' of schizophrenia can be described in terms of the patient's failure to recognize the metaphoric nature of his fantasies. In what should be triadic constellations of messages, the frame-setting message (e.g. the phrase 'as if') is omitted, and the metaphor or fantasy is narrated and acted upon in a manner which would be appropriate if the fantasy were a message of the more direct kind. The absence of metacommunicative framing which was noted in the case of dreams. . . is characteristic of the waking communications of the schizophrenic. (Bateson, 1972:190)

Bateson (1972:191) points out that psychotherapy is a job that can get done because the situation is framed in a way similar to play: "Just as the pseudocombat of play is not real combat, so also the pseudolove and pseudohate of therapy are not real love and hate. The 'transfer' is discriminated from real love and hate by signals invoking the psychological frame; and indeed it is this frame which permits the transfer to reach its full intensity and to be discussed between patient and therapist."

19. They are not, however, trying to turn people into schizophrenics (see note 18 above). Even Shankara allows that we should behave as if the world is real until we have attained perfect enlightenment: "The world is true as long as one has not yet come to realize that All is Brahman. For such unenlightened ones, all worldly as well as all religious actions are to be practiced until such higher knowledge is realized" (Tuck, 1986:31).

20. Personal communication, March 1985. See Schechner and Schuman (1976) for more explorations along these lines.

It may be mentioned here that Michel Foucault has also been keenly interested in framing as an activity that creates orders of reality. *The Order of Things* (1970) is largely about this. Foucault is fond of analyzing paintings which are self-consciously concerned with frames—for example, the well-known discussion of Velasquez's *Las Meninas*, which constitutes chapter 1 of *The Order of Things*. Foucault has also written a small book, *This Is Not a Pipe* (1983), on the painting (or the visual thinking) of Rene Magritte, who explored the meaning of frames in canvas after canvas. The preoccupation of Foucault and many other thinkers in the last twenty years with "representation" is also a preoccupation with frames.

In his preface to *The Order of Things*, Foucault presents as the inspiration for the book Borges's fantastic taxonomy of animals: "Animals are divided into: (a) belonging to the Emperor, (b) embalmed, (c) tame, (d) sucking pigs, (e) sirens, (f) fabulous, (g) stray dogs, (h) included in the present classification, (i) frenzied, (j) innumerable, (k) drawn with a very fine camelhair brush, (l) *et cetera*, (m) having just broken the water pitcher, (n) that from a long way off look like flies" (Foucault, 1970:xv). Categories are a species of verbal frames. Though the categorization of animals that Borges attributes to "a certain Chinese encyclopedia" rather disrupts than enhances our sense of order, it still sharpens our consciousness of the activity of framing. The same insight about what might be called "the pure activity of category-making" which Foucault draws from Borges's fancy is available from a Sesame Street children's book called *Grover and the Everything in the Whole Wide World Museum*.

21. Yesterday and tomorrow happen to be the same word (*kal*) in Hindi.

22. Much of the remainder of this paper is based on my 1983 article, "*Ram Lila*: The Audience Experience," to which the reader is referred for a fuller discussion.

23. This account applies to committed devotees who attend the entire performance. There are many such devotees, although there are also many who come for only a part of the lila, or only for arati.

24. From my notes of September 27-28, 1977:

The word 'verisimilitude' is foreign to the *Ramlila*. Either it is complete unreality (the ocean represented by a little pit, 10,000 buffalo represented by a small paper quadruped) or overwhelming literal reality (Indra on a huge white elephant; crying naked babies as the four newborn avatars). Sometimes the two mingle: at the end of day 2, the princes mount four real horses to go out and shoot two paper deer. On day 4 there's a real deer in Sita's garden—held on a rope by a policeman. When Vishvamitra takes Ram and Lakshman to the forest, I think again how the word 'verisimilitude' quails before what we are experiencing. We move from the main street of town to narrow lanes, a troop of horsemen in front, the Maharaja on his elephant behind, the golden gods in the middle gliding along at shoulder level. Shopkeepers and laborers stop to watch the gods go by, saluting them with joined palms, just as Tulsidas described it: 'When the citizens received news that the two princes had come...they left their business and ran out of their homes like paupers looting a treasure.' We move steadily to a more rural setting. Roads change from pavement to cobblestones to dirt, houses from plaster to brick to mud, on varying levels, with glittering algae-covered ponds, fields of leafy vegetables and corn, moist green everywhere. If Ram really did go to the forest with Vishvamitra, would it not have been through lanes like this, past houses, from town to village, while the local people stopped to watch? The sky is brilliant pink in the luminous ten minutes before sunset.

25. For this scene in more detail, see Hess (1983:191–92, fn. 5).

26. In the *Manas* Valmiki has an important speech about the world as performance (2.126.1–4). See discussion in Hess (1983:183–84).

3

What's Taking Place: Neighborhood *Ramlila*s in Banaras

Thomas Parkhill

Arriving in Banaras in early autumn, 1984,[1] I intended to follow other scholars from the West across the Ganges River to study the Ramnagar *Ramlila*, a religious drama of widespread reputation.[2] Determined to learn how a religious story was treated in a performance context, I spent the first days of the *Ramlila* season negotiating the river currents and the sometimes soggy Ramnagar geography. One afternoon, after I'd literally missed the boat to Ramnagar, I began to explore my own neighborhood and discovered a *Ramlila* there. This was the first of many I found, most often by consulting the schedule that appeared daily in the Banaras newspaper, *Aj*. I would try to arrive at each neighborhood *lila* (play) site early in the evening, allowing some time for getting lost in the web of Banaras's narrow streets and some time to chat with the *vyas* (director), "decorator" (makeup artist), or other *Ramlila* functionaries. On occasions when I was late, the sound of chanting, drums, and cymbals led me the last of the way. Coasting up on my bicycle, I usually saw a number of men standing around a seated crowd, chiefly children and women. Their attention would be directed to a makeshift stage on which actors in ornate costumes presented scenes from the adventures of Ram. The distinctive sounds I had heard as I approached, however, did not come from these actors.

Within fifty feet of the stage, often on the same ground where the crowd hunkered down, sat the Ramayanis, a group of men of varying ages, chanting verses from a religious text, the *Ramcharitmanas*. The *Manas*, as it is also called, was written in the late sixteenth century by Tulsidas, a poetic genius and celebrated saint, presumably at his home on Tulsighat in southern Banaras. Each evening of the *Ramlila* the chanting of the *Manas* punctuates the acting out of the story of the conflict between, on one side, Ram, his wife Sita, his brothers Lakshman, Bharat, and Shatrughna, and the monkeys led by Hanuman; and Ravana and his demon hordes on the other.

Most of these roles are played by children. The child actors who play the main characters are understood by most of the audience as *svarups* (forms, likenesses) which, like the solid images in the Hindu temples, can provide temporary homes or seats for the deities the actors represent.[3] The only difference, I am told, between stone image and human image is that when the *Ramlila* is over, the svarups become boys again. The children who play Sita, Ram, and his brothers—or better, become Ram and his brothers—act out scenes from the story with stylized movements and speech patterns (Illus. 3.1, 3.2).

Consulting the newspaper *Ramlila* schedule daily during the *Ramlila* season and watching as neighborhood after neighborhood added its production to the list of available lilas, I became acutely aware of just how popular this religious drama is in Banaras.[4] At least sixty neighborhoods, or *muhallas*, in the Banaras area mount productions of the *Ramlila*.[5] Given the time, energy, expense, and expertise necessary for staging just one of these ordinarily nine-day productions of the *Ramlila*, that there are so many is staggering. Intrigued as much by the local variations in production as by the fact that there were so many *Ramlilas* going on all at once, I devoted the remainder of that season to visiting neighborhood *Ramlilas*. Reflecting on that experience now, I see two themes clearly: (1) the tension between those who favored traditional productions of the lila and those who implemented innovations, and (2) the role the *Ramlila* played in a neighborhood's sense of place.

Traditionalists and Innovators

It would make sense to begin an investigation of this theme by describing the typical neighborhood *Ramlila*; but there isn't one. When I was surveying the *Ramlilas* of Banaras neighborhoods, the first characteristic that struck me was their diversity. To be sure, most of the lilas move from place to place in the neighborhood, had children as svarups, men called Ramayanis chanting the *Manas*, intricate facial decoration, elaborate monkey and demon masks, and a vyas or director prompting from a script book, but there were exceptions even to this very general list.[6]

At some *Ramlilas* the Ramayanis sang *bhajans* (popular hymns) as well as the *Manas*, at some they did not; at some the chanting was strong and sweet, at some it was weak and uninspired; at some there were good morale and ample funding, at some there were ill humor and an obvious lack of resources. Some *Ramlilas* featured *sadhus* (holy men) in attendance (sometimes playing the roles of sages), at some there were

3.1

The *svarup* (human representation of the deity) of Ram during bow *lila* (play) at the Lallapur neighborhood *Ramlila* of Varanasi.

3.2

Svarups of Ram and Sita at the Lallapur *Ramlila*.

none; at some the svarups were properly detached but attentive, at some they chatted with one another and ate snacks during the lila; at some the masks and decoration were elaborate, at some they were not. In sum, the diversity included not just quality and style, but also the extent of innovation.

In all three matters it is the biggest *Ramlila* of them all, the Ramnagar *Ramlila*, that serves as the standard or basis of comparison.[7] The only *Ramlila* in the Banaras area that still retains the vestiges of traditional royal patronage, the Ramnagar lila is conservative in other ways as well.[8] The young *Brahmin* boys who become svarups are sequestered for the month of *Ramlila*, and great numbers of sadhus receive royal support and attend each lila. Ramnagar geography has been transformed into a lila-scape, and the Ramayanis are carefully chosen and trained. The production values reflect this conservatism: when artificial lighting is needed, it is provided by torches and lanterns; neither dialogue nor chanting is amplified; costuming and makeup remain unchanged from year to year; even the brass band required for Ram's marriage to Sita wears nineteenth-century British uniforms. By embracing conservatism in a culture which values tradition, the Ramnagar *Ramlila* has ensured its niche as a standard against which the neighborhood lilas of Banaras measure themselves.

Most neighborhood *Ramlila* committees, I found, were not adverse to challenging the standard, especially when it came to innovations. (Only the Chitrakut lila makes a credible claim to be even more conservative than the Ramnagar lila; it is an exception [Lutgendorf, 1987:420–28; Hein, 1972:105–10].) Although these innovations can reach into every detail of a neighborhood *Ramlila* production, I have noticed differences in three main areas of the lila-scape: lighting, amplification, and personnel.

Most neighborhood lilas used electric lights. Usually a few fluorescent tubes or floodlights lit the stage and the area where the Ramayanis sat. Sometimes strings of green Christmas-tree-like bulbs would encircle Ram's area, and, if Ravana was present, his domain, Lanka, would be set off by red bulbs.

Khojwan and Chaitganj featured more extravagant lighting. At Khojwan strings of white bulbs blinked and flashed. On the wall of the two-story "Decoration Center" the bulbs formed stars and long garlands, while fluorescent tubes made up the ribs of huge fans that flashed, sometimes in sequence. Later, on Ram's birthday, the lights were redone. The replacements were more extensive, framing and draping the whole of the left side of the box-shaped building with flashing intensity. Meanwhile, steady fluorescent tubes lit the main audience area, attracting masses of insects.

The Chaitganj Nakkataiya or "nose-chopping" of Shurpanakha, was a special event, an all-night procession of floats and performers that, while apparently consisting of deities and heroes, was in fact made up of shape-shifting demons belonging to the army of Shurpanakha, Ravana's demon sister. The lighting was extraordinary to match the occasion, with prizes offered to shopkeepers for the best displays (Kumar, 1984:252, 267–76). The lights were everywhere in many colors, blinking, almost pulsing, in crazy rhythm. The orange bulbs which formed a canopy over the street blinked in sequence, causing wave after wave of orange light to flow overhead. Whether they offered a lavish display of technical prowess, as at Khojwan and Chaitganj, or simply attempted to provide adequate lighting, most neighborhood lila-scapes challenged the Ramnagar standard of traditional torches and lanterns.

Less ubiquitous than electric lighting was the amplification of dialogue or chanting. For example, neither the Mauniji nor Lat Bhairav lilas had amplification, and at Lallapur there was amplification only for reciting poems for the bow sacrifice lila. Even at the more techno-logically daring lila sites like Khojwan the chanting was rarely amplified, although all the main stage activity—largely dialogue and singing— was. Although less prevalent than electric lighting, amplified sound was featured at the majority of lilas I visited.

At Mirapur, a neighborhood on the outskirts of Banaras, like Ramnagar outside the sacred circle of Kashi (Eck, 1982:350–53), I learned some of the details of acquiring this kind of technology for the lilas. The drama troupe contracted to perform the lila arranged for their own amplification and lights. The troupe's proprietor subcontracted this work to the same man at both the Mirapur and Varunapul lilas. In contrast to the West, where the technical director hides away or at least retreats to the back of the hall, at these lilas this man and his assistant were quite prominent, sitting right in front of the stage. From there they made adjustments and moved the stage microphone around, sometimes while the action and dialogue were going on. At Mirapur the sound was as substantial as at any *Ramlila* I witnessed: one could hear *Ramlila* sounds for at least a kilometer away.

All this new technology is not without its consequences. At Mirapur, just as the performance was about to begin, there was a power outage. As a result, I spent two hours in a nearby tea stall with one of the principals of the company. When the power returned, the lila began. Similarly, the creative lighting techniques featured on some of the floats of the Chaitganj Nakkataiya procession suffered from the lack of portable generators. On several occasions I saw an assistant, power cord in hand, running up the street in search of the next source of electricity for his float's light display.

The new arrangements can exacerbate human tensions as well. Initially at one lila the chant was being amplified. Then the vyas decided he needed the microphone for Ram's speech, so took it in mid-chant from the Ramayanis. At the same lila the lighting consisted of two floodlights, both of which helped illuminate the *Manas*. But there was an ongoing discussion, sometimes quite lively, about whether one of the lights should be turned off. The elder Ramayani wanted both lights in order to see better, and the younger technical director complained that they drew too many insects. There seemed to be tension at this lila between this senior Ramayani, the younger technical director, and a young vyas. This tension found a convenient vehicle in those innovations around which behavior is not yet regulated by the certainty of tradition. But despite attendant complications, most *Ramlila* committees have opted for some kind of technical innovation.[9]

More striking, at least to Western sensibilities, were the innovations in personnel. Stemming from a long history of the exclusion of girls and women from much of the public arena, the Ramnagar standard demands that the lila principals—svarups, Ramayanis, vyas, monkeys, and demons—be male (Awasthi, 1980:514; Mathur, 1978:31). Ram's wife Sita is played by a young boy, as are her attendants. Steeped in the lore of the all-male *Ramlila*, I was amazed when dancing women took to the Khojwan stage. There, to the accompaniment of a three-piece ensemble, was a purple-sari-clad woman dancing and singing, entertaining the old king, Dasharatha, and the rest of us with her vamping. The purple-saried woman was followed by a woman in red whose song apparently originated with a Hindi film soundtrack. The crowd had swollen by this time; the nearly empty schoolyard was now packed with attentive spectators. I'm not sure whether my initial amazement at encountering women on a *Ramlila* stage was muted or amplified when I realized that the women were *men* dressed as *women*. I learned they were *hijras*, cross-dressers with a caste *dharma* (duty) of their own whose visit to a household shortly after the birth of a male child is considered an auspicious event. Devoted to the goddess Bahuchara Mata, these liminal figures, like Shiva, hold the ascetic and erotic in powerful tension.[10] At Khojwan and Varunapul, and I suspect other lilas, the hijras play the roles of women (courtesans, Ravana's sister Shurpanakha, and his wife Mandodari) as well as other hijras at the birth of Ram.

At most neighborhood lilas that feature hijras, the standard proscription against women principals is, technically at least, upheld. But not so in one lila I visited. One night as I sat in the audience at Mirapur watching the *arati* or light offering ceremony, I suddenly realized that the officiant was a woman. Modest and devout looking, she was nonetheless a woman. I later learned, although I could not tell from where I sat in the audience, that Sita was played by a young girl. For the members of the drama troupe who staged the Mirapur lila, this event was as natural as casting a local sadhu as the sage Vishvamitra.[11] Not every lila aficionado would agree.

The tension between those who want to keep the *Ramlila* traditional and pristine and those who are introducing modern innovations runs deep, both in the conversation about the *Ramlila* and in Hindu culture itself. In Banaras the issue is emotionally charged. Innovations are either contemporary enhancements or unfortunate corruptions, depending on one's point of view. Traditionalists worry that the neighborhood lilas are becoming "disco."

The connection between disco and the *Ramlila* was first made for me by Virendra Singh, Hindi teacher and cultural guide to many of the foreign residents in Banaras. One day he began discussing *Ramlilas*. Upset with what he saw as the deterioration of one of the local *Ramlilas*, he predicted with disdain, "In ten years we will have disco lilas." Virendra Singh is very perceptive about the passing Banaras scene; no doubt many Banarsis share his concern. Without some notion of what *disco* means in this context, however, it may be hard to appreciate the depth of that concern.[12]

The word *disco* seems far removed from the world of the *Ramlila*, a sacred world of ritual drama, mask, pilgrimage, and transformed geography. Although *disco* has its slang roots in North America, it has been appropriated in a particular way into parts of India. Young, modern Indians in Banaras use *disco* to refer to something or someone who is "cool," "hip," or, I suppose, "far out": that is, it is a word that is best translated by the current slang for something or someone who displays a sophisticated awareness of the intricacies of local popular culture. To traditional Banarsis, *disco* has a more insidious connotation.

One *Ramlila* evening, a group of adolescent males approached me, pushed one of their number to the fore, and announced with fourteen-year-old surety that their friend was a "disco dancer." I was nonplused, as I often was in Banaras. What, I wondered, would happen next? Would this smiling youth, dressed in "smart" polyester shirt and pants, dance? No, the denouement had been reached: the young man acclaimed as disco dancer had been shown to the Western visitor: that was sufficient. This mundane, ersatz *darshan* served to point up a crucial aspect of things "disco" in the Banaras area: *disco* meant demonstrating an ability to imitate Western fashion and attitudes. Although I could see no significant difference between the disco dancer and his friends, it was because I did not have their eyes to see what was manifestly obvious: his dress, behavior, and attitudes were quintessentially modern and Western; they displayed perfectly these young Indians' perception of what it meant to be "cool," leading them to idolize this "svarup" of disco dancing. These young men probably approved of the "disco lilas" with their flashing electric lights, amplified movie music, dancing "women," and actresses. For people such as Virendra Singh, however, the newer, less traditional aspects of the local lila were distressing.

Although this tension between traditionalists and innovators rests on issues too complicated to reduce to personalities, it was helpful to meet and converse with articulate representatives of each position. I met such representatives in Dr. Bhanushankar Mehta, a traditionalist, and innovator Sarada Guruji.[13] On first meeting, the similarities between these two men are more striking than their differences. Both are Brahmins, gentle white-haired men with eyes prone to sparkling, and both are devotees of Ram and the *Ramlila*. Their devotion is impossible to measure but obvious, not only from the depth of thinking each has done about Ram and the *Ramlila*, but also from their behavior at the lilas they attend.[14] Their different attitudes toward change in the performance of the *Ramlila* are apparent not only from what they say about the production of the *Ramlila*, but also from the lilas they favor and frequent.

A medical doctor and an avid *Ramlila* scholar, Dr. Mehta noted he had been attending *Ramlilas* from the time he was five or six (I would estimate his age in 1984 at between fifty-five and sixty), and that he had seen perhaps twenty-five different *Ramlilas* but had focused his study on three: the Chitrakut, the Ramnagar, and to a lesser extent, the Tulsighat.

For Dr. Mehta the essence of the *Ramlila* was its ritual quality. The analogies he used to describe the lila—*japa* and *yajna* (mantra repetition and sacrifice)—are themselves rituals. "Any dutiful work for the benefit of the world, or even yourself, is yajna."[15] Thus staging a *Ramlila* for the "uplift of the character of the people"—an action, he said, that would provide a "rough copy" so that people might see the deeds of god—is yajna. Here Dr. Mehta quoted the *Ramlila* program motto from the Ramnagar lila: "Doing lila and seeing lila both give *punya* (merit)." In keeping with this understanding, Mehta considers darshan, seeing and being seen by god, the most important part of the *Ramlila* experience. The efficacy of darshan depends on the properness of the ritual, and the properness of the ritual hangs on its unvarying nature. When I asked about modern innovations, I did not get through my list of examples. Dr. Mehta interrupted: "They are not part of *Ramlila*. We don't use any magnification or electrification; we allow no change in the ritual. Even the decoration will not change from year to year. The most important thing is darshan."[16] All the ritual elements, like the opening and closing ceremonies (*arati*) and the "decoration" or makeup, he claimed, were not arbitrary; their specifications are set out in books. Those lilas using innovations are done by professional troupes. They "should not be called *Ramlilas*," he said, "they should be called *Ram katha* festivals." In other words, just performing the story (*katha*)[17] of Ram is not the same as doing the *Ramlila*. Simply performing the story of Ram, especially using electric lights, amplified sound, and dancing hijras, is mere "theater." What's missing, according to Mehta, is ritual. "There are no ritual elements. You will not see people touching the feet of the svarups for they are just actors." When I contradicted Dr. Mehta, saying I had seen this very thing, he said that maybe village people will touch their feet but that rural people were simple people. He emphasized that from his point of view, the actor had not been made god by the proper rituals.

Visiting different *Ramlilas* in Banaras, I kept remembering a line I heard first from a young Western researcher in Banaras. Describing the Khojwan lila he had visited the night before, he said with disgust, "People leave before arati."[18] That is, people leave before the last ritual offering of light (usually in the form of a brilliant magnesium railway flare) to the svarups. My colleague echoes both the words and complaint of Ram Chandra De, in 1978 the personal secretary to the maharaja of Banaras, quoted by Schechner: "Religious belief is fading. The *Ramlila* hasn't changed because the Maharaja is a conservative. After him? Elsewhere *Ramlila* has changed. Today people come to see friends, relations, make purchases...Some leave before *arati*" (1985:195). De provided what he took as the litmus test of devotion, a test based on this underlying notion that the essence of the *Ramlila* is ritual. It is important that the ritual be done correctly without shortcuts, and it is absolutely critical not to leave before the ritual is completed.

That not everyone shares this model of the lila is implicit in De's complaint. My experience is that *Ramlila* goers, whether at Ramnagar or elsewhere, are often not fully intent on the lila. Some come late; others leave early; many chat or snack or wander about, some even during the high ritual moments—arati, placing the *tilak* (ornamental mark) on King Ram's forehead, even the famous meeting of brothers at Bharat Milap. Clearly another model of the lila is at work here.[19] It may well be that Mehta's vision of the *Ramlila* is less a description of what is the case than an ideal that informs his devotion.

What seems clear is that there are competing visions and models of the *Ramlila*. Sarada, besides being a member of the Varunapul *Ramlila*

Committee and having a job "in agriculture," is a member of the Kabir Chaura Natik Mandali, a professional drama troupe. The troupe performs *Ramlilas* for six months of the year, and other dramas the rest of the time. Sarada himself had been involved in *Ramlilas* for forty years; he had been the svarup Ram when he was fourteen or fifteen, and has since played Dasharatha, Meghnad, Angad, and many other characters. When I first saw Sarada, it was in the Varunapul lila, where, as chief vyas, he was beginning arati. The Ramayanis and two hijras had started singing bhajans. Before beginning, Sarada positioned the svarups, placing his large, worn copy of the *Manas* between them. The boys held their pose, in frozen tableau called *jhanki*. While the bhajan went on, Sarada performed arati with a high-lipped stainless steel plate called a *thali*, piled high with flowers surrounding a single ghee lamp burning quietly. He traced the thali through the air in slow, graceful arcs, his eyes closed, head covered with his *Ram-nam* shawl. Later, this thali, light still burning, was passed among the audience; some crowded up to hold their hands over the flame; others placed coins there. At the end of the arati, Sarada scattered flowers over the svarups, and they relaxed again. The crowd let out its collective breath and began to buzz in anticipation of the rest of the evening's lila.

Weeks later in Mirapur, Sarada met us in the room that served as a dressing and decoration room during the lila. A number of other people were sitting around as we talked: the boy who was Ram, the proprietor, the woman who had done arati in last night's lila, the girl who played Sita, a hijra who played a number of female roles, and the man who played Hanuman. The hijra began a fire outside; eventually Sarada would be called away to cook. Caste proscriptions about handling food meant that he and some other Brahmins had to cook for the rest of the cast.

We were also joined in our discussion by Sarada's co-vyas, Jyoti Shankar Mishra, a thin, tall man with a wild grey beard and an unruly halo of grey hair; cockeyed, black-framed glasses set off his intense face. It was to Jyoti that I first put the question of the modern innovations, which, I guessed aloud, some might label corruptions. Misconstruing what I meant by "corruptions," he responded energetically:

At Ramnagar not everyone can see or hear. Some poor village people come just to see the Maharaja who they can't see otherwise, because they can't get into the fort. Here [at Mirapur] everyone can see and hear. At Ramnagar people go to wear a turban and a *kurta*, a *gumcha* and a *dhoti* and to take *bhang*. [That is, in general terms, one goes to "get dressed up and get high."] There is corruption already there.

Ram is great and sacred; his character and this atmosphere are part of the lila. But Ravana is neither great nor good; he is a different ideal, and this atmosphere must be created too. Both characters must be shown to the people, otherwise the conflict doesn't make sense. Because of who Ravana is he invites singers and dancers. So we put more spice in the food. And giving these many types [presenting the whole ethical range of characters] is pleasing to God. The loudspeaker addition is to aid the teaching— more can hear. (October 21, 1984)

The lighting, amplification, and even the dancing hijras were all used, according to Jyoti, to make the lila more accessible to more people. In addition, the hijras "worked" in terms of the internal logic of the lila. They were part of the lila because they fit. A king would want his courtesans to entertain in his court, and it was fitting that there be celebration at the birth of Ram: the courtesans would sing and dance, the hijra would come to sing and be propitiated, and when Ravana sang a bhajan to Shiva, whom he worshiped, his wife Mandodari would naturally join in. A happy bonus of these innovations, according to Jyoti, was pleasing God.

Innovation took place not only in the production, but in relation to the text as well. The *Manas* that is always chanted alongside the drama was not altered, but the dialogues of the actors were. The more Sarada and I talked, the more it became apparent that the dialogue, or *samvad*, was a fluid part of the drama troupe's *Ramlila*, not unlike a text-based oral exposition or commentary (Lutgendorf, 1987:544–58). Sarada began, as he often did, with a comparison to the Ramnagar lila:

At Ramnagar the people are there only for darshan. Here [at Mirapur] there are many different types of people—types of people who will get bored, so we put in songs and jokes, this kind of thing. The meaning is the same, but their interest is satisfied. In chanting like Ramnagar, when it is the time of the battle, then no one will know; so the samvad gives the power [shakti] to the actors by means of the words; simple Hindi words, they pass it on to the people in the audience.[20]

There had been, Sarada said, many many changes in the samvad in his forty years with *Ramlilas*. I asked when the dialogue was written and by whom. He chuckled and said that someone will read something in a book, like it, and show it to "Guruji," the proprietor. If he approves, then the suggester will work it into the samvad and remember it.[21]

In the lilas done by this drama troupe, the samvad is like "fluid" oral tradition complementing the "fixed" book-centered *Manas* recitation. The samvad is a way of adding to the *Manas*-based performance a fresh and contemporary element which deepens the devotee's experiences of the "text-made-flesh." I did not find innovation in the samvad in all the neighborhood lilas, even those that feature other innovations. At Khojwan, a neighborhood that Lutgendorf (1987) explains is producing an innovational *Ramlila* but using some of the Ramnagar time and space models, the dialogues are carefully written in unlined legal-sized copybooks, with illustrations that are reminiscent of illuminated manuscripts. As illustrator Shobanath Gupta showed me these beautiful books, I had a sense I was seeing something permanent. The dialogue at Khojwan does not have the same fluidity it has in the drama troupe lilas of Sarada. A different kind of innovation comes at Khojwan, however, through its uniquely droll character, whose main purpose is to provide some comic relief by ad-libbing throughout the dialogue (Lutgendorf, 1987:465–76, 557). Of all the Banaras lilas, save perhaps Chitrakut, the Ramnagar lila offers the least contemporary exposition or commentary on the *Manas*.[22] Proponents view this as a maintenance of purity, a hedge against popular currents, whim, and fancy; critics counter that this recalcitrance renders the *Manas* inaccessible to many in neighborhood audiences, thereby excluding them from the possibility of a full experience of Ram.

In this matter the sides are clearly drawn. From one point of view the very essence of the lila—the darshan effected by proper ritual—is threatened by these modern "disco" corruptions. From the other, when lilas place all their emphasis on correct procedure and traditional production values, they can become elitist, excluding many people who work until dusk or who can't afford the time, energy, or money to make the journey to another neighborhood to take darshan of the svarups, just wander about absorbing the atmosphere, or listen to (and understand) the *Manas* chanted. Despite this disagreement, people on both sides spend untold time and resources producing what they see as the most effective *Ramlila* possible.

Taking Place in Banaras Neighborhoods

Whether the greatest emphasis was placed on traditional production values or modern innovations, there was frequently intense emotion and occasionally bored indifference among members of all audiences. The representatives of both positions understood this. Sometimes the svarups are home to God himself; sometimes they are just children.[23]

It is not just the actors who shift in and out of divinity; the physical neighborhood goes through a comparable transformation from ordinary landscape to "lila-scape" and back. Discussing the *Ramlila* season, Lutgendorf writes,

> During this [*Ramlila*] season, *mances*—the elevated platforms used for staging important scenes—sprout like mushrooms at major crossroads and on many ghats. To a daytime visitor, these dilapidated wooden structures might hardly seem to warrant notice, but the same visitor returning at the proper hour of the night would see them transformed, through rich draperies and backdrops, into palaces and battlefields, to be trodden by the feet of tiny gods in gilded and spangled costumes. (1987:445)

This movement of both "actors" and "set" in and out of sacredness suggests the "pivoting of the sacred," an essential characteristic of ritual (Van Gennep, 1960:12-13). Jonathan Z. Smith explains: "There is nothing that is inherently sacred or profane. These are not substantive categories, but rather situational or relational categories, mobile boundaries which shift according to the map being employed. There is nothing that is sacred in itself, only things sacred in relation" (1982:55).

The foregoing link between ritual and the pivoting of essential *Ramlila* elements in and out of sacredness suggests we would do well to attend more closely to the claim by both traditionalists and innovators that the *Ramlila* is before all else a ritual. They may well disagree as to which lilas are rituals and which are not, but it is clear that all of those Hindus working to produce a neighborhood lila understand that they are engaged in ritual.[24]

What does it mean for the *Ramlila* to be a "ritual"? One answer which I think is fundamental (but of course not exclusive of other meanings) is that the lila ritual consecrates the space in which it is done, whether that space is spectacular Ramnagar or a modest neighborhood. One result of this consecration is that for the duration of the lila ritual the ground becomes a "place of clarification," a place where attention is focused to reveal significance. Jonathan Z. Smith explains: "A sacred place is a place of clarification (a focusing lens) where. . .[human beings] and gods are held to be transparent to one another. It is a place where, as in all forms of communication, static and noise (i.e., the accidental) are decreased so that the exchange of information can be increased" (1982:54).

As a focusing lens, the *Ramlila* ritual is exceptional. Even at the most modest neighborhood lila there exists the possibility of an intimate interaction with God minus the distractions that complicate everyday life. In the lila, what Smith calls the "exchange of information" between humans and deities is made free of distortion through *Manas* chanting and the dialogue between likenesses of God always on the edge of becoming temporary residences of that God. It is by means of this lila ritual that lila-goers bring Place into being; it is by such means that they confer meaning on space, transforming and consecrating it into Place.[25]

The kind of "transparency" a *Ramlila* offers is special in many respects. Foremost is the fact that the image of God in the sacred *Ramlila* place is alive. Not only is the image alive, but his is a memory that lingers. One afternoon when *Ramlila* season was over, Lutgendorf and the chief Ramnagar Ramayani met the boy who had played Ram only months before in that famous *Ramlila*. Lutgendorf did not recognize the boy, who invited the two for tea. The scholar repeatedly declined until, prompted by his friend, he suddenly realized who this ordinary boy had been: ". . .Just for an instant the sharp contours of the mundane seemed to dissolve into transparency, and another familiar world came back into focus. . .I looked again at the face I had seen. . .at the sunrise *arati*. Then we all had tea" (1987:538). The Ramayani, an especially devout man, understood that tea to be *prasad*, a divine gift, God's grace in physical form. By consecrating space, the *Ramlila* affords an experience (and lingering memory) of the divine, fine-tuned to filter out the static of the everyday.

Perhaps the most graphic example of a neighborhood in which the lila ritual is used to consecrate space is Lallapur. The obliging head of the *Ramlila* committee, Bholanath Varma, began his story by telling me of the history of lilas in his neighborhood dating from the time of Tulsidas. This story of beginnings, like many I heard without variation in other neighborhoods, featured the teller's muhalla prominently. The Lallapur Varma described is a place of central importance, surrounded by five sacred ponds called *kunds*—the Pitri Kund, Matri Kund, Pishachamochana Kund, Surya Kund, and Chakra Kund. Thousands of years ago, he said, powerful sages picked this spot to do their austerities because it was so auspicious.

A temple in Lallapur called Yajnavan Baba Mandir verifies that long ago this muhalla was a preferred site for sacrifice. This origin story described a place that was an important center for religious activity. Varma's story of more recent events told of adversity, struggle, and success. About forty-five to fifty years ago (c. 1940), he went on, Muslims in this predominantly Muslim muhalla objected to the lila, and it was stopped. Their objections in all likelihood stemmed from the thoroughly Hindu religiosity and political ideology conveyed by the *Ramlila*. This issue was taken to court, and, according to the story, the Allahabad High Court ruled that the lila could continue. Although the lila has since gone on without fail, from time to time there have been "incidents," a euphemism for communal violence. One especially noteworthy incident stood out. About twenty-five years ago, according to the committee head, the Muslims tried to take possession of the seven acres of land around Matri Kund by forceful means. This area, Varma pointed out, had been part of Hindu lands on a map of the area issued by the local British official. It was Varma's perception that the Muslims were attempting to usurp Hindu religious space. The *Ramlila* committee of the time decided to regain control of this land by filling in the kund and turning the land into the lila ground. This was done, and now every lila is performed at Matri Kund.[26]

It is worth pointing out three details in Varma's story. First, his description of the Lallapur neighborhood situates it as an exceptional place from the time when all Banaras was a forest, and that, in mythological reckoning, was a very long time ago (Eck, 1982:29–31, 55–56). Second, when the very sacredness of the place was threatened, the Hindus of the neighborhood responded with the lila ritual. By means of the *Ramlila*, the story goes, Hindus reclaimed the land and made it their place again. Third, this reclamation project is maintained, that is, reconsecrated, by the yearly performance of the lila.

Although Lallapur provides the most graphic example, I would argue that the *Ramlila* ritual functions to claim and maintain Hindu space in virtually all the neighborhoods in the Banaras area, and perhaps throughout north India.[27] By means of the lila ritual ordinary space is temporarily transformed into a sanctified, Hindu Place. Further, the *Ramlila*'s characteristic pivoting of sacredness in and out of both svarups and lila-scape works to indemnify Hindu Place against desecration.

The significance of Lallapur's story of reclamation is made clear by numerous stories of the violation of sacred space in which order is eventually restored. Here is an example: About midway through the 1984 *Ramlila* season a Shiva *lingam* was removed from its small shrine near Durga Kund Temple in the Asi Ghat neighborhood. I heard some discussion as to whether sacrilegious Muslims or ultraconservative Hindus intent on increasing communal tensions were the culprits. There were arguments and violence: fights broke out in Asi between Hindus and Muslims. Within a week of the disappearance of the lingam, divers recovered it from the waters of nearby Durga Kund. Once the lingam had been ritually reconsecrated and installed in the little shrine, iron bars were fitted around it. This protected it from vandals but also limited access to devotees wishing to place their offerings at the base of the lingam—a less than satisfying conclusion.

Any sacred place in Banaras—temple or mosque, tomb or shrine—is vulnerable to desecration and attendant violence (Eck, 1982:xv, 46, 66, 77, 82; Kumar, 1984:253). Less so the *Ramlila*. The lila ritual consecrates neighborhood space without the commensurate threat of desecration. Characteristically, the svarup pivots easily from sacredness to ordinariness, allowing for gods quickly to become boys, thus making desecration difficult. In a sense desecration, or better, "unconsecration," is an integral part of the lila ritual. At the end of each performance, I was told, when the svarup's crown is removed, he no longer has the potency of being God; he returns to being an ordinary boy.[28] Similarly, the neighborhood ground—whether a neighborhood corner consecrated as Ayodhya, Chitrakut, or Rambag, or a permanent "lila ground" like the reclamation project at Lallapur—returns to its ordinary status after the lila is over. Most grounds look like what in the West would be called "vacant lots."

Another story first pointed me toward the *Ramlila's* near invulnerability to desecration. I first visited the Adi Lat Bhairav neighborhood's *Ramlila* on a night when the exiled Ram was leaving his home city of Ayodhya for the forest. As the svarups, in ascetic garb appropriate for the forest, wended their way through the streets of Lat Bhairav (transformed into Ayodhya), they were stopped repeatedly by ordinary householders who did *puja* (worship) to them, offering fruit, sweets, and flower garlands. The svarups accepted these offerings and invariably returned them to the worshipers as prasad, a tangible sign of God's grace. Prasad in hand, the beaming householders returned to their homes to share with guests, who crowded the verandas watching, waiting, and listening to the *Manas* being chanted (see also Awasthi, 1980:513).

On the veranda from which I watched the procession and received prasad from its generous householder sat Chedi Lal, a large man with the beginnings of grey in his hair, reminiscing about *Ramlilas* gone by. I was struck by how communal violence figured in his recollections. On another occasion he told me his story in some detail. That story provided evidence that even in the worst of all situations—a violent confrontation in a neighborhood with at least 175 years of communal tension[29]—the lila, although not immune to the ravages of violence, could resist virtually any desecration.[30] Chedi Lal told me that in 1933 or 1934 the magistrate forbade the lila procession, especially the band, from going up onto that evening's lila ground, a site sacred to both Hindus and Muslims.[31] Determined that the lila must go on, the organizers arranged for three wrestlers to be bearers for the three svarups.[32] The procession was stopped at the steps of the raised *Ramlila* area; fighting broke out. Soon utter chaos reigned in a pitched battle that included mounted police and flying bricks. Lal was one of the young men who ran with the wrestler-borne svarups up into the lila area. He recalls being worried that in the melee "God might be hurt." The men managed to protect their divine charges, eventually escaping to safety. The Lat Bhairav lila was closed down the next day, and all the *Ramlilas* in Banaras the day after that. Repercussions followed; a semblance of normalcy was restored only after much negotiation. The point is that by later in the evening of the ruckus the svarups looked just like ordinary boys again, vulnerable to attack like any other boys, but not to desecration. Chedi Lal's story, recalled in the midst of a peaceful *Ramlila* procession, served to teach me and remind his neighbors that Hindu Place established by lila ritual could not be easily desecrated.[33]

That processions—Hindu and Muslim—serve in part to mark neighborhood boundaries in all of urban north India is undeniable. The *Ramlila*, however, goes beyond simply setting the borders. True, *Ramlila*-as-ritual, by virtue of its processions, sets neighborhood boundaries, but like a temple or mosque it also gives a neighborhood a religious core, a holy focusing lens. With the *Ramlila* the muhalla is not just any place; it has become a Hindu Place.[34]

What is uncommon about the phenomenon of *Ramlila*-as-ritual in the Banaras neighborhood context is that Place (the quality of consecrated space) is simultaneously temporary and enduring. For a time, ordinary neighborhood spaces are themselves "focusing lenses," encouraging the lila-goers to attend to whatever might be revealed there, especially in the persons of the svarups. Yet, when the lila ritual is over, there is rarely anything tangible left vulnerable to desecration. Stages are often torn down or moved to be used elsewhere; the lila ground is returned to its former status as secondary school yard, vacant lot, or street. The svarups of God go back to school. Whether it lasts six days or thirty, the consecration effected by the *Ramlila* ritual is fleeting.

Paradoxically, however, the *Ramlila* ritual is also enduring. The sacred may have pivoted from the neighborhood boys and locales, but the experience of sacredness—of taking darshan of Ram in Videha where he broke Shiva's bow, or receiving prasad from God as he made his way to forest exile—remains in the hearts and minds of the lila-goers. The memory of that intimate experience of the divine—jogged by the daily trip to the bazaar past the field once transformed by dramatic ritual to the Place where the demon Ravana was destroyed, or by a glimpse of the svarup of Ram in a tea stall, and reinforced as well by the myriad *Manas*-related activities throughout the year (Lutgendorf, 1987:passim)— continues to maintain the neighborhood as Place until the lila is done again the following *Ramlila* season.

If the two themes of this chapter have a point of contact, it is here: both traditionalists and innovators in Banaras are intent on claiming and maintaining Place. Both want to provide an efficacious lila ritual, one that casts a paradoxically temporary yet enduring sacred aura over their neighborhood. They disagree on how best to do this. Electrification or no, amplification or no, hijras or no—each decision has larger implications. Each neighborhood *Ramlila* committee must struggle with how best to respond to change, especially change from the West, and still maintain and know their Place. It is a struggle in which we all to some degree share. If the rich diversity of responses I witnessed is any indication, Hindu Banarsis will continue to take their Place in Shiva's city for a long time to come.

Notes

1. This study is based in part on fieldwork done during the *Ramlila* season of 1984. From early September until the season was cut short by the assassination of Indira Gandhi on October 31, I spent virtually every night at a *Ramlila*, visiting a total of fourteen, some of them as many as four times. In this work I was guided, both geographically and linguistically, by my research assistant, Om Prakash Sharma. A number of people helped me revise versions of this chapter. They are Bradley Hertel, Linda Hess, Cynthia Ann Humes, Russ Hunt, David Kinsley, James and Jackie Reither, Doug Vipond, and an anonymous reviewer.

2. Here I refer particularly to the works of Linda Hess, Richard Schechner, and Philip Lutgendorf. Their work devoted to the *Ramlila* is essential for all who wish to understand the Ramnagar version of that lila specifically and the *Ramlila* phenomenon generally.

3. A number of consultants consistently referred to the svarups as *murtis*, the word also used for stone images in Hindu temples.

4. See Lutgendorf, "The Life of a Text: Tulsidas' *Ramcaritmanas* in Performance," passim. Besides giving a thorough and enjoyable discussion of the *Ramcharitmanas* and its expositors, Lutgendorf explores in detail some of the more specific reasons for the *Manas*'s popularity, for example, for Marwari

industrialist patrons, for whom the story is important both as a family *Dharmashastra* (code of ethics), and as a source of "peace of mind" (693–706).

5. Nita Kumar (1988:65) notes that during most of the past one hundred years Banaras has been divided into eight wards. At present, each ward is divided into approximately fifty smaller neighborhood units known as *mohallas* (also, *muhallas*), each with about one thousand residents.

6. The fixed stages of Shivapur, Daranagar, and Lallapur, the vyas of the drama troupe who takes various roles instead of prompting, and the lack of decoration at Chitrakut come to mind.

7. Unfortunately, most of the people involved in the production of the larger neighborhood *Ramlilas* did not have time to go to the Ramnagar lila. It was evident that many of the people I interviewed had not been to the Ramnagar lila; most seem to rely on secondhand information. For example, one consultant told me that at Ramnagar they had no need for electric lights because the lila started at 4:00 and was over at 6:00. Although it is true that the maharaja stops the *Ramlila* every evening so he may attend to his prayers, the lila begins again, often carrying on way past dark into the early morning hours.

8. Lutgendorf (1987:596) traces the pattern of *Ramlila* patronage from kings in the eighteenth century through to merchants and industrialists in the twentieth. Schechner and Hess are especially helpful for understanding the Ramnagar *Ramlila* (Schechner and Hess, 1977:51–82; Schechner, 1985: 151–211; Hess, 1983:171–94).

9. Schechner (1985:199) links modern innovations ("modernization") with a lack of financial resources. This is not my experience.

10. See Nanda (1990:20, 29ff.). The presence of hijras in neighborhood *Ramlilas* may derive historically from the *Svang/Nautanki* tradition, which featured among other things "female impersonators" (Hansen, 1989:64).

11. On the advent of women performers in *Manas*-based expository performances called *katha,* see Lutgendorf (1989b:56).

12. Alter explores a similar tension between Banarsi wrestlers and those they typify as having a "disco mentality" in his chapter of this volume.

13. We were joined in conversations with Sarada by his assistant vyas Jyoti Shankar Mishra. Everyone in the drama troupe referred to Sarada by the appellation "Guruji."

14. I am grateful to Cameron Barr for his report of Dr. Mehta's response to the Chitrakut Bharat Milap.

15. Mehta's identification of the *Ramlila* with sacrifice places him in a long tradition of thinking about the lila. Consider, for example, the current maharaja,

Vibhuti Narain Singh: " '*Ramlila* is not a play, it is a *yajna . . .'* " (Gargi, 1969:34). Gargi (1967:270) also notes, "*Ramlila* in Varanasi is not a dramatic spectacle, it is a ritual." Lutgendorf has given much thought to the many ways yajna relates to the *Ramlila*. See, for example, his description and interpretation of the "Great Sacrifice of Nine-day [*Manas*] Recitation" at Gyan Vapi (Lutgendorf, 1987:135–59); his thoughts on yajna as a subtle means of appropriation or "Veda-ization" (1987:719); and his conclusion: "For four hundred years the *Manas* has functioned as something like a living *yajna*—a performance of meaning which *samskar*-ized and thereby changed its performers: made them over into what they aspired to be, while simultaneously bringing transcendence to earth in the form of human language and song" (1987:723). See, too, his comments on the "present vogue for *yajnas*" in Lutgendorf (1989b:60–61).

16. Dr. Bhanushankar Mehta, personal interview, October 30, 1984.

17. Lutgendorf unpacks the performative dimension of katha in detail (1987, 1989b: passim). Mehta's pejorative use of *katha* here has nothing to do with the expository form of katha about which Lutgendorf writes.

18. Cameron Barr, personal communication, September 21, 1984.

19. Mehta seemed to recognize this as well. He noted that his narrow definition of the *Ramlila* (to include Ramnagar, Chitrakut, and Tulsi Ghat lilas only) "was not so popular." See also Schechner (1985:187).

20. Personal interview, October 21, 1984. Lutgendorf argues that the perception that "people don't understand Avadhi," the sixteenth-century literary dialect of the *Ramcharitmanas*, is too simplistic. According to Lutgendorf, the *Manas* is understood by more people than is commonly thought (1987:684–93).

21. A favorite source of dialogue is the *Radheshyam Ramayana*, composed in the twentieth century. For a range of dialogue composing techniques and sources, see Mathur (1978: 34–37), who reports that at the Daranagar *Ramlila* the dialogue was composed at each lila and dictated to the actors. There was no written script, according to the vyas, because the actors were forever throwing their scripts away.

22. According to Lutgendorf (1987:552–53, 557), Ramnagar production lore has it that even a seemingly insignificant detail can take as long as several *Ramlila* seasons to work out, and may include a debate for the maharaja to settle. This refusal to innovate does not, of course, prevent the Ramnagar lila, or any neighborhood lilas, from providing enlightening "spatial articulation" of the *Manas*.

23. Mehta noted in an interview (October 15, 1984) that the transformation from boy to svarup is unpredictable. Sometimes it happens, he said; sometimes it does not. Discussing the attitudes of the audience toward the svarups, Jyoti said, "This is the belief of the people, for some people these are boys, some

say these are gods. It's the same at [the] Sankat Mochan [Temple, dedicated to Hanuman]: some say [the image] is stone; some that it is god. There are bad people and good everywhere." Sarada indicated that since the time royal patronage of *Ramlila* has all but ended, the audience has been able to become too familiar with the svarups as mere boys. This, according to Sarada, has increased the number of disbelievers. Ironically, on this point Sarada sounds like a traditionalist. Lutgendorf (1987:706–13) rejects the perception that the *Ramlila* is in decline.

24. Sarada (October 23, 1984) said the most important thing in *Ramlila* was arati. The most efficacious moment for taking darshan of the god, arati, whether during *puja* or the *Ramlila,* is the moment the god is "awakened" to this world, most commonly by the swirling movement of light, or, in the *Ramlilas,* by the glare of the magnesium flare.

25. On this process of conferring meaning on space, see Smith (1987:28, 96–117).

26. I cannot verify the historical accuracy of the details of Mr. Varma's story. Kumar (1984:115) does not list Matri Kund as one of the kunds which have been filled in, although she makes no claim that her list is exhaustive. For our purposes, however, story, not historical accuracy, is most useful in understanding "Place."

27. Certainly this is the case in Ramnagar, where, according to Awasthi (1980) and Lutgendorf (1987:435–36), the maharaja established the *Ramlila* at a time when the population of his realm was predominantly Muslim. The situation is, however, far more complicated than simple opposition. Kumar (1984:324) has demonstrated that Hindus and Muslims in Banaras share a cultural identity deriving from a sense of local tradition. Freitag (1989b) writes that class differences may be operating as much as religious differences. Indeed, my colleague Scott Exo (personal communication) pointed out that the audience at one of the Lat Bhairav lilas we attended included a few Muslims.

28. That the svarup pivots back to ordinariness at the end of each *Ramlila* performance seems to be belied by the Ramnagar Ramayani who insisted that Lutgendorf take prasad/tea from the former svarup of Ram. However, both the intensity of the Ramayani's devotion to the *Ramlila* and the context of the Ramnagar "neighborhood" are unusual when considered against the backdrop of Banaras neighborhood *Ramlilas*. In my experience, most people attending the *Ramlila* do not respond this way to the svarup boys once their role in the lila is over. As for Lutgendorf's momentary experience of the trasnparency of divine and ordinary realms, I am sure that to those who can see and recall the *Ramlila* ritual, an ordinary boy can serve as a window to God. This reinforces the enduring quality of making Place discussed below.

29. Freitag (1989b:211–12) gives the early nineteenth-century history of violence at Lat Bhairav; Eck (1982:196–97) also provides an overview of almost

two centuries of tensions there. Kumar (1984:325–26) discusses the dynamic that fuels the acceleration of Hindu-Muslim conflicts. Often at the Lat Bhairav lila my research assistant and I were told that two processions, one Hindu and one Muslim, were heading for one another, but that the police prevented trouble. Chedi Lal told us this occurred in the current year (1984) as Bharat Milap and Moharram processions moved toward collision. Another consultant, Tripathi, told us that the year before a lila procession had been stopped by the police inspector, who, he said, had been bribed by "other parties," that is, Muslims. Tripathi, who once played the svarups Laksman and Ram and is now a temple priest and assistant vyas, also established Lat Bhairav's prominence among lilas. At the Lat Bhairav lila, he said, just as at the famous Bharat Milap (Lutgendorf, 1987:448–59), a devout person could have a vision of Ram. After all, he went on, the lila ground (often the site of conflict) *is* Chitrakut; "it is the forest where Ram, Lakshman and Sita stayed. That type of place you can't find just anywhere."

30. In neighborhoods with a high proportion of Muslim residents— Alaipur, Lallapur, and Lat Bhairav—I had some difficulty finding the lilas, even with the help of my research assistant and cooperative cycle-rickshaw drivers. Time and again we would be told that the lila was already over or that it had been postponed. It was not that we were asking only Muslims. Rather, I suspect it was that we were strangers. There seemed to be an assumption in these neighborhoods that everyone who needed to know where the lila was already knew. The lila's location in these neighborhoods seemed very much a local matter, perhaps as a hedge against encouraging conflict.

31. Another consultant, Bhegeluram, gave the date as 1937.

32. In many neighboorhood lilas the svarups' feet are not allowed to touch the ground once their tiaralike crowns are in place. Often the svarups are carried short distances on the shoulders of devotees. It is a well-known characteristic of Hindu gods and goddesses that their feet never touch the ground. I found it remarkable that Chedi Lal remembered the names and muhallas of the three wrestlers, whom he also called "goondas," a version of which (goon) has been appropriated into English. Elsewhere in this volume, Alter shows why wrestlers, devotees of Hanuman and warriors on the front lines in the battle for preserving Banarsi culture, would be natural allies of the *Ramlila* and its svarups.

33. Even as presented in Chedi Lal's biased story, the situation that unfolded was a recipe for violence. The ingredients were the site, where Hindu pilgrimage place and Muslim mosque and sacred tomb shared the same ground with a permanent armed police guard which had fired weapons during fighting three times in the last twenty years (Kumar, 1984:329); the time, a Muslim holy day that prohibited the playing of joyful music; and a *Ramlila* wedding procession that, by lila standards, required the presence of a noisy, Western-style brass band. Given this situation, once there was confrontation, violence was all but inevitable.

4

Hanuman and the Moral Physique of the Banarsi Wrestler

Joseph S. Alter

In this paper I will develop an interpretation of the symbolic meaning of the Banarsi wrestler's body, showing how this body becomes a medium for moral self-expression through association with the iconographic physique of Hanuman, the patron deity of all wrestlers. In this process the wrestler's physique takes on nationalistic tones as it comes to symbolize ethical reform.

Although this paper is specifically about wrestling (*pahalwani*), as it is practiced and conceptualized throughout much of northern India, it is also about Banaras. Many who have studied Banaras point out that the city has a character or ethos that is all its own (Eck, 1982; Freitag, 1989a; Kumar, 1986, 1988). What is intriguing about this ethos is its somewhat ineffable quality: the notion that it has to be experienced in order to be appreciated, and can only be really understood on a purely sensory level. The tendency among scholars has been to celebrate this ethos by focusing on that which makes Banaras a unique milieu: the sacred precinct of the inner city, the culture of the *ghats* (steps) along the banks of the Ganga, rituals of morning bathing, *pan* (betel leaf), *bahri alang* (the recreational activity of crossing to the "farther shore" of the Ganga, to leisurely relieve one's bowels and wash one's clothes with one's friends), the annual cycle of pilgrimage and *puja* (worship), ascetic sects, craft and textile production, *katha* (recitation of and commentary on sacred stories) performance, and of course the spectacular *Ramlila*. As a result the city appears as an enchanted environment vibrant with meaning and teaming with cultural significance—all of which is true, as Kumar (1988), Lutgendorf (1989a:272–88), Parry (1980, 1982a, 1982b), and others have well illustrated. It must not be forgotten, however, that behind the enchanted culture of katha performances, *Ramlila* dramas, reveries induced by *bhang* (a *cannabis* concoction popular in Banaras), *bhakti bhajans* (devotional hymns), and countless other artifacts of an idealized life plan lurks, on another more pervasive level, the alternate reality of modern hedonism, commercialization, and immorality: a world of crass sensuality manifest in cinema halls, "disco music," and self-indulgent fashion.

It is, in part, modern hedonism which makes the enchanted culture all the more inspired, for crass commercialism and immoral materialism serve as stark backdrops for a well-crafted and self-reflexive culture. And this inspired culture seems all the more resilient as it holds back the tide of urban malaise and cheap self-indulgence. The cultural life of Banaras is, in some respects, best seen in these terms, that is, as a somewhat self-conscious response to rampant, generic modernism that threatens to undermine a prized way of life. My purpose in this paper is to demonstrate this point through an examination of Indian wrestling as it is practiced in Banaras.

Throughout northern India, and most certainly in Banaras, wrestling has developed into an elaborate way of life which extends well beyond the bounds of what in the West would be termed simply a "sport." In Banaras in particular it has become an artifact of inspired culture which defines an important aspect of the Banarsi ethos. As Kumar (1985:33–37) has pointed out, going to the *akhara* (a public gymnasium for wrestling) is regarded as a structured form of leisure which creates an aesthetic sense of well-being. Many Banarsi men frequent akharas in order to relax in a structured, healthful environment. They lift weights, do a few exercises, and massage one another in a casually energetic fashion. Strictly speaking, these men participate in the culture of wrestling, but they do not subscribe to the rigorous regimen of the committed wrestler. For wrestling is not just a leisure activity; it is a disciplined way of life—an ideology of moral and physical fitness—which stands in sharp contrast to the undisciplined, hedonistic narcissism which many feel has come to characterize the modern Indian scene.

Harsh, subjective, and self-righteous criticism of the modern Indian milieu is as much a feature of Indian wrestling as are tournaments, exercises, and training sessions. Why this is so, particularly in Banaras, will be made clear, but it is first necessary to briefly outline some basic features of Indian wrestling if only to override and dispel some possible preconceptions.

Wrestling

The competitive aspect of Indian wrestling is perhaps its most superficial, although certainly dramatic, form. As I have discussed elsewhere (Alter, 1989), Indian wrestling is a way of life bent on a holistic psychosomatic reform of the wrestler's sense of self. As a result, many noncompetitors engage in wrestling as a regimen of health and fitness.

In the city of Banaras, where I conducted twelve months of field research, there are between one and two hundred akharas ranging in membership from five to seventy. Most akharas have between twenty-five and thirty members, who range in age from about eight to sixty-five, and the five most popular ones are considerably larger. Other northern Indian cities and towns also have a large number of gymnasia. Similarly, many large villages sponsor akharas and associated wrestling activities.

Although wrestling is commonly regarded as a lower-class or rural activity by members of the upper middle class, in fact the range of people who engage in wrestling includes college professors, wealthy merchants, artisans, peasant farmers, bank clerks, lower- and middle-level government bureaucrats, and a host of other people from a wide range of caste and class backgrounds. Regardless of this heterogeneity, or perhaps because of it, the wrestling way of life is remarkably homogeneous and uniform because of its strict regimentation. In principle, it brings all participants, regardless of background, up to a common, high level of psychosomatic health consciousness. In this regard wrestling effectively cuts across other criteria for self-evaluation. (See Illus. 4.1 for a photograph of wrestlers in Banaras.)

The Akhara

The central feature of every akhara is a twelve- to fifteen-meter-square earthen pit which is usually covered over with a cement pavilion. The pit is surrounded by an expanse of packed earth which is used as an exercise area by the members. The akhara compound also includes a number of shade trees and a water source in the form of a well or hand pump. Regardless of size, every akhara also has a temple or small shrine dedicated to Lord Hanuman, the revered monkey general who helped Ram free the kidnaped Sita.

The overall aesthetic of akhara space is of vital importance to the whole wrestling enterprise. Words such as *cool, calm, peaceful, relaxing, spiritual,* and *pure* are used to define the general aura of a gymnasium compound. This aura emanates from the confluence of Hanuman's divine power, the cool water of the well, the shade of the trees, the purity of the earth, and, most significantly, from the wrestler's body as he takes part in the rigorous discipline of training and exercise. As such, the akhara is an aesthetic cum moral space which is physically

4.1

A group of wrestlers at the Akhara Bara Ganesha in Banaras.

as well as conceptually regarded as dramatically opposed to the teeming chaos of modern urban life.

The Daily Regimen

A wrestling way of life is characterized by strict adherence to a regimen of physical exercise and dietary practices. Significantly, however, the regimen to which a wrestler subscribes is not simply a single aspect of his life; it is, in fact, his whole life envisioned as a discipline of health.

The regimen, somewhat simplified and abbreviated, is as follows. Waking at 3:00 A.M., a wrestler performs his ablutions and relieves himself. He then runs between five and ten kilometers, depending on his ability. Before entering the akhara precinct he bathes in the cool water of the akhara well, puts on a *langot* (g-string), the traditional garb of a wrestler, and rubs his body with mustard oil.

At about 5:30, when most of the akhara members have assembled at the compound, one wrestler takes responsibility for making the morning supplication. Three or more sticks of incense are lighted in front of the image of Hanuman. The wrestler holds these in his hand and walks backward into the freshly dug earth of the pit. Starting at the point nearest to Hanuman, he walks around the perimeter of the pit in a clockwise direction. At each corner of the pit the suppliant wrestler takes a fistful of earth with his right hand and lets the earth trickle through his fingers as he circles his hand around the sticks of incense. After circumambulating the pit he walks backward to the center and plants the incense in the earth. He continues walking out of the pit while facing the image of Hanuman. Together the assembled wrestlers chant a short prayer to Hanuman which invokes his blessing and protection, glorifies his courage, and praises his love and devotion to Lord Ram. The incense is then removed from the pit and taken and presented to all of the wrestlers. Each in turn draws his hands through the smoke and bows his head in an act of reverence, supplication, and communion.

Many wrestlers mark their foreheads with earth before they begin to wrestle, and some swallow a small piece of sacred earth before they actually enter the pit. In a gesture signifying respect that is common in many Hindu religious settings, all wrestlers touch their hands to the edge of the pit before they engage in practice.

Wrestling practice begins when two senior wrestlers enter the arena and begin to spar. Gradually other wrestlers pair off and begin to practice moves and countermoves on each other. This sort of sparring is a form of general exercise referred to as *jor* (exertion or force): see Illus. 4.2. Jor continues for about two or three hours, and many wrestlers spar with ten or twelve different partners until the morning session ends at approximately 8:00 A.M.

The evening exercise schedule, known as *vyayam*, begins at about 4:30. Two simple exercises, *dandas* and *bethaks*, form the cornerstone of the vyayam regimen. Dandas are like Western-style push-ups except that the body is bent at an angle rather than held rigid and perpendicular. *Bethaks* are virtually identical to Western deep knee bends. What is unique about dandas and bethaks is partly the form of the exercise, but more significantly the sheer number that wrestlers perform. A wrestler in the prime of youth will do anywhere from 1,000 to 1,500 dandas and from 2,000 to 2,500 bethaks at a stretch. Even a fairly casual wrestler does hundreds if not thousands every day.

Eating is also an important part of the wrestler's commitment to overall health and fitness. Although wrestlers eat many things common to the diet of other north Indian Hindus, the nature of their diet, referred to as *khurak*, is unique in a number of ways. For one thing, wrestlers drink huge volumes of milk: up to two or three liters a day. They also consume large amounts of ghee (clarified butter): up to a half kilogram or more per day. Ghee is mixed with milk and drunk as a tonic after the morning workout. In addition to this, wrestlers eat upwards of a kilogram or more of raw almonds and chickpeas. Being able to consume a diet as rich as this is as much a reflection of strength and good health as it is a way of building a strong body.

Space does not permit me to give a full account of the wrestler's entire regimen. It must be noted, however, that the schedule of fitness and health goes well beyond the obvious dimension of jor, vyayam, and khurak. The regimen extends into the most minute facets of everyday life: where, when, and in what position to defecate; how, when, and with what to brush one's teeth; when and in what temperature water to bathe; what quality, texture, and style of clothes to wear; which oil to use as a body lotion and hair tonic; when, where, and in what position to sleep; what to think about when relaxing; what appropriate leisure to engage in; and how best to be of service to elders, teachers, and the larger community. There is no time or situation in which a wrestler is not first and foremost a wrestler. He may be called upon to perform other functions and to play other roles—father, worker, brother, community leader—but even these "distractions" can be interpreted and thus logically integrated into a pervasive ideology of health whereby a strong wrestler is a good citizen.

4.2   *Jor* (sparring) at Kedarnath Akhara in Banaras District.

The regimen of health to which a wrestler subjects himself produces a physique of a specific type. Size is important, insofar as a great wrestler is usually big, broad-shouldered and thick-necked, but texture and a general sense of balance and proportion are of more vital importance. An ideal physique is referred to as a "body of one color," meaning that it is whole, solid, and pure. It radiates health and vigorous energy. As one author writes:

> When thousands of people stop to look at a famous wrestler then one may say that the character of the wrestler calls out; it beckons. So what is this character? A wrestler has a majestic body. He has strength. He has stamina, skill, experience and if he is educated and well-read then he has knowledge and wisdom. He has humility and is well mannered. He is skilled. . .and who knows what all else. Any number of these traits define his character, and as long as they are maintained they will be the reason for the wrestler's fame. But most of all a wrestler's character is defined by his strength. . .Character is fostered by strength, and in turn strength is the aura of character. A wrestler builds his character through his own efforts, and reaps what he sows. *Brahmacharya* (self-control/celibacy) is the paramount means by which a wrestler establishes his character. He is a disciple of celibacy. (K. P. Singh, 1972b:21)

The Moral Physique and the Immoral Everyman

Insofar as wrestling is a form of physical and moral self-discipline, the wrestler sees himself as standing in sharp contrast to all that is wrong with modern India; and what is wrong with modern India is embodied in the person of the narcissistic, self-indulgent young man. Many of the senior wrestlers with whom I spoke had a clear image of who this delinquent everyman of India is: a product of his times. In general terms he is undisciplined, lazy, boisterous, self-serving, effeminate, garrulous, sexually preoccupied, promiscuous, materialistic, trendy, fashion conscious, and depraved in the most extended sense of the term. In a more specific and sensual vein the marks of hedonism are as easily distinguished by the wrestler as they are common to the public street life of urban Banaras. Young men who have fallen victim to the encroachment of modern values are seen wearing tight, synthetic trousers, well-groomed "hippie-cut" hairstyles, fitted Western-style shirts, heeled, zip-up pointed boots, thin, trimmed mustaches, and manicured nails. They wear scented talc powder, deodorants, and perfumed after-shave. These young men promenade in public, flaunting their leisure life-style by spending hours idly drinking tea and eating fried, salty snacks from street-side stalls. They frequent *pan* shops, where gossip often turns to the subject of sex and promiscuous, sensual pleasure. They smoke, often drink, and act intoxicated.

If not most egregious in a literal sense, the single most dominant metaphor of overall moral depravity—again, in the wrestler's judgmental eye—is the popular Indian cinema. Film, and film music in particular, has come to be regarded by wrestlers (and probably other moralists) as the burlesque swan song of a beleaguered nation, the overt cele-bration of hedonistic self-indulgence. So-called filmy fashion evokes notions of gross materialism and sexual promiscuity. The cinema hall is a veritable den of iniquity, festooned as it is with posters which advertise and glorify the fantasy of an alternative, dark reality. The world of film is populated by glamorous, busty heroines, debonair criminal masterminds, drug lords of countless varieties, and, of course, heroes who escape the pitfalls of real life in the most unreal and enchanting fashion. Cinema halls, commercial television and radio, tape decks, and film magazines have redefined the landscape of modern India as surely as have mopeds, diesel tube wells, and Maruti cars. Those who celebrate the terms of this modern landscape and consume its products (as opposed to those who simply put up with it) are characterized by wrestlers as having a "disco mentality," the term *disco* having the connotation of cheap, trendy and commercial. Although modern Indian cinema is, of course, a legitimate art form[1] and I do not wish to cast aspersions on it, it must be understood that in the view of the wrestling ideologue, film has no redeeming features; it is, as most put it, disgusting in a vulgar way.

What place does all of this have, one might ask, in the City of Light? From the wrestler's perspective at least—and my feeling is, from that of other Banarsis as well—the debauchery of modern life is central to what wrestling is all about. In talking with people in Banaras I was given the distinct impression that, far from being immune to filmy fashion, Banaras has become the frontline of an ideological battle-ground. This is not simply to say that Banaras has more than its share of cinema halls, tea shops, street-side vendors, motorcycles, liquor stores, and pan shops. It is that for Banarsis all of these institutions (including the pan shop, which has a legitimate place in the high culture of Banarsi leisure) have come to represent a foreign reality which is nevertheless a permanent, troubling, and ambiguous feature of everyday life.

On a mundane level—and it should be clear that the affliction of modernity which is regarded as most egregious by wrestlers is mundane in a common, tactile, and everyday sense—what this means is that, for many who live in Banaras and feel an affinity for the city's culture, there is an ever widening and troublesome gap between what is idealized and what is real, what is imagined and what is experienced. This is not just the usual feeling of urban anomie and depersonalization that can afflict city dwellers in any part of the world; the Banaras experience is more subtle. It has to do with the perceived erosion of an envisioned community: with children who no longer take education seriously, temple priests who put self-interest above devotion and beatitude, milk that is adulterated with water and sugar with sand. Wrestlers believe that most people are corrupt and dishonest, that liquor stores share common walls with temples, that temple custodians build latrines on their temple roofs, that police constables, railway clerks, postal inspectors, lawyers, and civil servants take bribes, and that young men on fast motorcycles no longer take the time to show the proper reverence to the gods in local shrines.

Amidst all of this, life goes on, but more out of habit than inspiration. Banaras still has its character—its structured leisure, and its atmosphere of auspicious grace and devotion—but for many these popular and meaningful traditions have become jaded and, indeed, fetished almost to the point of parody.

I was crossing the Ganga with some wrestlers and other friends in a boat borrowed from an acquaintance. Halfway across we encountered a not uncommon sight, a bloated baby floating in the current. The floating baby knocked against one of our oars and caught our attention. One of our party, the thirty-two-year-old son of a senior wrestler, leaned over on the opposite side of the boat, took a palm full of water, and drank. He then made the point, more as a proclamation than as a casual statement, that dead baby or not, the sacred water of the Holy River was always pure and clean. Others in the boat spat over the side in disgust, while a few nodded in somewhat ambivalent and uncertain agreement. The point of this vignette is not to argue that the water is either pure or impure. The point is that, as with other primary dimensions of life in Banaras, it has become necessary to overstate the meaning of certain primary icons of culture that have in the minds of some become somewhat dubious but which are still regarded by others as irrefutable facts of life.

In fact, this is what has happened to wrestling in Banaras. It has taken on the tone of overstatement: not of self-parody in a pejorative sense, but of a fetished form of meaningful cynicism as regards the nature of tradition and identity in the face of dramatic change. Wrestlers in general are moralists and advocates for national reform, and in Banaras they are particularly adamant. They see themselves, quite literally, as crusaders who look toward a utopian future, as contemporary critics of a degenerate world, a world at radical odds with that of the idealized Banaras. The wrestler's criticism of the world follows from his ability to be dramatically self-conscious about himself and the meaning of the endeavor which he advocates. As I have written elsewhere (Alter, 1989), the wrestler is always on stage and therefore always making a statement about his cultural environment. The moral physique of the Banarsi wrestler takes on the character of an icon juxtaposed to the degenerate world of filmy fashion. The absolutely disciplined regimen of training and self-control creates a sense of self which is the antithesis of that which is expressed through the disco mentality. It is the shadow figure of the degenerate everyman, like the questionably pure water of the river Ganga, which prompts the wrestler along the utopian path of moral and physical reform.

And if it is a critique of hedonism which inspires the wrestler to develop a moral physique, it is a vision of power, self-control, and devotion which draws the wrestler up to greater heights. This vision is manifest in the character of Hanuman, the epic hero of the *Ramayana* and patron deity of all akharas. Hanuman is the antithesis of "filmy fashion" and in this regard he provides the moral coordinates around which a theme of ethical, somatic nationalism is spun.

Hanuman as Icon

If an ideology of health and fitness pervades every aspect of a wrestler's life, Hanuman adds a dimension of moral purpose and gives this ideology an iconographic form. Largely because of his epic role in the *Ramayana* drama, Hanuman is a popular deity among northern Indian Hindus. When verses from the epic texts are sung, the most common and popular recount Hanuman's pugilistic and martial exploits: his leap across the ocean to Lanka and subsequent destruction of the demon king Ravana's fortress capital; the grandeur of his body as revealed to Ram's captive queen Sita; and his countless wrestling bouts with the giants of Ravana's demon army.

But Hanuman is not simply a martial hero of superhuman proportions. In Banaras he is a ubiquitous figure in the drama of everyday life. He is found in niche shrines on street corners, at the base among the roots of old, sacred trees, near ponds and tanks, above gateways and astride columns. He is painted on walls, etched on medallions, and tattooed on arms. Hymns in his praise can be heard broadcast from loudspeakers. In his most common guise he appears hewn in rock or sculpted from cement or wood. Form is not, strictly speaking, of any great importance in defining his character, but he is commonly regarded as having a simian body of divine proportions and human motility. In niche shrines he is often "cleaned" with a bright coat of vermillion color and often appears carrying a mace in one hand and a mountain in the other. In popular calendar art his form varies almost to the degree described by the poet saint Tulsidas: in one instance a chubby cherublike baby, and in others towering over the cowering ranks of Ravana's rank and file, body radiant, muscles thick and well textured, and eyes ablaze. He also appears as a contemplative suppliant prone at the feet of Ram and Sita, enraptured in devotion.

Hanuman is worshiped in a number of different ways under various different circumstances which I shall not go into here. I will restrict my remarks to a consideration of what he represents and how these representations are significant to the Banarsi wrestler's ideology of reform.

Those with whom I spoke, wrestler and nonwrestler alike, pointed out that Hanuman embodies three basic traits: *shakti* (divine energy), *bhakti* (devotion), and *brahmacharya* (celibacy). Two features stand out as the most important aspects of his character: his phenomenal strength and his absolute devotion to Lord Ram. Although brahmacharya is not often mentioned with regard to Hanuman's epic role, it too is an integral aspect of his character: a requisite condition for both his strength and devotion.

Shakti

Although shakti can denote a purely metaphysical notion of divine creative energy, it is also used to refer to a kind of manifest human strength which is both out of the ordinary and somewhat supernatural (Wadley, 1975). Shakti is distinct from *bal* (brute force or raw power) insofar as it transcends the merely physical nature of active, human strength. For his part, Hanuman evokes a notion of concrete, manifest shakti. This is not to say that Hanuman's shakti is different in kind from metaphysical divine energy; it is simply more tangible on a number of different levels. For instance, because he is as fast as the wind and as tall as a mountain with thighs the size of tree trunks and a body as radiant as the summer sun, Hanuman gives recognizable form to what is otherwise incomprehensible. Hanuman's shakti falls on a liminal plane between the supernatural and the simply human. His feats are superhuman in a natural kind of way. What this means is that Hanuman functions as a mediating symbol, or icon, through which human actions can be regarded in terms of divine shakti. For the wrestler this is a crucial point of translation.

Wrestlers use the term *shakti* to refer to their strength. They do this because for them strength is never something which is simply physical. As pointed out, reverence and prayer are integral to the exercise regimen; and propitiation of Hanuman is regarded as emanating from the confluence of basic physical strength, devotion, and self-control. *Shakti* refers at once and unambiguously to the size of a wrestler's neck and thighs, the gleam in his eye, his appetite, and the radiance of his oiled body, and also to his devout, passive, and self-controlled disposition. In this regard shakti is not so much a latent capacity as it is a facet of personal character. When one wrestler refers to another as being *shakti shali* (energized or invigorated), he is referring to the embodied form of a larger corpus of factors that correlate strength with identity. The shakti of the Hanumanlike wrestler is the antithesis of the weak moral fiber of the thin everyman.

Bhakti

As manifest in both the wrestler's body and Hanuman's physique, shakti is a direct result of both devotion and self-control. As devotion, bhakti is an experience of mystical bliss and complete absorption into God, an experience of total release and dependence on divine grace. Although there are many who are regarded as devout disciples, it is generally recognized that Hanuman personifies a pervasive attitude of pure devotion and perfect love for Lord Ram.[2] It is only by "thinking of Ram" that he is able to perform feats of great strength and courage. Popular art often depicts Hanuman either humbly touching the feet of Ram and Sita or else blissfully contemplating their form while singing hymns of praise.

For the wrestler the lesson of Hanuman's bhakti is very clear. Just as Hanuman is powerless and practically devoid of any sense of self-worth without the shakti he derives from his love for Ram, so is the wrestler powerless without a similar commitment of devotion to Hanuman. Hanuman's relationship with Ram provides a model for the wrestler's attitude of adoration toward Hanuman.

But the wrestler is called upon to be more than an occasional devotee. There are some wrestlers who make Hanuman worship the express focus of their lives: by singing hymns, performing puja, and fasting on prescribed days. For the vast majority of wrestlers, however, bhakti is adopted as an integral but unself-conscious way of life. This may be explained as taking on a devotional attitude toward the routine

of life: a mundane devotional personality. The wrestler tries to live his
life as though every thought is of Hanuman and every breath a devotional prayer. He must think on Hanuman as he performs thousands
of dandas and bethaks and as he engages in jor. He must also think
on Hanuman as he bathes, eats, and relaxes. The wrestler's devotion
and discipline are sharply contrasted to the degenerate everyman's
sensual addictions.

Brahmacharya

From the wrestler's perspective, Hanuman's most important
character trait is his brahmacharya, his complete celibacy and self-
control. The extent of Hanuman's self-control is not explicated or
elaborated upon in any great detail, either in the epic literature or in
more popular folklore. It is simply taken for granted. Significantly,
Hanuman's shakti is de facto evidence of his extreme brahmacharya;
that is, his radiant strength is a reflection of his embodied self-control.

Brahmacharya may be regarded as a key feature of the wrestler's
identity as it relates to the ideology of health and fitness. There is a
direct relationship between a wrestler's shakti and his ability to exercise
self-control over base and carnal human instincts. In Indian thought,
semen is regarded as a vital fluid which contains the essence of
masculine strength.[3] In order to have shakti it is essential that one not
lose semen. For the wrestler, sex is anathema and self-control both a
moral and physical imperative. As a general principle of moral self-
control, brahmacharya extends beyond the bounds of sexual abstinence
to include and define other arenas of both obligatory and prohibited
behavior. A *brahmachari* must renounce the material world and lead a
simple life. He must adopt an attitude of humility and service, discipline
and contemplation. He must commit his life to the pursuit of greater
knowledge and direct this knowledge, as a civic responsibility, to the
common good. In all of this, however, celibacy serves as the dominant
metaphor for personal self-control redirected to the end of moral reform.
The popular, technicolor images of Hanuman which appear in calendar
art mimic, in a sense, the immoral iridescence of lusty, busty, and
bombastic film heros and heroines who are also portrayed in this genre.
As Hanuman's glowing aura is a reflection of internalized sexuality
directed toward higher goals, so the radiance of the film posters conveys
a sense of unchecked, overt sensuality.

The Embodiment of Hanuman's Three Virtues

Shakti, bhakti and brahmacharya are abstract principles with
broad religious significance and multiplex symbolic meaning. Through

wrestling and the strict regimen of health, the wrestler comes to embody these virtues which Hanuman represents. Two examples will make this clear.

As pointed out, ghee is an important ingredient in the wrestlers' diet. Many authors have shown that ghee is the symbolic equivalent of semen, and both represent shakti. Wrestlers point out that semen is to the human body as ghee is to the oil lamps of devotional worship: both are substances which fuel the fire of a vital life force. In a fairly explicit way, eating ghee evokes the moral imperative of brahmacharya. It symbolizes the internalization of shakti.

The highly repetitive danda-bethak exercises which constitute the core of a wrestler's regimen are often compared to the rote recitation of devotional prayers. Exercises are done and jor is performed in front of, or facing, the image of Hanuman. Thus, exercise specifically, and wrestling in general, become an embodied form of devotional worship. The strong body is not simply a metaphor of devotion: it is a form of devotion made manifest. To exercise in a haphazard and irreverent manner is a waste of energy: to exercise with spiritual conviction builds both strength and moral character.

The Body, Hanuman, and Ethical Nationalism

Since wrestling is a highly structured and disciplined way of life, and the wrestler embodies moral and ethical virtues as an essential component of physical health and strength, it is not surprising that the wrestler's body represents a kind of utopian ideal. As modeled on a vision of Hanuman's grandeur, the "body of one color"—tremendously strong, radiant, self-controlled, and eminently powerful—is taken to represent a form of nationalized health consciousness.

Hanuman's particular and dramatic heroism is sharply contrasted to the commonplace hedonism of the modern everyman. Banaras seems to lend itself to this kind of radical juxtaposition, one that helps to make sarcasm a condition of truth, as Barthes (1972:12) has written in a different but not dissimilar context. Sarcasm implies criticism, which, for the wrestler, is expressed as a kind of critical awareness that modernity is in fact a myth—again, in Barthes's sense of the term. Hanuman's character provides for a sarcastic deconstruction of the modern world, and in the space provided stands a new ideal figure embodied in the person of the wrestler.

Although I have spoken of the discipline which gives this moral physique a recognizable form, it is also important to note that an elaborate rhetoric serves to explicate the meaning of morality by extending the significance of wrestling beyond the akhara. This rhetoric is overtly nationalistic, not in a militant or communal sense (a sense which is reaching alarming proportions in many parts of India), but in a utopian, moralistic sense. To conclude, I will discuss the nature of the wrestlers' appeal for an ethical nationalism.

If the medium for moral reform is the physique of the wrestling everyman, one medium for expressing the ideology of this reform is poetry, expository prose, and letters. A fairly extensive popular literature on wrestling can be found in many northern Indian cities. A prominent journal is *Bharatiya Kushti*, published quarterly in Indore by Ratan Patodi. This journal, as well as other pamphlets and books, contains essays which expound the virtues of a wrestling life-style and poems which exalt the discipline of exercise and self-control.

In Banaras there are a number of writer/wrestlers who have contributed to this literature. Shanti Prakash Atreya, Govardan Das Malhotra, Gupteshwar Misra, and Jatindar Kumar Pathak in particular deserve mention. The essays written by these and other authors are interesting for a number of reasons. Specifically, essays such as "The True Wrestler Is God," "A True Wrestler Is One Who Turns Others into Wrestlers," and "Wrestling and Character" make explicit the correlations between physical fitness, morality, and national reform; see Atreya (1973b) and K. P. Singh (1972a, 1972b; 1972–73). Wrestler/writers such as Atreya and K. P. Singh lament the immorality of modern times and challenge young men to take control of their lives by joining an akhara. Their poetic rhetoric makes explicit the sarcastic critique of the disco mentality: "Who does not know how poor is the health of our citizens? Our youth appear as apparitions with sunken cheeks, hollow eyes and dried up scaly skin. Yes, the very same youth on whose shoulders is placed the burden of protecting the nation, religion and society. . . Are these youth, with their skeletons of dried, brittle bones, up to the task?" (Sharma, n.d.:4). The author continues his harangue by stating that modern youth are not up to the task because they have not followed the path of brahmacharya. He then calls for action.

Brothers! If we are to revive our true and natural condition, if we are to shatter our naivete, if we are to champion the people's concern for ethical reform and establish programs for morality in everyday life, if we are to reestablish the primacy of the race through the revival of religious and moral values, and if more than anything else we are to protect our national freedom, then the most important task which is before us is to banish once and for all every vestige of carnal sensuality that we secret within us. (Sharma, n.d.:4)

Once carnal sensuality has been banished, the image of the perfect citizen comes more sharply into focus. Paraphrasing the *Gita*, Atreya makes the following remarks:

> Free from egoism, desire, anger, vanity and attachment, everything is under his control—the body, mind and speech. All his selfish interests get merged with the social interest. He is engaged in bringing about social welfare without any selfishness. He is really a model of ideal and pure behavior. He is not governed by anyone, but his very nature is ethical. Right actions are performed by him naturally. (Atreya, 1973a:41–42)

As it is envisioned, Banaras is a city of right action, a sacred and special place which is structured according to a well-defined cosmology. For many Hindus it is the center of the world. And because it is so special, it is also in many ways most vulnerable. Cinemas have replaced bahri alang as the leisure of choice, or at least that is what is feared (Kumar, 1986). Consequently, wrestlers feel it necessary to reconstitute the moral fiber of the Banaras citizen in an effort to recenter the city in a modern, changing world. To mix myths, this is a Herculean task. One visionary advocate put it like this: "Practice self-denial. Go to the villages. Be an ascetic for your work. Spread the word and do it with missionary zeal. If a wrestler only gives a fraction of himself and goes to the villages, thousands of young people will crowd around him and dig an *akhara*. The roots will then run deep and it will not take long to build up a tower [of moral and physical strength]" (K. P. Singh, 1972a: 47).

The wrestler's physique is the essence of his character and so it is the aim of those who envision a new moral order to turn wayward men and boys into upright wrestlers. In the editorial of a Banaras-based wrestling journal, one author made the following appeal: "Now is the time, the demand of the hour, the appeal of history and the nation's urgent call: Go to the *akharas!* We must denounce the path of delusion and insincerity and turn instead along the path of health and strength. There we will find *shakti* and our competence will grow. There we will realize our full potential" (H. B. Singh, n.d.:3–4). In a real sense, the wrestler translates Hanuman's divine character into a practical form of ethical nationalism. Hanuman's moral character is given human, embodied form in the person of the wrestler as a nationalistic culture hero.

Notes

1. Dissanayake (1988), Kakar (1980), Rangoonwalla (1975), Barnouw and Krisnaswamy (1963), Haggard (1988).

2. Aryan (n.d.), Bulcke (1960), Shastri (1986), Gotham (1980), Dixit (1978), Wolcott (1978).

3. Carstairs (1957), Kakar (1982), Obeyesekere (1976, 1981), O'Flaherty (1973).

5

Religious Division and the Mythology of the Past

Mary Searle-Chatterjee

Recent accounts of mythological and cognitive systems in Banaras, a city sacred to Hindus and central to the cultural world of Hinduism, focus on themes central to the elucidation of that world, for example, on Shiva and Bhairava, death and sacrifice (Parry, 1981; Chalier-Visuvalingam, 1989). These sources commonly stress Hindu priestly perceptions even when they include reference to the actions and perceptions of a diverse group of devotees. Accounts derived primarily from studies of texts are even more Brahminical in focus (for example, Eck, 1982). But another cluster of myths that is also central to an understanding of the city today varies in different religious groups and economic classes. Its social significance is completely overlooked if it is seen from the point of view of only one group.

In this chapter I discuss two sets of symbolic narrative. I include in the sets local oral tradition and folk legend, books of local history, and the standard school history textbooks used in the state of Uttar Pradesh. These all show striking structural similarities in their presentation of key symbolic Hindu-Muslim encounters involving the destruction of the temples and images of Shiva, also known as Vishvanath and Somnath. I use the term *myth* in the manner conventional among anthropologists and philosophers, as an account of events charged with dramatic and symbolic meaning. In this sense, an account of events that did in fact occur may be regarded as mythical if the ordering of events and the form of the framing context create symbolic meaning. Much historical consciousness partakes to some degree of the nature of myth: "history should admit that it never completely escapes from the nature of myth" (Levi-Strauss, 1966:91). This is particularly true at the local level. It is clear, too, that in much academic writing, by both British and South Asian historians as well as by others, mythical elements are present in the type of context that is provided and in the selection of facts that are emphasized (see White, 1973, for examples from the historiography of Europe). It is not always easy to make a neat distinction between myth and history. Some of the local "mythical" traditions in question refer to real historical persons, and some refer to events that may have happened and about which historians debate.

The two sets of myth both refer to powerful Muslim leaders and relate to the issue of the legitimacy of certain types of power. The names of the folk hero Ghazi Miyan and of the later Moghul, Aurangzeb, are widely known in the city by both Muslims and Hindus. Muslims are far more numerous than popular images of Banaras would have us believe: they constitute 26 percent of the city's population, which means that Muslims are about as numerous in Banaras as *brahmins* (members of priestly caste) (Engineer, 1984:55). Unlike Banarsi Brahmins, however, Banarsi Muslims have been greatly neglected in studies of the city.

My account is based on six months of research in 1986, though some of my comments are based on my more general experience in the nine years in which I lived in the city from 1963 to 1965 and from 1970 to 1977.[1] The alternative, usually "Muslim" versions of the narratives which I discuss are mostly derived from conversations with groups of people, often Weavers by caste, at ten tomb shrines, mosques, and *imambaras* (other Islamic religious sites). Such accounts also emerged in private interviews with twenty to thirty informants, mainly men, of a range of social backgrounds. On some occasions the issue of particular narratives was not raised because it seemed too sensitive or inappropriate. A similar number and range of interviews were held with Hindu informants. Additional group interviews were held with exuntouchable Sweepers, including Muslim ones, in two localities. It is significant that Sweepers showed very little interest in this particular set of divisive symbolic narratives.

Symbolic Narratives on Ghazi Miyan and Mahmud Ghaznavi

This set consists of oral legends about the Muslim saint and folk hero Ghazi Miyan, one of the powerful dead of north India, and of the historical figure of Mahmud Ghaznavi. These are commonly referred to in Banaras and are very similar to versions found in school textbooks. They show striking structural parallels in the form of inversion to some variants of the legend of Ghazi. The Ghaznavi accounts refer to a national context, and the Ghazi variants to a local one. Although it might be considered surprising to conflate these, I do so because I believe that in popular Muslim consciousness these narratives are part of one symbolic set and may indeed have been historically linked.

Version A (standard in the larger Hindu-dominated society, relating to the historical figure Mahmud Ghaznavi)

This narrative may be mentioned spontaneously by the literate classes when they discuss historical dimensions of "ethnic" or communal issues, and is found in the standard Hindi secondary school history books used by the overwhelming majority of schools in Uttar Pradesh. "Mahmud Ghaznavi was an Afghan" (one of the most famous rulers of the medieval Muslim world) and "the first Muslim invader of India, who descended on the country in the eleventh century, plundering and destroying. He looted vast quantities of treasures, seeking out particularly the fabulously wealthy Somnath temple in Gujerat. This was due to religious fanaticism as well as to greed."

No mention is made in these versions of Ghaznavi having reached Banaras, though the city is said by historians to have been looted later by Muhammad Ghori and Ahmad Niyaltigin, the governor of Punjab appointed by Masud, son of Mahmud (Haig, 1958). Academic historians disagree about the likely causes of Ghaznavi's actions and about the type and amount of contextual information that needs to be provided to present an adequate account.

Version B (alternative form found among the Muslim masses, relating to the folk hero Ghazi Miyan)

These descriptions of Ghazi's life were first related to me by groups of Muslims at six tomb shrines in the city. Answers to my questions about the saint revered at any particular tomb often expanded into accounts of the much greater importance of Ghazi and his tomb. Such narratives invariably showed something of the following form. "Ghazi Miyan was the nephew of Mahmud Ghaznavi. He was the first Muslim Banarsi. In the eleventh century he fought and defeated Banar, the last Hindu king of the city for hundreds of years. Ghazi was a warrior [a couple of informants in individual interviews described him as a *pir*, or "saint," as well] who performed many miracles" (see version C).

On one occasion he came to the help of a Hindu woman whom he found weeping hysterically. She told him that every day in Banaras one person was sacrificed by lot at the temple of Somnath where sorcery was used. The lot had fallen on her only son. It was his wedding day. Ghazi at once offered to stand in as a substitute. He took a bath in the Ganges to purify himself. Then he put one foot inside the temple. As he did so, the floor fell in beneath the image and only the head remained visible with its tuft of hair. Ghazi grabbed the tuft and kicked the head. The image disappeared below the ground. Ghazi threw the tuft as far as he could. Wherever it fell there grew a type of grass used for making stools [patlo].

Another common variant runs as follows:

One thousand years ago there was a Raja Banar at Rajghat, the oldest site of the city. His astrologer had told him that he should sacrifice someone every day. Victims were selected by lot and sacrificed in the Somnath temple in the fort. One day the lot fell upon the son of an old woman. Ghazi heard of her plight and came to her rescue. He instructed her to pretend to the Raja's police that he was her son. Consequently, the next day he was taken away to the fort where he began to argue with the astrologer. In his anger he broke some of the images. The king asked the astrologer what he should do. The astrologer said, "It is not possible to fight this man with the sword. He is a man of spiritual powers [wali]. We must break his purity [wazoo]." Accordingly, hundreds of naked women were brought in. Ghazi then took off his own head and put it under his arm so that he could not see the women. Then he angrily overturned the fort with his hand. Everything sank under the ground. Ghazi was never able to marry because he was always fighting evil.

In brief, then, Ghazi, a Muslim founder of the city, demolished the image or temple of Somnath, another form of Shiva (Haig, 1958), the deity with whom Banaras is very closely associated. He did this because of his opposition to human sacrifice and because a Hindu woman had requested his intervention.

This account of Ghazi was presented in contexts where few, if any, Hindus were present. Some Hindus may well believe in this version too; on no occasion did I hear it contested. I have no evidence as to the age of this variant and do not know whether it represents an early local form, part of which has become forgotten by Hindus, or whether it is a later reworking of a Hinduized legend, reacting against widespread claims of Muslim iconoclasm. In this version, the Muslim is exemplary in opposing evil Hindus. The legend is defensive of Muslim self-respect and justificatory of past power. This legend is not referred to in the Urdu books on Banaras written by Muslims, *Murukhai*

Banaras, by Chaudhuri Nabi Ahmed Sandelvi (1939), or *Tarikh Asar-i Banaras* by Abdus Salaam Nomani (1963). Nomani, who is head of the central Jnan Vapi Mosque (or Jama Masjid) and an active promoter of certain versions of the life of Aurangzeb to which I shall refer shortly, refuses to discuss Ghazi on the grounds that there is no reliable evidence available. Educated or wealthy Muslims are generally not interested in this corpus, which they class more as folk legend than as history.[2]

Version C (nonethnic form related by lower-level Hindus and Muslims, particularly when in the presence of Hindus)

Another shorter form of the Ghazi Miyan legend was recounted to me by Hindus visiting Muslim tomb shrines, as well as by some Muslims. This third version consists of a "nonethnic" portion of version B.

> Ghazi Miyan, otherwise known as Saiyid Salar Mashood, was the nephew of Mahmud Ghaznavi, the first Muslim invader of India in the eleventh century. Ghazi was a great and good man who helped both Hindus and Muslims in trouble. He made seven unsuccessful attempts to marry. Each time he was prevented by some untoward event. On one occasion the bride-to-be died, on another there was a violent thunderstorm, on others Ghazi had to be involved in battles. He had miraculous powers.

These powers are variously elaborated. This version has a pragmatic concern with the virtue and power of Ghazi.

The variants of the Ghazi/Ghaznavi corpus of symbolic narrative can be summarized as follows.

Version	*Proponents*
A. Wicked Muslim king attacked innocent Hindus, destroyed Somnath/Shiva temple (national reference).	Local school history books. Local conversation of literate Hindus.
B. Muslim warrior overthrew evil Hindu who was oppressing Hindus in the Somnath/Shiva temple (local reference).	Lower-level Muslims.

C. Hero happened to be   Lower-level Hindus and
Muslim, defeated opposi-   Muslims.
tion who happened to be
Hindu (local reference).

The Cult of Ghazi

Worship, prayer, and petitioning at the tomb of Ghazi Miyan at Bahraich, a town further west in Uttar Pradesh, is extremely popular among the masses, both Hindu and Muslim, though disapproved of by higher-strata coreligionists. On the annual saint's day, the tomb attracts vast gatherings.

Booklets in Hindi and Urdu relating to the life of Ghazi are available for pilgrims. These make no mention of his having ever visited Banaras. The replica of Ghazi's tomb, *yadgah*, in Banaras in Jaitpura, a densely Muslim area near the old city center, draws large crowds annually for the symbolic enactment of the wedding of Ghazi. Devotees insist that the wedding was never completed in his lifetime. The wedding procession moves from the Jaitpura crossing to the tomb, accompanied by drummers and other musicians. Men dance and sing *qawwalis* (Muslim songs of praise). People in the procession carry gifts of cloth, flower garlands, and live chickens which are later sacrificed and eaten. Weekly worship occurs primarily on Sundays, though to a lesser degree on Thursdays as well. Hindus and Muslims perform identical actions at the tomb but use different as well as shared terms and concepts. When Hindus worship, they do *puja, darshan, swagat* (welcome), or *manate* (meditation), whereas Muslims pay their respects and remember Ghazi in prayers, do *durbar* or *phatiya* (Muslim oblation to dead ancestors). Some Muslims use the Hindi and Sanskrit terminology general among Hindus as well as Arabic and Urdu terms. I have not heard the reverse pattern, though it would not be surprising if it occurred.

Devotees wash themselves before coming to the tomb, then remove their footwear and cover their heads before entering the domed mausoleum housing the "tomb," which is covered with red and green drapes. At its head is a high pillar. Knotted colored strips of cloth, tied by devotees who have made a vow or whose boon has been granted, hang from the pillar and from the surrounding stonework. Worshipers, many of whom are women, bring offerings of flower garlands and sweets. They bring bottles of water which are left beside the tomb for a week or more to acquire "virtue." Devotees may drink some of the water or sprinkle it on themselves before carrying the bottles home.

The *mujahar* who tends the shrine gives devotees consecrated sweets, known as *prasad* by Hindus and *tabaruk* among Muslims. Some people prostrate themselves before the tomb; most extend upturned or cupped hands. Men sometimes lay their hands on the tomb for a few moments. Women remain at a slight distance.

Historical sources on the city do nothing to shed light on the Ghazi tradition. They have little to say about any ancient temple of Somnath. My informants located this in several places, usually at Rajghat (the ancient center of the city), sometimes at Sarnath, the ancient Buddhist center outside the city (where a Someshvara temple still exists), and occasionally near Jnan Vapi, the modern center. Even Sukul (1977) has nothing to say of the demolition of any Somnath temple, despite the fact that one of the major themes in his lengthy historical account of the city is the destruction of its shrines and temples by Muslims. He refers to five Someshvara temples in various eras and to the earlier existence of a Someshvara Ghat on the river near Pandey Ghat. Today there is only a small Someshvara temple above Man Mandir Ghat. It is, however, important enough to be a major stopping place on the Panchakroshi pilgrimage around the city. The temple is not very old, having been built in the early British period by a Brahmin from Mysore, Parsottamanand Giri. The owners of it know of no legend of destruction. There is a reference to "the sacking of the fabulous temples of Somnath in Gujerat, Mathura and *Banaras* [emphasis mine] by Mahmud Ghazi in the year 1001" in the Government of India ITDC Guidebook to Rajasthan of 1975. However, no historical source is quoted.

Outside the city in Sarnath is a temple of Saranganath and Somnath. According to its priest, the icon (*lingam*) of Somnath was consecrated more than a thousand years ago by the philosopher Shankaracharya to commemorate his defeat of Buddhism. The priest had not heard of any tradition of human sacrifice on the site but was in no way outraged by the question. Banaras Hindus sometimes refer to stories of human sacrifices in the past, associated particularly with the worship of Shiva and the Goddess. I can make no comment on the veracity of these claims. Newspapers even today often report sporadic incidents of human sacrifice, particularly during the autumn months.

The Ghazi legends are of interest mainly to the lower classes and do not appear to be the subject of contention. In the case of versions and images of the life of the historical figure of the Emperor Aurangzeb, it is the educated classes and more prosperous groups who are most actively involved, though his name is very widely known in the city. In this case the divergence between "Hindu" and "Muslim" versions of the past is much more confrontational. Aurangzeb ruled in Delhi in the seventeenth century and was the last of the major Moghul emperors. Perhaps because of this and because of his religious orthodoxy, he has become both for Hindus and Muslims a prime symbol of Muslim identity.

Symbolic Narratives on the Historical Figure Aurangzeb

Version A (standard in the larger Hindu-dominated society)

"Aurangzeb destroyed many temples in the city of Banaras, particularly the central shrine of Vishvanath, Lord Shiva in Jnan Vapi. He provocatively built a mosque on the ruins of the temple. This was due to religious intolerance."

Every tourist or pilgrim to the city is taken to see the dramatic ruin in question. The outsider who enters the large mosque may be accosted afterwards by a priest from the present Vishvanath temple shouting out that it was Aurangzeb, the builder of the mosque, who destroyed the great temple of Shiva. Over the centuries there have been many riots and court cases concerning the use of space around the mosque and the new Vishvanath temple (Eck, 1982). Aurangzeb is often referred to spontaneously in conversation with higher-caste Hindus. For many he is the iconoclast par excellence. He is popularly believed to have destroyed the Lat Bhairava temple as well and also the Bindhu Madhava temple at Panchaganga Ghat, where the most impressive monument on the city skyline today is not a temple but a mosque carrying the name Aurangzeb. Folk tradition has it that Aurangzeb's attempt to destroy the Kedarnath temple, a major sacred place in the south of the city, was foiled only by the supernatural strength of three men in the temple.

Aurangzeb's name appears in every guidebook to the city. Hindu and Anglo-American contributors to the Hindi and English literature on the city all reproduce the tradition of his destruction of temples. Every child who has had a secondary education in Banaras using the standard Uttar Pradesh schoolbooks has learned of Aurangzeb's violence and iconoclasm. The only Hindus who tend to be ignorant or hazy about the supposed deeds of Aurangzeb are members of the very lowest castes who constitute around 15 to 25 percent of the population. Although only one of the Muslims I interviewed expressed belief in version A, several informants said that it is held by quite a few Muslims.

Version B (alternative form held today by many Muslims in the city as well as by some Hindus)

Variants of this version were related to me at two imambaras, two mosques and four tombs, as well as in private homes, by Sunni Muslims of a wide variety of backgrounds.[3] This was in response to my questions about the origin of the central ruin in the city. The issue is a delicate and contentious one.

Variant 1. "The major ruin in the center of the city is not that of a temple. It is the remains of a building constructed by Akbar, the earlier Moghul emperor" [much admired by Hindus] as part of his attempt to establish the new religion of Din-i-Ilahi [uniting Hindus and Muslims and focused on himself]. The building collapsed or was pulled down by the order of Aurangzeb due to his hostility to Akbar's approach to religion. The new religion had required its adherents to repudiate Islam." My informants claimed that this oral version is very widely held.

Variant 2. "The ruin is the remains of a Hindu temple that was destroyed either by a Hindu, Jnan Chand, or at the command of Aurangzeb, but for reasons unconnected with religion. The cause was the looting, rape or murder by priests of a Hindu woman or women worshipping in the temple, either the 'fictive' sister of Aurangzeb or the daughter or wife of one of his officials or commanders." Many of my informants claimed that the Jnan Chand version is believed by many Muslims. It is also held by some elderly Hindus. "Jnan Chand from Jaunpur sacked the temple when the heavily ornamented women of his family failed to return from worship. Their bodies were found in the underground passages of the temple." In another variant, the temple was destroyed because it was being used as a center of rebellion against the Moghul government.

Supplementary arguments such as the following were often used. "Aurangzeb always built mosques away from temples or temple sites. Since he is the one who built the Jnan Vapi Mosque, it must be the case that there could not have been even a ruined temple adjacent to it." Others, however, claimed that the Jnan Vapi Mosque was built much earlier. Another argument was that "there must have been communal conflict in the course of which the temple was destroyed. Muslims are not unreasonable and could not have started fighting without cause. Hindus must have refused space to Muslims for building a mosque on the desired central site."

All of the B versions are supported by arguments to the effect that it is unlikely that Aurangzeb destroyed a temple for religious reasons since many documents and inscriptions survive showing that he made donations to various temples and monasteries in Banaras. In the Banaras Hindu University Museum is his edict (*firman*) instructing that, although no new temples were to be built, existing temples in Banaras were not to be damaged.

The *iman* or prayer leader of the central Jnan Vapi Mosque, Abdus Salaam Nomani, is also a bookbinder and printer. In 1985 and 1986 he published articles in many Urdu papers, both local and national, including *Awaz Mulk* (October 30, 1986), *Qami Morcha* (November 11, 1986), and *Nai Duniya* (November 4, 1986), as well as in *Blitz* (January 4, 1986). These promote the view, mainly among Muslims, that Aurangzeb did not destroy the Vishvanath temple. They refer to the edict mentioned above as well as to letters and inscriptions in Banaras relating to donations Aurangzeb made to various Hindu establishments. These establishments are said to include the Jangambari Monastery in Madanpura and a Hindu school for sadhus (*pathshala*) near the Jnan Vapi Mosque, both referred to in inscriptions; an Aparnath temple in Luxa, a nearby Kali monastery, and a Sita Ram temple, all referred to in letters. Several educated informants suggested the British may have encouraged the idea that Aurangzeb and Muslims were the destroyers of temples among Hindus. They argued that specific crucial documents were wrongly translated by British writers, either deliberately or because of their own unconscious prejudices.

Variant 3. This was a very unusual version expressed by one intellectual and one cleric. "The ruin was that of a Buddhist temple destroyed in ancient times by Hindus. Thai monks at Gaya have said that many Buddhist temples were destroyed by Hindus."

Many educated Muslim informants claim that in the last few decades schoolbooks have presented Aurangzeb in an increasingly negative light mainly because of the growing tendency to present the brilliant Maratha military leader Shivaji, one of his opponents, as a Hindu crusader rather than as simply another regional contender for power. Most of my Muslim informants saw Aurangzeb as a model of simple living and straightforward incorruptibility. The only exceptions were a handful of Sweepers and persons of elite background who criticized him for his puritan approach and opposition to alcohol.

This set of symbolic narratives on Aurangzeb can be summarized as follows.

Version	*Proponents*
A. Evil Muslim king destroyed central Hindu Vishvanath/Shiva temple and built a mosque on it.	Wide variety of Hindus, especially of middle and upper classes, school textbooks, Hindi and English histories and guides of the city.
B. 1. The central ruin is not of a Hindu temple but is the result of action by a Muslim king acting against Muslim heresy.	Widely held by Muslims.
2. The ruin is of the temple, which was destroyed, perhaps by a Hindu, because it was being used for evil purposes.	Many Muslims and a few Hindus.
3. The ruin is of a Buddhist temple destroyed by Hindus.	Several intellectuals.

Discussion

It is not my purpose to discuss the historical validity of these competing narratives. From the point of view of this paper the historical issues are irrelevant, since it is clear that whatever the facts were, accounts of the origin of the central ruin are now functioning as symbolic narrative, providing a "charter" for contemporary attitudes and behavior. In many contexts and environments, the events of the seventeenth century and earlier would be considered quite irrelevant today. I should add, however, that academic historians themselves debate the actions and particularly the motives of Aurangzeb. They disagree about the significance and meaning of the facts (see Chandra, 1972, 1987, 1988; Ali, 1966). In the seventeenth century, looting and destruction of temples and villages by marauding armies was widespread, including those of the Sikhs and Marathas, as was destruction of major monuments symbolic of the power of others. One notable historian at Banaras Hindu University contests the view that Aurangzeb destroyed the Vishvanath temple (Bhatnagar, 1975). The priests of the temple refused to discuss the issues with him. Bhatnagar points out that in

parts of the medieval era there was not even a Vishvanath temple at
all in Banaras, contrary to popular belief. It is interesting that a Sanskrit
account of a visit to the temples of Banaras during the reign of
Aurangzeb mentions only an Adivishveshvara temple near Bindhu
Madhava near Panchaganga Ghat. The modern editor expresses his
surprise that no reference is made to the Vishvanath temple and
supposes that the Adivishveshvara temple must have been the
Vishvanath temple (Varadaraja, 1960).

In the last decade there have been considerable changes in Hindu-
Muslim relations because of new economic competition from a rising
class of middle-level Muslim merchants both at local (Khan and Mittal,
1984) and national levels (Engineer, 1984). Cash flows from the Middle
East—remittances sent home by migrant workers as well as occasional
donations to educational institutions by governments of oil-rich Arab
countries—have also contributed to the rising prosperity among Indian
Muslims. This development occurs in the context of increasing political
competition at the national level. Congress party dominance has been
shaken by the emergence of the "bullock capitalists" in rural areas. The
use of religion as a tool in struggles for power has increased (Rudolph
and Rudolph, 1987). At the local level, right-wing parties and sometimes
Congress I benefit from Hindu fear and resentment of Muslims (see
Juyal, 1970, for an earlier discussion of this problem). Other parties,
including sometimes Congress I, may benefit from a bloc of fearful
Muslims. Some Muslim leaders find possibilities of power and personal
benefit in the existence of a self-consciously Muslim constituency.

The 1986 February legal decision on the contested Baburi Mosque
site in Ayodhya in favor of Hindus has had numerous repercussions
in Banaras that cannot be discussed here in detail (rioting, curfew, Urdu
posters urging Muslims to march on the site and do *jihad* [holy war,
literally "exertion"], and speeches from leaders of the fundamentalist
Bharatiya Janata party urging Hindus to reinstate the icon of Vishvanath
in the Jnan Vapi Mosque now that "the time is ripe"). The case for
permitting Hindu worship inside the mosque had been on file in the
High Court since the nineteenth century. It was revived in the 1950s
and restricted rights were conceded. In 1986 a case for full access was
suddenly put before a lower court and a decision was made in favor
of removing all restrictions with unprecedented speed, in fact, within
several hours (Noorani, 1989). Since then the Vishva Hindu Parishad's
campaign to mobilize Hindus to bring bricks from all over India for the
construction of a large temple on the site has proceeded apace, and
was instrumental in contributing to V. P. Singh's fall from the prime
ministership in late 1990 when he moved to inhibit their efforts, and
to the rise of the Bharatiya Janata party in the 1990s.

The growth in Hindu-Muslim tensions is rooted in economic and social competition. It expresses itself in increasing emphasis on discordant myths of the past and in asserting prior rights to the use of contested sacred space. In recent years, Urdu, Hindi, and English presses in India have commonly carried articles and letters concerning temple demolitions and other turmoil at sacred sites.

It is significant that, in Banaras, alternative minority versions of the Aurangzeb narrative indicate much sharing of values with Hindus. The destruction of a Hindu temple is said to have occurred to avenge the dishonoring of a woman, particularly a Hindu woman. Such a theme is familiar to Hindus and is indeed a major preoccupation. Women often recount tales of other women who are said to have disappeared into the underground passages of the Vishvanath temple. It is implied that the women were raped, perhaps as part of tantric rituals. Such stories are part of the popular consciousness and were so even in the early 1960s and doubtless long before that. In the 1970s a popular film, *Sangharsh*, touched on this theme. It was set in Bananas and portrayed a struggle within the family of priests who managed a temple. Women and their male relatives were shown being robbed and murdered for their sumptuous jewelry and other possessions.

Minority versions of the Ghazi legend referring to destruction of the Somnath temple, though not generally known to Hindus, similarly refer to aspects of distortions of the Hindu tradition, about which the majority of Hindus are negative or at least ambivalent. They appeal to values shared by Hindus, that is, purity and male honor as expressed in upholding female "virtue": Ghazi bathes in the Ganges, his purity makes him invincible, and he removes his head rather than gaze on naked women. Both sets of myth stress male honor, *izzat*, a value much neglected in studies of Indian society, and the legitimacy of valiant forcefulness in protecting females. This is a theme often referred to by men in Banaras. Ghazi was both fearless and pure. He remained celibate in his lifetime even though he was active in the defense of *Hindu* women. It was only after his death that he was married to a *Muslim* woman, Jeelan Bibi. His chaste life and endogamous marriage showed him to be the reverse of a raping and looting invader.

The alternative narratives can be seen as subverting the perceived social inequality of being a minority group by insisting that Muslims are decent and nonviolent, acting with force only when confronted with horror. The "Muslim" accounts make their appeal, significantly, by accepting the "Hindu" premise that the descendants of iconoclastic destroyers of images and temples are not worthy of full respect and trust. They simply insist that Muslims were not iconoclasts. Those who debate these images of the past thus share a language of value in the present. Culturally, the similarities between the two groups are great (Kumar, 1988). However, perceptions of the past may provide a basis for religious division or mobilization even when cultural differences are few, as Epstein (1974) showed in his examination of the bases of Jewish ethnicity in the United States. The question of how far these images shape perceptions of social and political realities, and hence actions in the present, and how far they are simply manipulated to support present interests, is beyond the scope of this chapter.

Notes

1. I am grateful to Manchester Polytechnic for financial support for one term of research in Banaras in 1986.

2. I base this statement on interviews with twenty individuals who were clerics, professionals, teachers, and Merchant Weavers.

3. Private interviews discussing this issue were held in twenty-five homes or workplaces. In five of these, a large group contributed to the discussion. Informants were professionals, teachers, clerics, weavers of various levels, and servants. Lengthy group interviews with Muslim Sweepers held in two localities are not included in this discussion since these groups showed hardly any interest in Aurangzeb despite an awareness of various historical and mythological figures.

6

The Monastic Structure of Banarsi Dandi Sadhus

Dana W. Sawyer

The Shaiva ascetics known as Dandi *sannyasins*, for their characteristic carrying of the *danda* (staff), are an important component of the current religious montage in Banaras (see Illus. 6.1 and 6.2). First, they are an important presence on the basis of numbers alone. Though statistics are very difficult to trust for reasons that will soon be made clear, Sinha and Saraswati (1978:68) claim that in 1978 Dandis accounted for almost one-fifth of all the city's many ascetics. Second, the Dandis, like their founder Shankara, the ninth-century C.E. philosopher, are famous as advocates and defenders of the *shastric* tradition, or the conservative Hindu textual tradition which includes strict caste divisions. Even among Hindus of other sects, Dandis are referred to as *rudhivadi* (orthodox). Because of this reputation, they enjoy wide prestige among conservative Hindus, influencing their attitudes and behavior. The four Shankaracharyas ("teachers of Shankara's philosophy") are always Dandis, and as representatives of orthodoxy, are often asked to speak at pan-Hindu religious festivals to increase the general auspiciousness of these events.

Banaras is the most important center of Dandi monasticism in all of India. One-quarter to one-half of all India's Dandis can be found in Varanasi at any given moment. Estimates of India's Dandi population range from a low of five hundred[1] to a high of one thousand (Cenkner, 1978:114). The number of Dandis in Banaras has been estimated at between two and three hundred.[2] Putting these figures together in any combination, one realizes that a very significant percentage of the Dandi population is in Banaras. In the present essay, based upon field research conducted in the summer and fall of 1988, I will discuss Dandiism in Banaras primarily in terms of its monastic structure. I will show how Dandi monastic complexes originate and develop around charismatic gurus rising within their brotherhood. The guru is the pivot and

6.1

Swami Shri Ram Ashrama at Pushkara Math with *danda* (staff) covered to protect it from pollution.

6.2

Swami Shivananda Saraswati at Dharma Sangh,
the largest Karpati *math* (monastery) in Banaras.

foundation of the entire monastic structure, *maths* (monasteries) forming and dissolving as gurus come and go. The effect of guruism (having the living guru at the top of the monastic hierarchy) is a very volatile, ephemeral, and plastic monastic structure.

As a way of orienting ourselves, let us begin our investigation with a short general introduction to Dandi practice itself, including their relationship to other orders of Hindu ascetics.

Dandis, Paramahansas, and Nagas form the three main branches of the Shaiva *sampradaya* (sect) of ascetics, that is, ascetics traditionally associated with Shiva. Shaiva ascetics are commonly designated as sannyasins in contrast to *bairagis*, ascetics of the Vaishnava sampradaya. Sannyasins belong to one or the other of the Dasnami ("ten names") orders of monks: Giri, Puri, Bharati, Vana, Aranya, Parvata, Sagara, Tirtha, Ashrama, and Saraswati. Though tradition maintains that Dandis may come from any of the orders, in actuality all Dandis are Saraswatis, Ashramas, Tirthas, or, much less common, Bharatis; furthermore, Dandis are drawn only from the *Brahmin* (priestly) caste. In contrast, Paramahansas commonly come from any of the three *dvija* (twice-born) castes, and Nagas may even be *Shudras* (lowest class). Also, unlike Paramahansas and Nagas, Dandis usually only accept initiates who have completed the earlier *ashramas* (life stages) recommended by the *Shastras*. This is not always thought essential and there are exceptions, but young Dandis are far less commonly encountered than young Paramahansas or Nagas.

Despite some limited evidence to the contrary,[3] Dandis are always men. When a man is ready to take initiation, usually after having had a long family life, he apprentices himself to a Dandi *swami* (religious preceptor) for at least a few months. During this period he is referred to as a *brahmachari* and is trained in the ascetic life-style. When his preparation is complete, the ceremony of *sannyasa* (initiation to become an ascetic) is performed by his guru, usually waist deep together in a body of water, preferably the Ganges. At this time, his head and face are shaven and the danda, made from bamboo, is conferred as a sign of ascetic restraint. The Dandi will carry this staff without letting it touch the ground for the rest of his life, at which time he will be buried with it (ascetics are generally buried rather than cremated because they have already undergone the purification that fire is said to provide). In order to preserve the purity of their staff, some Dandis keep it covered while in public, lest a low-caste person inadvertently touch it. Dandis often leave staffs uncovered when inside Dandi maths and other places free of pollution. Traditionally, once initiated, the monk must either continue to keep all hair shaved or let it grow. Usually, the new monk will follow whichever practice his guru maintains. Interestingly, south Indian Dandis almost always shave their hair, whereas north Indian Dandis commonly keep it long.

Regarding daily practices, Dandis eat but one meal, usually collected by *bhiksha* (begging) in the morning and then eaten at midday. Water is taken as needed. Their principal *sadhana* (religious practice) besides devotional *puja* (ritual worship) is *omkar*, that is, saying the mantra *om* while counting a *rudraksha* rosary, so called because of its dried reddish-brown berries known as "Rudra's (Shiva's) eyes." Dandis often worship deities other than Shiva, and though traditionally called Shaivites, they are generally opposed to sectarian rivalries and argue that the Vedic and Vedantic foundation which they find authoritative is common to all Hindu sects (Cenkner, 1978:144). Though Dandis are liberal in many sectarian matters, they are strict in their advocacy of caste division and, since India's independence, have received much criticism for teaching that position.[4]

Having made these general comments, let us discuss the Dandis more specifically.

Ideal and Real Social Structure of Dandi Monasteries

Though the Dandi order holds a position of general prestige among the Hindus of Banaras, and though they are a major presence in the city, very little has previously been written about them. For example, there is no book and few articles in English dealing exclusively with ascetics of the Dandi order. If one wishes to learn about them, one must rely principally upon brief and general accounts of Dandis found in books on Indian *sadhus* (holy men) by such authors as Ghurye (1953), Tripathi (1978), Giri (1976), Murdoch (1904), Oman (1905), and Sinha and Saraswati (1978). These accounts are useful but they do not go very far; some are even misleading at times. For example, Sinha and Saraswati give very specific statistics when dealing with the number of Dandi maths in Banaras and the number of Dandis in each math, but they do not sufficiently explain the extremely transitory value of these figures. Any facility housing even one Dandi, whether *gupha* (cave), *kutir* (cottage), or other tenuous form of domicile, can be called a math, so the exact number of maths changes continuously. Furthermore, Dandis take a vow to wander from place to place rather than live in one monastery—they are often called *ramta*, "wandering" ascetics—and generally they do so, unless prevented by illness, age, or the traditional three-month pause during monsoon, which is not always done at the same math from year to year. Consequently, exact figures for the number of "residents" in any given math may be accurate for only a few weeks or months, or even for only a few days.

However, when discussing discrepancies between the descriptions of Dandis found in introductory texts on Indian sadhus and the realities of Banarsi Dandi practice, perhaps the largest difference deals with the structure of Dandi monasticism itself. On reading these descriptions, one is surprised to find that the actual social structure of Dandi monasteries differs markedly from the descriptions that have prevailed to date. I will begin by briefly outlining the standard description and then provide what I believe is a corrective to this view.[5]

1. Shankara, advocating his *Advaita* (nondual) philosophy, traveled about India for several years until his death in his late twenties or early thirties. During this period he established ten orders of monks, the so-called Dasnami ("ten names") orders.
2. At *diksha* (initiation), all Dasnami novices were given a danda; those who chose to retain the staff after the initiation period were called Dandis, and those that chose to abandon it were called Tyakta Dandis ("those who abandoned the danda") or, more commonly, Paramahansas ("Supreme Souls"). Members of any of the ten orders of monks could become either Dandis or Paramahansas.
3. In addition to starting these monk orders, Shankara founded many monasteries for them to visit. Principal among these were four maths: Jyotir in northern India, Shringeri in the south, Govardhana in the east, and Sharada in the west. These four were to act as centers for propagating his teachings, and so they were called *vidyapiths* (seats of knowledge). All other Dasnami maths were to affiliate themselves with one or the other of these vidyapiths according to territorially defined jurisdictions.
4. The vidyapiths were left in the hands of Shankara's four major disciples: Trotaka, Padmapada, Hastamalaka, and Vishvarupa. These disciples were to preside as abbots of the vidyapiths, leaders of the affiliate maths, and gurus of Advaita philosophy. In turn, each of these men would pass the mantle of leadership on to their respective disciples, along with the title *Shankaracharya*.
5. Shankara was a Dandi, as were his four major disciples, and therefore Dandis have a special place in Dasnami tradition. The four first Shankaracharyas were Dandis, and therefore, as direct inheritors of the tradition, all others must be also.
6. As Dandis are special among Dasnami monks, and Shankaracharyas are special among Dandis, so the Shankaracharya of Jyotir Math is considered the special Dandi leader among Shankaracharyas, as Cenkner (1978) points out.[6] The usual reason given is that Trotaka, the first Shankaracharya of the math, was thought the favorite disciple of Shankara.

Studying these points from the introductory descriptions as partial preparation for field research, I anticipated finding certain specific lines of authority when I visited the Dandi maths. For instance, (1) since Shankara wished that all Dasnami maths, including Dandi maths, affiliate themselves with a vidyapith, I expected to find that the vidyapiths would have significant power, both financial and bureaucratic, over the maths. I supposed them to be the centers of the Dandi monastic hierarchy. In addition, (2) since the tradition says that the Shankaracharyas, and especially the Shankaracharya of Jyotir Math, are to lead the Dandis, I thought I would find them to be the establishers of public and private precedents for Dandi behavior, serving as monastic heads bearing the powers of excommunication and academic authority. Generally speaking, neither of these suppositions was found to be true. The Shankaracharyas do no actual leading of Dandis, and the Dandis do no actual leading of the Dasnamis. The vidyapiths are not the centers of the Dandi monastic hierarchy, and the Dandi maths have no authority over other Dasnami maths. Few monasteries of Banaras that I visited[7] maintain a direct affiliation with a vidyapith. These include Shri Shringeri Shankar Math, Kanchi Shankaracharya Pith, Sumeru Pith, and two or three others directly under the guidance of a Shankaracharya, which were therefore satellite rather than affiliate monasteries. Furthermore, the only Dandis I interviewed who said they felt themselves subordinated to or compelled by the guidance of a Shankaracharya were those few who had a Shankaracharya as their personal guru. Ironically, given his supposed special position, the Shankaracharya of Jyotir Math was the current Shankaracharya most Dandis were least able to name correctly.[8]

At first, I was surprised by the discrepancy between what I had read and what I actually found practiced at the maths. The introductory accounts, and especially those of Ghurye (1953), Giri (1976), and Murdoch (1904), present a picture of Dandi practice in which the real and the ideal levels of behavior are not clearly delineated. Consequently, I was confusing the ideal conception of Dandi monastic structure with the real. However, I believe this problem in the introductory accounts was generally passed on to the authors by the Dandis themselves. After checking the sources of the introductory accounts, I found the accounts are largely based upon descriptions of Dandi monasticism offered by the monks. These accounts, perhaps thought by the researchers to reflect actual practice, are in turn based upon traditional descriptions of the ideal hierarchy of gurus and maths attributed to Shankara,[9] whereas, in reality, the monastic structure bears little resemblance to this traditional description. Hierarchical distinctions found in the traditional accounts are generally treated as mere nominal distinctions by Dandis today.[10] Tradition does influence the monastic structure in certain limited ways. For example, the gurus must be men and they must have been Brahmins before initiation. However, all actual monastic hierarchies are determined by what I term "guruism" and not by traditional ideas for affiliation. At the end of this essay, I will briefly discuss this potential inconsistency with tradition, but for now let us turn to a corrective of the prevailing view of the monastic structure.

Guruism's Influence on the Dandi Monastic Structure

Whenever an influential guru appears within the Dandi ranks, an ancient cycle is set in motion. As word of this guru spreads, brahmacharis are drawn to him for tutelage and possible diksha into sannyasa. Under his direction they will seek the peace they believe he has found. Others will also seek out the guru. Dandis who have already taken their ascetic vows under another guru are commonly attracted to this new personality for the sake of hearing his teachings. In most cases, this creates no conflict, since it is acceptable and even common-place to have one or more *vidya* gurus during one's life who convey wisdom or vidya in addition to the diksha guru by whom one was first initiated into the order. Religious training is seen as process, not as events that ever fully signify an end to the process. The new vidya guru is generally looked upon as a fresh spring rising from the same eternal lake of truth. New initiates and ascetic brothers alike gather around this well to drink. But it is not only monks who come before the new guru. Householders also come, and the support of these lay followers forms a crucial stage in the development of the monastic complex.

Dandis have taken vows of poverty, so they have no direct funds with which to build monasteries. Furthermore, they have renounced the practice of physical labor, devoting themselves exclusively to spiritual pursuits, so they cannot even participate in the construction of a monastery. Therefore, the involvement of householders is essential for a monastic complex to grow, and that involvement depends directly upon the inspiration of a charismatic guru. If a guru becomes popular, resources will flow from the lay community. Giving money to a sadhu is generally considered inappropriate because this compromises their vow of poverty. However, to present one's spiritual preceptor with a monastery is an acceptable and even a supreme gift. It is through such gifts that physical complexes arise, with the guru acting as the seed crystal for growth in the monastic structure nourished by both ascetics and householders.

The central importance of the guru in Dandi monasticism is not surprising, for reasons discussed below. Traditionally, whenever men or women have appeared who are believed to possess great spiritual powers, influence and prestige have gravitated in their direction. This has been true throughout the history of India from the time of the founders of Buddhism and Jainism, the Buddha and Mahavira, six centuries before the common era. It remained true many centuries later when Shankara and the other founding *acharyas* (teachers) of the Hindu sampradayas rose in prominence as gurus. It was true for the nineteenth- and twentieth-century Hindu Renaissance, including the great personages of Swami Vivekananda, Shri Aurobindo, and Dayananda Saraswati. Recent examples of gurus who have inspired large spiritual movements include Maharishi Mahesh Yogi, Sai Baba, and Swami Shivananda. Dandis themselves have many explanations for why the guru is critical, two of which include the following: the guru is the living embodiment of truth and therefore a clearer source of knowledge than books; and the guru is the embodiment of purity, so his or her *darshan* (visibility) has an uplifting and purifying influence on the disciple. Although explanations of his importance vary, that the guru is important is undeniable.

As the prestige of the guru increases, so do his resources. Wandering Dandis learn of him and in turn spread his fame. Soon many monks and lay followers alike gather around him. Facilities are built to aid the work of the guru. Usually a small monastery is built or rooms are secured for the guru in a math which has been abandoned (Illus. 6.3, 6.4). Then, if the guru becomes more influential, the small math will be expanded or replaced to accommodate the growing number of visitors. A small house is sometimes built for the guru to secure his privacy. Also, since any place where one or more Dandis live is considered a math, even if only either a small apartment or kutir (cottage), a guru can very rapidly find himself the spiritual head of several monasteries. In fact, it is often pointed out that a guru may ironically find himself in control of more physical and financial resources than he ever did before he renounced worldly life.

In Banaras today, Swami Kashi Ashrama is an example of a very successful guru, around whom has developed a powerful monastic complex. Kashi Ashrama related that he has initiated 250 men into sannyasa, and though they wander, he estimates that there are at least 50 of them in Banaras at any given time. Though his major monastery is Annapurna Bhavan, which dominates the river at Asi Ghat, there are five other maths under his direct control. Unlike the nominal affiliations which all maths claim with a vidyapith, this is a true

6.3

Five Dandi *swamis* (religious preceptors) at Ananta Vijna Math.

6.4

Four Dandis at Bhuma Adhyatma Pith. Note that three hold their *dandas* (staffs) uncovered.

monastic hierarchy, with all affairs of the subordinate maths, financial
and bureaucratic, decided by the guru or his appointees.

In addition to maths for Dandi ascetics, other buildings are usually
built as part of the monastic complex: *ashrams* or hermitages and
dharmashalas (literally "abodes of dharma") to house visiting lay pilgrims,
mandirs (temples) to various deities, *goshalas* to care for and shelter
untended cows, *pathshalas* (Sanskrit schools) for young boys, soup
kitchens and/or hospitals for the poor, and so on. Furthermore, growth
is seen not only in the number of buildings but also in their quality.
The principal monastery of a successful guru may become very large
and lavish. In fact, it usually becomes larger and more wealthy than
the monasteries of the present Shankaracharyas, the traditionally
conceived heads of Dandi monasticism. For example, Swami Bhumananda's monastery in Haridwar is much larger and more complex
than the maths of the Shankaracharyas at both Jyotir and Puri. In
Banaras, Mumukshu Bhavan and Dharma Sangh are good examples
of maths which are larger than the Shankaracharya vidyapiths with
which they are traditionally affiliated.

As a guru's monastery may grow larger than the vidyapith of a
Shankaracharya, so also his power may far outstrip that of his nominal
leader. A very good example of this phenomenon in Varanasi involves
the late Swami Hariharananda Saraswati, commonly called "Karpatri."
Until his death in 1982, Karpatri was the most influential Dandi in
Banaras, in fact, in all of India.[11] Sinha and Saraswati (1978:223) refer
to him as "the most learned, the most loved and the most controversial
Sanatani [orthodox] ascetic of post-Independence India," and Tripathi
calls him the "leader of Dandi Swamis" (1978:64). Karpatri was so
influential that he actually directed the activities of the Jyotir vidyapith
even though he was not a Shankaracharya.[12] For reasons which are now
unknown, that vidyapith had been without a Shankaracharya for a very
long time, its guru-to-disciple lineage broken. Cenkner (1978:111) states
that some records say it lacked a Shankaracharya for nearly three
centuries but that authorities there admit a break of only 165 years. I
found the latter claim made when I visited there in 1988, but whatever
the actual duration of the vacancy, the acharyaship could not be
conferred in the traditional way, directly from teacher to disciple.
However, so great was Karpatri's influence that his recommendation
of Swami Brahmananda Saraswati was generally supported, and in 1941
Brahmananda became the first Shankaracharya of Jyotir Math in the
modern age. Brahmananda himself became a charismatic guru, helped
by the influence of a charismatic disciple named Maharishi Mahesh
Yogi, made famous in the West by his connection with the Beatles and

the Transcendental Meditation movement. In turn, this furthered the credibility and prestige of Karpatri. A few years later, when Karpatri suggested that a disputed vidyapith in Banaras[13] should be revitalized, several senior Dandis in the city suggested that Karpatri himself should mount its *gaddi* (throne). According to Prakash Mishra, the secretary of Karpatri's major ashram at the time, Karpatri reportedly said: "I am the maker of Shankaracharyas. I need not be one myself." Instead, he recommended Swami Maheshvarananda Saraswati, who then received the Shankaracharyaship. Because of the great power of Karpatri, even this vidyapith, whose legitimacy was contended, gained a great measure of respect.

Having considered the linear development of Dandi monasteries, let us turn to the cyclical development. Since the guru is the center of monastic development, monastic structures fade as his influence wanes, just as they grow as his influence increases. The living guru is the center of the matrix, and after his death this matrix immediately begins to dissipate, like planets no longer held in orbit by the gravitational pull of their sun. In Banaras today, the largest Dandi monastery is Mumukshu Bhavan, measuring nearly five acres and once a thriving monastic center under the direction of Swami Ghanashyamananda, who established it in 1929. Today, long after his death, the math is supported by a trust and some governmental support, but much of it is in dire need of repair. Twenty-five Dandis were staying there when I visited, but all maintained that the math was failing without a new leader to attract disciples. Similarly, Dharma Sangh at Durga Kund, once the principal monastery of Karpatri, is waning. In the early 1960s when Karpatri lived there, it grew very large. Eventually Karpatri moved to a math at Narod Ghat on the Ganges, which is still well maintained and brightly painted, but after his death in 1983 his *samadhi* shrine (commemorative monument) was built at Dharma Sangh. Without Karpatri, the future of Dharma Sangh is uncertain. The present Shankaracharya of the Sharda Math, Swami Swarupananda, who owes his position to Karpatri, gives some financial support to the math of his old guru and there is a trust, but nowadays the math attracts little attention and only three Dandis were there when I visited. Without Karpatri, Dharma Sangh is definitely declining as a monastic center.

Some monastic complexes may continue intact for a time after the death of their guru. Such complexes generally survive because of (1) trusts established during the life of the guru, (2) government aid after his death,[14] or (3) the presence of a disciple who himself has become a charismatic guru. However, after the death of the founder most maths dwindle. As no new followers are attracted and old ones die off, the lifeblood of the monastic complex begins to dry up and monasteries collapse. As a consequence of this phenomenon, the fortunes of Dandi maths can change very rapidly. Monasteries which are flourishing at one time can entirely disappear within just a few years upon the death of the guru.

One becomes very aware of the ephemeral nature of monastic complexes while reading Baldev Upadhyaya's (1972) *Kashi ki Panditya Parampara*, an excellent sourcebook of guru lineages in Banaras. From Upadhyaya's text we get a sense of how rapidly the central figures of religious life in Banaras have changed. Some monasteries which were large and powerful in the nineteenth and even early twentieth centuries cannot even be accurately located today because their walls have long since deteriorated or been cannibalized to make other structures. Gurus whose influence was once comparable to a king's may barely be remembered even twenty years after their passing. For example, in the nineteenth century, there was a very respected Dandi named Swami Bhaskarananda Saraswati (d. 1903) who is said to have been an advisor to the maharaja of Banaras.[15] Many kings visited him to receive his counsel. He also met with and, if tradition is to be trusted, greatly impressed Mark Twain. However, in Varanasi today there are few people who have even heard of him. At Durga Kund there is a samadhi shrine dedicated to the swami still maintained by a small trust, but few people in the neighborhood can correctly identify whom the shrine is meant to honor. Focus on the living guru and, despite a general respect for the past, a traditional disinterest among Indians in the details of history can lead even the greatest Dandi leaders to soon be forgotten.[16]

Examples abound of how rapidly the fortunes of Dandi monasteries rise and fall in modern times. Following up the fieldwork of Sinha and Saraswati, I was amazed at how many of their findings were obsolete only ten years later. Some maths, such as Purshottama Math in Asi, had completely disappeared, while others, such as the large Bhuma Adhyatma Pith at Kedar Ghat, had come into existence. In fact, so rapid are the changes in maths as a result of guruism that I found almost none of Sinha and Saraswati's statistics currently accurate and many of their descriptions to no longer hold. For example, Sinha and Saraswati (1978:70–72) speak of Muchhali Bandara Math in Nagwa as "affluent." They say it is "one of the biggest in Kashi" and "provides accommodation to more than 400 Dandis" (though I think that here they meant that it could provide such accommodation, not that 400 Dandis were actually in residence). Today, the monastery is far from affluent. The valuable collection of tantric manuscripts mentioned in Sinha and Saraswati has been partially sold off to pay creditors, and when I visited, there were only two Dandis stopping there. In accord with what I have been arguing, the change in this math was also caused by its being directly tied to the fortunes of its guru, Swami Krishna Ashrama. Sinha and Saraswati testify to the fame of the old guru, who at 103 years of age at the time of their visit was "well known for his spiritual attainment": "People flock to him specially on Tuesday and Thursday when it is believed that whatever he will say will come out true." By the time I visited, the guru had died. Crowds no longer flocked, their offerings of rupees were no longer forthcoming, and the math was affluent no longer.

Other maths mentioned by Sinha and Saraswati have been abandoned. Purnananda Swami Math, which was declining in their time, is now overrun with squatting householders, and Dandis no longer stay there. Kali Math, which still continued in 1978, is now closed and nearly a ruin. Its walls are falling down and its remaining rooms are now occupied by monkeys rather than monks. Sumeru Pith, the disputed Shankaracharya vidyapith mentioned earlier, was doing quite well in the 1970s. Karpatri was still alive and his influence gave the math a measure of respect. Also, as Sinha and Saraswati mention, the first Shankaracharya appointed by Karpatri, Swami Maheshvarananda Saraswati, had a reputation as a learned scholar. However, with the passing of these two respected Dandis, the math is now in trouble. The present Shankaracharya has a reputation as a materialist,[17] and I met no Dandis in the city who respected either him or his claims to an acharyaship. One pandit at Dharma Sangh told me that once Swami Shankarananda, the present Shankaracharya of Sumeru Pith, was bragging that as a Shankaracharya he was more important than Karpatri. The pandit replied to him, "When Karpatri pissed he created hundreds of Shankaracharyas such as you." Today the Sumeru Pith survives on money collected from personal appearances of the Shankaracharya at religious festivals and functions. How long the Sumeru Pith can continue without support of the Dandis themselves is difficult to predict, but one can assume not long.

In contrast to these failing monastic complexes, the math of Swami Bhumananda at Kedar Ghat is just beginning its growth phase. Opened in 1986, it has now become the most affluent Dandi math in Banaras. Fueled by his prestige in Haridwar, Bhumananda has the resources to become the next major Dandi leader in the city.

In general, I believe it is guruism which prevents the Dandi monastic structure from having the monolithic hierarchy suggested by the traditional descriptions. All Dandis have their guru affiliations, but these gurus in turn need not be, and usually are not, affiliated. Dandi monasticism is not a unified venture in which all Dandis cooperate. Gurus appear and disappear among them in an unpredictable fashion, and so the Dandi monastic structure is very organic. When a guru appears, monastic complexes grow around him; when he disappears, attention flows elsewhere. Once their purposes have been served, few, whether Dandi, lay follower, or Banaras city official, generally see any point in preserving the math for sentimental reasons (one of the few exceptions to this is the Chausatthi Math, which is maintained by a trust given by a wealthy industrialist enamored of the previous guru). All this is not surprising given the Dandi emphasis on ties between living gurus and their followers rather than on buildings or other material associations with earlier gurus. Sinha and Saraswati tell us that 73 percent of the maths they visited were built between 1800 and 1968, and that only four out of thirty-seven claim to be older than the fifteenth century.[18] Monasteries arise and then crumble into ruin. Furthermore, since the prevalent methods of building construction in Banaras rely mostly upon mud bricks, the monsoon rains contribute to the swift passing of a dead guru's monastery into the unremembered past. Nature conspires with the cyclical evolution-devolution of Dandi monasticism, demonstrating the swiftly changing complexion of Dandi complexes in the city.

To conclude this discussion of guruism's influence on the Dandi monastic structure, I would like to make one final point. Since it is not a unified movement, I suppose it should not be surprising to learn that Dandiism is in fact at times divisive. Rivalries certainly exist in Banaras today between maths associated with different gurus. For the past ten or fifteen years, the main rivalry has been between Dandis associated with the two most wealthy maths, those of Swami Kashi Ashrama and the followers of Swami Vishvarupa Ashrama. These two belong to the same Dandi suborder, the Ashramas, and therefore one would expect them to be on friendly terms. Two informants at the math of Swami Vishvarupa Ashrama at Chausatthi Math indicated that the problem involves a woman who lives at the Annapurna math of Swami Kashi Ashrama who reportedly advises him and plays an important role in running the affairs of the Kashi group. The Chausatthis believe that it is wrong for sannyasins to let women have such contact with them. But whatever the cause of the rivalry, it certainly exists. The two groups will not attend publicly sponsored banquets for Dandis together, nor do they generally associate. However, ultimately it is not differences on points of practice which form the basis of factionalism among Dandis but rather lines of guru alliance. The Dandis associated with the two monasteries are simply acting in accord with the policies of their masters. The gurus decide which points of practice are critical and which are not.

Since guruism creates the lines of alliance, differences of opinion between gurus creates factionalism. Factionalism has occurred to such an extent among Indian Dandis today that one south Indian Dandi whom I interviewed in Uttar Kashi told me that "Varanasi is hardly the place to study Dandis" because of his belief that north Indian Dandis are guilty of many infractions of traditional directives.[19] When I pointed out that Banaras had more Dandis than all southern cities combined, he was nonplused and held to what he had been told by his guru.

The Dandi Ideal of the Living Master and Monastic Structure

Having completed my argument, there is but one more point to consider. I mentioned earlier that I would address why the monastic structure, based upon guruism, differs from the prevailing descriptions of Dandi monasticism in traditional works. Often I questioned Dandis themselves in this regard and usually received the same answers. They argue that the traditional configuration is only meant to be nominal; that the Shankaracharyas are only meant to be figureheads for the benefit of lay followers; that since all Dandis renounce the world, including its bureaucratic hierarchies, they are all equals in asceticism. (Dandis do, however, generally show polite respect for those monks who are their seniors, seniority being based on years observing sannyasa and not chronological age.) They also point out that since most Dandis wander there is little need for monastic hierarchies anyway. In defense of this, they would argue that hierarchical positions are not clearly delineated in the traditional accounts and therefore discrepancies and ambiguities exist. Furthermore, it is usually explained that these rules are simply directives, not laws. They are based on *smriti* ("remembered") texts, not the more authoritative *shruti* ("heard") texts such as the Vedas. The tenets of Shankara's philosophy come from the *Upanishads,* part of the sacred Veda, but the rules of the Dandis and the maths are only bureaucratic directives, the breaking of which involves no infraction of Shankara's ideals. This is also true for many of the daily rules regarding Dandi practice. For example, traditionally Dandis are supposed to travel only by foot, but daily one can observe them in Banaras boarding and disembarking from all types of vehicles. When questioned on this point, they will usually say that travel by foot is best, but if one is ill or inconvenienced by foot travel, then rickshaws and other means of transport are allowed.

One might argue that these differences are little more than the rationalizations of men who do not wish to comply strictly with their rules. Could Shankara have intended that the Shankaracharyas do no actual leading of the Dandis, or that the vidyapiths not actually be centers for the monastic hierarchy? Could he have meant that the structure he established should become only a series of nominal affiliations after his death? I believe the answers to these questions could, surprisingly, all be yes. Of course, this is only an educated hypothesis anticipating further research, but there is evidence to support the position. Certainly Shankara was aware of guruism; his success was itself an example of the phenomenon. Furthermore, I believe there is strong evidence in the tradition that he approved of it. Though he must have been aware of the Buddhist Pratimoksha text which provides rules regarding monastic organization and expressly intends to avoid guruism (Buddhist monks had mentors but monastic complexes did not depend upon charismatic gurus), Shankara placed at the pinnacle of his monastic hierarchy four Shankaracharyas—four living gurus. In addition, his advice that the acharyaships be passed directly from one master to the next supports the idea that he wished the Dandis to always be led by living gurus (Cenkner, 1978: 39-40). Shankara may have been well aware that the positions he was establishing could from time to time be compromised by the realities of guruism. In other words, the unpredictable nature of guru appearance might necessitate that if living masters are to be followed then they would need to be followed where found, even if outside of the desired structure, in which case the traditional structure becomes relegated to an ideal rather than a real position.

What I have suggested is that ideally Shankara would have liked to see his monastic structure remain intact and not become only a nominal hierarchy. But through interviews I have learned that this is also the case for most Dandis today. Ideally they also would like to see the vidyapiths become actual monastic centers and the Shankaracharyaships once more dominant guru traditions. However, given the precedent of following a living master, a precedent in Indian culture since before recorded history and one which Shankara himself probably endorsed, realizing that ideal is difficult. As I have said, gurus must be followed where they are found. In the meantime, tradition is not thrown to the wind. As much of the tradition as can be followed, given the Dandi's priority of following a living guru, is followed. Gurus form the pivot and foundation of the real monastic structure, but even a guru who has attracted much attention is likely to lose it if he begins flaunting tradition, for example, by allowing women or nonBrahmins to become

Dandis.[20] Tradition does provide its constraints, like riverbanks directing the flow of a living river, though they themselves must give a little in the process. The ideal monastic structure is continuously maintained, if in name only, awaiting the day when it might once again be realized.

Conclusion

There is little left to say but the obvious. Given the substantial discrepancy between the ideal vision and actual manifestations of Dandi monastic structure, it is important for researchers working with this material to make clear which level of things they are describing. Lack of care in this regard can result in tremendous confusion, as I myself was confused by the difference between what I had read and what I saw, and it is likely that there are instructors and professors in the field right now who are teaching the ideal structure of Dandi monasticism as if it actually existed. Finally, I would strongly recommend to others investigating Hindu ascetics and monasticism that they consider the possible effects of guruism on their own subjects of study. Perhaps similar discrepancies exist between ideals and realities within their sects, and, given the prevalence of guruism in India, for similar reasons.

APPENDIX: Banaras Dandi Maths Surveyed for this Report

Mumukshu Bhavan
B 1/86-87 Asi

Sumeru Pith
Dumrao Begh Colony

Kashi Kaivalya Math
Ghasiyari Tola (Durga Kund)

Dharma Sangh
B 27/97 Durga Kund

Bhuma Adhyatma Pith
B 6/99 Kedar Ghat

Shri Shringeri Shankar Math
B 14/111 Kedar Ghat

Go Math
Ck. 8/21 Gadhavasi Tola

Annapurna Bhavan
Asi Ghat

Purnananda Swami Math
B 4/20 Hanuman Ghat

Kanchi Kamakoti Math
B 4/7 Hanuman Ghat

Kali Math
D 17/35 Lakshmi Kund

Pushkara Math
B 1/88C Asi Ghat

Purshottama Math
B 1/113 Asi

Ananta Vijna Math
Asi (at main crossing)

Dakshinamurti Ashram
B 1/127 Asi

Ganeshavara Math
B 1/90 Asi

Baladevashrama Math
B 5/77 Awadhagarvi

Madhavananda Math
Ch. 41/21 Pathara Gali

Dwarka Shankaracharya Math
Hanuman Ghat (on river)

Chausatthi Math
D 21/12 Chausatthi Ghat

Muchhali Bandara Math
B 30/247 Nagwa

Gauda Math
D 5/110 Mira Ghat

Bhinga Raj Dandi Sevasthana
B 29/25 Sankatamochan

Maheshvar Math
B 1/78 Asi

Shankara Math
B 8/19 Bara Gambhir Singh

Notes

1. This estimate was given to me by Swami Rama at his *ashram* (hermitage) in Rishikesh. Swami Rama was from 1949 to 1951 the Shankaracharya of the disputed Karvir Pith in south India.

2. For example, Sinha and Saraswati (1978:51) counted 239 Dandis.

3. Sinha and Saraswati (1978:68) report the presence of two female ascetics living in Dandi maths. At Dakshinamurti Ashram they found that "a female ascetic resides permanently with her *gurubhais* [spiritual brothers]." And, at Purnananda Swami Math, they found a woman from Tamil Nadu, called "Gaura Ma," whom they describe as the head of the math and the successor to its *gaddi* (throne). Since these cases would constitute serious anomalies in Dandi practice, I was careful to investigate them during my own research. I was unable to locate any female ascetic at Dakshinamurti Ashram. If one had lived there, it is unlikely that she would have undergone the Dandi initiation or claimed to be a Dandi. In the second case, I found only squatting householders residing at Purnananda Swami Math. They were very familiar with "Gauri Ma," as they called her. She died the year before (1987), but I was told she neither carried the Dandi staff nor sat on the gaddi. She considered herself an ascetic and had affiliated herself with the Dandis, but they were her teachers, not her brethren.

4. The most recent conflict on the issue involves the Govardhana Shankaracharya at Puri, Niranjan Dev Tirtha, who in June of 1988 publicly advocated that Harijans (Untouchables) be excluded from Hindu temples (See

Times of India, July 2, 1988). Cenkner (1978:143) notes that this same Shankaracharya "brought forth the wrath of Maharashtrian Buddhists in 1969, in Poona when he said that untouchability was integral to Hinduism."

5. For the accounts of Dandi monasticism in question, see Ghurye (1953:70–97), Tripathi (1978:63–68), Oman (1905:153–67), Giri (1976:4–19), and Sinha and Saraswati (1978:59–74).

6. Cenkner (1978:114) notes, "The guru of this religious center [Jyotir Math] is the spiritual head of the Danda Samnyasis, . . . and as such engages in the role of *rajaguru* which distinguishes him from the others."

7. See the Appendix at the end of this chapter for a list of the maths I have surveyed.

8. Several factors contribute to the general ambiguity surrounding Jyotir Math. First, it has a very remote location, and second, there is a legal dispute between Swami Swarupananda and Swami Vishnudevashrama, both of whom claim to be the legitimate Shankaracharya there.

9. Traditional descriptions, differing slightly from monastery to monastery, are all based upon similar sources: (1) traditional biographies of Shankara, such as *Shri Shankara Vijayam*, which is attributed to his disciple Anandagiri; (2) the *Mahanushasana*, a text on Dasnami asceticism attributed to Shankara himself; (3) Shankara's *bhashyas* (commentaries) on various sacred texts; and (4) oral traditions passed on by pandits and gurus. Commonly, these sources are accessed and a general account of the tradition is written up as a small booklet, usually called *Yati-Sandhya*, which the maths pass out to those interested.

10. This was briefly noted by Sinha and Saraswati (1978:74), but they make no point of presenting its ramifications for the ideal monastic structure they describe.

11. For a brief life sketch of Karpatri, see Tripathi (1978:224–25). For a comprehensive discussion, see Baxter (1969).

12. For my information regarding the influence of Karpatri on the Shankaracharyaship, I am relying upon interviews with two of his chief disciples, Swami Nandanandana Saraswati and Swami Hansananda Saraswati, both of Rishikesh; two pandits at Dharma Sangh, Shri Prakash Mishra and Shri Markandeya Brahmachari; and Swami Swarupanandi of Shankaracharya Pith.

13. Most Dandis believe only four vidyapiths were established, and none at Banaras.

14. Usually such aid is shunned by caretakers of the monasteries because of governmental controls which accompany it, including rules against untouchability.

15. Besides Upadhyaya's material, much information can still be gained on Bhaskarananda because there is a trust supporting his samadhi shrine. In a small office near the main *chawk* (square) of Asi, his affairs are still looked after and a life-size statue of the swami is maintained.

16. For a very good, brief discussion, see "Problems of Chronology" in Organ (1974:4–9). As Organ (1974:5) notes, "Kings and princes did not leave precise records of their own achievements on the monuments they erected. Military leaders did not hire secretaries to record their exploits, and authors did not sign nor date their work." One reason commonly expressed for the ahistorical nature of Indian civilization is reiterated by Dhan Gopal Mukharji (cited in Organ, 1974:5): "The consciousness of history as an asset of life and as an expression of our people, does not seem important to us. History is the record of men's relation to time, but the Hindu does not believe in time, and all our life, according to the Hindu's vision, is all illusion and something to be transcended."

17. I myself noted that he tries to keep his mouth closed when smiling to hide his habit of chewing *pan* (betel), expressly forbidden in the traditional Dandi rules regarding intoxicants.

18. Sinha and Saraswati (1978:68). Among the older maths, I was told by several informants that Go Math at Gadhavasi Tola and Gauda Math at Mira Ghat are the oldest. However, the dates that I was given varied greatly from source to source, and it was clear that the claims rested upon tradition rather than research.

19. In general, north and south Indian Dandis disagree on several specific directives. South Indian Dandis believe that they may only wear one cloth, which must be seamless and unsewn. In the colder north, Dandis often wear clothes with sleeves and sometimes even sweaters. South Indian Dandis generally shave their faces and cut their hair every two weeks. Many northern Dandis, including the Shankaracharyas of Jyotir and Sharada, wear their hair and beards long.

20. Cenkner (1978:126) relates an interesting situation in which there was potential for strong conflict between guruism and the fixed traditional guidelines of Dandiism. He explains that though Maharishi Mahesh Yogi was the favorite disciple of Swami Brahmananda, he could not become a Shankaracharya because of his being born a *Kshatriya* (warrior caste). In deference to his status as a master, the Shankaracharya following Brahmananda, Swami Shantananda, addressed Mahesh Yogi as "gurudeva," and Cenkner witnessed him celebrating Guru Purnima (annual celebration honoring gurus) publicly for Mahesh Yogi in Delhi. However, Maharishi, for all his prestige as a guru, would still not be able to assume the acharyaship without overstepping the rules.

7

The Goddess of the Vindhyas in Banaras

Cynthia Ann Humes

Banaras is said to be the city of 330 million gods, but its preeminence among Hindu pilgrimage places predates the arrival of all Hindu deities: Banaras is "not such a great *tirtha* [pilgrimage place] because all the gods are there; all the gods are there because it is such a great *tirtha*" (Eck, 1982:157). These deities perform *Kashivas*, or fulfill their vow to reside in Kashi for the remainder of their lives. The famous goddess Vindhyavasini, "she who dwells in the Vindhya mountains," is one of the myriad deities who are believed to have come to Banaras precisely because of its status as the greatest tirtha. Since Hindu texts teach that Banaras is a microcosm of the world with everything that is powerful and auspicious found there, it is natural that the Great Goddess Vindhyavasini chose to dwell within its borders as well (Eck, 1982:23).

Hindu philosophical views of goddesses are diverse and complex. The most common understanding held by many people today seems to embrace two complementary views simultaneously. The earliest conceptualization of goddesses viewed them as distinct from each other and exercising separate spheres of dominion defined either geographically, in which case the goddess was a "regional goddess," or in terms of a specific function, such as the cure of a disease. Over time, a belief in the unity among goddesses arose, positing all as being manifestations of a single Great Goddess. Today, although most devotees each still tend to worship one goddess in particular, preserving the uniqueness of each goddess's mythology and reign, many believe that all goddesses are manifestations of a single Great Goddess.[1] A related view of goddesses is common in *Shaktism,* a movement centered on *Shakti* or Power, which personifies that power as feminine. In Shaktism, the Great Goddess is the unitary, primeval, unmanifest First Power or *Adi-Shakti,* and the multiple goddesses are the manifested plural *shaktis* who are related to male deities as their "power." In Shri Vidya, one of the most important philosophical forms of Shaktism, this single Great Goddess, or Parashakti, is understood in a quasi-Advaitan or nondual sense. In the Kevaladvaita (pure nondual) philosophy of Shankara, Brahman is the unitary, impersonal Absolute and deities are a subordinate form of Brahman, and further, the dualistic world is a product of ignorance understood to be *maya* or illusory. In Shaktic Advaita, Parashakti is the original theistic unity which transforms itself by its own free will into a dualistic, phenomenal, and totally real universe. The theme of power arises in a related but different way in conceptions of the goddess as consort or spouse of one of the male deities, and this source of "power" is controlled or contained by the male through marriage. Some scholars argue that this "spousification" is a later development which seeks to "tame" raw female divinity by shedding it of its ambivalent ancient origins in the worship of uncontrollable regional goddesses and the all-powerful Great Goddess (Gatwood, 1985). Nowadays, most devotees worship a specific goddess associated with the cure of a particular disease or other function or with a reign over a particular region. Many or even most devotees simultaneously regard the specific form which they worship as a manifestation of the One Goddess. Thus, at a conceptual level, it is possible to distinguish between little and Great Goddess, but worshipers themselves ordinarily do not hold to a sharp either-or distinction.

Vindhyavasini was probably originally conceived as the regional goddess of the Vindhyas,[2] yet for nearly two millennia she has been identified as the spouseless "Great Goddess." Some scholars argue that the extensive mythology of her cult may have contributed to the development of the concept of the Great Goddess itself (Tiwari, 1985; Vaudeville, 1984). Because Vindhyavasini specifically rejects marriage to any deities in her most popular myths, she is almost never portrayed as a consort of a deity.[3]

In her most famous myth, Vindhyavasini is recognized as the single Great Goddess who incarnated herself in order to come to the assistance of Lord Vishnu.[4] Vishnu had decided to incarnate himself as the two brothers Balabhadra and Lord Krishna from the womb of Devaki in order to save the world from the oppression of Devaki's brother, the evil King Kamsa. When Kamsa learned he was destined to die by the hand of one of his sister Devaki's children, he resolved to murder each of her babies at birth. Vishnu appealed to the Great Goddess first to transfer the embryo of Balabhadra from Devaki to Vasudeva's other wife Rohini's womb. He then requested that she take birth from the womb of a humble cowherdess named Yashoda and act as a substitute for him in his incarnation of Krishna. He requested her to delude all the persons involved through her powers of illusion, to ensure that the replacement remained secret. Devaki's husband Vasudeva substituted the baby Krishna for the Goddess incarnate. Kamsa picked up the child by her ankle and attempted to strike her head against a rock. However, the baby flew from his hand into the sky and assumed her celestial form, predicting that Kamsa would later be defeated by Krishna. She then flew off to the Vindhya mountains and became known by the name of Vindhyavasini.

Most Indians and Westerners familiar with her today are taught that Vindhyavasini dwells at a single residence in a village called Vindhyachal—"Vindhya Mountain"—near Mirzapur, in southeastern Uttar Pradesh about fifty miles southwest of Banaras. In the many references to Vindhyavasini in Sanskrit and Prakrit literature, she is described as ever dwelling in "Vindhyachal." The term *Vindhyachal* can refer to the whole Vindhya mountain range or to this specific town, but modern interpreters usually associate the term automatically with the town now known as Vindhyachal. There is no doubt that this site has been the main focus of Vindhyavasini's cult for centuries; however, she is worshiped in many other temples, including at least six in Banaras alone. Moreover, I have visited five extant Vindhyavasini temples outside Vindhyachal and Banaras, and there are at least four others in north India.[5]

Ancient texts suggest that there used to be many more such temples on the "Vindhya Mountain" than these now known to be dedicated specifically to Vindhyavasini.[6] Vindhyavasini was worshiped in both temple and wilderness, by the highest to the lowest in social rank, from the west to the east coasts, within and beyond the Vindhya mountain range. Elaborate mythologies connecting her to these various sites have evolved. Indeed, so pronounced was her habit of leaving her main abode in Vindhyachal that some current devotees of Vindhyavasini at Vindhyachal told me that her temple priests had to intervene to keep her there. In the past, Vindhyavasini has been "attracted" by some powerful devotees who convinced her through eye contact to accompany them elsewhere. These secondary manifestations threaten to deplete her "power" at Vindhyachal, so until several years ago, during the crowded days of Navratra, the "nine days" of the Goddess worship in the fall and spring, her face used to remain covered by Vindhyachal priests to ensure that she not be lured away.[7]

For at least the last several centuries, however, the Vindhyachal Temple has come to be understood as "the" dwelling of the Goddess of the Vindhyas. Perhaps, over time, as the popularity of the cult of

the Great Goddess grew, together with Vindhyavasini's close identification with the Great Goddess, the more popular and less geographically
specific epithets of the Great Goddess, such as Durga, obscured the
original identity of temples dedicated to the "regional" but "Great
Goddess" Vindhyavasini. Further, the ambiguity of the term *Vindhyachal*
allowed Vindhyachal priests to assert that all references to Vindhyavasini
temples refer to theirs near Mirzapur. These factors may have facilitated
a decline in the breadth of Vindhyavasini worship across north India
while forging a single site of intense devotion in Vindhyachal village.

The Vindhyachal Temple site near Mirzapur has long had a special
relationship to Banaras and its inhabitants. It is included in the great
Chaurasi Kroshi Parikrama, a large pilgrimage circuit popular for
centuries which connects Banaras to many major pilgrimage sites in
northern India. The numerous tour buses between Banaras and Vindhyachal further attest to the temple's popularity among Banarsis today.
The Vindhyachal Temple has received patronage by the kings of Banaras
for centuries. Even today in the month of Magh (January/February) the
king makes a formal yearly state visit there, and all royal family members
undergo *mundan* (ritual tonsure) at Vindhyachal.[8]

Currently, there are at least six places in Banaras open to the public
where Vindhyavasini is worshiped. Considering that there appear to
be fewer than twenty Vindhyavasini temples in all of India, this is a
remarkable concentration of worship sites, and it confirms that Banaras
is a special locus of worship of the Goddess of the Vindhyas. In part,
this number reflects the proximity of Banaras to Vindhyachal and the
regional prominence of Vindhyavasini. However, most of the creation
stories of the six Banarsi temples stress that it is the special sanctity
of Banaras, not its convenient location, that attracts this goddess. The
Banarsis' perception of their city necessarily paints its famous neighbor
Vindhyavasini as pilgrim and dweller in the eternal, ideal Hindu Place
par excellence.

All of my informants know a miraculous story, or *mahatmya*, which
describes the glorious history of the Goddess coming to dwell at their
respective temple. I will trace the popularization and spread of this
regional Hindu cult and the relationship between the Goddess
Vindhyavasini and her Banarsi devotees by drawing on each temple's
mythological descriptions and historical background.

Vindhyavasini at the Durga Kund Temple

The earliest reference to Vindhyavasini's residence in Banaras is
found in the *Kashi Khand* (*KKh*), the fourth book of the *Skanda Purana*,

which is an elaborate mahatmya of the merits of Kashi. According to the *KKh*, when all the gods were defeated by the demon Durg, they appealed for help from the Great Goddess who dwelled in the Vindhya mountains. In their elaborate eulogy, the gods clearly identify her as the Great Goddess on whom all depend, and who creates, protects, and destroys the world. Assuming the agnomen *Durga* after her victory over the demon Durg, the Great Goddess Vindhyavasini took up residence in Banaras.

Exactly where Vindhyavasini came to dwell in Banaras is debated today. Eck (1982:167) explains that this myth refers to the Durga Kund Temple in southern Banaras, which has been included in the itineraries of most pilgrims to Banaras for centuries. However, a priest of the Kedar Nath Temple argues that the *KKh* passage refers to the Vindhyavasini image established at Kedar Nath. The owner-priest of a Vindhyavasini temple located adjacent to the famous Sankata Temple claims that the *KKh* passage refers to his family's shrine, an assertion which is confirmed by the founder of a Vindhyavasini shrine within the Shitala Temple. Finally, the priest at the Vindhyavasini Temple in Kashipura states that the *KKh* passage refers to the temple at which he now officiates. Although some of these men were aware of each other's claims, none of the four was aware that priests of the Durga Kund Temple also cite this same passage as proof that Vindhyavasini resides there.

The *KKh* appears to refer to the Durga Kund Temple, as its priests and Eck contend. The Great Goddess pledges to remain in Kashi forever and to protect all of its inhabitants; she specifically promises that "the man who bathes in Durga Kund [will be] freed from all difficulties" (*KKh* 72.87). The emphasis upon bathing in the adjacent *kund* (water tank) supports the location of Vindhyavasini's dwelling at Durga Kund, for no other Vindhyavasini temple in Banaras has such a water tank or bathing tradition. Even so, representatives of three other Vindhyavasini temples believe that the *KKh* proves the ancientness and sanctity of their religious sites in Banaras. This fact points to the continued importance of sacred texts in the growth and maintenance of local worship patterns in Banaras, as well as to the efficacy of repeated truth claims and creative textual reinterpretation.

The *KKh* passage repeatedly exhorts pilgrims to worship Vindhyavasini-Durga in Kashi. Since the phrasing *in Kashi* is so insistent, and the chapter explains that the Great Goddess comes from "Vindhyachal" and "rests" in Kashi after her battle, it appears that the author of the passage is attempting to popularize worship of Vindhyavasini-Durga at this local site, or at least to make devotees aware that this is the

Goddess of the Vindhyas who dwells in Banaras. If one cannot go regularly to her Banaras temple on her sacred days, that is, Tuesdays and the eighth and fourteenth days of the lunar month, one should at minimum make a yearly pilgrimage to her site at Durga Kund during the autumn Navratra. One may take *darshan* ("ritual seeing") of the beautiful *svayambhu* or "self-manifested" silver mask of the Goddess's face installed at the shrine, often referred to as the "Monkey Temple" today for its numerous simian inhabitants.

The mythological tie of Vindhyavasini to the Durga Kund Temple reflects both the popularity that this regional goddess must have had in Banaras prior to the formulation of the fourteenth-century *Skanda Purana* and the strong identification of Vindhyavasini with Durga, the Great Goddess. An entire Hindi *Vindhyeshvari Chalisa*, or "forty verses to the Queen of the Vindhyas," is inscribed in marble on the modern Durga Kund Temple's walls, affirming the ancient identification of Durga and Vindhyavasini. Although Durga Kund priests are aware of the *KKh* passage and confirm that this temple's goddess is in reality Vindhya-vasini-Durga, today's pilgrims do not appear to know of this connection. It is reasonable to suggest that the intention of the *KKh* authors was to popularize the worship of Durga as specifically Vindhyavasini at Durga Kund, or to encourage Vindhyavasini devotees to interpret Durga Kund as her dwelling in Banaras in contrast to other competing sites in Banaras and perhaps nearby Vindhyachal or Vindhya forest sites. If so, they do not seem to have succeeded up to today. If, rather, the *KKh* passage reflects the trend to popularize a strand of worshiping Vindhyavasini in Banaras as Durga, it has succeeded so well as to obscure the regional but Great Goddess Vindhyavasini's original identity.

The Vindhyavasini Shrine in the Kedar Nath Temple

According to Mukti Prasad Pandey, a priest at the Kedar Nath (Shiva) Temple, the image now worshiped there as Vindhyavasini was installed at the same time as that of Shiva. As previously mentioned, Mukti Prasad Pandey also claims that the *KKh* refers to the Vindhya-vasini image in his temple. When asked what connection this goddess has to Kedar Nath, Pandey explained that wherever Shiva is, so will be his shakti or power/consort, thus assuming that Vindhyavasini is in fact Parvati.[9] In answer to why Vindhyavasini-Parvati is established in Banaras, he reiterated the common claim that all deities live in Banaras: "Kashi is where one can find each and every deity. They all come to Banaras on pilgrimage and dwell here."

Mukti Prasad Pandey explains that devotees who come to the temple almost always do so to worship Kedar Nath in particular, not Vindhyavasini, although many devotees may worship her as they circumambulate this temple. The only day when she is specially worshiped is the eighth day of the autumn Navratra, and Navratra is not observed with much elaboration there. Besides greater decoration and a slightly expanded worship ceremony, there is nothing else done by the priests to mark the occasion. Vindhyavasini's birthday is also a muted affair; although known to be on the second day of the month of Bhadrapad, it is not celebrated in any special way. Pandey says that those who come to the temple are mostly from south India and Bengal, in part because of the nearby hostels that cater to them, and usually they pay attention only to Kedar Nath and Parvati, the main deities there. The *annakut* or "heap of food" festival is performed jointly for all the deities on Kartik Purnima, the day of the full moon of Kartik (October/November), the most common date for annakut.[10]

The icon declared to be Vindhyavasini at the Kedar Nath Temple is very different from those at other Banarsi Vindhyavasini temples, all of which closely resemble Vindhyachal's icon. I have been told that three hands bear a conch shell, a discus, and a lotus, and her fourth displays a gesture of fearlessness, although I could not see for myself since there was a barred door separating lay devotees from the image, which was partially shrouded. The head of the dark stone image is adorned with a very tall headdress, and there is a broken image of a smaller female deity to its right side whom the priest was unable to identify. This diminutive female icon on the right suggests that the major image next to it may have once been understood to be a male deity. Perhaps the original identity of the icon was changed to promote the Kedar Nath Temple by drawing upon the popularity of the cult of Vindhyavasini. Since I am not certain that Vindhyavasini's icon is even a female image, I am reluctant to accept without more evidence that this shrouded image was originally created to represent her. Although some local devotees are aware that the statue is Vindhyavasini, it does not draw the attention of many people these days, nor do the priests attempt to popularize her worship at the Kedar Nath Temple among their primarily south Indian and Bengali clientele. The lack of specific ceremonies dedicated to Vindhyavasini suggests that this image is either a relic from a time when she was more popularly worshiped at this temple, or perhaps points to a shift in patronage from regional devotees to outside devotees unfamiliar with her. In any case, at present the Kedar Nath priests are unanimous in their agreement that it is a statue of Vindhyavasini and point to the *KKh* as proof.

The Vindhyavasini Temple near the Sankata Temple

When they came to Banaras about nine generations ago, the Mishra family bought land near the Sankata Goddess Temple, and in the process became the owners of a private Vindhyavasini temple, which has existed there "for innumerable centuries." They owned vast property in Gwalior, Madhya Pradesh, and earned their living through tax collection, farming, and renting land. However, in 1952 land reform laws stripped them of much of their claims. Some of the family remain in Gwalior tending their reduced collective holdings, and others have moved to their Banaras home to seek employment. To offset maintenance costs of the temple and to alleviate increased property taxes, in the 1970s the family decided to open the temple to the public, thus providing employment for family member Ashok Kumar Mishra, who is the temple's priest.

Mishra explains that his temple actually dates from prehistoric times, and the image installed there is a svayambhu, or "self-manifested" statue. Further, it is this temple that is described in the *KKh*:

This statue of Vindhyachal [a common name for Vindhyavasini] came here by itself. This has always been here. When all the gods were coming to Kashi, the city of Baba Vishvanath, then she also came to do Kashivas. Just as ordinary people make pilgrimages to gain peace of mind, so Vindhyavasini came to Banaras to dwell in order to secure the mental peace the city provides all her pilgrims and residents...The *Kashi Khand* passage refers to this temple because I have heard this from the learned people of Kashi.

He is joined in this conviction by Shiva Prasad Pandey, a priest at the Shitala Temple who has established a Vindhyavasini image there. Patrons of the Vindhyavasini temple near Sankata seem to have accepted Mishra's confident assertions, so, at least in popular lore, it appears that more Banarsi devotees of Vindhyavasini believe that the Vindhyavasini temple described in the *KKh* is this temple near Sankata rather than Durga Kund. This development demonstrates that religious officiants and influential devotees who make repeated and convincing claims about the special sanctity or power of a site or a text can profoundly alter the way a site or text is perceived in religious practice.[11]

According to Mishra, Vindhyavasini establishes herself in different forms with different qualities. These forms are determined by the number and types of *kala* (qualities, or portions) she displays in the places she chooses to inhabit. When she flew from the hand of King

Kamsa she went to her temple site in Vindhyachal, where she can be seen in the *ugra* or violent expression, her face lit with bright power and displaying all sixteen qualities. In contrast, at her temple near Sankata, she resides in only fourteen qualities, because when devotees leave on pilgrimage they leave behind their two aggressive and destructive qualities and go with a cool and calm mind. Like the Vindhyachal icon, her Sankata image is made of dark stone and has wide silver eyes, and her body is draped modestly in a red sari. However, the Sankata Vindhyavasini image has a more peaceful expression and has a smoother, more human appearance than the cruder "birdlike" appearance of the Goddess famous in Vindhyachal. She is ever bedecked with flower garlands and a large silver crown ornately shaped like the fanned tail of a peacock. A common Hindu custom is the application of the sacred vermilion powder called *sindur* on the feet of the goddess. Not all people are believed to be entitled to touch the feet of a holy image, however, so to maintain an image's purity, alternate "feet" are provided near a temple's entrance; such is the case at this temple. Many red layers have obscured her white marble feet located at the barred doors to the shrine's entrance. The main image several yards away is untouched by all but the priest and certain privileged devotees.

Since the temple's recent opening to the public, its popularity has spread by word of mouth, especially among people living near the temple and those devotees who frequent the more popular Sankata Temple nearby. Although Mishra considers the "day of Vindhyavasini" to be Saturday, this temple is most crowded on Tuesdays and Fridays, the popular days of Sankata, because devotees who come to visit Sankata also visit neighboring temples. Because of this fortuitous proximity, this temple is more popular than all of the other Banaras Vindhyavasini temples except the Durga Kund, Kedar Nath, and Shitala Temples, none of which is best known for its connection to Vindhyavasini. The only rival in popularity among those dedicated specially to Vindhyavasini is the temple in Kashipura, which is conveniently located on a very busy commercial street today. These facts testify to the truth that spatial and temporal organization can have a dramatic impact on the popularity and ritual of Hindu temples.

There are three special days each year sacred to Vindhyavasini that are popularly celebrated at this temple. The most popular is the Annakut festival performed in Magh. Enormous mounds of grain and fruit are offered and shared with Vindhyavasini's devotees. Her birthday celebration begins on the second day of the dark half of the month of Bhadrapad (August/September). Its climax takes place six days later at midnight, and is called *Janamashtami*, literally "birth-eighth," that is, that eighth day of a month—in this case, Bhadrapad—associated with Krishna's birthday. This day is also celebrated as the birthday of Vindhyavasini. The celebration of her birthday includes an elaborate ritual bathing and decoration of her image according to the practice of *chathi*, the celebration of a child's first bath, which normally occurs on the sixth (chathi) day after its birth. The next morning, devotees come to see the deity and receive the *prasad*, or gracious leftovers of the sumptuous birthday offerings of dried fruits and nuts. The third most popular event occurs on the fourteenth day of the month of Chaitra (March/April) several days after the spring Navratra. On this day, the image receives the most elaborate decoration of the year, with many more flower garlands, special silver ornaments, and a fancier sari.[12]

In 1985, Mishra established a small shrine next to Vindhyavasini dedicated to Sharada, the "Autumn" Goddess, who has a popular temple located in Maiher, northeast Madhya Pradesh. He had many reasons to build this temple, none of which was "miraculous." First, it occurred to him that "all the gods dwell in Kashi." "But," he said, "I have never seen a temple built to Mother Sharada anywhere [in Banaras], . . . so the desire came to me to establish an image of her." Second, the two goddesses have a strong connection. At the Maiher Sharada Temple, there is a small cave shrine to Vindhyavasini as well, and pilgrims often journey to both Vindhyachal and Maiher.[13] Third, and perhaps most important, there were some people renting space within his home next to the Vindhyavasini shrine who were messy and troublesome. Because of strong protective tenant laws, Mishra could not evict them; by building a place for Sharada to dwell, however, he was able to rid his home of those pests. In one fell swoop, the establishment of Sharada dislodged entrenched renters and provided another impetus for worshipers to come to this temple.

Pilgrims often stand in front of Vindhyavasini and sing versions of the forty-verse hymn to Vindhyavasini called the *Vindhyeshvari Chalisa*, mentioned earlier. There is nearly always a steady stream of devotees. Patrons here appear to be more familiar with her mythology and special religious practices than those devotees who frequent all the other temples of Vindhyavasini in Banaras, except perhaps those devotees who frequent that temple which is located on Inglishiya Line described below. Mishra explains that this familiarity is due to his patrons being of "the ancient people of Banaras" or those religious persons whose families are longtime residents of Kashi and who are proud of belonging to, and constituting, "pakka" (genuine) Banarsi culture.

This assessment of his clientele is a source of great pride for Mishra. Pilgrims who come to the ideal city may visit only the most common ancient and well-advertised new sites, but that the "true" or "pakka" Banarsis frequent his temple supports its claims to ancientness and importance among the noncommercialized web of essential sacred sites in Kashi. It may also be true, however, that just as with the nearby Sankata Temple, Vindhyavasini's temple here is "in the labyrinthine lanes of the city where only Banarsis can find their way" (Eck, 1982:168).

Since acting as the priest of this temple is his only job, Mishra is dependent on cash offerings, and explains he has been fortunate that a wealthy paternal aunt has supplemented daily donations to help finance the temple's upkeep. Although he wants more people to learn about and patronize this temple, he is not making great efforts to popularize it because as the sole priest he would be unable to handle the religious needs of great numbers.

Some Banarsi pilgrimage tour businesses see this temple as a source of potential clients and a possible tourist attraction in its own right. At busy times of the year a small makeshift booth is set up near this temple where application forms are available offering pilgrimage bus trips. At the top of the pamphlets in bold print is the familiar refrain "Jai Ma Vindhyavasini!" ("Victory to Thee, O Mother Vindhyavasini!"), and the exciting descriptions promise the true devotee an uplifting triangular pilgrimage to different Vindhyavasini temples at each far-flung corner. From the Sankata Vindhyavasini temple, the pilgrim will visit the Vindhyachal Temple in Mirzapur, and then the journey continues on to the Sharada Temple near Maiher. The addition of the Sharada image in the Sankata Vindhyavasini temple in 1985 helps to symbolically connect all three sites, which together constitute a convenient and already popular triangular pilgrimage network. By advertising near this temple, pilgrimage businesses hope to sign up many clients already evidencing strong devotion to Vindhyavasini and Sharada.

The origin of this temple is steeped in miracle and mystery, yet its opening to the public is due entirely to economics; the impact of recent agrarian reforms and harsher property taxation precipitated an economic crisis for its owners. Ashok Kumar Mishra appears genuinely devout, but he sees the long hours he spends working in the temple as necessitated by political and economic change rather than super-natural inspiration. Although the mahatmya or spiritual history of Vindhyavasini's establishment here is as miraculous as that of any other of her temples in Banaras, the economic and political history of the temple reveals the important commercial function of religion and the dramatic intersection of "worldly" changes and the sphere of the "spiritual."

The Kashipura Vindhyavasini Temple

This small temple is located on a heavily trafficked street front in the crowded lanes known as Kashipura. Looking through the barred iron doors of the temple, the passersby can easily see at eye level the vehicle of Vindhyavasini, a large winged lion, white with a brilliantly colored mane, facing the Goddess five feet away. Like the Vindhyachal and Sankata Vindhyavasini icons, that of Kashipura is made of black stone and has wide silver eyes and a large nose ring. She is about two feet tall, traditionally dressed in a bright red sari and decorated with crimson flowers. Her feet, adorned with ornate anklets, are red from numerous applications of sindur by the priest, who alone is allowed to touch the image. As at the Sankata Vindhyavasini temple, a marble icon of her feet is located near the doors for convenient adoration. A framed picture of the elaborately decorated images of Vindhyavasini of Vindhyachal and of Kashipura (labeled "Varanasi" underneath, as if that of Kashipura were the only Banarsi Vindhyavasini temple) hangs nearby.

Ananta Prasad Sharma is the priest of this temple. This inherited position dates back at least four generations, Sharma explains, so the age of the temple is at least 150 years and is probably much older. Like the other Vindhyavasini Temples in Banaras, the Kashipura temple boasts of a miraculous origin. About two hundred years ago, there was a great Banarsi devotee of Vindhyavasini. This man was of the Kasera or potter caste, and lived in Kashipura. At that time, although there were fine connecting roads between Banaras and Mirzapur, journeying from Mirzapur to Vindhyachal was difficult. People would travel on foot, in large groups for safety from robbers and wild animals, and the seven-mile journey was very time-consuming because of the rugged terrain. Despite the hardship, this devout Kasera pilgrim often went to worship at Vindhyachal. After many decades, he grew too frail to complete the arduous trip.[14] Vindhyavasini then visited him in his dreams; she said, "On Lalita Ghat on the bank of the Ganges, there is a stone statue of me. You must go find it and then establish it in its proper place here in Banaras."[15] He found her statue there, and established it with great ceremony at her chosen site on the street now known as Vindhyachal Gulley. He then appointed Ananta Prasad Sharma's ancestor as the Brahmin priest to perform her worship.

Gir Shankar Shah was a wealthy Kasera related to the founder who donated five buildings to this temple a number of decades ago. The income generated by their rent covers all the temple's maintenance costs, including support of a full-time priest. A trust of five brothers related to Shah manages the temple and its property. Although the temple was founded by a Kasera and is now managed by a committee of Kasera caste fellows, it should not be mistaken as a "Kasera caste" temple. According to Peter van der Veer, new "caste temples" are being consciously constructed in prominent pilgrimage sites such as Ayodhya, Haridwar, and Banaras to symbolize the prestige of a caste and facilitate its upward mobility. The Kashipura Vindhyavasini Temple, in contrast, originated from the spontaneous hierophany of the Goddess to her devotee and, unlike these new "caste temples," has always been open to all castes (Van der Veer, 1988:275).

Friday is the "day of Vindhyavasini," so it is the busiest day. Hundreds of devotees pay their respects to the Goddess then. This temple is famous even outside of Banaras for its special decoration or *shringar* of Vindhyavasini, held on the eleventh day of the bright half of the lunar month of Chaitra, as it is in Vindhyachal. On that day thousands of people come from many surrounding areas of Banaras to see the decoration of the Goddess, explains Sharma, and other Banarsis corroborated this statement.

When questioned whether he had any promotional literature which extolled the merits of the site, Sharma said that "other than the *Kashi Khand*, there was nothing special." Asked to elaborate, Sharma said that the *KKh* describes in detail the story of Vindhyavasini coming to Banaras. Although the statue at Kashipura was established only about two hundred years ago, he explains, the statue is actually svayambhu or self-manifested, and it was when Vindhyavasini first came to Banaras, as described in the *KKh*, that this image appeared. She had remained near Lalita Ghat until the Kasera devotee found her, and was only then established in Kashipura. Once again, in this fascinating and creative reinterpretation we find an appeal made to the authority of the *KKh* to prove the auspiciousness and antiquity of another specific tradition of worship to the Goddess Vindhyavasini in Banaras.

The mahatmyas of the Vindhyavasini Temples near Sankata and in Kashipura both elaborate miraculous origins. However, in contrast to the obvious commercial motives for opening up the Sankata Vindhyavasini Temple, the Kasera opened his temple to the public in response to the Goddess' spontaneous appearance. All costs are covered by the rent of buildings donated by a single Kasera family. The Kashipura origin myth as told by its hereditary priest is an interesting fusion of the *KKh* myth and a modern tale of devotion which highlights the flexible and reciprocal nature of the human relationship with the divine in Hinduism. Whereas the devotee is expected to bear hardship in pilgrimage, when such difficulties preclude her worship, at times this kind Goddess may condescend to come to her devotee, lured away from her main site in Vindhyachal.

Vindhyavasini Comes to the Shitala Temple

For various reasons, including caste endogamy and similarity of occupations, families of priests who work in temples often intermarry with families of other temple priests. Accordingly, numerous Banaras temple priests are related to temple priests at the Vindhyachal Temple. While visiting their relatives, most of these Banarsis pay their respects to Vindhyavasini, and some may become very devoted to her. This connection has contributed to the creation of a new shrine to Vindhyavasini in the Banaras Shitala (Goddess of Smallpox) Temple.

In 1969, when the Shitala Temple priest Shiva Prasad Pandey was twelve years old, he visited his maternal uncle, who is a priest at the Vindhyachal Temple. His cousin allowed him to assist in performing the worship service of Vindhyavasini, and while performing the decoration he experienced a great love for the Goddess and saw her come alive in a vision. He asked her to come to Banaras in the same form as she has in the Vindhyachal Temple so that he could worship her daily in his family's hereditary temple. In 1982, the family considered establishing an image of the goddess Annapurna (bestower of grain) inside the temple. Before they could do so, however, Shiva Prasad's father, Bhavani Shankar Pandey, had a vision of Vindhyavasini. Vindhyavasini finally accepted Shiva Prasad's earlier invitation to come to the Shitala Temple in Banaras to be worshiped by him; she said in the dream, "I will sit there now." Instead of installing Annapurna there, they sent for some sculptors and ordered them to create a stone idol of Vindhyavasini just like she appears at Vindhyachal to be placed inside the Shitala Temple.

The artists had already made the body of the image when the Goddess appeared to Shiva Prasad and told him he must fashion her face himself. Even though he was not a sculptor, that very night he took a hammer and chisel and sculpted her face just as he had seen it in his vision at Vindhyachal. Her statue finished, some members of the Pandey family took it to Lalita Ghat, where she would spend her *jaladivas*, the tradition of placing an image in the sacred waters of the Ganges before its official establishment. Despite extensive search, however, they could not retrieve the submerged image. Bhavani Shankar, asleep at home, was told by Vindhyavasini in a dream, "Go— they are in trouble there. I am now on Manikarnika Ghat." Bhavani Shankar came to the river, and directed by Vindhyavasini, he located her statue at Manikarnika. With full musical band and parade, the family took the image and established it inside the Shitala Temple.

Miraculous circumstances continue to surround Vindhyavasini worship there, explain the Pandeys. Because the Shitala Temple is located directly on the riverbank, it usually floods during monsoon rains so that determined devotees must reach the half-submerged temple by boat. Vindhyavasini's birthday occurs during the monsoons, and the first year after the image of Vindhyavasini was established, it rained so heavily that the temple was completely submerged on that day, so the family decided not to hold any celebration at all. However, all of a sudden the water receded. The Pandey family sent a servant to clean the temple, who, while cleaning, was stunned to see a female cobra come out of Vindhyavasini's sari. No amount of coaxing by the servant and others would dispel the snake. Finally, Shiva Prasad himself was called. After much persuading, at about 1:30 A.M. Shiva Prasad promised Vindhyavasini they would hold a real birthday celebration. At that very moment, the cobra left. The Pandey family interpreted the snake as a direct appearance of Vindhyavasini herself; apparently she wished to ensure a proper birthday celebration by making it known that she was dangerous if not propitiated. Now there are two images of Vindhyavasini at the Shitala Temple, the large established statue and a transportable image which can be moved to dry ground for worship service during floods.[16]

The worship of Vindhyavasini at the Shitala Temple is the closest in philosophy and format to the worship of her in Vindhyachal, which is natural because of the priestly connections between the two temples. Shiva Prasad views Vindhyavasini as the Great Goddess herself, and he espouses the Shakta Shri Vidya philosophy. He explains that although devotees may take a vow to different gods or goddesses, in actuality it is Vindhyavasini who fulfills all desires. She incarnates herself in various forms, a phenomenon which is represented in her daily worship at the Shitala temple as it is in Vindhyachal; she is first adored in the form of an old woman at daybreak, at noon as a child, in the evening as a young maiden, and in the night as an adult woman in her full power. Selections from the *Durga Saptashati*, the Sanskrit text dedicated to the Great Goddess, are recited before her at all four ceremonies, and a *Vindhyeshvari Chalisa* is sung in the evening.

Like the Kasera founder of the Kashipura Vindhyavasini Temple,
Shiva Prasad believes that Vindhyavasini came to Banaras because of
the intensity of his devotion. She granted his wish that she come to
Banaras so that he could personally worship her, and now many
Banarsis and pilgrims worship her at the Shitala Temple. Although the
devotees usually come to worship Shitala, all stop for at least a moment
to adore the Great Goddess Vindhyavasini as well.

We have seen that the popularity of the Sankata Vindhyavasini
Temple is due in part to its fortuitous location next to the famous
Sankata Temple, a stop long favored by pilgrims and Banarsi devotees.
In the case of the Vindhyavasini shrine at Shitala Temple, we see once
again that the addition of "related" deities augments a major temple,
and provides devotees a great deal of convenience; without any stops
elsewhere, they may worship many major deities at once. In a pamphlet
published by Shiva Prasad and his family, they advertise Vindhyavasini's
residence there, and provide appropriate verses for her worship. This
active promotion may lead pilgrims previously unexposed to the cult
of Vindhyavasini to begin to worship her, perhaps even in Vindhyachal
as well, demonstrating a phenomenon that has helped in the past, not
only to rejuvenate regional cults at their roots, but also to universalize
them by spreading them further from their home base.

Vindhyavasini's "Direct Line" to a Woman in Her Home: The Inglishiya Line Vindhyavasini Temple

In 1975 Rama Rani Maharotra established a Vindhyavasini Temple
in her home on Inglishiya Line road near the Maldahiya area of Banaras.
Rama Rani Maharotra is believed to be specially blessed by Vindhyavasini with the gift of channeling the Goddess's healing powers.
Together with the assistance of her husband Jivan Lal and other family
members, Rama Rani conducts daily worship of the Goddess and
dozens of other deities established there. She welcomes visitors on
Tuesdays, Fridays, and Sundays, Vindhyavasini's "special" days, as
advertised on a sign in front of her home.

Rama Rani has a special love for Vindhyavasini which she believes
is reciprocated; she was cured by Vindhyavasini after years of ill health,
a miracle which convinced her to build a permanent shrine for the
Goddess in the family's new home. Her husband explains, "For the
last twenty years, she has had a *dhyan* [special vision] of the Mother,
and Mother's grace has fallen upon her." Because of this special vision,
she says she has a "direct line" (she used the English words in our Hindi
conversation) to Vindhyavasini and can channel the Goddess's power

for healing. People from all over India, and indeed many other countries, including England, the Middle East, and the United States, come to this "medicine shop" to ask that they be healed. Rama Rani communicates with Vindhyavasini by writing questions posed by devotees in her left hand with a simple metal key. She then relays whatever answer she finds in her palm, which is visible only to her. After she gives them prasad, the devotees perform whatever deeds or take whatever treatment the Goddess advises.

Unlike the Brahmin priests of all the other Vindhyavasini temples in Banaras, Rama Rani and her husband are unfamiliar with the KKh's passage about a Banaras Vindhyavasini Temple. Given Rama Rani's "direct line" to the Goddess, however, appeals to the authority of any sacred text are unnecessary to validate the prominence and special sanctity of the Inglishiya Line Vindhyavasini Temple.

The story of the temple's construction borders on what many would call sacrilege. When Mr. Maharotra was having their home constructed, he put off building the shrine because he was short of funds. Rama Rani became angry and told her husband that Vindhya-vasini's shrine must be finished before the second day of the bright half of Asadh (June/July) in order to coincide with Rathayatra, the chariot festival of Krishna-Jagannath, whose sister is Ekanamsha-Vindhyavasini. Mr. Maharotra, irritated at his wife's ordering him, took a large stone upon which his family used to sit while bathing and brushing their teeth, surrounded it with some stray bricks, and sarcastically said to his wife that there was her foundation stone for the beautiful silver Vindhyavasini image waiting to be installed. Mrs. Maharotra accepted this without comment. She established the purchased silver image "on the strength of her devotion," without the aid of Brahmin priests. She then worshiped Vindhyavasini in a jagrata, literally, "awake," an all-night singing celebration to the Goddess which is popular in north India, the songs of which are also known as jagratas. Worshiping for over twenty-four hours continuously, she burned the lamp of the Goddess and asked her to come dwell at her humble shrine. Mr. Maharotra, although he has always been a great believer in the power of Vindhya-vasini, laughed and shook his head in amazement as he explained that the Goddess not only accepted Rama Rani's invitation to dwell there, despite its humble foundation, but made this home shrine famous and Rama Rani a cult figure. The Maharotras said that had they known the shrine would become so popular, they would not have established it within their own home, but rather on adjacent ground outside.

Mrs. Maharotra used to observe purda, the custom of veiling herself to nonfamily members. "She was always covered with a sheet and stayed reserved. She never talked with a man from outside [the family], never so much as walked in front of an outside person," said Mr. Maharotra. He continued, "But I do not know what happened, but I suddenly lost all my strictness, and my wife became very bold." As more and more devotees appeared, Mr. Maharotra encouraged his wife to end her purda and spread Vindhyavasini's grace. Now Rama Rani meets hundreds of strangers who are related to her only in their devotion to Vindhyavasini. Rama Rani said specifically that the majority of vistors to the temple were Khatri women.

Unlike the officiants at all the other Banarsi Vindhyavasini shrines except at Kedar Nath, the Maharotras do not claim that the icon of the Goddess established there is svayambhu; the miracle of faith and divine healing, not the miraculous epiphany of the Goddess, sustains the spiritual aura of the temple. The shrine has beautiful silver images of dozens of deities resting on multileveled platforms. Vindhyavasini's image is graced with her customary silver peacock tiara, and it is smaller and more elegant than all the other temple images of Vindhyavasini in Banaras. Collections of devotional prints and marble plaques with inscribed texts cover the broad expanse of walls. One of these inscriptions is a popular jagrata song to Vindhyavasini.

The Maharotras are members of the high Khatri caste group,[17] which has performed special traditions of worship to Vindhyavasini of Vindhychal for centuries. This group, commonly called the Khatri Samaj—Khatri Society—is famous in Vindhyachal for its weeklong worship called the Ratjaga Mela, or "Fair of the Sleepless Nights," also known simply as the Khatri Mela, or "Fair of the Khatris." It officially begins in Vindhyachal on the eighth day of the waxing fortnight during the monsoon month of Shravan (July/August), but groups of dozens, even hundreds, come to Vindhyachal before and after that date, particularly from Banaras. Every year large groups of Khatri Samaj Banarsis gather in Banaras and start out together to the Vindhyachal Temple seventy-five kilometers away. Although nowadays some members go to Vindhyachal via modern conveyances, hundreds continue to journey by foot as their ancestors did. As they walk, they sing their own traditional songs, along with new and spontaneous ones to the Goddess Vindhyavasini and other deities. After arriving at Vindhyachal late on the second day of their journey, they light large ghee lamps symbolizing the Goddess. They perform jagratas in Punjabi and Hindi dialects before the Goddess's fiery image. For several days to a week they perform their rituals and stay at the Saraswat Khatri Dharmashala caste pilgrimage shelter which their Banarsi ancestors constructed early this century directly adjacent to the Vindhyachal Temple.

Rama Rani spreads the specialized Khatri Samaj tradition of worship at her home temple in many ways. When people come for help, she urges them to light a small flame to the Mother and do worship for just a few minutes daily in order to receive the grace of the Goddess. Even before their temple was completed, they had installed a ghee lamp which has been burning continuously since 1972. Mr. Maharotra explains, "By the light, everything in the world exists. When you burn the light, then you will get her grace," and through her grace, people gain her power and true affection for her. Although the use of ghee lamps is common in Goddess worship, it is noteworthy that the Khatri Samaj's emphasis on meditating upon the flame while singing special Vindhyavasini hymns is a central part in the ritual Mrs. Maharotra recommends. Many of the hymns she teaches devotees are peculiar to the Khatri caste. Further, it is on the eighth day of Shravan, the day on which the Ratjaga or Khatri Mela begins in Vindhyachal, that the Maharotras sponsor the Annakut. Thousands of people receive the prasad of Vindhyavasini on this day, including Khatris before they venture to the Vindhyachal Temple on foot for the most important annual celebration of Vindhyavasini.

Worship at the temple normally takes place twice daily, and three or four times on special days. The characteristic form of worship here is singing, and until 1988 the recitation of the *Durga Saptashati* in Sanskrit was also done by Mr. Maharotra. Recently, the Maharotras have begun to sing the songs of the famous Punjabi author Pandit Chaman Lal Bhardwaj, whose book *Shri Durga Stuti* is an adaptation of the entire Sanskrit *Durga Saptashati* into a Punjabi dialect spiced with ancient Sanskrit epithets. This version has been popularized by the famous singer Narendra Chanchal, who is considered a great devotee of the Goddess and a master of the jagrata genre of music, the devotional singing which is prominent during the Khatri Mela at the Vindhyachal Temple. In a set of three cassettes, Chanchal sings Chaman's version of the *Durga Saptashati* accompanied by a chorus of background singers and full orchestra. The Maharotras believe that this version of the *Durga Saptashati* is more accessible to their patrons, who they feel also enjoy the lovely melodies of Chanchal's interpretation. The vast majority of visitors to the temple, like Rama Rani herself, do not know Sanskrit. So that she and her visitors may understand the text and glorify the Goddess themselves, Rama Rani now sings and teaches Chaman's version of the *Durga Saptashati* as sung by Chanchal rather than have Mr. Maharotra performing the Sanskrit text.[18]

During the fall and spring Navratras, Vindhyavasini is decorated in different fashions for each of the nine days, corresponding to the nine forms of Durga. Great crowds come to sing hymns and see the ornately decorated Goddess. So popular is the temple during Navratra that "one cannot find any [free] space whatsoever from morning until two at night." Even famous Banarsi musicians come to the temple to sing special songs to all of the many deities established here, who are described as "Mother's family." So that the crowds may hear the musicians, a loudspeaker was installed in 1985. The Hindi weekly *Saptahik Hindustan* featured Rama Rani Maharotra and her temple in their October 8–14, 1989, edition on the fall Navratra. In addition to detailing her personal background and the origin and growing popularity of her temple, the author documented in words and stunning photographs Rama Rani's ability to channel Vindhyavasini's power to heal instantly the bloody wounds of a devotee who had whipped his back violently with iron claws while in an ecstatic trance.

An important change in the religious practices of the Maharotras is that they no longer go to the Vindhyachal Temple for darshan of the Goddess. Previously, the Maharotras would make frequent trips to see the Goddess there, but now they believe that to do so would indicate lack of faith. After making a trip to Vindhyachal for darshan ten years ago, Mrs. Maharotra had a dream in which Vindhyavasini slapped her and said, "Do you not have faith in me? Why have I come here?" Mrs. Maharotra tugged her ears and begged her pardon, realizing that since the Goddess is already dwelling in their home, they have no need of going anywhere else; if they go to any other Vindhyavasini Temple when the Great Goddess has already blessed them, they show they have lost their faith in her full and eternal presence there.

Home shrines are common in Hindu households. At these shrines, caste-specific and highly personalized forms of worship may be performed. When the Maharotra home shrine became popular among Rama Rani's Khatri friends and neighbors, and later among others who had heard of the shrine and Rama Rani's power, her particular form of worship began to spread beyond her family and caste members. Belief in Rama Rani's "direct line" to the Goddess Vindhyavasini and her special gifts of healing have helped raise this home shrine to an important position in the web of Banaras temples. It may in time further popularize a particular form of worshiping Vindhyavasini among a greater cross-section of Hindu society. The Vindhyavasini Temple near Sankata was originally a home shrine as well, but was opened to the public due to commercial reasons; in contrast, the Maharotras believe their home shrine was "forced" open to all who wish to be healed or helped by the will of the Goddess Vindhyavasini, with whom Rama Rani is in constant communication.

Conclusion

As I have shown, fascinating traditions particular to each temple reflect religious diversity, historical and economic change, and the impact of geographical and temporal conditions in the life of Vindhyavasini temple worship in Banaras. Each of these six Vindhyavasini temples in Banaras has its own distinct mahatmya. Four of these claim that their respective temple is the Vindhyavasini temple described in the *KKh*. Hindus believe that deities appear in multiple locations, so it could be argued that when Vindhyavasini first came to Banaras she settled in numerous temples. However, each of the four temple representatives citing the *KKh* does so to stress the uniqueness of Vindhyavasini's manifestation at his own temple and to deny that the *KKh* passage refers to the other temples. Their employment of the *KKh* fuels their claims to the greater sacredness and antiquity of their temples. The ancient reference in the *KKh* about Vindhyavasini is important even today among patrons and religious intermediaries at these temples dedicated to Vindhyavasini. The two temples which are not claimed to be the subject of the *KKh* partake of alternate sources of authority. In the Shitala Temple's mahatmya, the Goddess spontaneously manifests herself at the already very important and ancient Shitala Temple at the request of a devotee in modern times, just as at the Inglishiya Line Temple Vindhyavasini maintains a "direct line" with her favored devotee Rama Rani.

The origin of many of the Banaras Vindhyavasini temples is linked to the belief that all Hindu deities are pilgrims living in the Hindu city par excellence. This notion partially explains why there are more Vindhyavasini temples in Banaras than in any other city. The regional prominence of Vindhyavasini's temple in nearby Vindhyachal, Vindhyavasini's perceived willingness to follow her favored devotees to their homes, and the ancient connection of Banarsis' worship at that site are further contributing factors in the origin of Vindhyavasini temples in Banaras. Thus the sacredness of Banaras and the prominence of the regional but Great Goddess Vindhyavasini reinforce each other, resulting in a nexus of Vindhyavasini temples in Banaras unparalleled elsewhere.

Notes

1. Interviews with informants were conducted in Hindi on location in Banaras and Ramnagar during 1988 and 1989. I would like to thank my research assistant Ratnesh K. Pathak for helping me conduct most of the interviews for this study.

2. As Kinsley (1987:99) points out, Vindhyavasini's name underscores her ambivalent nature as the "regional goddess" of the Vindhya mountains. Early references describe her being worshiped by wild tribal peoples, who believed she was a fierce warrior goddess "fond of flesh and liquor" (*Hari Vamsha* 47:51). Even up to the ninth century, she was portrayed in the *Gaudavaho* by Vakpatiraja as accepting human sacrifice. In more recent centuries her associations with Krishna's birth and other more mainstream Great Goddess myths have been emphasized and prior "unorthodox" connections correlatively deemphasized. Today, her priests at her major temple near Mirzapur stress her identity as the Great Goddess, and eschew as "ignorant" prior worship practices viewed currently as "unorthodox" such as the acceptance of alcohol and meat.

3. In *Vamana Purana* 28, Parvati tires of her husband Shiva's teasing her about her dark skin. She resolves to do *tapasya* ("heated" self-discipline) until she receives the boon of a golden-colored complexion from Brahma. From the sheath (*Kosha*) that she sheds, Katyayani-Kaushiki is born. Indra approaches then and accepts Katyayani-Kaushiki as *dakshina* (payment for religious services), and asks Parvati that this goddess be granted as his sister. Indra then goes off to the Vindhya mountains and installs his sister there as Vindhyavasini, who will fight the demons for the benefit of the gods. The now golden or Gauri Parvati returns to her Lord. What I find interesting here is that although she is in a sense "spousified," for she comes from the dark skin of Shiva's wife, Vindhyavasini remains the "unmarried" "sister" of Indra, and further, as the battler of demons for the gods, she is the quintessentially "dark" side of the spousified Parvati.

4. Variations of this core myth reveal sectarian biases. She has many myths in earlier literature, but it is not in the scope of this essay to examine them.

5. I have examined Vindhyavasini Temples in the following locations: in Madhya Pradesh, the village of Tumain; and in Uttar Pradesh, the southern part of Lucknow City, and in the villages of Shuklapur and Musapur, and outside Bandha. Many of these temples appear to be at least several centuries old and have fascinating origin myths. The Tumain Temple was investigated by British archaeologists, who dated it circa ninth century. These researchers believed it was originally a Krishna temple, so its history as a Vindhyavasini temple remains obscure; as Krishna's "sister," Vindhyavasini may have been worshiped there since the creation of the temple. Other Vindhyavasini temples I have yet to visit include Alopi Devi in Allahabad; a village near Allahabad; at Maiher, Madhya Pradesh; a rural site in the Bhopal District of Madhya Pradesh; and according to personal testimony of Dr. N. N. Bhattacharyya, in a village of Hooghly, Bengal. A possible seventh site of worship to Vindhyavasini in Banaras is the Annapurna Temple near the Vishvanath Temple. According to Mr. Ratnesh K. Pathak, there is a twenty-foot-tall painting there of Vindhya-vasini as she appears in the temple of Vindhyachal. Personal communication, Ratnesh K. Pathak, April 23, 1990.

6. Ancient texts confirm the pervasiveness of the cult of Vindhyavasini long ago. In Dandin's c. 700 C.E. Sanskrit work *Dashakumaracharita*, a temple to Vindhyavasini is located on the banks of the Narmada River at Mahishmati, the capital of Avanti. Brahmin priests supervised worship to the large free-standing image of the Goddess (Acharya explains that Mahishmati [Maheshvara] was located about forty miles south of modern Indore [1983: 272ff.]). The *Avanti Khand* of the *Skanda Purana* also describes a temple to her on the Narmada River in Avanti, which may be the same temple described in the *Dashakumaracharita*. In the *Avanti Khand* myth, the sage Agastya practices austerities on Vindhya Mountain and worshiped Vindhyavasini, who became pleased with him. When the Narmada River began to flood the world, Agastya asked Vindhyavasini to come to Avanti and stay there permanently to control the river. That place where she came to dwell was called *Vindhyavasini vimalodatirtha*, the "purifying water pilgrimage place of Vindhyavasini" (*Skanda Purana* 5.1.55, as quoted in Kumar [1983:140]). The *Dashakumaracharita* also explains that at the request of a devotee Vindhyavasini took up residence in the city of Tamralipta in Suhma (now part of Bengal), having "forgotten her love of dwelling in the Vindhyas" (Acharya, 1983:13). In a second work by Dandin, the *Avantisundari*, some tribal people called Kiratas attempted to offer the child prince Upaharavarman to "the terrible" Vindhyavasini in the wilds of the Vindhya forest (Mann Singh, 1979:140). A Sanskrit version of the *Dashakumaracharita* describes this event as having taken place at a shrine at a temple of "Chandika," the "terrible one," not specifically Vindhyavasini (Acharya, 1983:206ff). This translation of the site as a Chandika shrine is also followed by Arthur Ryder (1960:12). Either the authors have used Sanskrit manuscripts which have variations, or Singh has rendered *Chandika* as an epithet of, or adjective describing, Vindhyavasini.

7. Alternate explanations for covering her face exist: to protect it from the crowds, and because some pilgrims believe that only her feet should be observed by the public.

8. Untaped interview, His Highness Vibhuti Narain Singh, September, 1987. The Vindhyachal Temple is a very popular site for mundan, in part because of Vindhyavasini's renown as bestower of children.

9. Recall that the Sanskrit literature supporting this indentification of Vindhyavasini as Parvati retains the unmarried status of the goddess of the Vindhyas. Ethnographic evidence gathered at Vindhyachal reveals that almost all of the several hundred devotees interviewed there consider Vindhyavasini unmarried, and the dozen or so who do claim she is married often depict her as the wife of Vishnu rather than of Shiva.

10. For an excellent analysis of the connections of Vindhyavasini and Krishna to the Annakut festival, see Vaudeville (1984).

11. See, for example, Vidyarthi, Saraswati, and Jha (1979:269–70), which quotes a priest of Dashashvamedh Ghat thus: "Myth perpetuation is the normal technique of a professional priest."

12. Her decoration takes place on the eleventh day of Chaitra in Vindhyachal.

13. Although he himself did not go there, the South-Indian Enugula Veeraswamy describes the Maiher Devi temple from reports of others he heard during his journey to Mirzapur-Vindhyachal in his 1830 journal. He explains that there were good roads between the two sites at that time. Ease in transportation may certainly have helped lead to a pilgrimage network, or vice versa (Sitapati, 1973:70). I have not visited the Maiher Temple, so I am accepting the testimony of pilgrims I interviewed at Vindhyachal that there is a Vindhyavasini cave shrine there, the dating of which I am also uncertain.

14. According to Veeraswamy, the journey took two hours and required crossing the river Ojhla by boat (Sitapati, 1973:83). In 1850 a bridge was built there by Mahant Parashuram Giri, of the Dashanami sect, and later a convenient road laid to Vindhyachal village, indirectly supporting the dating of the Kasera founder to at least pre-1850 (Mirzapur Municipal Board, 1972:24).

15. *Lalita* is the preferred name for the Parashakti among those who espouse the popular Shakta Shri Vidya philosophical view. Perhaps for this reason, Lalita Ghat in Banaras figured prominently in both origin myths of the Vindhyavasini temples of Banaras which involve the Ganges River, namely, Kashipura and the shrine at the Shitala Temple.

16. Transportable images of deities are common in temples subject to floods.

17. It is understood to be within the Kshatriya *varna* (the broad grouping of ruling, martial castes).

18. Pandit Chaman Lal Ji Bhardwaj (1988) and Chanchal (1987).

8

Lolark Kund: Sun and Shiva Worship in the City of Light

Ratnesh K. Pathak and Cynthia Ann Humes*

When a traveler comes to Banaras, whether as secular tourist or devoted "sightseer," one of the "must-see" attractions is the bathing in the Ganges at dawn. For many, bathing on the *ghats* (steps, river banks) of the most sacred Hindu river in the most sacred of all Hindu cities is living Banaras at its best; this is experiencing Kashi, City of Light, celebrating and participating in it as it shimmers in its watery abode.

Bathing in the gleaming waters evokes the primordial connection of water and light in Hinduism, the "protean fire-water" O'Flaherty describes (1978:97). Fire, personified as the deity Agni, assumes various forms: the sun in the sky, lightning and comets in the atmosphere, and the sacrificial, domestic, and human digestive fires on earth. In Hindu mythology, water and fire share many characteristics: they are purifiers, bridges between the sacred and profane, and closely related to fertility. In *Kashi Khand* (*KKh*) 46:67, the water of Asi River and the fire-power of the sun god Lolark work together to destroy the sins of those who come to Banaras. Their southern location ensures that any impurity flowing into Varanasi from the north-flowing Ganges is removed before it can pollute the sacred city. Asi is the bridge and barrier between the sacred city and the profane world south; as the *asi* or sword of the goddess Durga, the river slices away all evils. Lolark Kund, the "pond of the trembling sun," is the site near the Asi-Ganga confluence (*sangam*) where the sun god himself descended to earth and bathed, establishing his place as protector of the purity of all water *tirthas* (pilgrimage places) in Kashi. The sun burns up any evil that threatens to cross over into the sacred space of Banaras.

Although known in the *puranas* (collections of "old stories") particularly for its purifying powers, bathing in Lolark Kund today preserves all three protean fire-water motifs. Bathing there not only purifies the devotee of sin and disease, but it provides a means to touch, indeed to cavort with, the deities enshrined there, and it yields the ultimate blessing in life: fertility.

Lolark Kund is the most prominent of the dozen sites in Banaras devoted to the *adityas*, the twelve solar deities born of the Vedic goddess Aditi.[1] Eck explains, "Lolarka is not only the oldest and most famous of Kashi's *adityas*, but it is perhaps one of the oldest of all sacred sites in Kashi" (1982:177). Archaeological evidence found at the site includes eighth- and twelfth-century images of Surya and an eleventh-century female sun deity, Chakreshvari (Eck, 1982:180). But even here at this ancient solar worship site, devotion to fire on the earth and the sun in the sky has been surely and steadily eclipsed by the worship of an even more brilliant source of light in Kashi: the puranic god Shiva.

The Rise and Decline of Worship to the Sun God

The sun used to be the center of a flourishing cult in north India and is still highly venerated by many Hindus. The fourth to the thirteenth centuries was the classical age of sun worship in India. V. B. Mishra reports that during this time period the Hindu Trinity of Brahma, Vishnu, and Shiva was in some cases "a kind of quadrumvirate," with Surya finding a place alongside the three great gods. Surya evidently overshadowed Brahma and Vishnu in some places, as is demonstrated by his replacement of them in some eleventh- and twelfth-century sculptures of the Trinity. Finally, some icons of this period combined Surya with Shiva as Martanda-Bhairava and with Vishnu as Surya-Narayana (Mishra, 1973:34). In the various subpuranas devoted to the sun, Surya is portrayed as Supreme, and specific myths demonstrate his primacy over other deities in the Hindu pantheon.

Today there are few temples devoted to Surya alone, but sun worship does continue in alternate forms. When people bathe in the Ganges at dawn, for instance, the sun is clearly worshiped as it has been for millennia. Many Hindus recite verses from the Vedas sacred to the sun each morning before they begin their daily work. The Gayatri Mantra is recited by twice-born males every day. This prayer asks the Sun, evoked as the Shining Nourisher or *Savitar*, to stimulate the mind (Rig Veda 3.62.10). Millions ascribe to the *panchayatana-puja*, the worship of the five deities Vishnu, Shiva, Shakti or Devi, Ganesh, and Surya, a practice popularly believed to have been initiated by the ninth-century Advaita philosopher Shankara. As Eck explains, although a pilgrimage to all twelve adityas is outlined even today in Kashi guidebooks, it is not a common or "popular pilgrimage" (Eck, 1982:181). Even so, in mid-1991, a Calcutta devotee of the sun donated a sun shrine at the

Lolark Kund complex next to the Lolarkeshvara Shiva temple and under a huge pipal tree. He claimed to have donated sun statues depicting Surya in his chariot drawn by six white horses at each of the twelve aditya sites in Banaras.

But in many ways the case of the aditya Lolark demonstrates the decline of Surya worship since the fourteenth century. Lolark used to be the primary focus of worship in the southernmost area of the city long ago. In *Kashi Khand* 7:66, Banaras is personified as a goddess whose "tremulous eyes" are Lolark and Keshava, and whose arms are the rivers Varana and Asi.[2] Early texts describe the riverbank there as "Lolark Ghat."[3] The name "Lolark Ghat" has been forgotten, however, so that the river bank is now called Tulsi and Asi Ghat instead, for two other landmarks: the temple dedicated to the poet saint Tulsidas (situated just a stone's throw away from Lolark Kund) and the Asi River some distance further south.

The ancient *Panchatirtha* pilgrimage of Banaras, the journey between the "five tirthas," is first mentioned in the *Matsya Purana* as Dashashvamedha, Lolarka, Keshava, Bindu Madhava, and Manikarnika (Agrawala, 1963:283). In the *Kashi Khand*, this list of the five sites is Asi, Dashashvamedha, Adi Keshava, Pancha(ganga), and Manikarnika, but Asi is understood elsewhere in the text as Lolark Sangam. Today, Panchatirtha pilgrims are advised in pilgrimage guidebooks to visit Lolark while stopping at Asi, but they rarely bother to climb up the riverbank to honor Lolark at the *pakka* (brick) complex in which his worship is now contained. Instead, the Panchatirtha pilgrims worship Shiva *lingams* (phallic symbols) conveniently established there which are extolled as Asisangameshvara, "Lord of the Asi Sangam."[4] In the temple of Asisangameshvara at Asi Ghat is a marble plaque on which are inscribed verses "establishing the *puranic* heritage of the site"; one of these is the *KKh* verse "All the other *tirthas* that girdle the earth are not equal to a sixteenth part of the *tirtha* at Asi *sangam*" (Eck's translation, 1982:222). The preceding verse of the *KKh*, however, states specifically that "of all the *tirthas* of Kashi, Lolarka is primemost; its waters flow forth thence to all other *tirthas* [of Kashi]." No mention is made of Shiva in this passage, and the chapter explains that the water is purifying because Surya-Lolark "burns up" all evils. The Asisangameshvara Temple's marble placque omits the prior passages which clarify that bathing at the sangam draws on the power of Lolark, not Shiva.

Like many Vedic gods, although Surya reappears in puranic lore, he no longer remains central: "it is as if they have been demoted in favor of the famous Hindu 'triad' of Brahma the creator, Vishnu the preserver, and Shiva the destroyer" (Dimmitt and van Buitenen, 1978:9).

This demotion is effected in one of two ways: either by appropriating the mythology of Surya (and Agni) or by portraying puranic deities, especially Shiva, as conqueror and Lord of the Sun.

The lion's share of worship performed at Lolark Kund today is devoted to Lolarkeshvara, the "Lord of Lolark." This does not mean that worship of Lolark has been totally removed, however; like solar mythology, it is almost as if he has been fused with, and, for some devotees, confused with, Shiva into a hazy Lolark Baba. Many rural informants explain that they worship Lolark Baba, but are puzzled as to his precise identity: is he Surya or Shiva? And although theoretically Lolark Chath or "Lolark's sixth-day" is the aditya's festival, the fertility rituals revolve first around the lingam, and then bathing in the solar pond. It is possible that Lolark's worship at Lolark Kund has been associated with Shaiva lingam worship for centuries.

The mythological fusion of Shiva and Surya-Lolark does not represent a startling departure from worship patterns elsewhere in north India. The melding of Shiva's myths with the fire-solar deities is well known, as established by O'Flaherty; indeed, some texts identify Shiva-Rudra with Agni directly (O'Flaherty, 1973:104). In the *Shiva Purana* Shiva's identity is fused with Surya even as he is simultaneously declared the sun's lord: At the request of Brahma, Shiva causes the excess energy wrought by his *tapasya* ("heated" self-discipline) to enter the sun since he is "lord over the sun," and he allows Brahma and all the other immortals to live together in the energy of the sun. At the end of the eon, Shiva agrees to "take the form of the sun and burn this universe." Saying that "there is no good for this linga except for the creation of progeny," Shiva breaks it off and his lingam casts its brilliance from the subterranean hells to the sky, so deep and so tall even the gods cannot discover its limits (O'Flaherty, 1978:140). Just as Agni appears in the sky, in the atmosphere, and on land, so Shiva becomes the great lustre in all realms.

In addition to gradually adopting or fusing with fire-solar motifs, some Shaivite myths portray a violent substitution of puranic worship of Shiva for Vedic sacrifice to Agni-Surya and a concomitant transmutation of sacrificial themes. Specific myths demote Lolark to Shiva. The *Vamana Purana* illustrates these trends perfectly, and apart from the *Kashi Khand*, it is the most commonly cited text by learned Lolark patrons and thus merits a deeper look.

In *Vamana* 3.40ff., Shiva must journey to Varanasi in order to expiate his sin of cutting off Brahma's head, which remains attached to Shiva's hand. While in Kashi, he follows Vishnu's advice to go to three particularly efficacious places there: first, the place of the "destroyer of all sins, the Lord Lola Ravi"; second, Dashashvamedha Ghat; and third, (Adi)-Keshava. Finally, he visits the pond which becomes known as Kapalamochana, the "site where the skull was freed" (3:40–51). Whereas here Shiva actually worships Surya at Lola Ravi's site, the very next chapter portrays Shiva battling the adityas, and just thirteen chapters later he casts the Sun to earth and makes him "tremble" with his fiery glances.

When Shiva is refused his share in Daksha's sacrifice because of his status as *kapalin* ("one who carries a skull" [of Brahma]), his wife Sati commits suicide (*Vamana* chapters 4, 5). "Lustrous rays" then emerge from the enraged Shankara that become lion-faced *ganas* or "troops." Vishnu realizes he is outmatched and quickly withdraws, as do most of the other puranic gods, and the group of terrible ones called the Rudras merge into Shankara. Shankara's enemies are those that dare to remain: the gods of "light" and the Vedic sacrifice.[5] In particular, two forms of the Sun, or Bhaskara, namely, the adityas named Pushan ("nourisher") and Bhaga ("dispenser of wealth"), battle with Shiva. Pushan and Bhaga both try to overpower him with their fire but fail. Shankara scatters Pushan's teeth and twirls the hapless Sun round and round "in the same manner as a lion does the young one of a deer," sending the "effulgent Sun" himself senseless to the ground; he then turns to Bhaga and strikes his eyes to the earth.

Shankara reduces all remaining enemies to ashes with the fiery glances of his three eyes, and with an arrow he pursues the sacrificial fire,[6] who had assumed the divine form of a deer and leapt into the sky. Shiva benevolently spreads himself over the sky as the celestial bodies, and piercing the sacrifice with his arrows pins it in the sky. Of the constellations Shiva creates, Capricorn is known as the "deer-faced one" or Margashirsha, and it "moves over rivers and resides in oceans" (*Vamana* 5.57). Thus, Shiva is now the very source of all light and fire, and it is he who must be appeased through worship. The Vedic fire sacrifice is subjugated and relegated to the waters. The ancient mythological strands of astral symbolism, dismemberment, and the distribution of the seed into various life forms and the waters come together in the Shaiva-aditya myths (see O'Flaherty, 1978:29, passim).

In an earlier multiform of this myth from the *Shatapatha Brahmana*, Rudra pierces the animated sacrifice which becomes the constellation Margashirsha, but what breaks Pushan's teeth and blinds Bhaga's eyes is the fiery seed of Prajapati, understood to be an oblation into the fire-sun-sacrifice. Only the Sun Savitar can successfully accept the seed (O'Flaherty, 1973:116). We see in the *Vamana*, however, that Shiva takes the place of the scorching oblation and destroyer of the adityas, and in this variant, not even the Sun can consume the offering and survive the conflagration Shiva creates.

Returning again to the *Vamana Purana*, after describing the famous stories of Kama's incineration by Shiva and the ascetic god's fiery lingam, six chapters detail how and why Shiva cast the Sun down to Banaras at the Asi sangam. This myth is known by many educated devotees:

> Sukeshi was the son of demon king Vidyutkeshin. Shiva blessed the infant with the boon that he could neither be conquered nor slain by his enemies, and gave him an aerial city. Sukeshi, devoted to Lord Shiva, sought out sages to teach him *dharma* (religious duty) and righteous rule (chapters 11–15). One of the last lessons he learned was that "he incurs the wrath of Surya who forsakes the duties of his *varna* and stage of life." Under the tutelage of their devout king, the demons became very righteous and holy, clearly out of keeping with their expected behavior, and the glory of their aerial city grew to outshine the sun, moon, and planets. Surya, realizing that they had abandoned their own dharma and furious that their city rivaled his brilliance, burned the demon city with a scorching glance, sending it reeling from the sky. Sukeshi revered Shiva, and the celestial bards called out to Shiva that his devotee was falling. Shiva retaliated with a single stare at Surya, proving that his fiery power was more brilliant than that of even the Sun, the "Lord of the Gods." As Surya spiraled from the Solar region into the atmosphere, hermits on Earth called out, "If you wish to be saved, fall in the land holy to Hari [Varanasi]." The Sun landed between the Varuna and Asi rivers. Burning from Shiva's glance, the "restless sun" or *lulad ravi*, dipped first in the Asi, then in the Varuna, and "restless [*lulam*] by the affliction caused by the fire of the eyes of Shiva," he again splashed in the fords of Asi and Varuna. The gods, led by Brahma, appealed to Shiva on the Sun's behalf. Appeased by their worship, Lord Shiva left Mandara and came to Banaras, named the Sun "Lola," and put Lola in his own celestial chariot to return him to the sky. Brahma returned Sukeshi and his city of Rakshasas to the sky.

Lolark (from *lola*, "restless, trembling" and *arka*, "ray, sun god") is so named for he was made restless from the heat of Shiva's angry eyes. According to this myth, not only is the ancient Vedic deity Surya literally "put in his place" by the puranic god Shiva, but his efforts as preserver of *varna-ashrama-dharma* (duty defined by caste and stage of life) behavior are overruled. Although Surya was attempting to restore

natural (the days and nights) and caste-dharmic order, as in the majority
of puranic lore, Shiva holds devotion and a new morality independent
of caste to be a higher priority than fulfilling caste dharma. Finally, even
the rays of the Sun are dim in comparison to the brilliance of Shiva;
Kashi, the "City of Light," is so not because of the Sun, but because
of Shiva.

The *Vamana Purana* neatly demonstrates the progressive over-
shadowing of Surya by Shiva: 3.40ff. preserves the ancient preeminence
of Surya worship as Lola Ravi in Banaras even as its later chapters
portray Shiva's step-by-step domination of the solar deities and the
assumption of their realms of rule.

Kashi Khand 46 presents another widely known myth that explores
the complicated (inter)relationship of Shiva and Surya-Lolark, and it
offers an alternate explanation of Lolark's name and Shiva's place in
Banaras. Shiva wished to draw the excellent Buddhist king Divodasa
of Banaras away from the path of righteousness in order to capture
Kashi. He sent various groups to accomplish this task, including Surya.
Whereas in the *Vamana Purana* Sukeshi myth Lolark acts against the
(righteous) demons and is subsequently punished by their lord Shiva,
in the *KKh*, Lolark successfully avoids helping Shiva's endeavor to
encourage unrighteousness and remains unpunished because of the
protection afforded by the sacred city. We summarize:

After many attempts in various guises, the Sun realized it was
impossible to tempt the king. Surya abandoned the idea of
returning to Shiva's abode for fear of Shiva's anger, and instead
decided to take the ashrama of *kshetra sannyasa* in Varanasi (to
remain forever as a devotee in Kashi's sacred territory). Surya came
to be known as "Lolark," for when he saw the beauty of Kashi,
his mind became tremulous or desirous (*lola*). Surya-Lolark then
divided himself into the twelve adityas, the first of which is named
Lolark. Lolark constantly looks after the welfare of all Kashi
inhabitants, protecting the purity of the tirthas of Kashi, and the
reader is urged to bathe at Lolark Sangam at various times,
including the special day of the sixth or seventh of Margashirsha
when it falls on Sunday.

Here, in this *mahatmya* or eulogy of the sacred city, a power greater
than Shiva himself makes the sun tremble: the lovely Kashi. This
effulgent goddess protects all who live in her sacred grounds, and
Lolark, in turn, devotedly protects her purity.

Lolark Kund Today

Many still do worship Lolark as the Sun (Ravi) at the kund, especially on Ravivar (Sunday) and specific solar holidays. Many more worship both Lolark and Shiva together. But today, particularly popular folk rituals at the kund involve Shiva specifically; not only does bathing at Lolark Kund purify devotees from sin and disease, but devotees believe that the "Lord of Lolark," or Lolarkeshvara Shiva, graciously condescends to "marry" and beget children on his barren female *bhaktas* (devotees) from the fiery seed he spills into the waters there.

During the yearly Lolark Chath Mela or "Lolark Sixth-day Festival," the ancient popularity and nonBrahminical fertility practices of this site are reaffirmed by tens of thousands of villagers (Illus. 8.1). The *pandas* (Brahmin pilgrimage priests) at Lolark observe but do not participate in several of the most common rituals performed there for fertility and good health: "marriage" to Shiva and *totaka*, a kind of simple magic for protection and exorcism that involves the piercing of fruits and vegetables believed to embody one's enemies or problems. Eck asserts, "Its brahminical heritage aside, it is likely that Lolarka has an even longer history as a pilgrimage center for the non-brahminical folk tradition" (1982:177).

A Brief Tour of Lolark Kund

Lolark Kund is a deep pond surrounded by *pakka* or cemented walls of buff sandstone. Its rectangular shape measures thirty-nine feet from north to south and nineteen feet from east to west. Three long staircases descend into the kund on the west, north, and south. After thirty-five deep steps the walls of the kund begin. The east side is a wall which is bifurcated by a wide cut that allows water to flow from the kund into an adjacent well to the east and eventually into the Ganges (Illus. 8.1, 8.2). In winter and spring, when the water level is at its lowest, one must descend at least another ten to twelve feet past the stairs to reach the water, which is normally sixty feet deep during the monsoon season.[7]

Etched into one of the kund's walls is an image of a wheel of the Sun's chariot. Priests and residents of the temple's neighborhood tell a tale that during a battle between the gods and the demons a wheel of the Sun's chariot broke off. The wheel fell to the earth at the temple's present location, and the well that was created by its impact was called Lolark Kund for its zig-zag (lola-trembling) path.

Judging strictly by the number of worship sites devoted to him, Ganesh, the elephant-headed son of Shiva, used to have a more

8.1

The enormous crowds of devotees at Lolark Kund during Lolark Chath Mela.

8.2

A view of Lolark Kund on a normal day without any pilgrims. The waters of the *kund* are connected to the adjacent well via the long split in the wall of the *kund* on the right side. This photo also provides an aerial view of the small temple to Surya and Ganesh which is inside the square building pictured on the lower left-hand side.

important role at Lolark than he does today. A huge statue of Ganesh sits leaning against the northwest corner wall of the kund. There is also a small Ganesh temple which leans over the wall of the well. Down by the water is a five- by ten-foot stone structure, inside which is a small shrine to Surya and Ganesh (Illus. 8.2, 8.3). Like the kund, this temple's length is twice its width. Informants living near the temple opine that this smaller Surya-Ganesh temple is the "original" structure dedicated to Lolark and possibly Arka Vinayaka. Ganesh's popularity may have been inspired not only by his being Shiva's son but also by the tradition of worshiping Ganesh in Banaras in the form of the fifty-six Vinayakas. Arka Vinayaka, clearly drawing his name from Arka, the Sun, is to be worshiped first of the fifty-six at the Ganga-Asi sangam (KKh 57.59). Arka Vinayaka's shrine overlooks the Ganges just a short distance due east of Lolark Kund today. But for the houses now crowded around, this famous site would be visible from Lolark Kund.

Inside the kund at water level is a black stone plate inscribed in both the Saraswat Bangla language and Sanskrit which describes the temple complex as the property of a king named Bhu Pati. It is dated "1760" in the shatabd calendar popular before the more common shaka dating. Many of the letters are broken, so most of the plate is undecipherable.

According to popular belief, the plate confirms folk stories of a visit by a king of Kuch Bihar who was healed of leprosy and built the stone walls of the kund.[8] Long ago this king came to Kashi to be cured,[9] and while passing through the vicinity he felt the need to defecate, so he sent a servant for water. As the king washed, he noticed that wherever the water touched his leprosy was healed. When the servant was questioned, he apologized for bringing such muddy water, for at that time the pond was still clay-sided, or kaccha. The king reassured him that he was thrilled, not angry, and the servant led him to Lolark Kund. When the king jumped in, his leprosy was cured instantly. He was so pleased he wanted to build walls of gold around the pool, but eventually he decided to build them of stone, and installed a gold plate to commemorate the miracle. Lolark officiants claim that this gold plate exists somewhere inside the main tank but has not been found yet. The creation of the stone structure transformed the undistinguished pool into a prominent kund and temple "owned" by a famous royal patron. On the top wall of the kund today, a marble inscription states simply, "Owner: Kuch Bihar State."

Ordinarily, after entering the kund from the west staircase, one bathes and exits from the southern side; the northern staircase is closed except during busy festivals. Pilgrims then proceed to the small

8.3

The temple to Surya and Ganesh from water level. This temple often serves as a platform on which the *panda* (pilgrimage priest) or *Karinda* (assistant) sits.

Lolarkeshvara Temple above the kund near the southern exit which shelters a large Shiva lingam (Illus. 8.4). Beside the Lolarkeshvara Temple is a huge pipal tree. Underneath or near the tree there may have been an earlier temple, for a large number of small ruins, including fragments of various icons, can be seen lying here and there. In 1990, a new concrete image of Lolark was installed at Lolark Kund by a wealthy Calcutta patron. The icon depicts the Sun in a splendid chariot drawn by six white horses, and it was established up above beside the pipal tree. There is generous open space on all four sides of the kund, allowing freedom of movement except during the busiest festival times, when even such space is insufficient for the thousands of pilgrims.

Up above the kund on the northeast corner near the well is an open-air pavilion which serves as a *dharmashala* (pilgrim shelter). Located next to the dharmashala is a flat platform on which sit one large and two small Shiva temples. Immediately adjacent to these is a shrine devoted to Mahishasuramardini, the goddess who is the "Destroyer of the Buffalo Demon." This temple has a religious life independent of Lolark Kund which includes a consistent calendar and pilgrimage route, many regular devotees, and a great number of pilgrims during the "nine night" or Navratra festivals dedicated to the Goddess in the fall and spring.

Lolark Kund has enjoyed royal patronage for at least nine centuries. Brass inscriptions (c. twelfth-century) attest to the patronage of the site by Jayachandra, the Gahadavala ruler of Kanyakubja (Mishra, 1973:36). He donated half a village to Lolark, and the other half to a number of Brahmins "who might have been attached to the worship of the deity" (Mishra, 1973:36). Kubernath Sukul writes that a king named Govind Chand made a pilgrimage to bathe in Lolark Kund, and then donated a village to the priests of the temple (Sukul, 1977). Bal Mukund Varma remarks that Lolark Kund was renovated by the famous Queen Ahalya Bai Holkar of Indore in the late eighteenth century.[10]

Since independence there are officially no longer kings or kingdoms in India. The Kuch Bihar royal family, which ostensibly owned Lolark Kund, tended to its landholdings through officials of the Kuch Bihar Trust. These officials used to visit the properties periodically and dispense monies for upkeep of religious sites, including Lolark Kund. For instance, the whitewashing of Lolark Kund and its temples was funded by this trust. Since independence, the trust has been replaced by Bengali government officials who manage landholdings absorbed by the state. Today, the former royalty of Kuch Bihar still patronize Lolark Kund, but as individuals rather than heads of state.

8.4

A couple offering *karahiya* (cooked food) to Lord Shiva at the Lolarkeshvara Temple with the help of a *panda* (priest).

After many years of absence, in 1988 the current "king" of "Kuch Bihar," Brij Narayan—now a resident of Great Britain—visited Banaras. While at Lolark Kund, he appointed a *pujari* (temple priest) to perform *arati* (lamp offering) for his and the general welfare at the Lolark Kund complex and adjacent Mahishasuramardini goddess temple. Although not actually a king of what is now no longer a kingdom or even a state, this British citizen undertakes strenuous efforts to continue his family's traditional patronage of Lolark Kund. His actions attest to the continuation of the Indian pattern of royal patronage of Banaras religious sites. Although today royal patronage in Banaras is perhaps most poignantly demonstrated by the Banaras king's role in the Ramnagar *Ramlila*, those dispossessed kings from other parts of India who can afford to do so also support religious activities in Banaras. And in a general sense, the Kuch Bihar king's actions underscore the continuation of personal loyalty to sacred place in Banaras year after year, whether the kings live in India or abroad.

The Ritual Life of Lolark Kund

Like many major temple complexes in Banaras, Lolark Kund employs a range of religious practitioners and a well-developed network of commercial relationships.[11] There are three main ritual activities and thus arenas of commercial activity, and each of these is dominated by a particular group of officiants. The Brahmin *panda* (pilgrimage priest) oversees rituals in the Lolarkeshvara Temple and orthodox bathing in the kund. Pandas at Lolark employ *karindas* (Brahmin assistants) who perform the rituals there for them on a percentage basis. *Bhaddars* are lower-ranked Brahmin functionaries who are hired by the pandas only during busy times. The *nau* (barber) performs ritual tonsure or *mundan* of children. Peculiar to Lolark is the function of the *mallah* (boatperson) who cleans the kund and aids in folk fertility rituals in the waters.

At many, but not all, Hindu temples, the pandas who work there retain documents or seals presented to their ancestors by kings or local powers which grant their family the exclusive right to oversee religious services at a particular location. Pandas often have ledgers which list gifts of land as well, the proceeds of which maintain the temple and support the panda family. It is common to maintain lists of their most wealthy pilgrim patrons. Although Lolark Kund has received patronage by many important individuals in the past, as is proven by inscriptions and other documents, the panda family in control at Lolark today have no documents or seals that support their claims to that control. Bhavani Shankar Pandey, a member of the family of Raja Pandas (king of pandas) currently in charge of Lolark Kund, was unable to explain any details about the management of the temple at all before 1949.[12] He said his family does own the hereditary rights to oversee worship at Lolark and that these rights were donated to them by royal authority, but he was unable to recount anything about when, how, by whom, or to whom the rights were given; nor could his elder relatives. Pandey explained that there was no tradition at the kund of keeping written accounts of patronage, but having heard the stories about a king of Kuch Bihar building the pakka walls at Lolark, he surmised that it must have been this king who appointed someone in his family's past at some time long ago.[13]

A possible explanation for the family's inability to explain Lolark's economic history is that, except on the major holidays, Lolark Kund did not draw enough clients during earlier years to justify close attention. The recent recovery of the temple to a more prominent status after a break in popularity is supported by testimony of workers at Lolark Kund and the recent appointment of a family member to manage the temple site directly.

On most days, activities of patrons at Lolark Kund are overseen by karindas appointed by the Raja Panda family. The karindas are addressed by pilgrims as "panda," which is often used loosely to refer to any Brahmin officiant associated with a pilgrimage site, but in actuality there are many gradations of religious functionaries in terms of rank and status. The first karinda that can be recalled by our informants was Ram Prasad, who was appointed in either 1949 or 1950. When he passed away in 1960, his wife, popularly known simply as Pandayin (panda's wife) took over. It is not uncommon for a Brahmin woman whose panda husband dies to assume his duties as pandayin. Ram Prasad and later Pandayin paid the Pandeys a lump sum for rent, beginning at Rs. 10 and gradually increasing over the years to Rs. 36 per annum, and they surrendered 80 percent of the *dakshina* or gifts received from Lolark patrons.

Arguments over money are not uncommon between pandas and karindas. Pandey said they experienced problems with Pandayin—that is, she was deceiving the pandas about how much dakshina she earned, cheating pilgrims, and getting into arguments with residents dwelling close to Lolark Kund—so in 1963 his family fired her and appointed another karinda instead and fixed a modest monthly rent in addition to the percentage claims. From 1963 to 1983, five different karindas worked at Lolark Kund with little supervision by the Raja Pandas. In 1983, however, a prominent member of the Pandey family, Bhim Chandi Pandey, popularly known as Chahange Maharaj, or "the great six-fingered one," came to Lolark Kund to oversee worship directly, retaining then head karinda Vijay Kumar Mishra. Chahange Maharaj manages all the places of the Raja Panda family, including the Shitala Devi Temple. In 1987, Madan Dube began assisting Mishra (Illus. 8.5).

The number of people coming to worship at the site is increasing. For a short time before Chahange Maharaj's overseeing of duties at Lolark Kund in 1983, representatives of the panda family came in person only on the day of the great Chath Mela and other major festivals. They collected the total proceeds for that day, and in turn left the income from the other days to the karinda. According to Chahange Maharaj, the family was too preoccupied with their panda business at the Shitala Temple to be concerned with the "off-days" at Lolark. Now that business is picking up at Lolark and the Pandeys have more male family members to employ, they are motivated to oversee their properties more directly.

The average offering of ordinary devotees has risen considerably as well, and since more urbanites are coming to Lolark Kund, the site generates more income. The majority of devotees who come on special days, such as the sixth and eleventh days of the month, lunar eclipses, Sunday, and the great festivals of Lalahi Chath and Lolark Chath, are rural peoples. On these special days, the panda family keeps the whole income of Lolark Kund, merely paying the karindas a nominal sum or small percentage for their labor. Most urban devotees, however, prefer to come on ordinary days when the crowds are light. Urbanites offer cash rather than the grain or vegetables commonly given by the rural devotees. Since cash requires no middleman, it is more lucrative and easier to divide, so both pandas and karindas prefer their new urban customers.

Although the most famous local story of Lolark Kund's power is the healing of the king of Kuch Bihar, and the *KKh* specifically promises release from sin, the most frequent visitors to Lolark Kund are couples who wish to have children. When a couple arrives, they are usually first received by the mallah, who asks them what ritual services they require. If they want to bathe, the mallah inquires whether they have the requisite materials, and if not, provides them with the necessary fruits, vegetables, and so forth. Then, the panda, the karinda, or sometimes even the mallah briefly interviews the couple to determine their fertility problem. This may be an inability to conceive, continued miscarriages, or the failure of their progeny to thrive, each requiring different remedies. At this point, there is usually some bargaining between the pilgrim and the panda, who normally asks for Rs. 21, but he will usually accept as little as Rs. 5 for his participation, so it always pays to bargain.

8.5

Karindas (assistants) Madan Dube and Vijay Kumar Mishra waiting for customers on a normal day beneath the pipal tree. In the background, devotees prepare *karahiya* (cooked food).

The panda or karinda states the *sankalpa,* or ritual declaration of one's intention, chants appropriate mantras, requests Shiva to help the couple, and guides "normal" bathing done by both the man and wife. The couple bathe with their clothing tied together. (This also occurs when the couple "tie the knot" ritually during the Hindu marriage ceremony.) They release fleshy fruits and vegetables into the kund, then change their clothing and exit. The pair must leave behind their old clothes and the vegetables in the water. After the couple perform *pradakshina,* or circumambulating the Lolarkeshvara Shiva Temple, the panda gives final instructions to them, including common advice to women to omit salt and drink more milk, or men not to shave. The mallah then appears and asks for money for the fruits or vegetables provided and any auspicious gifts the pilgrim may agree to surrender. After the couple depart, the mallah removes the fruit and discarded clothing from the kund.

In addition to this quasi-Brahminical bathing practice, there are several folk traditions peculiar to religious life at Lolark Kund. For example, often the couple are accompanied or advised earlier by a village pandit, rural friend, or elder, who tells them to perform totaka. Totaka is a form of both curative and preventive magic. By inserting needles into the vegetables which represent the malevolent spirits that afflict them, the pilgrims remove their problems and believe they are then able to have children. The popularity of this folk tradition (observed by, but not involving, the Brahmin panda) is proven by the fact that the standard "package" sold by the mallahs includes needles for the practice.

Three mallahs preside over the waters of the kund and take turns tending to the nonbrahminical worship needs of Lolark pilgrims. As with mundan, Brahmin pandas are restricted by rules of caste purity from performing ritual functions at Lolark that are deemed "polluting." One of these rituals involves donning new clothing after bathing and discarding their used clothing inside the waters. The mallahs do not just clean the kund; they clean up financially. It is customary for pilgrims to place "secret" coin offerings inside the vegetables and fruits, which are carefully retrieved by the mallah. Mallahs sell the clothing, fruits, and vegetables left over from the fertility rituals (Illus. 8.6). According to a local cloth dealer who purchases some of the used saris from the mallahs, between thirty to forty thousand saris are left at Lolark Kund every year on the day of the great festival, and he alone bought Rs. 40,000 worth.

Hijras also purchase some of the used saris to resell. Hijras dress in saris and are often claimed to be hermaphrodites. They live and travel

8.6

Fruit and vegetable offerings being removed from Lolark Kund by the *Mallah* (boatperson) after the festival.

with each other and have close connections with birth rituals. In the Banaras region, hijras often support themselves primarily through musical performances of *sohar*, songs sung by women at the birth of a son, and they go "to the homes of newborn sons without being called, and are paid for their services in part because the groups will broadcast the family's stinginess in song to all neighbors and passers-by if they are not compensated as they see fit" (Henry, 1988:64). They claim to make excellent profits from reselling the Lolark saris. Thus, the bathing practices at Lolark generate enormous profits for a diverse commercial network.

All three of the mallahs who work at Lolark Kund are relatives of the former mallah, Banarsi Ram, who died without a child. Banarsi Ram's grandfather Budhu was supposably appointed to clean the pool by the king of Kuch Bihar State. After his death, Banarsi Ram's ownership of the right to remove foodstuffs and cloth from the kund was divided between his siblings' children, one niece and two nephews. His niece Sukhdeyi Devi owns the rights to work for two consecutive years. Her cousins Hira Lal and Panna Lal share their parents' inheritance, and so each works at the kund for one year apiece. Sukhdeyi Devi is financially secure even during her "off-years" because her husband is employed, and in 1988 she established a permanent *prasad* (food offerings to gods) shop at Lolark Kund from which she earns money by selling ritual offerings during Hira Lal and Panna Lal's years of tenure. In contrast, 75 percent of their time Hira Lal and Panna Lal must earn money by practicing their traditional caste craft: fishing and ferrying persons around the ghats.

In addition to reselling leftover foodstuffs, for several decades the mallahs have monopolized the right to sell the fruit and vegetables used in the rituals to pilgrims. Popular purchases include several varieties of squash, pumpkins, and wood apples, all round fleshy items, "signifying perhaps, the fertility for which [the devotee] hopes" (Eck, 1982:179). The yearly income from food sales alone is Rs. 8,000 to 10,000. An open market prevails during the Lolark Chath festival: only at that time may pilgrims bring their own offerings or purchase them from the many shops that mushroom temporarily near the entrance of the cobblestone lane off Asi Road leading to Lolark Kund.

The fruits and vegetables are often sold in "packages" which also contain a red piece of cloth, five red bangles, some needles for totaka, a little mirror and comb, and the red powder called *sindur*, which is used by women to line the part of their hair and indicates that she is married. Sukhdeyi Devi, the major mallah since Banarsi Ram's death, would not comment on the significance of these ritual objects, saying only that pilgrims requested the items so they provided them. Some pilgrims, however, responded that various *pandits* and "wise older women" who had come to Lolark Kund previously had recommended using these items in the popular folk traditions of totaka and marrying Lord Shiva or simply "Lolark Baba." The cloth, bangles, and sindur are necessary for "marrying" Lolark Baba to ensure progeny.

Clearly the most provocative folk tradition unsupported by pandas or ritual texts is this "marriage" of female devotees to the deity. Although no woman would discuss her "marriage" personally, an elderly woman who knew about folk advice given to infertile women agreed to a brief whispered interview. Kalavati Devi explained that women bathe in the kund, change their clothing, and then remove their bangles and all other symbols of marriage to their husbands. They then enter the Lolarkeshvara Shiva Temple in front of the kund and hug the Shiva lingam there five times. They don the red bangles, and return to the tank. After breaking these bangles, they toss them into the kund. By doing so, these women "marry" Lolark Baba and become fertile through dipping in the kund.

Pandas, mallahs, barbers, and shopkeepers all admit that the practice of "marrying" the deity is common, but they refuse to speculate on its ritual validity. Pandas are quick to emphasize that they do not participate actively in this uncondoned process. Wearing bangles is an accepted cultural symbol indicating a woman's marital status and is observed by females of all manners of castes and sects in India, including many Muslims. After bathing in the water, numerous women who wish to "marry" the deity can be seen openly breaking their bangles on the side of the kund, entering the Lolarkeshvara Temple, and hugging the Shiva lingam there five times (Illus. 8.7). When they bathe, they do so alone without their husbands. Breaking their bangles suggests that they symbolically divorce or at least separate from their husbands just before hugging and thereby "marrying" Shiva. After they leave behind their red glass bangles worn after the "marriage," they purchase a second set of bangles from the numerous impromptu bangle shops on Asi Lane and become respectably "married" once again to their human husbands.

Much can be said of this marriage ritual. There may be some variance in how the women interpret the events, although this was impossible to confirm since they were reluctant to discuss this secret rite. We will turn again to an analysis of this fascinating practice in some detail later.

In addition to those who seek offspring, many couples come to Lolark Kund to thank Shiva for giving them a child. Such pilgrims

8.7 Women breaking each other's bangles at Lolark Kund in preparation for their marriage to Lolarkeshvara.

usually have performed rituals earlier for offspring, and at that time vow to return to Lolark Kund to give thanks and often to perform mundan, the ritual tonsure of small children. Both thanksgiving festivals (*badhaeeya*) and mundan are popular rituals at Lolark Kund (Illus. 8.8).

There are approximately 200 to 250 thanksgiving or badhaeeya ceremonies during the year, and they are becoming increasingly popular among local Banarsis, for whom they are not a tradition. These rituals are not uniform; depending on the family tradition and economic status of the pilgrim, they may vary significantly. The more elaborate badhaeeya rites, for example, often feature hired bands and dancing hijras, whereas poor devotees may offer only simple prayers inside the temple in thanksgiving. While giving thanks, some patrons choose to perform mundan as well.

It is common to offer first *karahiya*, or food cooked in a large clay pot at the dharmashala above the kund, when performing mundan of one's child. Usually, if karahiya is offered the panda asks for Brahmin *bhoja*, or the money for a Brahmin's meal. Another common offering to the deity is a yellow waist cloth called a *piyari*. If a piyari is offered, pandas ask for the piyari or money equal to its value.

Three *nau* families work at Lolark Kund. Certain customs keep the economic position of these barbers fairly low. The panda or karinda must be given his dakshina before the barber is allowed to bring the Ganges water from the fecundating kund used to wet the child's scalp. The barber is expected to help ensure that the pilgrims give an appropriate sum to the Brahmin priest before bargaining for his own payment, and pilgrims sometimes come to resent the barber in the process. Whereas the barber helps the panda or karinda to secure a good amount, the latter do not help barbers. After deciding on a sum for the shaving, the barber completes the rite and sends the family back to the Shiva temple for the child to be blessed by the panda and to take *darshan* (viewing) of the deity. Although a pilgrim may not bring his own priest to perform religious practices at Lolark Kund, he is allowed to bring his own barber. The fact of there being three barber families—a large number for such a small temple complex—also increases internal competition.[14] Thus, even though barbers do not have to give any percentage of their income to the panda or anyone else, they earn only a modest amount. During the Lolark Chath Mela, when many mundans take place, approximately one to two hundred barbers come to work, for on that day Lolark Kund becomes an "open market." Still, because of the great demand for their services by thousands of pilgrims, the Lolark barbers acknowledge that they all earn a great deal on that day (approximately Rs. 200 to 250 each). Finally, one barber said

8.8

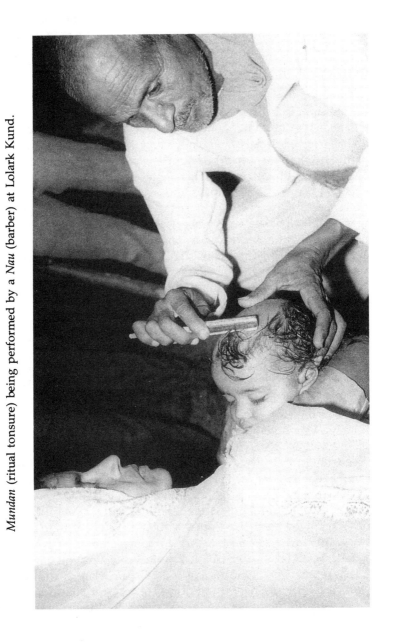

Mundan (ritual tonsure) being performed by a *Nau* (barber) at Lolark Kund.

that when some families come to Lolark Kund for fertility and are successful, they return only to give thanks and do not perform the child's mundan at Lolark, choosing instead to have tonsure performed closer to home.

Festivals at Lolark: Lalahi and Lolark Chath Melas

There are many pilgrimage traditions in and outside of Banaras which temporarily render an obscure site the focus of widespread and fervent religious devotion for one day of the Hindu religious year. Lolark Kund has such a special day: Lolark Chath Mela, or the festival (*mela*) occurring on the sixth (*chath*) day of the waxing fortnight of the sixth Hindu month of Bhadrapad (August/September). However, the site also attracts large crowds on Sundays and every eleventh day or *ekadashi* of the lunar month, which are sacred to the sun god; the sixth day of Margashirsha (November/December), which is specifically tied to the aditya Lolark in the *Kashi Khand*; and the fascinating festival called Lalahi Chath. Lolark Kund consistently draws crowds on days when it is important for Hindus to bathe or to perform mundan. This brings the total number of miscellaneous important occasions to approximately twenty each year.

The sixth or seventh of Margashirsha, when it occurs on a Sunday, is said to be a particularly auspicious date to bathe at Lolark (*KKh* 46:50). People do bathe at Lolark on that date nowadays, but it does not attract the numbers as Lolark Chath Mela does in Bhadrapad. As stipulated in the *Kashi Khand*, the hundreds who come to bathe at Lolark Sangam at that time do so even today in the pursuit of *moksha* (release from the cycle of rebirths) and good health.

Lalahi Chath is the sixth day of the dark fortnight of the month of Bhadrapad, exactly two weeks before Lolark Chath. This festival is observed almost exclusively by women from eastern Uttar Pradesh, who fast on that day for long life and better health of their sons. Nearly three hundred women come to Lolark Kund on that day for worship. In ethnographic interviews, devotees offered a wide variety of answers when asked why they worshiped at Lolark Kund at that time. For instance, this fast was said by some to be devoted exclusively to the Sun, who is asked to nourish and protect devotees' offspring. This practice is reminiscent of the ancient Vedic Gayatri Mantra, and women's folk songs commonly record the Sun's concern for children (see, for example, Chandramani Singh, 1979:57–58). The rituals performed on that day require devotees to worship at a site connected with the Sun and at a tank or river where they may bathe in the protective lustrous waters. Because of its correlation both with the Sun and with the

Ganges, the waters of Lolark Kund draw numerous women seeking to protect their sons' health and promote their longevity. Others expressed confusion on "six-es": Lolark Chath is so famous as a "six" that protection of children on the sixth two weeks earlier naturally is associated with the famous local deity worshiped on the sixth of the next fortnight. Still others expressed this confusion: isn't "Lalahi Chath" the local tongue's name for Lolark's wife? In short, there was no consensus on why Lolark Chath draws so many bathers on that day.

Finally, this testimony aside, some of the women were aware that Lalahi Chath is best known to be the festival dedicated to Shashti Devi, who has a widespread and diverse cult of her own (Dhal, 1979:12). Worshiped on the sixth day (*shashti*) of the month or six days after the birth of a child, she is generally believed today to be a protectress of children. However, in early mythological cycles (and even today in some places), Shashti Devi is portrayed as a frightening goddess who preys on the young and therefore must be propitiated; like Shiva, euphemistically extolled as the "auspicious one," Shashti Devi is appealed to out of a sense of fear.

Shashti's name stems from her mythological origin: she is the goddess who is born out of "one-sixth" part of original nature, or *mulaprakriti*. Also known as Devasena, Shashti Devi is the daughter of Daksha, who protects children and always remains by their side. In the *Devi Bhagavata Purana*, for instance, after the goddess brings back to life the stillborn son of the sage Priyavrata and his wife Malini, Shashti declares that it is she who bestows and protects children.

This, of course, still does not answer the question of why this festival, held on the sixth day of the dark fortnight of the sixth month of the Hindu calendar and dedicated to the folk deity Shashti or "sixth one," is observed at Lolark Kund of all places. Although the devotees expressed some chagrin at the question, in fact this is not such a surprising or necessarily fortuitous development. It so happens that Shashti Devi is the wife of Skanda, who is believed to be the son of either Agni or Shiva. In *Vana Parva* 231 of the *Mahabharata*, Skanda marries Devasena/Shashti and declares that he will function as a spirit which kills children to feed to his six ravenous and bloodthirsty mothers. Immediately after proclaiming this, "a terrible person just like Agni emerged from his body and it was called Raudragraha, which is known also by other names such as Skandapasmara, Shakunigraha, Putanagraha, etc. This Graha is supposed to cause children's death" (Mani, 1984:748).

This prominent festival may thus have begun or persisted at Lolark Kund because of this Skanda connection, which has been forgotten or (con)fused with the Sun's traditional benevolent protection of children.

Water, Sun, Shiva, and Sons: The Skanda Connection at Lolark

The peculiar "marriage" dip in the fecundating kund by the women alone involves bathing naked in the kund (they must change clothing, enforced by the rule that they must leave behind their old sari), breaking their bangles, hugging the lingam, donning new bangles, and then leaving these trinkets behind in the kund. This fascinating practice calls to mind a cluster of myths which combine water, fire-lustre-sun, Shiva, and fertility.

The Skanda myth is especially interesting in its connections to ritual behavior at Lolark for a number of reasons. First, Lalahi Chath, the second most prominent mela at Lolark Kund, is the festival which celebrates Skanda's wife Shashti Devi's powers to protect children. The Shaiva connection of Lolark Kund and the bloodthirsty mythology of Skanda as this *Raudra graha*, namely, the planet descending from Rudra, and the traditionally benevolent and protective function of the sun make Lolark Kund a natural place to hold the Shashti festival. But perhaps more interesting, the Skanda myth cycle provides a means to understand how Shiva and the aditya Lolark could be so closely associated in the first place, and suggests a mythological rationale for the curious bathing and "marriage" practices at Lolark Kund.

Both Agni and Shiva are the father of Skanda, the conquerer of the demon Taraka. In a myth from the *Mahabharata*, Agni, having come "out from the orb of the sun," became "heated" with passion after looking at the "golden" wives of the sages, who "shone" "like rays of the oblation-devouring fire, like marvelous stars." Realizing his heated passions were improper, Agni went off into the forest to try to abandon his body. Meanwhile, Svaha, goddess of the sacrifice and daughter of Daksha, became desirous of Agni. Disguising herself in turn as six of the wives of the seven sages, she seduced him six times, throwing the seed of each union into a golden pot. From this "kindling" of Agni and Svaha, Skanda was born, who like his father Agni is capable of scorching his foes with fiery breaths (O'Flaherty, 1978:108–15).

In later Shaiva myth cycles which depict Shiva as Skanda's father, the ascetic god does not completely take over Agni's role. Although it is Shankara's seed which begets Skanda, this son is born only after Agni consumes the burning seed. Since Agni is the mouth of the gods, his consumption of the seed leads to their becoming "pregnant" as well. The deities can vomit out the seed, but Shiva tells Agni he will relieve his "burning" only if the fire god leaves the seed in the womb of some good woman. Narada advises Agni to place it in the bodies of those women who bathe at dawn in the month of summer; he sits near the water, six of the wives of the seven sages bathe, and when they approach Agni to warm themselves, all the tiny particles of Shiva's seed enter their bodies through their hair, and Agni is thus freed of his feverish burning. The six wives leave the seed in the form of an embryo on the Himalaya mountain, but the mountain cannot bear the heat and throws the seed into the Ganges; even the Ganges cannot bear the heat, so she throws the seed into a clump of reeds, where on the sixth lunar day in the bright half of the month when the moon is in the constellation of Margashirsha (November/December), the very day sacred to Lolark in the *Kashi Khand*, Skanda appears. In a multiform of this myth, it takes the seed of both Agni and Shiva to produce the child. Agni releases Shiva's seed to provide the birthplace of the mountain and forest of reeds, and then places his own fiery seed into the Ganges to produce the actual child Skanda (O'Flaherty, 1973:105).

The mythological connection of fire, water, and creation abounds in Hindu lore. The Shaiva myth cycle of the fiery seed in the Ganges resonates with an earlier myth cycle, namely, the dismembered Agni who hides in the waters and is distributed (O'Flaherty, 1978:101, 285). Shiva is "fire under water"; and when the flame from his third eye enters the Ocean at its confluence with the Ganges, it spawns the submarine mare, Jalandhara (O'Flaherty, 1973:287, passim). Indeed, in many myths, Shiva marries Ganga, who, unlike Parvati, is capable of bearing children (O'Flaherty, 1973:231–33). Heat is believed to be the cause of desire, sexual union, seed, and birth (O'Flaherty, 1973:90). In south Indian mythology, bathing after menstruation is believed to be a common method of impregnation, and some believed that menstruous women had to be protected from the Sun lest they be impregnated by his rays (O'Flaherty, 1973:100). Bathing itself is widely believed to be a method of impregnation; the sages' wives become pregnant with Rudra's seed by bathing in the Ganges or by warming themselves by the fire after bathing (O'Flaherty, 1973:276–77).

Like the wives of the sages who are impregnated by dipping in the fecundative waters, those women today who bathe alone are still "married" to their husbands when first bathing at the site. Knowing and hoping that immersion at this fire-water site may impregnate them, these ordinary wives bathe, then choose to "marry" Shiva as well, returning to the kund to leave behind their symbols of marriage to the ever fertile ascetic god. Their actions resonate with the mythological cycle that combines the seeds of Agni and Shiva to impregnate the wives of the sages. Those who seek less divine intercession bathe literally tied to their husbands, an unsubtle reminder to the divine of exactly to whom this woman belongs.

Bathing at Shiva-Ganges sites to cure infertility is not unique to Lolark Kund. Saraswati reports that at Baidyanath Dhama, the site of the *manokamanalingam*, or *"lingam* which dispenses all desires," "the woman desirous of an offspring takes a bath in the Shiva-Ganga tank, usually with her husband, and then they lie down on the verandah performing a fast for three days and three nights" (1983:29–30). One can speculate that couples enter the water together for the purpose of rejuvenating the husband or their conjugal relations. Immersion in water is a direct link with the themes of conception and rejuvenation, and the knot linking the clothes of the married couple is a tangible metaphor for sexual union; recall the healing of the impotent elderly sage Chyavana cured by bathing with his young faithful wife (O'Flaherty, 1973:61–62).

Perhaps it is not mere coincidence that it is on the very day of Skanda's birth whenever it falls on Ravi's or the Sun's day, an astrological conjunction which fuses the Agni-Shiva-Surya cycles, that *Kashi Khand* 46:50 advises one to bathe at Lolark Sangam. Skanda appears to conquer Taraka, the demon threatening world order; bathing at Lolark on that date is said to achieve similarly lofty purposes: moksha and release from sin and disease. But people also wish for worldly prosperity, including fertility. And although the *Kashi Khand* is silent about the more popular Lolark Chath Mela, if Shiva and Surya-Agni can produce the glorious Skanda in such a fashion by impregnating the unsuspecting bathing beauties, then surely they can similarly bless their barren devotees who consciously seek but a momentary dalliance in the Ganges tank with the kindly (and ever fertile) Divine. Thus, on the sixth day of the bright half of the sixth month, these hopeful devotees imitate in ritual the "six-faced" Skanda's miraculous origin.

Lolark Chath Mela: Tradition and Change

When patrons were asked why bathing during the Lolark Chath Mela was so important and efficacious, the most common response was that bathing there yields a special effect by virtue of the power in the water combined with the auspiciousness of the day. The next most common reply was simply that it was "traditional" for their family to bathe at Lolark Kund on this day, and patrons pointed to the long-standing prominence of this festival primarily among rural devotees. More urban devotees are coming to Lolark Kund, however, both on Lolark Chath and other auspicious dates, as well as on ordinary days. In part this represents general demographic shifts in India; descendants of Lolark Kund devotees continue family tradition after they move from their native villages into the city. Many other urbanites are coming, however, whose families did not traditionally come to Lolark Kund.

The famous Banarsi astrologer Narayan Sharma explains that the power of Lolark Kund on the sixth day of Bhadrapad stems from a unique configuration of planets. On this day, there is a conjunction of three auspicious astrological events. The day occurs on the sixth or seventh; on a Saturday, Tuesday, or Sunday; and during the *purvabhadrapad nakshatra*, or constellation of the Bhadra month. When this configuration of the sun, moon, and planets occurs, it constitutes what is called a *Tripushkar yoga*. This makes Lolark Chath astrologically three times more effective than an ordinary day in yielding a result for bathers at the temple.

The performance of rituals varies greatly during the festival. The normal officiants cannot supervise the enormous crowd, so patrons can purchase ritual needs elsewhere, contract outside pandas or bhaddars,[15] omit certain practices, offer whatever sum they wish to the priests or barbers without much protest, and even perform the bath on their own. Pandas explain that bathing without supervision is the most dangerous alteration, for they believe priests must intervene on the pilgrims' behalf to conduct the sankalpa, or ritual intention, properly. The only strictly enforced practice during the Lolark Chath Mela is leaving one's old clothing behind after bathing.

There are a number of significant changes in the Lolark Chath Mela which contribute to greater economic opportunities for Lolark functionaries and more convenience for pilgrims. For instance, the festival no longer begins precisely at a time reckoned by knowledgeable astrologers and lasting for a single twenty-four-hour period, which caused a great deal of commotion and difficulty for the huge crowds. Since 1987 the event has unofficially become a two-day affair, beginning on the fifth of Bhadrapad and extending into the seventh. In addition, several temporary icons have come to be installed at the site during the festival to disperse the crowds and to provide other income opportunities. Since 1985, the Pandeys have placed a four-faced brass cover over a small Shiva lingam established on the eastern side of the tank up above by the well and have identified it as "Lolark Baba," claiming that worship of it is as effective as worship of the usual Lolarkeshvara lingam (see Illus. 8.9). Similarly, in 1987 pandas began the practice of placing a female deity's mask on the pipal tree near the Shiva temple, calling it "Lolark Mayee," or "Mother Lolark"[16] (see Illus. 8.10).

Pandas admit that the people who make offerings to the new icons are generally uneducated rural people who have come for the first time and are unfamiliar with Lolark Kund, but they insist that by giving the pilgrims more places to worship they are actually assisting them. At

8.9

The brass bust of Shiva placed over a *lingam* (phallic symbol) on top of the well adjacent to Lolark Kund.

8.10

Image of Lolark Mayee on the pipal tree several feet from the Lolarkeshvara Temple surrounded by crowds of devotees.

the very least, the crowd is decentralized, making the festival more pleasant for everyone. When asked how he could justify pilgrims worshiping the new Lolark Baba rather than the more ancient one, one panda said that from the religious point of view all of the Lolark Kund area is invested with power and is the place of Shiva: "Brother, no matter what practice one performs or where one performs it, if it is close to the site its benefit goes directly to the deity, and in Kashi, each and every piece of stone is Shiva himself." The orthodox belief that every pebble in Kashi is a Shiva lingam is no doubt a pervasive one, and the incentive to add new icons in Kashi where Shiva may be worshiped is indubitably powerful as well.

As mentioned earlier, an eleventh-century statue of the sun goddess Chakreshvari was found at Lolark Kund (Eck, 1982:180). An epithet of Bhairava-Shiva is Chakreshvara, and the goddess Chakreshvari may be interpreted to be his consort. Chahangey Maharaj explained that since all male deities are associated with a female half or *shakti*, it is appropriate that they have installed an icon of Parvati, Shiva's wife. Further, he added that "women from the rural areas are more attracted to female deities than male deities," a fact affirmed by their singing *mata git*, folk songs to the Mother Goddess, at Lolark Kund; Lolark Mayee's establishment has been embraced enthusiastically. Thus, although once again the placement of Lolark Mayee may appear to the skeptical as a clever way to make more money for this growing panda family, it may actually result in the resurgence of an ancient tradition of worship to Chakreshvari at Lolark Kund, and in any case provides a focus of worship for goddess devotees.

Lolark Chath used to be an overnight affair for groups coming from neighboring villages, but with the advent of modern transportation most pilgrims come to the tank, bathe, perform any other religious practices desired, and return to their villages on the same day. This development has had an impact on some folk traditions, such as *kajali*, folk songs popular in Eastern Uttar Pradesh during the rainy season. Kajali singing at Lolark Kund has almost entirely disappeared, and those that continue to do so lament that kajali is a dying tradition there. In contrast, sohar and mata git are commonly sung by women today adjacent to the temple. Their strong connection to fertility keeps these folk traditions alive in contrast to Kajali, which does not purport to yield mundane benefits such as children.

In the 1950s, it became very popular for pakka or "genuine" Banarsi devotees to worship Lolark during the day and proceed to Krim Kund on the evening of the great festival for a night of singing. The site is popularly known today for the ashram there of Baba Kinaram, who was an eighteenth century Aghori (practitioner of the *aghor*, or terrible Tantric practices associated with Shiva).

Qawwali is a style of entertainment music popular in the Varanasi area. Qawwali derives from Sufi songs, which carry the same name and have a history which dates back to the thirteenth-century Indo-Persian poet and musician Amir Khusrau (Henry, 1988:211). Islamic singers of qawwali perform a number of genres, including the praise of Mohammed (*nat*), descendants of Ali (*manqabat* or *sahidi*), and Allah (*hamd*), and their singing sessions may also include *ghazals*, a poetic form often lamenting unrequited love. The basic format of the qawwali is solos in free rhythm alternating with heavily rhythmic and repetitious refrains sung by a chorus (Henry, 1988:215). Most Hindu singers of the qawwali retain the use of Urdu and musical styles but utilize Hindu rather than Muslim imagery, for example, mythology of Ram adapted from the *Ramcharitmanas*, the various exploits of Krishna, and even the "foibles of a villager in the city, and devotion to the nation" (Henry, 1988:217).

According to informants, the performance at the ashram there on the evening of Lolark Chath attracts very famous singers of the qawwali genre. They also said that many hijras and *laundas* (female impersonators who dance and sing suggestively but are not considered hermaphrodites or to live the part of a female) come to the singing sessions and perform. The singers and dancers of Banaras are said to have been cursed by Baba Kinaram, so they come to appease his anger in order that they may pursue their calling.

According to the folk story, once Baba Kinaram was passing through the lanes of Dalmundi, the "red light" district of Banaras. He was carrying a dead body on his shoulder that was so rotten its stench could be smelled hundreds of meters away. The king of Banaras at that time took offense and ordered his officials to remove the corpse. Furious, Baba Kinaram cursed the king and all of the dancers of the area: the king would not sire an heir, and the dancers would lose their capability to perform. In order to remove the curse, the dancers began to go to his ashram and perform in his honor. Some informants speculate that the king began the practice of first bathing in Lolark Kund for fertility and then proceeding to Kinaram's place to ask that the angry ascetic remove his curse.

Whereas three decades ago only the local Banarsi peoples would attend the qawwali sessions, nowadays, after bathing in Lolark Kund, virtually all festival patrons, whether Banarsi or not, swarm together to this site located a quarter-kilometer away. The crowds are so great that they completely fill the roads and make all vehicular traffic impossible. After arriving at Baba Kinaram's ashram, they bathe again and sing various religious songs. Outsiders who intend to stay in Banaras overnight do so increasingly at this site rather than at Lolark Kund.

Although it may have originally been merely coincidental that Banarsi devotees of Lolark went to Krim Kund on the night of the festival, a specific religious reason is offered today by the new rural participants in this pilgrimage circuit. They claim that Krim Kund has a special power to heal childhood diseases; in contrast, Lolark Kund yields fertility. Thus, by bathing in both Lolark and Krim Kunds, devotees are assured of both fertility and good health of children.

Conclusion

The earliest references to Lolark worship in Banaras do not describe a deep pond such as that at Lolark Kund today. Even in the relatively late *KKh*, compiled during the waning period of Surya worship, bathing is to be done at Lolark's site ambiguously described as "at the Ganga-Asi confluence," which the text also calls "Lolark Sangam." Given that the text specifies other sites, such as Durga Kund, having ponds, and given that the mythology places Lolark as falling in the confluence, the aditya Lolark may have been worshiped by simply bathing within the sangam of the Asi rivulet and the Ganges River itself. Perhaps people adored a Lola Ravi icon of some kind established near the sangam, as is the case today with Shiva's lingam called Asisanga-meshvara. After all, once one has witnessed the beauty of the sun rising across the Ganges while bathing at Asi, it is clear that no temple, kund, or even an image of Surya, for that matter, would be necessary in order to worship Lola Ravi at his station there.

The kund as it exists today thus may have originally been dedicated to this aditya, but perhaps not. Perhaps it was dedicated to an even earlier folk deity, such as a *Naga* or serpent deity connected with well worship, as Eck hypothesizes (1982:177). In any case, today Lolark Kund is a Solar-Shaivite site of worship that reflects a complex history of gradual mythological fusion, and it remains a powerful attraction that draws thousands of Hindus who "vote with their feet" to confirm its popularity among Banaras religious sites (Eck, 1982: xv–xvi).

Notes

* Ratnesh K. Pathak provided the anthropological perspective of this chapter: he conducted all of the ethnographic interviews, observed the *mela*

(festival) and daily rituals, and took all of the photographs. He is responsible for the information on folk perceptions of Lolark mythology, the archaeology of Lolark Kund, and the history of religious functionaries. He also contributed to some of the *puranic* analyses. Cynthia Ann Humes provided the textual and theoretical perspective of this chapter: she translated the Sanskrit passages and examined the secondary sources. She is responsible for the analysis of the textual evidence in relation to the ethnographic materials, and she shaped this essay into its present form.

1. The particular grouping of the twelve adityas varies from text to text. The accepted list for those of Banaras is elaborated in *Kashi Khand* 46:45–47, and their mythology is found in *Kashi Khand* 46–51.

2. The name *Lolark* offers an interesting wordplay on *vilola lochana*, or "tremulous eyes." The depiction of Lolark as the "eye" of Banaras also resonates with Surya's epithet as Jaggachchakshu, or "eye of the world" (*Kashi Khand* 46:7, 44), and it underscores Banaras's nature as the microcosm of the world and Lolark's preeminence within that sacred place.

3. The major references to Lolark specifically include the *Avimukta Mahatmya* of the *Matsya Purana* (185.69), a brief note in the *Avimukta Mahatmya* of the *Kurma Purana* (1.33.17), and the extensive myths of the *Vamana Purana* (3:40ff; 11–16), all dating from approximately the eighth to eleventh centuries; the *Kashi Khand* of the *Skanda Purana* (7, 46), whose final compilation may date from the mid-fourteenth century; and the *Kashi Rahasya*, ostensibly of the *Brahmavaivarta Purana*, dating between the fourteenth and seventeenth centuries. This dating follows Eck (1982:347–48).

4. Worship of Asisangameshvara in the south is paralleled by worship of Sangameshvara at the confluence of the Varana and the Ganges in the north of Kashi (Eck, 1982:222, 203).

5. These astrological and sacrificial deities are the Vishvedevas (grand-sons of Daksha, who sponsors the sacrifice), the two *ashvins* (twin sons of the Sun and a mare), the *sadhyas* (twelve celestial beings who dwell in the region between the sun and the earth), *maruts* (literally "flashing," the storm gods of the atmosphere), Agni (fire god), and finally, the forms of the Sun (here, *Bhaskara*) and the two adityas, Pushan and Bhaga.

6. The Margashirsha myth is quite ancient. A variant from the *Aitareya Brahmana* depicts Prajapati as the incestuous stag punished by Rudra (O'Flaherty, 1978:29).

7. Ratnesh K. Pathak's family home actually abuts the southeast corner of Lolark Kund's brick walls. Among his favorite childhood memories are breathtaking dives into the kund from the roof of his home: three stories from above into the waters sixty feet deep, located fifty feet further from ground level.

8. Kuch Bihar was a royal state which was incorporated into West Bengal in the Land Acquisition Act of 1961. It was located near the borders of northeastern Assam's Dhuburi District and West Bengal and extended to Darjeeling, Assam (specifically, near Highways 56 and 83). There used to be a Kuch Bihar Trust Office in Calcutta which took care of the properties the royal family owned all over India, especially in religious sites such as Banaras, but since Kuch Bihar merged with West Bengal, the State Government has taken primary care of them.

9. Samba, son of Krishna, is said to have been cured of leprosy at Surya Kund, where Surya as "Sambaditya" dwells (*KKh* 48). The Sun God at the famous temple of Konarak is also believed to cure leprosy (Saraswati, 1983:30).

10. Bal Mukund Varma, *Kashi ya Banaras*, 68 and 32. Queen Ahalya Bai Holkar of Indore was responsible for various projects at other Banaras temples, including the reconstruction of the Vishvanath Temple and the erection of a large temple at Manikarnika.

11. In particular, see Saraswati (1975); Sinha and Saraswati (1978); and Vidyarthi, Saraswati, and Jha (1979).

12. Bhavani Shankar's family also manages the famous Shitala Temple near Dashashvamedha Ghat. This panda family has recently established a Vindhyavasini shrine inside the Shitala Temple which is becoming popular. Their associations with Vindhyavasini and pilgrimage priests at Vindhyachal, near Mirzapur, Uttar Pradesh, are described by Humes in the preceding chapter.

13. According to a prominent journalist of a Hindi daily newspaper who wished to remain anonymous, in the mid-nineteenth century there was a major historical change in the tradition of pandaship at Lolark Kund, as at many other Banaras temples. Two powerful groups of pandas at that time fought to gain ownership of temple services, and employed *goondas*, or toughs. Their conflict is one chapter in the story of *goondai*, or "goondaship," in Banaras among the brahmin priestly sector. Lolark Kund is said to be one of the sites which underwent a change in ownership through the advent of priestly violence. This informant said that the popular 1970 film *Sangharsh*, literally "struggle," which depicts violent factions within a panda family of Banaras, is "perhaps more truth than fiction." Fighting among pandas over rights to practice the business of religion in Banaras during the nineteenth century is a well-documented fact today. Van der Veer (1988) discusses the rise of priestly violence at pilgrimage sites in Ayodhya. Not all temple priests may keep records, but since historical references describe Gahadavala kings bathing and making charitable donations at the site, and since this family does have such documents for their other sites, the fact that no records exist which affirm any gifts of temple lands or the rights to perform services at Lolark to this particular panda family is somewhat unusual. Their claim to the title *Raja Panda*, or "the king of all the pandas or the panda community," implies a firm authority. In any case, there has been

no conflict whatsoever among recent generations of priests over worship rights at Lolark, nor is it a subject of any dispute today, even if it remains a subject of local gossip.

14. This position is an inherited one; sons replace their father. In one case, when barber Sadho died without an heir, a Bengali barber took his place, but this was unusual.

15. During the Lolark festival, outside bhaddars are allowed to perform ritual services ordinarily reserved only for the more highly educated pandas and assistants associated with Lolark Kund. During the major festivals bhaddars perform the sankalpa, recitation of mantras, and oftentimes some Tantric practices for pilgrims, and in return are supposed to give a percentage of their income to the Raja Pandas, as the karindas do ordinarily. Field observation indicated that the length of both the ordinary sankalpa and the Tantric rituals tended to reflect how much money the bhaddars received from their patrons. Further, neither their pronunciation nor their performances were done very well. The type of Tantra they practice is called Shabara, a form which uses vernacular rather than Sanskrit mantras, and is generally considered more accessible to the common person.

16. The image of the goddess at the Durga Kund Temple nearby is a silver mask as well.

9

Language Choice, Religion, and Identity
in the Banarsi Community*

Beth Simon

> The language in common use [in Banaras] is Bihaarii which is spoken
> by 90% of the population, while Western Hindi (chiefly Hindustani) is
> spoken by 7%.
>
> —(*Imperial Gazetteer*, Varanasi District, 1908)

> Varanasi is a polyglot city, but the majority of the. . .population of the
> district speaks Bhojpuri, and even the educated people speak it in their
> homes. The number of such persons is included in the figure of Hindi-
> speaking people which, calculated on the basis of the census of 1951,
> is 87.5 percent.
>
> —(*Uttar Pradesh Census, District Gazetteer of Varanasi*, 1965)

The Complexity of Banaras

Banaras has always been a city of language. Some of the oldest
continuously inhabited urban sites on earth, even today, the original
areas of Banaras are composed of "pockets of ethnicity" (Sinha and
Saraswati, 1978), concentrations of people with antecedents from
regions or ethnic groups throughout South Asia. Demographically, most
of original Banaras is divided into neighborhoods (*muhallas*) known
informally by linguistic or ethnic labels associated with the origin of
the residents. Streets and alleys often define regional or ethnic borders.[1]
A walk through the older areas of Banaras may take one from a Nepali-
speaking area to a Gujerati enclave centered around a temple, or from
the Tamil neighborhood fragrant with roasting coffee beans into the
substantial and influential Bengali section.[2]

Banaras has its own community of native Banarsis, who live in neighborhoods infacing those of outside language groups. Like the others, this community too has its own local language, Banarsi Boli. In this study, a family was considered "Banarsi" if it had been based in Banaras for at least three generations and had a sense that Banaras was its home place.[3] This means that the Banarsi community is both Hindu and Muslim, and hence is demographically divided within itself along religious lines.

The Banarsi Community and Banarsi Boli, the Speech of Banaras

Traditionally, Banarsis, both Hindus and Muslims, have been the people who provide the services and produce the goods that are basic to the socioeconomic foundation of the city as a Hindu pilgrimage site, as a center for ritual and practice, and as a tourist draw. Banarsis make their living from "sacred" Banaras by performing rituals, poling boats on the Ganga for tourists and pilgrims, performing classical and semi-classical music, and fashioning objects from the materials traditionally associated with Banaras, for instance, the silk brocades and brass.[4]

A common language, Banarsi Boli, and a common economic ground make a Banarsi community distinct from other linguistic or ethnic groups in Banaras. Banarsis talk to each other, within and across religious lines, in Banarsi Boli. Banarsis are identified by others in Banaras by their language, and most Banarsis claim their speech as part of who they are. Banarsi Hindus claim to speak Hindi, and many do use regional standard Hindi. Increasingly, Banarsi Muslims claim Urdu, and again, because of education being allowed or provided in Urdu, many are Urdu speakers. Nonetheless, whatever other speech they use, Banarsi Hindus and Muslims are related in the same way that they differ from the others, including the Hindi and Urdu speakers, around them.[5] Banarsis use language to identify themselves, and alternate between languages to structure discourse and to convey differences between themselves.

The presence and influence of Hindi and Urdu means that Banarsis are a bilingual group. There has been stable bilingualism within the Banarsi community over an extended period of time. Because much of Banaras economic life is still largely based on pilgrimage, ritual performances, and tourism, most Banarsis who are employed outside their immediate neighborhoods, especially in any service capacity, are actively bilingual in regional Hindi. Although not all Banarsis speak Hindi with grammatical accuracy, "street" fluency is common, and most are able to interact appropriately in situations where Hindi is the dominant language.[6] One participates in Hindi situations by inserting formulaic and idiomatic phrases. Adept Banarsi monolinguals "Hindi-ize" their speech (just as local Hindi speakers "Banarsi-ize" their speech) by substituting better-known parallel features of one language for the other.

The following anecdote demonstrates nicely how, especially for some Hindus, being part of the Banarsi speech community can result in an interesting dynamic between Banarsi Hindu identity and Hindi language association. A Hindu male friend invited to me to sit with his father, a brahmin astrologer[7] and a man of standing in his neighborhood. Several mornings a week, neighbors and friends would come to their front room, where the astrologer would recite verses, direct conversation, make charts, provide refreshment, and offer insights. Earlier, my friend had stressed that his father, a "true" (*pakka*) Banarsi, spoke only "pure" (*shuud*) Hindi, but since I seemed to be taping everyone else they knew, his father had decided I should tape him as well.

On the morning in question, we sat at the front of the room, closely observed by a group of neighbors. We began in Hindi. I offered my standard opening, "When did your family first come to Banaras?" and he replied

Ham log to banaaras aaye kariib DeRh sau varsh.
(we [plural morph] then came to Banaras about a hundred and
    fifty years ago)

HunDreD phiphTi iyars baek ham log aaye the.
(hundred fifty years back we [plural morph] came.)

"As for us, we came to Banaras about a hundred and fifty years
    ago. A hundred and fifty years back, we came here."

His reply, code-switching between Hindi and English, both with Banarsi Boli phonology, was an efficient social statement. He indicated that he knew English, that I knew Hindi, and that he was a true Banarsi. He continued speaking in Hindi for over an hour, commenting on neighborhood *Ramlilas*, and explaining how illness and death have been defeated in Banaras. He brought each topic to touch on religious practice or ethics, and he adorned his conversation with appropriate verses from *shastras* (Hindu law books) and Tulsidas. Several times the room echoed with "Wah! Wah!" when a verse was particularly fitting and the diction beautiful. Finally, he inquired whether there was anything else I wanted to know, and I asked why he hadn't spoken in Banarsi Boli. The following was said in Hindi.

"Banarsi Boli, what is that?"

"Isn't it the speech (*bhasha*) of Banaras?"

"The bhasha of Kashi is Hindi."

Giggles in the room. I'm nonplused. His son is my field worker, so he knows quite well what I'm talking about.

"But, isn't there another bhasha people use around here?"

Long pause, then: "Do you mean Bhojpuri?"

"Yes, exactly, the Banaras style of Bhojpuri." And in Banarsi Boli he says: "Bhojpuri is the language of Bihar. Here we don't speak Bhojpuri. We don't even understand it." Everybody laughs and then we all have tea.

Bhojpuri is an Indo-Aryan language with five main variants.[8] The *Linguistic Survey of India* (*LSI*; Grierson, 1901, 1903, 1904) recognized Banarsi Boli as a distinct dialect of Western Bhojpuri,[9] particular to "Banaras City." Later official publications confirm the *LSI* recognition, although some change the language label. The 1908 *Imperial Gazetteer* calls it "Bihaarii,"[10] and the 1965 *District Gazetteer* calls it "Banarsi Boli," reiterating that it is a "western counterpart of Bhojpuri." The 1965 *Gazetteer* states that (Banarsi) Bhojpuri is the first language, or home/neighborhood variety, or "mother tongue" of the Banaras community. (See opening quotes.)

To the west, the Banaras district is contiguous with a variety of Eastern Hindi known as Awadhi.[11] In all other directions Banaras district conjoins areas of the other Bhojpuri dialects. More important than geography, however, is the fact that Banaras lies within the historical and political purview of what has become regional standard Hindi. Banarsi Boli has, over time, come to exhibit phonological and grammatical features similar to regional standard Hindi,[12] and thus it has become increasingly unlike other Bhojpuri varieties. These linguistic changes are a product of ongoing complex language contact, and the noticeable points of similarity between Hindi and Banarsi Boli have encouraged a sense that Banarsi Boli is "a kind of Hindi."

Historically, Banaras has been a center for Sanskrit preservation and learning.[13] Beginning early in this century, Banaras became a base for the Hindi national language movement.[14] The lexicon for this consciously developed Hindi was derived, directly or indirectly, from Sanskrit. Today, modern standardized Hindi is more than a partially engineered linguistic variety. It is a sociopolitical entity, one with which many local Banarsi Hindus identify.[15] For a Hindu, identification with regional standard Hindi may mean self-identification as a Hindi speaker and a perception of Banaras as part of the Hindi regional language area. There is strong motivation for this view. Such identification carries with it potential political and economic benefits that do not follow from being a Banarsi Boli speaker.

The converse association has occurred as well in Banaras. Because Sanskrit is a hallmark of Hinduism, and Hindi is associated with Sanskrit, Hindi has come to be associated with Hindu, particularly educated Hindu, identity. Finally, there has been a third effect, less obvious but pervasive nonetheless. Insofar as Banarsi Hindus identify themselves with Hindi, Banarsi Boli is then identified with Banarsi Hindus.[16]

Language, Religion, Bilingualism, and the Census

For a number of reasons, the Census of India has never been a reliable source for language data. Documentation of mother tongue claims or of multiple language use has often been vitiated by political and bureaucratic definitions of "language." These definitions change from one decade to the next.

Until the 1961 census, in Banaras as elsewhere in India, all "Urdu" responses were merged with "Hindustani" or "Hindi," and consequently any correlation between Urdu and Muslims was obscured. Beginning with the 1961 census, Urdu responses were recorded separately. Since 1961, the number of recorded Urdu speakers has steadily increased, and identification of Banarsi Muslims with Urdu language has become much more explicit.[17] The 1971 census count for mother tongue in Banaras showed a 300 percent increase in reported Urdu speakers.

On the other hand, while the number of reported Urdu speakers has become more accurate, the number of individuals who speak languages not listed in Schedule VIII of the Constitution of India, and the number of bilingual or multilingual speakers reported, is now far less accurate than previously. This loss is due to changes in language definitions. The *Census of India* for 1981 (*Varanasi District Handbook*, 1987: 1.1) expanded the parameters of Schedule VIII languages such that twenty-eight speech varieties previously considered separate were included within, and hence not named or counted separately from, the official languages. For instance, the 1981 Census called "Hindi" what had been eighteen other varieties. Bhojpuri was one of the eighteen languages now called "Hindi." Bhojpuri was considered to have anywhere from sixty to seventy million speakers.[18] As of the 1981 census, any response naming Bhojpuri, including Banarsi Boli, was officially counted as "Hindi." These new definitions provide for a radical decrease in the number of mother tongue labels recorded, and ultimately in the number of bilinguals.

The Banaras Urdu returns of 1981 were recorded separately, but here too, there were still potential problems. The instructions were not clear as to whether "Urdu" was recorded only when the respondent was Muslim but not when Hindu. Again, if a Muslim responded with a variety other than "Urdu" but included under "Hindi," the census taker may well have recorded "Hindi."

The 1981 census created millions of monolingual mother tongue Hindi speakers. In Banaras this meant that a fairly representative number of Muslims returned themselves as Urdu speakers, and all others, by and large, were returned as Hindi speakers.

Since most other languages in which a Banarsi might be bilingual were officially considered Hindi, almost no one was returned as bilingual.[19] In fact, though, whatever the census instructions, few individuals reported themselves as bilingual. In 1951, census takers were specifically instructed to ask about multiple language use. The data show that only 1.2 percent of the urban population reported themselves as bilingual. Of those who did, almost 98 percent claimed "Hindi/Hindustani/Urdu" as the second language. The censuses of 1961 and of 1971 each show "Bhojpuri" responses increasing, but the absolute number was still very small.

Coincidentally, what the census recorded for Banarsis may reflect their own view. Most Banarsis simply do not see themselves as either monolingual Banarsi Boli or Bhojpuri speakers. Nor do they see themselves as bilinguals. Although most Banarsis have Banarsi Boli either as their first language or alternate language, few Banarsis, Hindu or Muslim, female or male, give "language" status to Banarsi Boli. Almost no one associates himself or herself with "Bhojpuri." This denial is interesting, because it is of language label and language status, not of that individual's actual use or association with use.

Gender, Religion, and Linguistic Identity

Language label and status are sociocultural considerations, and among Banarsis, as elsewhere, formal affirmation of them appears to be influenced by gender, and hence, education level. In urban Banaras overall literacy rates are higher than in the rest of the district (and are very high compared with the rest of Uttar Pradesh), but literacy rates for Banarsi females are well under those for males. The 1981 census showed not only substantially lower literacy rates for urban Banaras females than males, but also a far lower number of females educated past the primary levels.

Throughout Uttar Pradesh, public education from primary level on is provided in Hindi,[20] and at the secondary level Hindi is either the only medium of instruction or is a compulsory offering as a language along with English.[21] One can assume, then, that an individual's level of formal education is a good indicator of access to and identification with standardized Hindi. Since the number of Banarsi females educated past the primary level is far below that of males,[22] uneducated Banarsi females tend to be monolingual Banarsi Boli speakers, and to see themselves as speakers of a lesser, nonstandardized localized dialect.[23] I spent an afternoon recording a group of Banarsi Boli–speaking women of a low-caste group geographically isolated within Banaras. They told me repeatedly that they didn't know "good" or "real" Hindi, and that their own speech did not have a formal name because it was particular to their group. When I asked whether they thought their speech and Hindi were related, they said that what they spoke was "like Hindi" but different, and that it was not what most people speak. These women were typical of most of the Hindu women with whom I spent time. Most said the language they spoke was Banarsi Boli.[24]

The Hindu males with whom I had contact represented themselves quite differently. No matter how accurately or frequently they spoke Hindi, most of the adult Hindu males whom I knew identified themselves as Hindi speakers. Those who claimed a second "language" usually named English, not Banarsi Boli or Urdu as that language. Of interest here is that almost every Hindu male said that, at least part of the time, Banarsi Boli was used at home. Every Hindu male I asked said that Muslims spoke Urdu (although several who made this statement had no close, informal contact with Muslims).

Most Banarsi males are educated beyond primary level. Since second language education begins at secondary level, most Banarsi males receive formal education both in Hindi and in a second language.[25] Education beyond primary level, a male domain, is both *in* Hindi and *of* Hindi. Hence, there is a strong institutionalized basis for Hindu males to identify with Hindi. Among my own acquaintances, most of the Hindu males said they spoke Banarsi Boli, but few claimed to be Banarsi Boli speakers. They said Banarsi Boli was a "dear" or "special" or "home" speech they used with loved ones, at the tea stalls, with close friends, among Banarsis.

Muslims, Banarsi Identity, and Banarsi Boli

There are those who assert a strong association with Banaras, but not with "Banarsi" identity. I was acquainted with a Muslim tailor (*darzi*).

He spoke his language and I spoke my university Hindi-Urdu which I adapted with Banarsi Boli verb endings, lexical items, and phonology. One day without my asking, he invited me to his house, saying that his family had lived in Banaras for several generations and I should tape them. I was complimented but surprised, and said that I hadn't realized he was a "true" (*pakka*) Banarsi. After a silence he said, "I am not a pakka Banarsi. I am a Muslim. Pakka Banarsis," he said enunciating clearly, "are milkmen and thieves."

His response was a sophisticated and complex insult to Hindus. Because the products of the cow are sacred, dairy people in Banaras are a particular caste, and, as most Banaras residents know, some dairy people water the milk. According to the Muslim's insult, milkmen are Banarsis, and milkmen are thieves. Since milkmen are Hindus, Hindus are Banarsis, and Hindus are thieves.

The tailor made another point with this insult. In daily life, this man spoke the same language as his neighbors, Muslim or Hindu. He and his family were not Banarsis, however; they were Muslims. This suggests that within the local Muslim community it is the Hindus of Banaras who are the recognized Banarsis.

Hindi and Banarsi Boli: Alternate Languages

Diglossia

Going around public Banaras—at the bazaars, in shops, around temples, on ghats—one commonly hears Banarsi Boli and Hindi used in alternation; that is, people alternate between languages depending on the participants, topic, and function. This pattern of language alternation is called "diglossia."

Diglossia names a situation in which two languages coexist with an almost symmetrical relation between each language and the function or social context in which that language is used. This type of functional or contextual specialization is related to the status of each language.

Throughout the plains of northern India east of Bengal, Hindi is the major regional language; it is standardized and has a fairly extensive, recognized body of written literature. It also has a higher explicit social prestige. Hindi is the language medium of public school. Finally, Hindi is, with English, the official national language. It is the language of public life, public education, and public politics.[26]

In Banaras, it stands in contrast to Banarsi Boli, which is not standardized, has little formal literary tradition, and has a lower explicit social value (see Ferguson, 1972).

Expanding the concept of diglossia to include stylistic register means that in Banaras Hindi is the language choice for formal or official public events and for nonlocally based workplaces such as civil service and quasi-government offices. Because it is the regional lingua franca, Hindi can serve as the neutral choice for interchanges between new acquaintances, for people who are not members of the same first language group, or for those who are socially unequal and meeting in formal situations.

Language alternation between Hindi and Banarsi Boli expresses language-function relations specific to Banaras. I was invited to the home of a Banaras Sanskrit University–educated Brahmin whose family had held controlling interest in one of the most important temples in Banaras. Beside fulfilling his priestly duties, he also performed at home as a Tantric. When I arrived he was seated on the floor conversing in Banarsi Boli with a mother and daughter from whom an object had been stolen.[27]

The mother requested the Tantric to use his power to discover the thieves and restore the object, and the daughter made an offering of coconut and sweets. The Tantric began his *puja* (worship), reciting in Sanskrit and in Hindi with Sanskrit case endings. Then he became possessed. Rocking and calling, he invited his goddess, praised her, propitiated her, and commanded her, all in Banarsi Boli. Finally, snatching up the coconut and smashing it on the floor, he ceased being possessed. He reported the goddess's judgment and distributed *prasad* (food blessed by the deity), and his clients left. We two then sat on chairs, and with great courtesy he told me his life story in flowing regional standard Hindi.

Banarsi Boli and Hindi within the Hindu family

Especially in educated or higher-caste Hindu families, both Banarsi Boli and Hindi are part of a shared family speech repertoire, each used to signal subtle notes of intimacy, respect, and hierarchy. In these households, intrafamily relations are incorporated and expressed partially through language alternation. For instance, Banarsi Boli will be used between grandson and grandmother, and Hindi between the same boy and his father. If the family includes daughters-in-law originating from outside Banaras and their mother-in-law is a Banarsi Boli speaker, then the incoming females learn Banarsi Boli and in turn pass it to their children. Within the household, adult males use Banarsi Boli with females but Hindi with nonadult males, particularly once they reach school age. Thus, Banarsi Boli is maintained in the family while at the same time Hindi is confirmed as the language of educated males.

My impression is that in educated and upper-caste Hindu families Banarsi Boli is maintained across generations through female use.

Code-switching with Banarsi Boli and Hindi

Among Banarsi bilinguals, one finds not only diglossia but also "code-switching," and these are different in important ways (see Romaine, 1989:111). In Banaras, Hindi of one sort or another has been used on an everyday basis both by outsiders and by Banarsi Boli speakers for at least two centuries. The result is that the speech repertoire of most Banarsi Boli Hindus includes a Hindi end of the verbal spectrum. This is evidenced in code-switching between Hindi and Banarsi Boli.

Code-switching is "the juxtaposition within the same speech exchange of passages of speech belonging to two different grammatical systems or subsystems" (Gumperz, 1982:59). Romaine expands on how code-switching works. "In code-switched discourse, the items in question form part of the same speech act. They are tied together prosodically as well as by semantic and syntactic relations equivalent to those that join passages in a single speech act" (Romaine, 1989:111). Code-switching, then, is a linguistic phenomenon and is structurally different from diglossia, a social phenomenon. Both have become means of passing, incorporating, and expressing community and religious identity.

In Banaras, code-switching is common. One type of code-switching is "intrasentential." In this type, a speaker switches between Hindi and Banarsi Boli within a sentence boundary. Intrasentential code-switching is evidence that functional specialization, a hallmark of diglossia, has been naturalized into a unified Banarsi speech repertoire. For many bilingual Banarsis, Hindi and Banarsi Boli exist in a linguistic continuum and language choice is a matter of stylistics and discourse functions conditioned by shared social norms.

Code-switching in a Stable Multilingual Community

Bilingual Banarsis have open to them more strategies for conversational interactions than do monolinguals. Each language choice can be a device for structuring discourse, controlling focus, and guiding interpretation and response. Unconscious, spontaneous code-switching is a natural expression of who one is. Conscious, controlled code-switching is a ready means for exploiting shared group background. Gumperz makes the point that dialect differences can "serve both as reflections of indices of social identity and as symbols of shared cultural background. . .[S]uch symbols serve as effective carriers of information and powerful means of persuasion" (Gumperz, 1978:401). It is in the daily acts of dual language use, and of code-switching in particular, that we see how both Hindi and Banarsi Boli are "effective carriers of" social and cultural "information" for Banarsis. "If conversational inference depends on shared social presuppositions, and if conversational continuity is a function of the success of such inferences, then the mere fact that two speakers can sustain an interaction over time is evidence for the existence of at least some common level of social knowledge and agreement on interpretation." (Gumperz, 1978:401)

In order to investigate just how Banarsi Boli and Hindi function together, the rest of this chapter will examine two acts of code-switching. These two examples are typical of daily, informal conversation among Banarsi bilinguals. They have the same primary situational features: Hindu males who have a long-standing relation with each other. The first case provides a typical example of bilingual behavior in a community where multiple language use is common and unremarkable. The second case differs primarily because the person controlling the discourse uses code-switching to focus attention on languages and cultural features associated with them. By consciously code-switching, the speaker controls participant response in order to draw a relation between religious identity and Banarsi identity.

Hindu Males Pass the Time of Day: Unmarked Code-switching

In Banaras, Hindi and Banarsi Boli are used in rapid alternation within a sentence boundary. This intrasentential code-switching occurs within the body of the sentence itself, or between the main part and the "tag"—phrases such as "isn't it," "and then," and so on. Code-switching at these points is typical of informal, spontaneous conversation. In the first conversation, intrasentential code-switching separates what the participants know as "facts" from what the speaker says about those facts. The code-switching itself differentiates these discourse functions, and each speech variety is assigned a function.[28]

The conversation is between two Brahmin males, twenty-four and thirty, educated beyond secondary level, and married. These men are friends, neighbors, and cousins. The immediate topic is the convalescence of a popular and wealthy film star, Amitabh Bacchan, who has suffered extensive injuries in a motorcycle accident. In this portion, one man speculates on the star's medical treatment.

Banarsi Boli
    aitnaa siriiyas rahal, na, u ta, sunaat rahal
(It was so serious, wasn't it then I heard)

"It [=the accident] was so serious, that I heard"

Hindi

    ki agar yahaã nahĩ hogaa, to
(that if it [=the operation] doesn't happen here, then

    "that if the operation can't be done here, then"

    londan jaayegaa, ruus jaayegaa.
he will [may] go to London, he will [may] go to Russia)

    "he'll go to London, he'll go to Russia."

Banarsi Boli

    u, ta, prashan hau ki, paisa hau
(he, then, this is the question, he has money)

    "The point is—he's got the money!"

    ta, kahĩ bhii ja sakelaa, ar-e
(then, wherever ! he is able to go, EXCLAMATION)

    "He can go wherever he damn well wants!"

The following is mixed, with expressive, noncontent words in Banarsi Boli, and content words in Hindi.

    u ta jitna kharch lagii
(that then however much it costs [treatment and recuperation])

    "Whatever the costs are,"

    utna ta aik sinemaa mẽ u khaam karke nikaal lagii."
(that much comes out of the work in one film)

    "that much is what comes out of making just one film."

The commentary is in Banarsi Boli, for example: "It [=the accident] was so serious [*siriiyas*—occurs as a naturalized item]" and "Here's the point: money. He can go anywhere [with a Banarsi exclamation *ar-e*]." Naming actual locations and details about the actor's income, what pass here for facts, are in Hindi: "He will/could go to London, He will/could go to Russia." The speaker puts the point or "moral" of the story in Hindi with Banarsi Boli demonstrative adjectives and fillers: "Whatever it costs, he makes that much from working in one film."

    Here are two Banarsis, passing the time of day. They talk movies, they talk politics, they talk weddings and prices, and the way they do it involves unself-conscious code-switching.[29] Neither participant is explicitly demonstrating or asserting anything about himself to the other. The above speaker code-switches because it is part of who he is: a fluent, unself-conscious bilingual. The code-switching pattern demonstrates that both Hindi and Banarsi Boli are deeply embedded in the social speech repertoire of these two participants.[30] It is an essential part of the unconscious knowledge that bilingual Banarsi community members share about how to talk with each other.[32]

Romaine holds that intrasentential code-switching involves. . ."the greatest syntactic risk, and may be avoided by all but the most fluent bilinguals" (1989:113). The frequency with which intrasentential code-switching occurs in the informal conversation between Banarsi bilinguals is strong evidence that bilingualism itself is common, accepted. It is a basic characteristic of Banarsi identity.[32] It is natural, unself-conscious code-switching which occurs as a part of natural, unself-conscious speech acts. Such code-switching appears to be a stable feature of conversational interaction among Banarsis, and as such it is indicative of the positive (albeit often covert) value of Banarsi identity.[33]

Marked Code-switching: A Performed Narrative in Ordinary Conversation

Another type of code-switching is the intentional shifting of languages within conversation for strategic purposes. Structurally, this type of code-switching occurs at sentence or clause boundaries; this is called "intersentential" code-switching. Such switches assume fluency in separate linguistic codes *as* separate codes. Intersentential code-switching seems to be more conscious and can be used to manipulate conversation and focus participants on a particular issue or point of view. What underlies significant code-switching in a close social group is a deep agreement, a commonality, in the way participants use language to signal "cultural presuppositions." Given that agreement, known differences can be exploited. The different languages the group shares are marked for sociocultural differences and thus can be used as reminders of in-group membership and its consequent obligations. Hindi–Banarsi Boli code-switching stands out among bilingual Banarsis when code-switches point to a pertinent shared social norm. Group interaction utilizing language differences depends on this deep agreement.

In this second example, the speaker's confidence in his use of code-switching depends on sharing the same speech repertoire with his audience, one in which Banarsi Boli and Hindi stand not as separate languages per se but as symbols of social norms. The following is part

of a long conversation that took place on a weekday morning in a side
street in an old Banarsi neighborhood near the ghats. In this piece, the
two verbally active participants are Hindu males. Both are mother
tongue Banarsi Boli speakers. The dominant speaker is an older man.
He is the launderer (*dhobi*) for most of the present group. The other
is upper caste, in his mid-twenties, and employed in a government
office. The younger man comes from a household in which both Banarsi
Boli and Hindi are the home speech. He has been educated through
college in a Hindi-language medium. The launderer, without any formal
education, knows Hindi in the same way that most uneducated Banarsi
males in service occupations know it. These two participants directly
address only each other.

In this portion, the launderer complains to his audience about
the vicissitudes in his business caused by the growing popularity of
polyester blend fabrics. The launderer then tells about his stay in Delhi.
He says that he lived in Delhi for one year, and he worked for a Muslim
employer in a dry-cleaning establishment.

The Lead-in: The Economic Situation. The laundryman tells his
audience how things have changed in the laundry business over the
years.

> Earlier, everyone, like your family [=the younger man's], had
> dhobis take care of their clothes. Nowadays of course we're in great
> demand during the festival season. Everyone gets new clothes,
> they want their clothes pressed, and we have a lot of work. I'm
> very busy right now, but later, well, you understand, I don't know.
> Will there be work later? Well, brother, I don't know.

The other man asks what has changed. The launderer says that these
days, people buy much more terrycot.[34] Worse, people now do more
of their own daily washing. It is only at festival time that all the old
clients, "like you brother, come looking for me. At festival times, you
understand," but not, it is implied, at other times.

The Lead-in: Employment in Delhi. The launderer says that ten years
earlier he had gone to Delhi. He points to his iron, a heavy brass
implement, and gives a local equivalent for "have brass iron, will travel."
In Delhi, he says, the traditional social and economic relationships based
on kinship and caste are missing. Everyone is a stranger, without kin.
One is on one's own. The launderer says:

I worked for a Muslim employer, you know; he was a Muslim, a Muslim, in a Muslim neighborhood. He paid me 300 rupees, this employer a Muslim you understand.[35]

In Banaras, by contrast, laundry charges are a set amount per piece of clothing. The younger man asks about this 300 rupees. Wasn't the launderer paid by the piece?

Launderer: No, brother, this [wage arrangement] was for time. I worked from eight in the morning until six in the evening.

The younger man suggests that those hours aren't so good.

Launderer: Understand that at twelve [noon] there was a two-hour break, you know two to three hours.

Younger man: I understand, you were at the employer's for two to three hours a day, and you were someplace else for two to three hours.

Launderer: Yes.

Younger man: Given that much *break*,[36] well, doing ironing here, do you get more money or less?

Launderer: No, you can't explain it like that. Here, there's housekeeping, I have children, things cost. There, I was alone. There I had 300 rupees, from this employer, a Muslim you understand. Here, I set up in that park across the way, and I send my little girls around [to pick up and drop off the clothes]. They don't go to school, they can't read. *We're* not literate people you know.

Younger man: Okay fine. But what I mean is, if you worked for about four hours here, then how much can you make?

Launderer: Okay, let's say I do ironing for about four hours. Then, brother, understand, that I've gotten maybe 10 rupees.

Younger man: By that account, you earned less *there*, right?

Launderer: All right, maybe, but look, that was ten years ago. And that doesn't tell the story. At that time, 300 rupees was adequate (or serviceable).

Younger man: Yet, you left?

The Story

Launderer: Well, I got a letter. They [=the family] asked me to come back. I had this letter. I returned to Banaras, to here. I have a household you understand, I have children.

| *Younger man:* | You mean, the work there was finished. |
| *Launderer:* | No, the work wasn't finished. There was work there. But my household was here. The [Delhi] employer didn't want to permit me to return here. |

The launderer then reconstructs the final conversation between himself, a Banarsi Hindu, and his employer, a Delhi Muslim. The launderer presents the narrative framing utterances ("then I said to the employer," "then the employer said") in Banarsi Boli. The signal for the shift from frame to direct speech is the transitional conjunction *ki*, "that." The launderer gives the Delhi employer's speech within the body of the narrative in Hindi.

The Launderer Performs His Narrative

Banarsi Boli—launderer
  bahut jabrii kailii maalik se ki hame ek haptaa me cal aiib
  "I said very firmly to the employer, 'in one week I will leave.' "

Banarsi Boli
  Ta u kahe,
  "Then the employer said,"

Hindi—Delhi employer
  Nahĩ, mat jaao Ihaa kaam kaun karegaa?
  'No, don't go. Who will do the work here?'

Banarsi Boli—launderer
  Ham kahilii, Ham ruukbe na karab.
  "I said, 'I won't stay.' "

Hindi—Delhi employer
  Nahĩ, mat jaao. Ihaa kaam hau.[37]
  'No, don't go. There is work here.'

Banarsi Boli—launderer
  Ta bahut jabrii maalik se kahalii, Cal aiib.
  "Then I said quite firmly to the employer, 'I will go.' "

At this point the launderer returns to indirect speech and finishes his story in Banarsi Boli.

Then the employer said a lot of things to me. Then he allowed me to leave. Later, I got a letter from him. You know, he asked me to come back.

What Does the Launderer Accomplish?. As represented by the launderer, the Delhi Muslim's pleas, given in the simplest Hindi, are notably repetitious within the dialogue itself, and some are nearly identical to the launderer's direct interchange with the younger man, for instance, "there is work here"—"there was work there." The employer is presented as the alien because he appears to speak Hindi, and the repetitions then mark his speech as significant.

Earlier the launderer had reminded the younger man that they have a long-standing relation, one that has never been strictly that of employer-employee. He notes his own obligations, mentioning specifically his young children. As a Hindu husband and father, in a group of Hindu husbands and fathers, there is no need to mention the rest of the extended family. This juxtaposition of topics—changes in laundry patterns against his children's illiteracy—should prod the younger man into agreeing that he too has certain *moral* obligations which in the past have been fulfilled by giving the launderer work. No one challenges the launderer's inference: in Delhi, work was plentiful, money was easy, and he had a choice many of them never have had. The launderer uses his performed narrative to articulate his personal grievance with the younger man and to extend it to include the others.

The launderer's switch from Banarsi Boli to Hindi helps move the discourse from conversation to drama. The status quo is no longer identified with Banarsi Boli. In the story, it is *outside* the community, *away* from Banarsis, that the launderer is treated as he should have been at home. By presenting the Delhi dialogue as direct speech, in "Hindi," the launderer uses code-switches to signal identities based on religion as social grouping. He can then make a moral point, to the detriment of the entire audience.

The insertion of Hindi into a Banarsi Boli conversation lets the launderer call upon an attitude regarding Hindi: a Hindi speaker is not a Banarsi. A Banarsi speaks Banarsi Boli. Therefore the Hindi speaker must be the outsider. Yet it is the outsider, someone without social or cultural or traditional or familial ties to the narrator, who offers a fair, generous arrangement. This is the pivot upon which the narrator turns the moral of his story. The means by which he establishes his moral superiority is language alternation in a performance. The launderer makes his audience watch while he once again chooses family over personal independence, group over individual, Banaras over Delhi, Hindu over Muslim. He does this when he performs the Muslim outsider in Hindi, and himself—the Hindu, the home, the family, "Banaras"—in Banarsi Boli.[38]

For Banarsis, Banarsi Boli and Hindi are available as flexible metaphors. The potential for such use is present in the Banarsi bilingual situation. The launderer calls on shared cultural knowledge that Banarsi Boli and Hindi can be "marked" as symbols of a fundamental division in Indian culture: Hindu and Muslim. In this instance, Banarsi Boli and Hindi function as metaphors for belonging and otherness. The launderer uses code-switching to insist on the interdependency of Banarsi Hindus and the responsibility such interdependency implies.

The Significance of Language Choice among Banarsi-Boli Speakers

These two examples demonstrate different aspects of the bilingual situation in the Banarsi community. In both instances, code-switching is used as a structuring device. In the second case, however, it allows the speaker to assert a set of rights and obligations that, he implies, are particularly Hindu. This suggests three things. First, there is a defined set of relations between linguistic choices in the shared speech repertoire and the outer, social manifestations of these choices. Second, speakers "know" this. Third, this knowledge can be used by virtue of the equation between religious identity and social group.

The very commonness of code-switching in this bilingual community indicates that the relation between language choice and language function is integral to the norms for language use. Code-switching structures spontaneous, informal conversation. Therefore, we must assume that it is embedded in a deep cultural knowledge.

Notes

* The research upon which this article is based was conducted in Banaras (Varanasi) between 1981 and 1982 and was funded by the American Institute for Indian Studies and the National Science Foundation. The data were collected by tape-recording largely unstructured, spontaneous conversation. When I was a participant, I occasionally asked such questions as "When did your family first come to Banaras?" or "What changes have you seen here?" Otherwise no particular topic, style, features, or setting was disallowed. I did not use prepared questionnaires or survey instruments. At the time of the recording, participants were asked if I could tape them. I recorded in two types of situations. The first consisted of small groups of people (two to six) who normally got together, and they were taped at such a gathering—having tea, during the long afternoon hours on a street, in the courtyard. Participants were connected by kinship or marriage, friendship, or long-term work-related activity. There were forty-one participants, all over eighteen years old: twenty-two men

and nineteen women. Thirteen men were over forty years old; nine were Hindi educated, one was Urdu educated; the others had primary level or less education. Only four of the twenty-two were not active in both Hindi or Urdu and Banarsi Boli. Eight of the nineteen women were over forty; two were Hindi educated, both under forty. Seven women were at least minimally active in Hindi as well as Banarsi Boli; six of those were under forty years old.

The author gratefully acknowledges all assistance given by the American Institute for Indian Studies and the individuals staffing the offices in Delhi and Ramnagar, particularly that of Mr. Pradeep Mehendiratta.

The author also wishes to acknowledge and thank her advisor, Professor Manindra K. Verma, for his interest, guidance, and patience. She would also like to thank Professor Sheela Verma, without whom she would not know Hindi.

All errors and faults in this article are the sole responsibility of the author.

1. This type of urban spatial isolation is conducive to maintenance over several generations of the residents' original language and culture. Simultaneously, because of proximity, shared markets, and so on, there is impetus to develop some facility with the languages of other neighborhoods. Neighborhoods, although fairly discrete, often interface.

2. The *Linguistic Survey of India* (Grierson, 1903:270) gives the following description of the languages in use by nonnative Banarsis.

The city is, of course, largely inhabited by people from other parts of India, who speak corrupted forms of their mother-tongues, Panjabi, Gujarati, Marathi, Bengali. The influence is felt by the native inhabitants, and the true Benares language is every year becoming more and more uniform. Rather than being due to the influence of all the outside languages, it is much more likely that the increasing uniformity in Banarsi Boli noticed by the *Survey* is, even at that time, due to the influence of Hindi in the form of long-term and complex patterns Banarsis have had with Hindi speakers—both Awadhi dialect speakers and regional standard Hindi speakers.

3. Not all Banarsi families have been based in Banaras for more than three generations, and in many cases this geographic (re)location does not sever a family's ties with their earlier regional base. Banarsi families I knew had strong feeling for two home places: Banaras *as well as* their region of origin—Rajasthan, for instance—where members of the extended family still reside, and where the Banaras branch of the family may look for suitable marriage candidates.

4. More recently the children, especially males, from Banarsi families have gotten university-level degrees and gone into government and professional careers. But at the time of this research, most of the Banarsi families with whom I was acquainted still identified themselves in terms of caste, historical place of origin, religious considerations, and occupation.

5. I have tapes of interactions between Muslim and Hindu males who have known each other over time in a work situation. In each of these interactions, participants spoke Banarsi Boli. The data from those tapes show interesting differences in verb forms between the Hindu and the Muslim speakers, but I have no data that allow for correlation between speech and religious identity. This is not to say such evidence is not there. My method of finding participants for my research depended on getting to know a person who would then introduce me to another. Because my first contacts were with Hindus, I have far more material from Hindus than from Muslims. Furthermore, all Muslim participants were male.

6. See Dorian (1982). Anyone who has attended a Hindi-language film in an audience for whom Hindi is not the first language knows that almost everyone is following the story quite well. In Banaras and elsewhere in northern India, it is "filmy Hindi" rather than the regional standard Hindi of public education that appears in the local idiom.

7. He mentioned to me several times that he had never worked for money and he wanted me to remember that.

8. Bhojpuri, with Assamese, Bengali, Magahi, Maithili, and Oriya, are part of a language family labeled the "Eastern group" (Grierson, 1901) or "Magadhan group" (Chatterji, 1926) of the greater Indo-Aryan language grouping. Of these six, Bhojpuri is geographically the western-most language, and linguistically the most dissimilar to the others.

The *LSI* divides Bhojpuri into "three main varieties,—the Standard [subdivided into Northern Standard and Southern Standard], the Western, and Nagpuria. It has also a border sub-dialect called Madhesi, and a broken form called Tharu. . .Western Bhojpuri is spoken in. . .Fyzabad, Azamgargh, Jaunpur, Benares, the western half of Ghazipur, and South-Gangetic Mirzapur" (Grierson, 1903:42, 44).

Most of the people I asked in Banaras identified Bhojpuri as the language of Bihar. In one group, I was told that Bhojpuri was not spoken in Banaras, although everybody agreed that what they spoke at home was not Hindi.

9. Banarsi Boli is also known as Banarsi Bhojpuri, a more informative and technically accurate label. In this article I have chosen to use the term *Banarsi Boli* rather than *Banarsi Bhojpuri* because the former is the term used often by native Banarsi Boli speakers.

10. Grierson, 1903:264: "The dialect spoken in the District of Benares [*sic*] is Western Bhojpuri, the same as that of Azamgarh. It is locally known as Banarasi." Ibid., 270: "The language spoken by the natives of Benares City varies considerably according to the castes of the speakers." Ibid., 273 (Following a transliteration of a "middle class" reading of the Parable of the Prodigal Son): "The dialect of the lowest dregs of the populace has many marked peculiarities and has occupied more than one native scholar."

11. Banarsi Boli exhibits certain morphophonemic similarities with Awadhi, particularly in the pronominal and verbal systems. These similarities are part of what distinguish Banarsi Boli from other dialects of Western Bhojpuri (Simon, 1986).

12. The *LSI* notes that Banarsi Boli differs from other varieties of Western Bhojpuri. Tiwari attributes these linguistic differences to contact with Awadhi. My data show that where Banarsi Boli differs from other dialects of Western Bhojpuri, it matches either Awadhi or regional standard Hindi. I suggest that the morphosyntactic parallels between Banarsi Boli and Hindi are due to the immersion of Banarsi Boli speakers in Hindi-language situations in most of the important aspects of Banarsi social and economic life.

13. In 1965, Banaras housed over eighty-four Sanskrit *pathshalas* (traditional schools where Sanskrit is taught by memorization and repetition), many of which are over 150 years old.

14. As early as 1917, Gandhi argued that Hindi should be the national language. Among other reasons, he said that it would be easy for "the whole country" to learn Hindi, and that it was "the speech of the majority of the inhabitants of India." "Thus Hindi has already established itself as the national language of India. We have been using it as such for a long time. . .The birth of Urdu is due to this fact." (Gandhi, "Hindi Swaraj," in Gopal, 1966:90).

15. The influence of Hindi in the Banaras area is remarked, for instance, in the *Uttar Pradesh District Gazetteer* of 1965: "Linguistically, the district of Varanasi is a Bhojpuri speaking area, the social development of which, from the cultural and literary points of view, has been intimately related to the Hindi speaking regions of the State."

16. In general, Muslims feel they have not quite gotten their due in Banaras. Over the centuries, the population in Banaras has been between a quarter to a third Muslim, but usually among the poorer segment. Muslims are often employed by Hindus in the labor-intensive, low-wage occupations such as silk production, much of which is used for elaborate brocades purchased by wealthier Hindus for weddings. The same attitude toward cross-religion employment is implied to different purpose in the laundryman's story in the section on marked code-switching.

17. Until recently, only well-educated but politically naive Banarsi natives would return themselves as first language or mother tongue Bhojpuri speakers. Between 1961 and 1971, however, the number of "nonstandard" or nonregional language returns has increased because of several factors, among which is the change in instructions regarding recording responses as given.

18. "Variants have been grouped in some cases under the relevant languages [languages named in Schedule VIII to the Constitution of India]. This has been done on the basis of linguistic information readily available or

in light of studies already made. These identifiable variants which returned 10,000 or more speakers each at all-India level. . .are. . .*Hindi*—Awadhi; Bhojpuri; Braj Bhasha, Bundeli/Bundelkhandi, Chhattisgarhi, Garhwali; Haryanvi; Jaunsari, Kangri, Khariboli, Kumauni; Magadhi/Magahi; Maithili; Marwari; Nagpuria, Nimadi, Pahari; Rajasthani" (*Census of India, 1981*:5).

19. For each census where the individual's response was to be recorded as given, the census taker was allowed to record only two languages, and to do so in the order given. Even here, the census taker determines whether the variety named is a "language." "Banarsi Boli" would not have been included. Thus, in Banaras, an individual returning Hindi and Banarsi Boli is counted as a monolingual Hindi speaker. An individual claiming three languages—Urdu, Hindi, and Bhojpuri—is recorded as bilingual in Urdu and Hindi, and Bhojpuri is not counted at all.

Predictably, most Banaras natives, and almost all Banaras Hindus, have always been returned as Hindi speakers. In 1951, for instance, no "Bhojpuri" responses were recorded, although over 6,500 people claimed areas of western Bihar as "place of birth."

20. When the language medium for education is determined, the regional language is taken as the "first language" in most states. This means that although each state is required to provide education through the primary level in whatever mother tongue is requested (within certain student minima), the number of "mother tongues" is considerably reduced by using the *regional language* label as an umbrella for any number of mother tongues within the state.

As of 1961 at the primary level, Uttar Pradesh provided education in Hindi, as well as in Bengali, English, Marathi, Punjabi, Sindhi, and Urdu. (Neither Uttar Pradesh, nor Bihar—with a substantial Bhojpuri-speaking population—officially provided education in Bhojpuri.) (Goel and Saini, 1972:41.)

In practice, as Pattanayak has pointed out (1981), when teachers and students are from the same locality, the language medium is often the speech of that locality, although it is often given the regional language label and is often perceived *to be* the regional language.

21. At the university level, Banaras Hindu University offers English, Hindi, Sanskrit, Bengali, Pali, and Urdu; the classroom language medium is officially Hindi. At Varanasi Sanskrit Vishvavidyalaya, the language offered is, of course, Sanskrit; those language media are Sanskrit and Hindi. Kashi Vidyapith offers Hindi and Sanskrit; the official medium is Hindi (Goel and Saini, 1972:49–55).

22. The District Varanasi *Primary Census Abstract* gives the number of *literates* ("a person who can both read and write with understanding") for urban Banaras in 1981 as 376,410: females number 128,770 and males 247,640. The literacy rate for urban Varanasi is nearly 46 percent, compared to 27 percent for Uttar Pradesh in general. The rate for females of the whole Varanasi *tahsil*

(subdivision of a district) is somewhat higher than for the rest of the state (16.25 percent against 14 percent). With regard to the relation between gender, literacy (at least via public education), and language identity, the literacy rate for Varanasi tahsil males, compared with that of both the rest of the males in the state and with the females of Varanasi, is particularly revealing. Literacy rates for Varanasi tahsil males compared with those for females show 46 percent against 16.25 percent. (Males of Varanasi tahsil show a literacy rate of nearly 46 percent against about 39 percent for all males throughout Uttar Pradesh.)

23. See Humes's chapter in this volume for a discussion of how female participation in religious activities is in part determined by education and access to the "higher" language of Sanskrit. Women worshiping with the Khatri female guru use a new form of devotional singing of a Sanskrit text in their mother tongue of Punjabi.

24. Among the Hindu women I knew, it was the poorest and least educated, and hence most isolated, who identified Banarsi Boli as some form of Hindi. Those with more outside contact distinguished between Banarsi Boli and Hindi, and between their own speech and that of the males in the household. I was not studying this type of valuation, however, and the remarks from these participants may not be at all representative.

25. Government records on education show that the second language is usually English or Sanskrit for Hindus.

26. Diglossia is present to some degree in the urban areas of most of the northern Indian plains, which constitute the Hindi regional language area. In this area, Hindi coexists with a given local speech variety.

27. I thought I was barging in, but he was insistent that I not only stay, but also tape the proceedings.

28. Ferguson (1972:236) has suggested typical language situations in which speech varieties are function specific, and notes that there is little overlap. For instance, in a situation where bilinguals are fluent in both speech varieties, speakers may read from the newspaper in the "high" variety and then discuss what was just read in the "low."

29. That is, no individual code-switch can be "attributed to stylistic or discourse functions" (Poplack, 1988).

30. Neither man commented on his code-switching during the conversation, nor seemed to notice it later when listening to the tape.

31. This type of code-switching is frequent. Very few conversations did not include Banarsi Boli–Hindi code-switching at some point. However, my data do not show it to be the predominant stylistic or discourse strategy: that is, no single speaker whom I recorded used intrasentential code-switching throughout a whole conversation.

32. Several—for instance, Poplack (1988), Scotton (1988)—see this overall pattern of unmarked, intrasentential code-switching as analogous to monolingual discourse.

33. Within the Banarsi Boli–speaking community, intrasentential code-switching is, in itself, unremarkable. As is common in Chicano Spanish-English, or Puerto Rican Spanish-English bilinguals in the United States, or French-English bilinguals in Canada, the speaker and the other participants may be unaware of code-switching.

The frequency of unmarked intrasentential code-switching among Banarsis supports the current hypothesis that such code-switching "is only frequent when both varieties are indexical of identities which are positively evaluated for the specific exchange type" (Scotton, 1988:166).

34. This is a loan, a blend of terry and cotton, which has been naturalized with retroflex initial and final [T] and the mid-back rounded open. Terrycot is a polyester blend that is not only substantially more expensive than cotton, but also one that lasts longer and requires little pressing.

35. Among Hindus in Banaras, Muslims are reputed not to pay very good wages, especially to Hindus.

36. Again, an English loan, naturalized with a retroflex [R].

37. *Ihaa* has the Banarsi Boli vowel rather than the Hindi semivowel; *hau* has a Banarsi Boli diphthong.

38. It is, of course, unlikely, that the actual conversation of ten years earlier took place in this pattern of language alternation.

Appendices

Cynthia Ann Humes

Appendix A
The Thirty-One Day Program of the Ramnagar *Ramlila**

Day 1   The maharaja arrives at the performance scene two kilometers outside of Ramnagar. Ravana is born and subdues the world. The frightened gods assemble to determine what actions to take, and ask Brahma to seek help from Vishnu. This scene of Brahma beseeching Vishnu's intervention features the famous portrayal of Vishnu and Lakshmi reclining on the serpent Shesha, who floats atop the Kshir Sagar.

Day 2   Births of the four sons of Dasharatha (Ram, Bharat, Lakshman, and Shatrughna) and Ram's play as a child.

Day 3   Vishvamitra comes to Ayodhya and asks Dasharatha to allow Ram and Lakshman to accompany him so that they can go into the forest and rid it of the demons who have been destroying the sacrifices of the seers. Various demons are killed, including the demoness Taraka, and Ahalya is released from her curse. The brothers reach Janakpur, home of Sita.

Day 4   A tour of Janakpur is presented. Ram sees Sita in her garden and they fall in love. Parashuram arrives.

Day 5   The Svayamvara contest for Sita's hand in marriage takes place: whoever can lift and break Shiva's bow is to win Sita. After ten thousand other princes try but fail, Ram easily lifts and breaks the bow.

Day 6   The great procession from Ayodhya to Janakpur, and the wedding ceremonies of Ram and Sita.

---

* This calendar of the Ramnagar *Ramlila* is adapted from Schechner and Hess (1977).

Day 7   Ram's party, including the brothers and their new brides, leave
         Janakpur for Ayodhya; celebrations in Ayodhya.

Day 8   Preparations for Ram's coronation halt when Kaikeyi asks that
         her son Bharat be coronated instead in fulfillment of Dash-
         aratha's promises. Three dramatic scenes: the hunchback
         maid Manthara convinces Kaikeyi to extract the promises from
         Dasharatha; confrontation between Kaikeyi and Dasharatha;
         and Ram's calm acceptance of exile.

Day 9   Ram, Sita, and Lakshman begin their exile by leaving Ayodhya
         and proceeding into the forest.

Day 10   The Nishada tribal chief Guha offers humble but sincere
         hospitality to the royal party and joins them.

Day 11   Ram crosses the Jamuna and Ganga rivers. A tender scene
         in the *Ramlila* is the washing of Ram's feet by the boatman.
         The party is accompanied by Guha. A Shiva *lingam* is
         worshiped, with an actual priest conducting the *puja* and Ram
         performing the *arati*.

Day 12   Bharat learns of Kaikeyi's treachery and Dasharatha's death,
         and immediately leaves Ayodhya to meet Ram in Chitrakut
         in order to ask him to return to the city and accept the crown.

Day 13   Bharat arrives at Ram's site of exile in Chitrakut, where a
         conference is held with the sage Vashishta, King Janaka, and
         others. Ram refuses to return, for he has vowed to endure
         the hardships of exile.

Day 14   Bharat heads back to Ayodhya and rests at Nandigram after
         placing Ram's sandals on the throne to show his respect for
         Ram.

Day 15   Jayanta pecks Sita's foot. Having left Chitrakut Ram now
         dwells in Panchavati, located deeper in the forest. A series
         of meetings with sages takes place, and Sita learns from
         Anasuya the virtues of being a good wife.

Day 16   The *rakshasa* demoness Shurpanakha appears and attempts
         to seduce Ram and Lakshman. After appearing in her
         demonic form and threatening Sita, she is punished by
         Lakshman, who lops off her nose and ears. After two of her
         demon brothers are bested by Ram, Shurpanakha then
         beseeches her brother Ravana to come to her aid. He sends
         thousands of demons to revenge her, who are promptly killed
         by Ram. Ravana, using the ruse of Maricha as a golden deer,
         kidnaps Sita. Jatayu attempts to stop Ravana but is mortally
         wounded.

Day 17   Ram mourns the loss of Sita, and Jatayu is cremated. Ram meets Shabari and Narad. Sugriva and Hanuman become Ram's allies.

Day 18   Ram slays Bali, the tyrant king of monkeys, and Bali's younger brother Sugriva assumes the throne.

Day 19   Hanuman leaps across the sea at Rameshvaram after evading the giantess Surasa, who seeks to consume him. His flying (in the *Ramlila*, actually crawling) in and then out of her mouth is a favorite scene.

Day 20   The queens' quarters in Ravana's Lanka palace where Sita sits prisoner in the *ashoka* garden is displayed. Upon crossing the sea by constructing a bridge at Rameshvaram, Ram and his army worship Shiva.

Day 21   Ravana hears counsel, who unanimously agree that Ram is invincible. Vibhishana asks Ram for refuge. Ram's army crosses and invades Lanka; the news reaches Ravana that his warriors are suffering severe losses, but he merely laughs.

Day 22   A day of battle. Lakshman is wounded and Hanuman is sent to the Himalayas to get the herb to save him. To be sure he gets the right plant, Hanuman returns with the entire mountain.

Day 23   More battles.

Day 24   Ravana wakes his brother Kumbhakarna, who after consuming great quantities of water buffalo and wine fights Ram's army. His defeat by Ram is portrayed as a drawn-out dismemberment of a huge effigy.

Day 25   Ravana himself enters the battle. Ram tries to behead Ravana, but each time he cuts off one of the demon's ten heads it grows back. Sita expresses fear that she will never be rescued.

Day 26   (Dashahara) Ravana dies. This event is portrayed twice. In the first portrayal, the human figure (*svarup*) portraying Ravana removes his mask of ten heads and rigging of twenty arms prior to clasping Ram's feet. The second portrayal features the dramatic burning of a seventy-five-foot effigy of Ravana.

Day 27   Sita is rescued; she proves her chastity in Lanka through the fire ordeal. After Ravana's brother Vibhishana is crowned, Ram's party sets out for Ayodhya on the pushpaka, the aerial vehicle.

Day 28   The reunion of the four brothers (Bharat Milap) takes place, signifying the end of the exile.

Day 29   The coronation of Ram; farewells to forest companions and fellow soldiers. Only Hanuman is allowed to stay; the departure of Bali's son Angad is a highpoint, as is the *arati* at the end of the night's performance. The *mela* continues all night in Ramnagar, and at dawn the *svarups* of the four brothers and Sita and the maharaja return for another *arati* ceremony.

Day 30   The two royal parties of Ram and the maharaja ride together to a garden, where Ram offers his teachings.

Day 31   The events of this day are unique to the *Ramlila* of Ramnagar. The five *svarups* arrive at the maharaja's Fort late in the afternoon atop two elephants. There the maharaja greets them as a humble devotee of Ram, and the twelve Ramayanis recite the *Ramcharitmanas* in its entirety. The Kot Vidai, or farewell ceremony, takes place.

Day 32   The maharaja summons the *svarups*, who are paid full fees for their performance.

Appendix B
An Encapsulation of the *Ramcharitmanas* by Tulsidas

I. *Balkand:* "Childhood" (portrayed on days 1–7 of the Ramnagar *Ramlila*)

The longest of seven sections, *Balkand* is a description of Ram's "childhood." In actuality, the description spans tens of thousands of years, for it seeks to provide the reader with an elaborate reference to the history behind the story: connections of Ram to other deities, cosmic incidents that affect and effect later actions, and Tulsidas's perspective on religion and different deities. Tulsidas offers a lengthy description of the myths of Lord Shiva, who is narrating the story to his wife Sati. The author documents Shiva's reverence for the great Lord Ram in a bid to obviate sectarian divisions. Tulsidas then proceeds to the Ram incarnation story itself, beginning with the necessity for this particular incarnation of Vishnu as Ram, son of Koshala king Dasharatha.

As Ram, Vishnu sets aright a number of disharmonies in the universe. Tulsidas carefully details the prior lives of numerous demons, gods, and heroic figures and the curses or blessings which lead to their subsequent rebirths as characters described in the *Ramayana*. Through the actions of Ram, good or bad deeds are rewarded or punished, and in many cases tragic destinies are altered by devotion to Ram.

When the great demon Ravana overpowers the gods and begins to terrorize the entire world, the deities urge Vishnu to take birth. Peacefully reclining on the coils of the serpent Shesha floating on the ocean of milk, Kshir Sagar, Vishnu resolves to incarnate himself as the sons of Dasharatha, who performs a sacrifice for the birth of a son. Tulsidas briefly describes the childhood and adolescence of the four brothers Ram, Lakshman, Bharat, and Shatrughna.

Ram's mission to restore righteousness begins when he is still but a youth. The sage Shukracharya, enraged when his daughter was violated by King Danda, had cursed Danda's forest so that it would be overrun by demons. The great seer Vishvamitra requests Dasharatha to send his adolescent sons Ram and Lakshman to remove the demons who were disrupting the austerities of *sadhus* dwelling in the Dandaka Forest. Dasharatha agrees after his family priest and personal guru Vashishta advises him that no harm will come to the boys. Within days, Ram kills the demoness Taraka, thrusts Maricha away a thousand miles south beyond the sea with a headless arrow, and slays Subahu with a fiery missile. Vishvamitra tells Ram he should witness the great contest of the bow (dhanushyajna), and Ram sets out for Janakpur, where this contest is to take place. Along the way, Ram hears numerous stories told by Vishvamitra and learns great secrets of battle from this sage. Ram restores the beautiful Ahalya from stone to life, and finally arrives in Videha, the city of King Janak.

Ram and Sita (the incarnation of Vishnu's consort, Shri-Lakshmi) meet while she sits in the *ashoka* garden worshiping Girija (Parvati). They instantly fall in love with each other, and Sita asks the Goddess to grant her wish to marry the handsome prince of Ayodhya. To win the contest, the successful suitor is required to lift and break Shiva's great bow. Ten thousand hopeful princes attempt to do so, but even working together they still cannot lift the bow. Sita appeals to Shiva and Parvati to rob the bow of its might, and Ram then not only lifts but playfully snaps it in two.

The princes are furious that the impertinent young boy has achieved this so easily, and refuse to regard him as rightful victor. At that moment, Vishnu's own incarnation of Parashuram ("Ram with an axe") arrives. The princes draw back terrified of the angry anchorite Parashuram. Ram asks the wrathful Parashuram to become calm. Tulsidas does little with this myth, assuming most know that Parashuram descended to protect the *Brahmins*, who were being overpowered by the *Kshatriyas*. When Parashuram begins to offer Vishnu's bow to Ram and the bow miraculously leaps into the arms of the prince himself, Parashuram recognizes the youth's true identity, and he returns to the forest to perform austerities, bringing to a close the sixth avatar of Vishnu. The chapter concludes with the marriage celebrations of all four brothers with the daughters and nieces of Janak, king of Videha, and their triumphant return to Ayodhya.

II. Ayodhyakand: "Ayodhya Kingdom" (portrayed on days 8–14 of the Ramnagar *Ramlila*)

This second long section concerns itself with the issue of why and how Ram is sent into exile. On the human level, it appears to be due to the scheming of an evil stepmother and the weakness of Ram's father; on a transcendent level, it is due to the necessity of Ram's ridding the earth of demons and restoring *dharma*, or righteousness.

After Ram returns to Ayodhya with his bride Sita, Dasharatha decides he is getting older and should formally name Ram as regent. He instructs his minister Sumantra to begin the proceedings for his favorite son's installation. The gods are unhappy, however, for they need Ram to come to their aid against the demons. They therefore appeal to the goddess Sarasvati, and she agrees to manipulate circumstances so that Ram will be forced to dwell in the forest and eventually destroy the enemies of the gods. Sarasvati deludes Manthara, the evil hump-backed handmaid of Kaikeyi. Manthara convinces the queen to force Dasharatha to make good on two boons he had promised long before, and thus place Kaikeyi's son Bharat on the throne and thrust Ram into exile. Kaikeyi succeeds in her efforts, unbeknownst to Bharat and Shatrughna, who are located away from the city. Ram calmly accepts his fate and dutifully prepares to leave Ayodhya. The citizens and royal family are in great distress. Sita, asked by her husband to remain at home as a source of strength for the family, tells Ram she will die if separated from him, and Ram, realizing this to be true, allows her to accompany him into the forest. Similarly, Lakshman also insists on going with Ram, so all three set off for the forest in a chariot driven by Sumantra and followed by many sorrowful Ayodhyans.

The next morning, the exiled party leaves before the crowd awakes. The group meets the low-caste Nishada chieftain Guha, who receives them humbly in his village and joins the party in their exile. After arriving at the Ganges riverbank, Sumantra explains that Dasharatha had secretly instructed him to bring the party back to Ayodhya, but Ram refuses to return for it would mean his father's promise to Kaikeyi would be broken. Recognizing Ram's divinity, the ferryman insists on washing the Lord's feet before transporting the party across the Ganges River. The party meet various figures, including the sage Valmiki, who advises them to dwell near the Mandakini River at Chitrakut in the Dandaka Forest. After arriving in Chitrakut, Ram sends Sumantra back to Ayodhya. Dasharatha, heartbroken by Ram's decision to remain in exile, dies. Family guru and priest Vashishta sends for Bharat and Shatrughna, and when the two sons learn of the tragic events, they are furious with Kaikeyi and in profound grief that their father is dead and Ram and Lakshman are in exile. After consoling the two innocent brothers, Vishvamitra leads them and Dasharatha's wives (including the now remorseful Kaikeyi) to Ram. Meanwhile, Sita's parents learn of the procession and they also come to Chitrakut. Surrounded by Ayodhyans, Sita's parents, and others, Bharat pleads with Ram to return to Ayodhya and assume the throne. Ram forgives all concerned, but he refuses to return because he wishes to fulfill his father's vow to Kaikeyi. After lengthy debate, Bharat agrees to go back to Ayodhya, but he enthrones Ram's sandals before retiring to Nandigram to live an austere ascetic life while ruling until Ram returns.

III. *Aranyakand:* "The Forest" (portrayed on days 15–16 of the Ramnagar *Ramlila*)

This short chapter begins with the famous story of Indra's son Jayanta. Wishing to test Ram, Jayanta assumes the form of a crow and pecks Sita's foot. Ram becomes infuriated by this audacious act and releases an arrow which pursues the terror-stricken Jayanta until he appeals to Ram for forgiveness. Jayanta loses an eye in punishment for this deed. Ram now realizes that everyone is aware of his true identity and location, so in order to be free of constant interruptions, he resolves to leave Chitrakut, and thus turns away from civilization and enters the wilds of the forest.

The story now revolves quickly. The exiles Ram, Sita, and Lakshman enter the forest and meet the hermit Atri. Sita is taught by the sage's wife Anasuya on the virtues of a good wife. They meet Agastya, who advises the group to go to Panchavati. The *rakshasa* Shurpanakha, sister of Ravana, sees the handsome brothers and is infatuated. When she is teased, she assumes her demonic form and threatens Sita. When Lakshman retaliates by mutilating her face, Shurpanakha asks two brothers to punish them. In the ensuing battle, however, Ram and Lakshman easily defeat them and their armies. Ravana hears of their deaths and the beauty of Sita, and he resolves to take action. At Ram's request, Sita enters the fire and an "illusory Sita" steps out to experience the kidnapping in Sita's stead (thus removing potential questions of her "purity"). Ravana forces Maricha to aid his venture to steal Sita away from Ram. Sita espies Maricha disguised as a golden deer and requests its hide. Ram, although knowing the true nature of the situation, consents to do the will of the gods and shoots Maricha. In his dying breath, Maricha mimics Ram's voice as he cries out for help. Sita urges Lakshman to go to Ram's aid. When Lakshman at last agrees to do so, Ravana approaches Sita in the guise of a *Brahmin* and seizes her. The noble vulture Jatayu attempts to rescue her and is mortally wounded in battle with Ravana. Jatayu tells the brothers of Ravana's treachery, dies, and goes to Hari's realm for his devotional service. The brothers slay many *rakshasas*. The tribal Shabari woman adores Ram, naively offering him fruit which she has "taste-tested" for its sweetness; so benevolent is Ram that he accepts even this "impure" offering. Gifted with foresight, the elderly Shabari devotee advises Ram to go to Lake Pampasar and there befriend Sugriva. After fulfilling her duty to guide Ram on this journey, she too attains release. The brothers arrive at Pampasar, and the chapter concludes with the puckish sage Narada's appearance, who requests a boon from Ram. When Ram agrees to grant his request, Narada asks that the name 'Rama' be the greatest of all names for the divine, capable of "snaring" the "birds of sin."

IV. *Kishkindhakand:* "Kishkindha Kingdom" (performed on days 17–18 of the Ramnagar *Ramlila*)

In this brief section, the party meets the great monkey god Hanuman, who immediately recognizes Ram as his Lord. Bali, previously crowned King of Kishkindha, was furious that his younger brother Sugriva had been installed as the king of monkeys in his stead while he was away engaged in battle. Bali deposed Sugriva, retook the throne, and sent him into exile. Ram and Lakshman make an alliance with Sugriva against Bali, in exchange for which Sugriva will aid their quest to recover Sita. Ram quickly kills Bali and Sugriva assumes the throne. (Although in the Valmiki *Ramayana* this decision has ambivalent overtones, including Bali confronting Ram for shooting from a hidden position and unrighteously conspiring with a younger brother, in the *Ramcharitmanas* this dubious alliance of Ram with younger brothers who seek their elder brothers' thrones is consciously down-played. Tulsidas portrays Bali as a wicked ruler and Sugriva as righteous up to a point: Sugriva still must be forced to aid Ram in his quest after the Monkey King dallies for quite some time.) In search of news about Sita, Hanuman meets Jatayu's brother Sampati, who learns of his brother's heroism, performs his funeral rites, and tells them they can find Sita across the sea in the *rakshasa* kingdom of Lanka.

V. *Sundarkand:* "The Beautiful" (performed on day 19 of the Ramnagar *Ramlila*)

Here Tulsidas sets the stage for the great battle in Lanka between the forces of righteousness led by Ram and the forces of evil led by Ravana. Hanuman resolves to leap across the ocean to find Sita, but the giantess Surasa is sent by the gods to test Hanuman's strength and wisdom first. Surasa attempts to swallow Hanuman, but after he enters and exits her mouth by assuming a tiny form, she blesses his venture. Hanuman jumps across the waters to Lanka and encounters Ravana's brother Vibhishana, who proves to be a devotee of Ram. Vibhishana leads Hanuman to the ever faithful Sita, who asks that her husband come to save her personally. Ravana catches Hanuman and orders his tail to be burnt to humiliate him, but instead Hanuman sets Lanka ablaze and succeeds in returning to Ram. Mandodari urges her husband Ravana to give up his evil intentions, but again Ravana pays no attention; Vibhishana asks his brother to worship Ram and is not only spurned but kicked by Ravana. Vibhishana then goes to Ram and asks for his grace. Ravana's spies are caught and allowed to return in order to deliver Ram's ultimatum to return Sita and make peace with him. The frightened spies tell their king that Ram's forces are too great to conquer; Ravana laughs outwardly, even though trembling within. Ram takes action to cross over to Lanka by burning up the personified Ocean, who hastily agrees to allow the creation of a bridge across his waters.

VI. *Lankakand:* "Lanka Kingdom" (performed on days 20–27 of the Ramnagar *Ramlila*)

Lankakand features Ram's great battle against the forces of evil, resulting in the restoration of rule to the gods and Sita to her Lord Ram.

Ram's army masses at Rameshvaram, and the bridge to Lanka is constructed by the monkeys Nila and Nala. His forces advance while biting off demons' ears and noses in spite. Mandodari again asks her husband to abandon his quest, but he refuses. Bali's son Angad meets Ravana and asks the intransigent Demon King to seek Ram's forgiveness. When mocked, Angad challenges anyone to move his foot, but none can succeed because of the power of Ram. After giving Ravana plenty of time to surrender, Ram and his forces begin the battle in earnest. Lakshman is wounded by Ravana's son Meghnad, and Hanuman retrieves a physician from Lanka who sends him to the Himalayas to get the herb to save Lakshman. To be sure he gets the correct herb, Hanuman returns with the entire mountain, demonstrating his tremendous physical strength. Ravana wakes his brother Kumbhakarna, who consumes great quantities of water buffalo and wine. Kumbhakarna blesses brother Vibhishana's battle against the demon forces and resigns himself to his unhappy fate of fighting against righteous Ram. After a horrible battle between the demons and the hosts of monkeys, Ram finally slays Kumbhakarna. Meghnad consoles his worried father with confident boasts of his eventual success, but

Garuda swallows the magical serpents Meghnad conjures, allowing
Lakshman to slay him. Ravana himself finally enters the battle. Ram
tries to dismember Ravana, but each time that he cuts off one of the
demon's ten heads or twenty arms it grows back. The kind demoness
Trijata informs Sita of the battle's events and Sita expresses fears that
she will never be rescued. Ram at last kills Ravana. The "shadow" Sita
is summoned by Ram and she proves her chastity to all when she steps
into a blazing fire; the true Sita steps out of the fire back to Ram. The
gods rejoice and Vibhishana begins his rule of Lanka. The party returns
to Ayodhya in an aerial car, stopping at several sites for the blessings
of sages and to bathe in the Ganges.

VII. *Uttarkand:* "The Epilogue" (performed on days 28–30 of the
Ramnagar *Ramlila*)

The joyous reunion of the four brothers in Ayodhya opens this
final section. Ram comforts the remorseful Kaikeyi, showing he bears
no ill will toward her. He is at last installed on the throne while the
entire city rejoices. Ram bids farewell to his forest companions and
fellow soldiers, allowing only the faithful Hanuman to stay. Ram is asked
to deliver his teachings to an audience of devoted citizens and the gods
themselves. Tulsidas describes the happiness in the kingdom of Koshala
now that Ram has been righteously installed, and very brief mention
is made of many events. (For example, the birth of the handsome sons
Lava and Kusha to Sita merits only a sentence, and there is no mention
of her banishment, as in the Valmiki *Ramayana*.) A number of "frame
stories" are presented, as Hess describes in her chapter. These stories
reveal the many layers of "tellings" of the *Ramcharitmanas* by different
individuals, and how actions in their own life pertain to the story.
Tulsidas ends with a traditional promise that readers will receive great
fruits from hearing and chanting this work.

Appendix C
Major Characters of the *Ramayana*

Agastya   A sage who through various curses and boons affects
             many of the developments in the *Ramayana*; he also
             gives Ram divine weapons and advises him to build
             an ashram in nearby Panchavati.
Ahalya   Beautiful wife of the *rishi* Gautama who is seduced
             by Indra and cursed by the seer to remain as stone
             until Ram restores her to life.

Anasuya	Wife of the hermit Atri renowned for her devotion to her husband, who lectures Sita on the virtues of a good wife.
Angad	The son of Bali who is made crown prince of Kishkindha by his uncle Sugriva and fights against Ravana in battle.
Atri	A great sage and husband of Anasuya; both are visited by Ram's party in the forest.
Bali	The monkey king of Kishkindha killed by Ram in order to gain the aid of Bali's younger brother Sugriva in the battle against Ravana.
Bharat	Son of Dasharatha and Kaikeyi; he is loyal and devoted to his brother Ram and remorseful of his mother's efforts to gain him the throne.
Bhardwaj	A sage visited by Ram, Sita, and Lakshman who advises them during their sojourn in the forest; he entertains Ram's brother and his troops; he is the listener to the story of Ram as told by Yajnavalkya at his ashram in Prayag.
Bhushundi	Also Kakabhushundi. The crow devoted to Ram who relates the story of Ram to Garuda.
Dasharatha	King of Koshala and father of Ram.
Garuda	Part bird, part man King of Birds who serves as the vehicle of Vishnu; he comes to Ram's aid during his battle with Meghnad, consuming the serpent-snare that binds Ram; he listens to the story of Ram as told by Bhushundi.
Girija	"Born of the Mountain"; an epithet of Parvati, Shiva's wife.
Guha	King of the tribal Nishadas who is befriended by Ram despite his low caste.
Hanuman	The monkey god, famous as the faithful servant and model devotee of Lord Ram.
Indrajit	"Conquerer of Indra"; an epithet for Meghnad, who had defeated Indra by using his magical ability to become invisible while Indra battled with his father Ravana.
Janak(a)	King of Videha and father of Sita.
Jatayu	The loyal vulture who attempts to stop Ravana's capture of Sita but is mortally wounded and then sent to Vishnu's world after informing Ram of the kidnaping.

Jayanta	Indra's son who upon assuming the form of a crow and biting Sita's foot is pursued by an arrow of Ram and loses an eye in punishment.
Kaikeyi	A wife of Dasharatha; mother of Bharat. When urged by her maidservant, she contrives to have Ram supplanted by her own son and banished to the forest in fulfillment of two previously promised boons by Dasharatha which were granted after Kaikeyi saved his life in battle.
Kakabhushundi	See Bhushundi.
Kaushalya	A wife of Dasharatha; mother of Ram.
Kumbhakarna	The *rakshasa* brother of Ravana famous for his lengthy periods of sleep and slain after extended battle by Ram.
Lakshman	Son of Dasharatha and Sumitra; Ram's favorite brother who loyally accompanies Ram and Sita during their forest exile.
Lakshmi	The goddess of fortune and wealth who is known as the wife of Vishnu. Whenever Vishnu incarnates himself, she does so as well; hence in one of her forms she is Sita.
Mandodari	Favorite wife of Ravana who tries to talk him out of his nefarious actions against Ram.
Manthara	The humpbacked handmaid who, deluded by the goddess Sarasvati, convinces Queen Kaikeyi to call for her son Bharat's (rather than Ram's) installment as regent.
Maricha	The demon who is thrust thousands of miles away with a headless arrow by the youth Ram and then later compelled by Ravana to assume the form of a golden deer in order to lure Ram and Lakshman away from Sita and thus facilitate her capture.
Meghnad	Eldest son of Ravana and Mandodari; he is slain by Lakshman after ensnaring Ram in a magical net of snakes, which was devoured by Garuda, Vishnu's avian vehicle, who is the enemy of serpents. Meghnad is also known as Indrajit for having defeated Indra and carrying him off to Lanka.
Nala	Together with Nila, this monkey warrior constructs the bridge to Lanka.
Narad(a)	The mischievous *rishi* devoted to Vishnu who plays an important role at a number of junctures in the *Ramayana* tradition.

Nila   Together with Nala, this monkey warrior constructs
                the bridge to Lanka.
Parashuram   "Ram with an axe"; the sixth incarnation of Vishnu
                as a *Brahmin* born to repress the *Kshatriyas*, who
                were abusing the *Brahmins*.
Parvati   "Daughter of the mountain"; the wife of Shiva. In
                one of the early frame stories of the *Ramcharitmanas*,
                Sati doubts that Ram could be the immortal Vishnu.
                To test his powers, she assumes the form of his wife
                Sita; when Ram knows who she is, she is humiliated
                and lies to her husband Shiva about her deception.
                Shiva vows not to touch Sati because she had caused
                her body to assume the form of Sita, his "Mother."
                In order to regain her husband, Sati resolves to
                commit self-immolation, which she does at her
                father's sacrifice, and then takes rebirth as Parvati.
Raghu   An ancestor of Ram. Numerous epithets of Ram are
                generated from this name: Raghuchanda, Raghu-
                nanda, Raghunatha, Raghunayaka, Raghupati,
                Raghuraja, Raghuvira, and so on, meaning "delight
                of," "leader," "lord," "king," and so on, of the house
                of Raghu.
Ram (Rama)   Son of Dasharatha and Kaushalya; the hero of the
                Ramayana; seventh incarnation of Vishnu.
Ravan(a)   The Rakshasa king of Lanka who steals Sita from
                Ram and whose defeat by him is told in the
                Ramayana.
Sampati   Brother of vulture Jatayu; he helps Hanuman locate
                Sita.
Sati   The wife of Shiva who asks to hear the story of Ram
                from her husband in the *Ramcharitmanas*.
Shabari   The woman from the low-caste Shabara tribe who
                worships Ram, advises Ram to go to Pampasar and
                make friends with Sugriva, and then attains
                liberation.
Shatrughna   Son of Dasharatha and Sumitra; he remains behind
                in Ayodhya with Bharat.
Shesha   King of Serpents who has a thousand heads and
                forms the couch of Vishnu when he resides on the
                Kshir Sagar.
Shiva   So-called auspicious deity who narrates the story of
                Ram to his wife Parvati (*Ramcharitmanas*).

Shukracharya	The great sage who served as guru to the *daityas* or demons. He cursed the Dandaka Forest to be overrun by *daityas* after his daughter was violated by King Danda.
Shurpanakha	Sister of demon king Ravana; when she makes amorous advances toward Ram and Lakshman and is refused, she attacks Sita and is then mutilated by Lakshman as punishment; in revenge, she urges Ravana to abduct Sita.
Sita	Devoted wife of Ram who is kidnapped by Ravana.
Subahu	A demon who disturbed Vishvamitra's sacrifice and is slain by Ram with a flaming arrow.
Sugriva	Bali's younger brother who becomes the monkey king of Kishkindha when Bali is killed by Ram; in return, Sugriva aids Ram in the battle against Ravana.
Sumantra	Ayodhyan chief minister who acts as the charioteer for Ram's party in exile.
Sumitra	A wife of Dasharatha; mother of Lakshman and Shatrughna.
Surasa	The giantess mother of serpents who attempts to swallow Hanuman during his leap across the sea to Lanka, but after failing, blesses him.
Taraka	Mother of Maricha; a huge demoness who despite being a woman is slain by Ram at Vishvamitra's command.
Trijata	A kind female *rakshasa* who watches over Sita in the *ashoka* garden of Lanka and who is a devotee of Ram.
Valmiki	A sage who is attributed to be the author of the famous Sanskrit *Ramayana*. In the *Ramcharitmanas*, Ram visits Valmiki who advises the royal party to dwell in Chitrakut.
Vashishta	A Vedic sage who has an extensive mythology but in this story is the family priest of Dasharatha and Ram's personal guru.
Vibhishana	A brother of Ravana who had been a sage in a prior life but was cursed to be reborn as a *rakshasa*. He recognizes Ram in the wilderness, adores Ram, and assumes the throne when Ravana is overthrown.
Vishnu	The "Expander" who periodically incarnates himself to restore *dharma*, or righteousness.

Vishvamitra	A Vedic seer who has an extensive mythology but in this story he is the sage who asks Dasharatha for the aid of Ram and Lakshman to destroy the demons who are disrupting his sacrifice in the Dandaka Forest.
Yajnavalkya	A sage, reputed author of various texts, who recites the story of Ram to Bhardwaj.

Appendix D
General Glossary*

acharya	A spiritual teacher who guides disciples along their path.
aditya	"Portion of [the goddess] Aditi"; one of the twelve suns or solar deities.
Advaita	"Nondual"; the monistic school of Hindu philosophy positing the identity of the *atman*, or essence of the individual, with the *brahman*, or transcendent Unity, and which interprets the phenomenal world as illusory in some sense.
Agni	The Vedic deity of fire; the sacrificial fire itself.
akhara	Public gymnasium for wrestling, associated with the patron deity Hanuman.
Annakut	"Heap of food"; the grain festival which is usually celebrated on Kartik (October/November) *purnima*.
Annapurna	"She who [bestows much] food"; name of a grain goddess, usually portrayed as the consort of Shiva.
arati	The waving of ghee lamps before a divine image; also refers to the entire sequence of giving offerings to the deity.
ashoka	A type of flowering tree.
ashram	A hermitage where renunciants, known for their holiness and learning, live and teach.
ashrama	One of the four stages of the ideal life: celibate student, householder, forest dwelling hermits, and renunciant.

* The following terms are given in the forms used by the authors, which tend to reflect usage of vernacular rather than Sanskritic pronunciation and spelling. For names of *Ramayana* characters not listed here, see the list of major characters of the *Ramayana* (Appendix C).

ashvamedha	The Vedic royal horse sacrifice; a ceremony performed at the consecration of a king which signifies fertility and creative power.
Asi	Literally, "sword"; the name of the river that borders Varanasi on the south and enters the Ganges at Asi Ghat.
atman	The Self; in Advaita philosophy, the universal spirit which is identical with *Brahman* but which is used to refer to that essence within the person.
Aurangzeb	Late seventeenth-century emperor of the Mughal Dynasty.
avatar	A "descent" of a deity manifested in different forms; an incarnation, especially of Vishnu or the Goddess.
Avimukta	"The Never Forsaken"; another name of Banaras.
Balabhadra	Name of the elder brother of Krishna born to Rohini in the cowherd village; also Balarama.
Bhairava	The "terrible, frightful" one; a fearsome form of Lord Shiva; in the plural, a group of ancient frightful deities usually identified with Shiva.
bhajan	A song of devotional love.
bhakta	A devotee; one who worships God with fervent love.
bhakti	"Devotion, honor, love"; an attitude of devotion, love, and surrender toward a deity. Capitalized, Bhakti refers to the devotional schools of Hinduism.
Bharat(a)	The land of India, named for an ancient king, Bharata; name of a brother of Ram; name of the author of the *Natyashastra*, the Sanskrit text on performance and the arts.
Bharat Milap	Ram and Lakshman's meeting with brothers Bharat and Shatrughna after years of exile in the forest.
Bhavani	Another name for Parvati.
bhavna	Intense devotional feeling for God.
Brahma	The "Creator" God; the first member of the Hindu Triad or Trinity.
brahmacharya	The first of the four ideal stages of life or *ashramas*; celibacy, discipleship.
Brahman	The essence of life; the supreme, transcendent One; the Reality which is the source of all being and knowing; in Advaita, identical with *atman*.

Brahmanas	The name of the priestly and ritual texts attached to the Vedic *Samhitas*.
Brahmin	The first of the four Hindu *varnas*; the priestly class or a member of the priestly class, charged with the duties of learning, teaching, and performing rites and sacrifices.
Buddha	Religious figure (c. sixth century B.C.E.) who rejected the Upanishadic notions of self (*atman*) and founded a new order of renunciation. Regarded by some Hindus to be an *avatar* of Vishnu.
Daksha	The creator demigod who insulted his daughter Sati and her husband Shiva by not inviting them to a great sacrifice and refusing to give Shiva his rightful share of the offerings.
dakshina	A payment given to *Brahmins* for their ritual service.
danda (Dandi)	"Club, stick, staff"; as an adjective, *Dandi* refers to those ascetics who carry a *danda*; also a kind of push-up performed by wrestlers who simulate "sticks" by prostrating on the ground.
Dandaka Forest	A forest in the Indo-Gangetic valley where Ram dwelt during exile and the site of numerous key events in the *Ramayana*, including the mutilation of Shurpanakha, Sita's capture by Ravana, and the deaths of Maricha and Jatayu.
darshan	The "auspicious sight" of a deity.
Dashahara	A major festival celebrating Ravana's defeat by Ram, and the final day of the Navratra festival celebrating the Goddess's defeat of the Buffalo Demon. Also known as Vijayadashami and Dashera.
Dashashvamedha	The famous *tirtha* of the "Ten Horse Sacrifices" situated on the Ganges in Banaras.
Dashera	See Dashahara.
deva	A god, deity.
devi	A goddess; used to refer to the innumerable local goddesses, the consorts of the various gods, and also to the Great Goddess, called simply Devi or Mahadevi, "Great Goddess."
dham	The "abode, dwelling" of a deity; the four primary *dhams* in relation to Vishnu are Ayodhya, Chitrakut, Mathura, and Brindavan.

Dhanushyajna   The "Bow Sacrifice"; the contest at Sita's
                   Svayamvara in which the one who can lift and
                   break Shiva's bow wins Sita's hand.
dharma   The first of the four Hindu aims of life, usually
                   translated as religious and social duty, law, or
                   righteousness; often used to connote the general
                   religious tradition of Hindus or other faiths.
dharmashalas   Literally, "abodes of dharma." Places where
                   pilgrims may stay at religious sites.
digvijaya   The warlike traditional display of kingly might.
Divodasa   A legendary Buddhist king of Kashi reknowned
                   for his righteousness who expelled all the gods
                   from Banaras.
durbar   Coronation ceremony; Muslim term for paying
                   one's respect at a site of worship.
Durga   One of the names and forms of the Great Goddess.
Durgapuja   Durga's worship; See Navratra.
Dvaparayuga   The third of the four ages, or *yugas*, which together
                   constitute a *mahayuga* or eon.
Gahadavala   The twelfth-century dynasty of Hindu revivalists
                   whose centers of power were Kanauj and Banaras.
gana   The "group, troop" of demigods who are
                   attendants of Lord Shiva and are led by his son
                   Ganesha, "lord of the *ganas*."
Ganesh   "Lord of the *ganas*"; the elephant-headed son of
                   Shiva and Parvati; the "remover of obstacles" to
                   be honored at the doorway and at the outset of any
                   venture.
Ganges (Ganga)   Sacred river of north India, also personified as a
                   goddess, Ganga.
Gauri   The "fair one"; a name of Parvati.
Gaya   A site of pilgrimage in Bihar famous as an ideal
                   place for making offerings to ancestors.
Gayatri Mantra   Rig Veda 3.62.10; the Sanskrit mantra named for
                   its meter which requests the Sun to stimulate the
                   mind and which is recited by Hindu twice-born
                   males; often personified as a goddess, Gayatri or
                   Savitri.
ghat   "Step"; the steps leading down to a sacred river
                   or temple tank; the landing places or banks along
                   a river or coast, particularly where pilgrims may
                   bathe.

goonda	A ne'er-do-well; a hired tough; a gang member who engages in violence for economic or political reasons.
guru	Teacher; a spiritual preceptor who has himself attained insight.
Hanuman	The monkey god, famous as the faithful servant and model devotee of Lord Ram; because of his chastity and virile power he is the patron deity of Hindu wrestlers.
Hara	A name of Shiva.
Hari	A name of Vishnu.
Harishchandra	A legendary king and hero of the *Mahabharata*; famous for keeping his word at any cost.
hijra	A male transvestite who is a member of a castelike group of dancers that is often associated with birth rituals.
Indra	The most prominent Vedic god of the skies, wielder of the thunderbolt and drinker of the intoxicant soma.
Ishvara	"Lord"; designation used especially for Shiva; often connected with other names to refer to particular manifestations of Shiva, such as Lolarkeshvara, the "Lord of Lolarka."
jagrata	Literally, "awake," all-night singing celebrations, the songs of which are also known as jagratas.
Jagannath	"Lord of the Universe"; epithet of Vishnu-Krishna, especially as he is worshipped in Puri, Orissa, with his brother Balabhadra and sister Ekanamsha-Durga or Subhadra.
Janamashtami	"Birthday-eighth"; Krishna's birthday on the eighth day of the waning fortnight of Bhadrapad (August/September).
japa	Repetition of a *mantra*.
jhanki	"Glimpse"; the frozen iconic moments during the *Ramlila*.
jihad	Literally "exertions"; "Holy war"; a war considered by Muslims to be in defense of Islam.
Jnan Vapi	The Well of Knowledge, now located adjacent to the Vishvanath Temple in Banaras.
kaccha	"Unripe; rough, not fully formed," not settled or confirmed. *Kaccha* ponds or houses, for example, are made of clay, as opposed to *pakka*, or fully formed, brick construction.

Kajali	Folk songs popular during the rainy season.
Kali	The "Black One"; the dark form of the Goddess who is both giver and destroyer of life.
Kaliyuga	The "dark age"; the fourth *yuga*, or age of the *mahayuga* (eon).
kama	"Passion or pleasure"; pursuit of passion as one of the four aims of life.
Kama	God of love and pleasure.
kand	See khand.
Kapalamochana	"Where the Skull was Freed"; a famous pool in Banaras where the skull of Brahma fell from the hand of Shiva.
Karinda	A Brahmin priest functionary, subordinate to a panda.
Kashi	Another name of Banaras; "The Shining [City], the Luminous."
katha	"Story"; the exposition of a literary passage or a story, often revealing religious or philosophical import, such as in the *Ramcharitmanas* tradition.
Kathavachak	An oral expounder of a (usually sacred) story or *katha*, such as on the *Ramayana* or *Ramcharitmanas*.
Keshava	An epithet of Krishna, meaning the "long-haired god."
khand(a) (kand)	A "section" of a literary work, such as the *Kashi Khand* in the *Skanda Purana*, or the *Balkand* of the *Ramcharitmanas*.
khurak	Wrestlers' diet of milk and other dairy products, nuts, and other rich vegetarian foods.
kirtan	A song expressing the glory of a deity.
Koshala	The kingdom of Dasharatha whose capitol is Ayodhya.
Kot Vidai	The farewell ceremony of the *Ramlila*.
Krishna	Hero and advisor in the *Mahabharata* war; ancient cowherd god; playful lover of the milkmaids in Vraja (Braj) near Mathura; although understood as an *avatar* of Vishnu, he is so prominent as to be honored and loved in his own right and worshiped as Vishnu himself by some devotees.
Kritayuga	The first *yuga*, or age of the *mahayuga* (eon).
Kshatriya	The warrior or noble *varna*; traditionally, kshatriyas rule the land and protect the people.

Kshir Sagar	"Ocean of Milk"; the cosmic ocean where Vishnu floats sleeping upon Shesha, his serpent bed.
kund	A pool, especially a sacred bathing site.
Kurma	The tortoise incarnation of Vishnu; the name of one of the *puranas*.
Lakshman	Ram's brother who loyally accompanies him during exile.
Lakshmi	"Wealth, fortune"; the goddess who embodies auspiciousness, wealth, and fortune, and who is the wife of Vishnu.
Lanka	The island of Sri Lanka or Ceylon; the kingdom of Ravana in the *Ramayana*.
lila	"Play"; used in the sense of both the free, sportive, and playful nature of the deity and the theatrical portrayal of divine activity.
linga(m)	"Sign" or "characteristic"; the male sexual organ; the phallic representation of Shiva and the focus of his worship, understood as symbolizing his transcendent, formless nature.
mahatmya	The "glorification" or "praise" of a deity or a sacred place.
mallah	Boatperson.
Manas	Affectionate abbreviation for *Ramcharitmanas*. As part of the *Ramcharitmanas*, it may refer to the proper noun Manas, a Himalayan lake, or it may symbolize calm "mind," or consciousness.
mandir	Temple.
Manikarnika	The famous *tirtha* of the "Earring" situated on the Ganges in Banaras, now a site of cremation.
mantra	A sacred syllable, word, or verse; a prayer.
mata git	Folk songs to the Mother Goddess.
math	Solitary hut of an ascetic or student; a monastic school, monastery.
Mathura	A sacred city located in north central India on the banks of the Jamuna River; birthplace of Lord Krishna.
Matsya	The fish incarnation of Vishnu; the name of a *purana*.
maya	Illusion; the mysterious, illusory quality of the Divine; in Advaita, the mistaken perception that the phenomenal universe is permanent and the superimposition of the unreal onto the truly Real, or *Brahman*.

mela	A religious fair or festival, especially one which draws hundreds or more people on pilgrimage.
moksha	Liberation, or release; freedom from the rounds of birth and death; one of the four aims of Hindu life.
mudra	A mystic and symbolic gesture of the hands and fingers to convey particular meanings.
muhalla (mohalla)	Neighborhood, often divided into fairly distinct linguistic or ethnic entities.
mundan	Ritual tonsure; the first haircut of a child performed at a sacred site.
murti	Form or likeness; the material image of the deity as a focus for worship and *darshan*.
naga	Snake deity.
Nau	Barber.
Navratra	The "Nine Nights" of the Goddess; a festival of the Goddess, celebrated in Chaitra (March/April) and more elaborately in Ashvin (September/October).
nemi	"Devoted" spectator; a person who attends the *Ramlila* regularly.
nirguna	"Without qualities" or attributes; in Advaita, it is a designation commonly applied to Ultimate Reality conceived as transpersonal and about which nothing may be predicated; in personalistic Bhakti, *nirguna* often connotes the sense of being devoid of limiting attributes; see *saguna*.
nirvana	The "extinguishing" of earthly attachments and desires; *moksha*.
om	The most sacred *mantra* of the Vedas; symbol of Ultimate Reality itself.
pakka	"Ripe"; fully formed, settled, or confirmed; genuine. *Pakka* or "ripe" ponds or houses, for example, are made of brick. Antonym: *kaccha*, clay construction.
Panchaganga	"Five Gangas"; a famous Banaras *tirtha*.
Panchakroshi	"Five *krosha*"; a five-day circular pilgrimage route around Banaras, said to have a radius of five *kroshas*, or about ten miles.
Panchatirtha	The "five-*tirtha*" pilgrimage along the Ganges at Banaras: from north to south the *tirthas* are Adi Keshava, Bindumadhava or Panchaganga, Manikarnika, Dashashvamedha, and Lolark-Asi.

panda	A priest, especially at a pilgrimage site; a generic term applied to many different categories of ritual officiants who are usually *Brahmin*.
Parvati	"Daughter of the [Himalaya] Mountain"; the wife of Shiva.
pathshala	Traditional Hindu school where Sanskrit is taught by memorization and repetition.
pradakshina	"Keeping to the right"; circumambulating a religious site for reverence or merit, keeping it to one's right to reflect and maintain its purity.
prasad	"Purity, grace"; the food left over after being offered to the deity and returned, consecrated, to be distributed to devotees.
puja	Worship of any image of a deity or deities.
pujari	The *brahmin* priest who performs the worship ceremonies, or *puja*, in a temple.
punya	"Auspiciousness"; a good or meritorious act.
purana	A category of Hindu texts which contain "ancient stories"; collections of popular stories and legends about Hindu gods, epic heros, and ritual; often numbered as eighteen major *puranas* and many more *upapuranas* or sub-*puranas*.
Purnima	Full-moon day of the Hindu lunar calendar.
pushpaka	An aerial chariot stolen by Ravana from Brahma, who had received it from Lord of Wealth Kubera. After the conquest of Lanka, Ram flew it back to Ayodhya and presented it to Kubera.
qawwali	A popular type of entertainment music, often concerning love, and derived from Sufi mystics' songs.
rakshasa	Semidivine demonic beings who haunt the night and who are a perpetual threat to harmony at other times as well, particularly ritual occasions.
Ram(a)	Virtuous king and hero of the epic *Ramayana*; worshiped as a god, an *avatar* of Vishnu.
Ramayana	The Hindu epic celebrating the legend and deeds of Ram; two of the most influential versions today are the Sanskrit text attributed to Valmiki and the Hindi work composed by Tulsidas known as the *Ramcharitmanas*.
Ramayanis	The chanters of the *Ramcharitmanas* by Tulsidas during a *Ramlila* performance.

Ramcharitmanas	Often translated, "The Holy Lake of the Acts of Ram," a sixteenth-century Hindi interpretation of the *Ramayana* epic, composed by Tulsidas, which forms the basis for north Indian *Ramlila* performances.
Rameshvaram	A sacred site located in the far south of India on a small island near Sri Lanka.
Ramlila	The "play" or "*lila*" of Ram; the performative reenactment of the deeds of Ram.
Ramnagar	"Town of Ram"; location of the Banaras kings' palace across the Ganges from Kashi, and site of the famous thirty-one-day *Ramlila*.
Ramraj	"Rule of Ram"; a golden age of righteous rule.
Rathayatra	"Journey of the Chariot"; the yearly festival of Jagannath's procession.
Ravan(a)	The *rakshasa* king who steals Sita from Ram and whose defeat by him is told in the *Ramayana*.
Rig Veda	The oldest and most important *Samhita* or collection of Vedic hymns and mantras.
rishi	"Seer"; a sage or hermit.
Rudra	A Vedic god, later identified with Shiva.
rudraksha	"Eye of Shiva"; the large, bumpy, reddish brown berries used for rosaries, especially among wandering holy men.
sadhu	A general term applied to all holy men.
saguna	"With qualities"; the term connoting that aspect of the Transcendent which is describable with qualities, attributes, and adjectives; see *nirguna*.
samadhi	The final stage in yogic discipline; perfect concentration of the mind; a shrine containing the remains of a perfected one or dedicated in memory to a saint.
sampradaya	A sect or school of thought, often centered around a charismatic founding guru.
samsara	Passage; the impermanent world into which the individual souls are born; the ceaseless round of birth, death, and rebirth.
samvad	Dialogue in the *Ramlila*.
sandhya puja	"Twilight prayers"; worship at dawn, noon, and dusk.
sangam	A confluence of rivers, usually considered sacred.
sankalpa	The vow of intent taken at the outset of any ritual activity.

sannyasin	A person who has renounced the world and entered the fourth and last *ashrama* or stage of the ideal human life, *sannyasa* or renunciation.
Sati	The wife of Shiva who kills herself because of her father Daksha's insult and is reborn as Parvati.
Shaiva	Pertaining to the cultus of Shiva; a worshiper of Shiva.
Shakta	Pertaining to the cultus of Shakti; a worshiper of the Goddess as Shakti.
shakti	"Energy, power"; divine energy or strength, as in the character of the reverential wrestler; female creative power; when capitalized, another name for the Goddess, either alone or as the consort of the male deity.
Shankara	The famous eighth- to ninth-century philosopher who was the greatest exponent of the Advaita philosophy; another name of Shiva.
Shankaracharya	A teacher of Shankara; a teacher elected or appointed to lead ancient centers or *maths* established by the philosopher Shankara.
shastra	Teaching; a sacred treatise or body of learning on religious topics such as the Hindu aims of life.
Shatrughna	Son of Dasharatha and Sumitra; younger brother of Ram.
Shitala	The goddess of pustular diseases such as smallpox.
Shiva	The "Auspicious"; the third member of the Hindu Triad or Trinity: the "Destroyer."
Shivaji	A Maratha folk hero and military leader of the seventeenth century popularly portrayed today as a Hindu crusader.
shruti	"That which is heard"; revealed scriptures, usually synonymous with the four groups of the Vedas, the most ancient of Hindu texts which long existed as oral tradition.
Shudra	The lowest of the four *varnas*; not being twice born, *Shudras* are theoretically relegated to labor and service.
sindur	Decorative red powder used by married women to line the part of their hair to symbolize their marital status and also used for anointing the images of certain deities such as goddesses.

Sita	Wife of Ram who was kidnapped by Ravana; worshiped by many women today as the model of wifely devotion.
Skanda	The God of War, son of Shiva and Parvati.
smriti	"That which is remembered"; the later texts composed on the basis of the revealed texts or *shruti*.
sohar	Songs sung at the birth of a son by women and sometimes hijras.
Surya	Sun Deity.
svarup (swarup)	"Essential or true form"; icon; the human figures who portray the divine characters during *Ramlila* performances.
svayambhu	"Self-manifested"; a term used to describe certain *lingams* and other icons which are claimed to be uncreated by humans and to have appeared on their own.
Svayamvara	The ritual contest in which a bride chooses her own husband, as in Sita's choice of Ram. See also Dhanushyajna.
swami	A religious preceptor.
Tantra	An esoteric religious movement emphasizing the union of opposites, especially symbolized by male and female; that widely censured movement whose self-consciously unorthodox "five m" *panchamakara puja* utilizes five forbiddens, all beginning with the letter m in Sanskrit: wine, meat, fish, *mudras*, and ritual copulation.
Tantric	An adherent of, or pertaining to, Tantra.
tapas (tapasya)	"Heat"; the heat generated by intense self-discipline as a source of great spiritual and physical power.
Taraka	A male demon who received the boon of being unassailable by all except a son of Shiva, and who after terrorizing the gods is finally slain by Shiva's son Skanda-Kartikeya; a demoness who is slain by Ram at Vishvamitra's command.
tilak	Ornamental or sectarian marks made with various substances and usually placed on the forehead; the ritual application of such marks.
tirtha	"Ford, crossing place"; a place of pilgrimage.
tirthayatra	The journey (*yatra*) to a sacred place; pilgrimage; a pilgrim.

Tretayuga	The second of the four *yugas*, or ages of the *mahayuga*.
Tulsidas	Late-sixteenth, early-seventeenth century Bhakti poet and author of the celebrated Hindi interpretation of the *Ramayana*, the *Ramcharitmanas*.
Upanishad	Ancient philosophic and speculative texts constituting the fourth subset of the Vedas.
Vaishnava	Pertaining to the cultus of Vishnu; a worshiper of Vishnu.
Vaishya	The third of the four *varnas*, traditionally merchants and farmers.
Valmiki	A mythic sage and poet who composed the foremost Sanskrit *Ramayana* and who is an advisor to Ram in the *Ramcharitmanas*.
Vamana	The dwarf incarnation of Vishnu whose three strides claim the whole universe; the name of one of the *puranas*.
Varana	The river that borders Banaras on the north, entering the Ganges at Adi Keshava or Varana *sangam*.
Varanasi	The city between the Varana and the Asi rivers.
varna	Literally "color, category, rank"; the four divisions of Hindu society: *brahmin, kshatriya, vaishya, shudra*.
Veda	"Wisdom, knowing"; the seminal Hindu sacred literature, considered to be "heard" or "revealed" (*shruti*) and consisting of four subsets: the *Samhitas, Brahmanas, Aranyakas*, and *Upanishads*.
vidya	Wisdom.
vidyapith	"Seat of wisdom"; a place of learning.
Vijayadashami	"Victory Tenth"; a major festival celebrating Ravana's defeat by Ram, and the final day of the Navratra festival; also known as Dashahara or Dashera.
Vishnu	"Pervader"; the third member of the Hindu Triad: the "Preserver"; also worshiped in the form of many *avatars*, such as Ram and Krishna.
Vishvanath	Shiva, the "Lord of All."
Vyas(a)	The "arranger" or "editor" of the Vedas and the compiler of the *Mahabharata*; in lowercase, a vyas is a director of *Ramlila* performances.
yajna	Sacrifice.

Yashoda   Krishna's foster mother who raised him in the
                 cowherd village; the woman by whom the Great
                 Goddess Vindhyavasini took birth to aid Krishna.
yuga   "Age"; the four periods (*chaturyuga*) of the eon or
                 mahayuga—Krita, Treta, Dvapara, and Kali—
                 believed to gradually deteriorate from perfection
                 during the Kritayuga to the evil characterizing the
                 Kaliyuga.

Bibliography

Acharya, Narayan Ram. 1983 (Ed.) *Mahakavidandiviracitam Dashakumaracaritam*. Bombay: Nirnaya Sagara Press (first published 1951).

Agrawala, Vasudeva S. 1963 *Matsya Purana—A Study*. Varanasi: All-India Kashiraj Trust.

Ahmed, A. 1964 *Studies in Islamic Culture in the Indian Environment*. Oxford: Oxford University Press.

Ali, A. 1966 *Mughal Nobility Under Aurangzeb*. Bombay: Asia Publishing House.

Alter, Joseph S. 1989 *Pehlwani: Identity, Ideology and the Body of the Indian Wrestler*. Ph.D. dissertation. Berkeley: University of California.

Aryan, K.C. n.d. *Hanuman in Art and Mythology*. Delhi: Rekha Prakashan.

Atreya, S. P. 1973a *Health and Yoga*. Banaras: Shri Hari Press.

_____. 1973b *"Saccha pehlwan devta hot he."* *Bhartiya Kushti* 10 (nos. 7, 8, 9):21–26.

Awasthi, Induja. n.d. *"Ramcharitmanas* and the Performing Tradition of *Ramayana."* Unpublished manuscript.

_____. 1980 *"Ramacharitamanas* and the Performing Tradition of *Ramayana."* Pp. 506–16 in V. Ragavan (ed.), *The Ramayana Tradition in Asia*. New Delhi: Sahitya Akademi.

Babcock, B. 1978 *The Reversible World*. Ithaca: Cornell University Press.

Barnouw, E., and S. Krisnaswamy. 1963 *Indian Film*. New York: Columbia University Press.

Barthes, R. 1972 *Mythologies*. New York: Hill and Wang.

Bateson, Gregory. 1972 "A Theory of Play and Fantasy." Pp. 177–93 in his *Steps to an Ecology of Mind*. New York: Ballantine Books.

Baxter, Craig. 1969 *Jana Sangh*. Philadelphia: University of Pennsylvania Press.

Bharati, Agehananda. 1970 "Pilgrimage sites and Indian civilization." Pp. 85–126 in Joseph W. Elder (ed.) and A.K. Narain (special consultant), *Chapters in Indian Civilization*: Vol. 1, *Classical and Medieval India*. Dubuque, Iowa: Kendall/Hunt Publishing Co.

Bhardwaj, Pandit Chaman Lal Ji. 1988 *Chaman ki Shri Durga Stuti*. Amritsar: Brij Mohan Bhardwaj Library.

Bhardwaj, Surinder Mohan. 1973 *Hindu Places of Pilgrimage in India*. Berkeley: University of California Press.

Bhatnagar, G. D. 1975 "The Banaras farman of Aurangzeb." Pp. 227–32 in A. Lallanji Gopal (ed.), *Koshambi Memorial Volume*. Banaras: Banaras Hindu University.

Borges, Jorge Luis. 1964 "The Fearful Sphere of Pascal." Pp. 189–92 in his *Labyrinths, Selected Stories and Other Writings*. New York: New Directions Publishing Corporation.

Brooks, Charles R. 1989 *The Hare Krishnas in India*. Princeton: Princeton University Press.

Bulcke, C. 1960 "The Characterization of Hanuman." *Journal of the Royal Asiatic Society* 10:393–402.

Carstairs, M.G. 1957 *The Twice-Born: A Study of a Community of High Caste Hindus*. London: Hogarth Press.

Cenkner, William. 1978 *A Tradition of Teachers: Shankara and the Jagadgurus Today*. Delhi: Motilal Banarsidass.

Census of India. 1951, 1961, 1971, 1981 *Uttar Pradesh: District Census Handbook— Varanasi District*.

———. 1987 "Households and Household Population by Language Mainly Spoken in the Household," Paper 1.

Chalier-Visuvalingam, Elizabeth. 1989 "Bhairava's Royal Brahmanicide: The Problem of the Mahabrahmana." Pp. 157–229 in Alf Hiltebeitel (ed.), *Criminal Gods and Demon Devotees: Essays on the Guardians of Popular Hinduism*. Albany, New York: State University of New York Press.

Chanchal, Narendra. 1987 *Shri Durga Stuti*. New Delhi: Super Cassette Industries.

Chandra, S. 1972 *Parties and Politics at the Mughal Court—1707–1740*. New Delhi: Peoples Publishing House.

———. 1987 *Indian Ocean: Explorations in History, Commerce and Politics*. London: Sage.

———. 1988 (Ed.), *Essays in Medieval Indian Economic History*. Colombia, Mo.: South Asia Books.

Chatterji, S.K. 1926 *The Origin and Development of the Bengali Language*. Vol. 1. London: Allen and Unwin.

Chaudhuri, Nirad C. 1979 *Hinduism: A Religion to Live By.* New Delhi: B.I. Publications.

Coomaraswamy, A.K. 1941 "Lila." *Journal of the American Oriental Society* 61:98–101.

Dante. 1961 *The Paradiso,* translated by John Ciardi. New York: New American Library.

Das, Veena. 1977 *Structure and Cognition: Aspects of Hindu Caste and Ritual.* Delhi: Oxford University Press.

Dhal, U.N. 1979 "A Folk Deity in Purana Literature." *Purana* 21:9–22.

Dimmitt, Cornelia, and J.A.B. van Buitenen. 1978 *Classical Hindu Mythology: A Reader in the Sanskrit Puranas.* Philadelphia: Temple University Press.

Dimock, Edward C., Jr. 1963 *The Thief of Love.* Chicago: University of Chicago Press.
_____. 1982 "A Theology of the Repulsive: The Myth of the Goddess Sitala," Pp. 184–203 in John Stratton Hawley and Donna Marie Wulff (eds.), *The Divine Consort: Radha and the Goddesses of India.* Berkeley: Religious Studies Series.

Din, Jayram Das. 1942 *Manas Shanka Samadhan.* Gorakhpur: Gita Press.

Dissanayake, V. 1988 *Cinema and Cultural Identity: Reflections on Films from Japan, India, and China.* Lanham, Md.: University Press of America.

District Gazeteer of Varanasi. 1965 No author or publisher listed.

District Varanasi. District Census Handbook, 1981, Primary Census Abstract. 1987 Part XIII-B. Aligarh: Printwell Printers.

Dixit, R. 1978 *Hanuman Upasna.* Delhi: Dehati Pustak Bhandar.

Dorian, Nancy. 1982 "Defining the Speech Community to Include Its Working Margins." In Suzanne Romaine (ed.), *Sociolinguistic Variation in Speech Communities.* London: Edward Arnold.

Dumont, Louis. 1980 *Homo Hierarchicus: The Caste System and Its Implications.* Trans. Mark Sainsbury, Louis Dumont, and Basia Gulati. Chicago: University of Chicago Press (first pub. 1966).

Eck, Diana L. 1982 *Banaras, City of Light.* New York: Alfred Knopf.

Engineer, A. A. 1984 *Communal Riots in Post-Independence India.* Bombay: Orient Longman.

Epstein, A. L. (ed.). 1974 *Ethos and Identity.* London: Tavistock.

Ferguson, Charles. 1972 "Diglossia." Pp. 232–252 in P. Gigliolo (ed.), *Language and Social Context*. New York: Penguin.

Foucault, Michel. 1970 *The Order of Things* (translator not listed). London: Tavistock Publications.

———. 1983 *This Is Not a Pipe*, translated by James Harkness. Berkeley: University of California Press.

Freitag, Sandria B. 1980 "Religious Rites and Riots: From Community Identity to Communalism in North India, 1870–1940." Ph.D. dissertation. Berkeley: University of California.

———. 1989a *Culture and Power in Banaras: Community, Performance, and Environment, 1800–1980*. Berkeley: University of California Press.

———. 1989b "State and Community: Symbolic Popular Protest in Banaras's Public Arenas." Pp. 203–28 in Sandria B. Freitag (ed.), *Culture and Power in Banaras: Community, Performance, and Environment, 1800–1980*. Berkeley: University of California Press.

Gargi, Balwant. 1967 "The Ramayana in Folk Theatre." *Cultural Forum* 9: 25-29.

———. 1969 "Ramlila in Ramnagar." *Sangeet Natak* 13: 27–34.

Gatwood, Lynn E. 1985 *Devi and the Spouse Goddess*. Riverdale, Md.: Riverdale.

Ghosh, Manomahan (trans.). 1967 *Natyashastra*, attributed to Bharatamuni. Calcutta: Granthalaya.

Ghurye, G.S. 1953 *Indian Sadhus*. Bombay: Popular Prakashan.

Giri, Swami Sadananda. 1976 *Society and Samnyasin: A History of the Dasnami Samnyasins*. Varanasi: Samnyasi Sanskrit Mahavidyalaya.

Goel, B. S., and S. K. Saini. 1972 *Mother Tongue and Equality of Opportunity in Education*. New Delhi: National Council of Educational Research and Training.

Goffman, Erving. 1974 *Frame Analysis: An Essay on the Organization of Experience*. Cambridge: Harvard University Press.

Gonda, Jan. 1987 "Visnu" in *The Encyclopedia of Religion*, ed. Mircea Eliade. Vol. 15: 288-91. New York: Macmillan.

Gopal, Ram. 1966 *Linguistic Affairs of India*. Bombay: Asia Publishing House.

Gotham, C. 1980 *Shri Hanuman Charit*. Bareilly: Sanskrit Sansthan.

Greeven, R. 1892 "Benares—an Account of the Worship of the Panchon Pir." *North Indian Notes and Queries*, pp. 3-184.

Grierson, Sir George A. 1901 *Seven Grammars of the Dialects and Subdialects of the Bihari Language.* Varanasi: Motilal Banarsidass.

_____. [1903] 1968 Linguistic Survey of India, Vol. 5, *Indo-Aryan Family, Eastern Group,* Part 2. Varanasi: Motilal Banarsidass.

_____. 1904 *Linguistic Survey of India:* Vol 6. *Indo-Aryan Family, Mediate Group.* Calcutta: Office of the Superintendent of Government Printing.

Gumperz, John. 1978 "Dialect and Conversational Inference in Urban Communication." *Language in Society* 7:393–409.

_____. 1982 "Conversational Code-switching." Pp. 59–99 in his *Discourse Strategies.* Cambridge: Cambridge University Press.

Gupta, A.S. 1968 *The Vamana Purana with English Translation.* Varanasi: All-India Kashiraj Trust.

Haggard, S. 1988 "Mass Media and the Visual Arts in Twentieth Century South Asia: India Film Posters 1947–Present." *Society for Visual Anthropology Newsletter* 4:26–34.

Haig, W. 1958 *The Cambridge History of India.* Vols. 3, 5. Delhi: Chand.

Hansen, Kathryn. 1989 "The Birth of Hindi Drama in Banaras, 1868–1885." Pp. 62–92 *in* Sandria B. Freitag (ed.), *Culture and Power in Banaras: Community, Performance, and Environment, 1800–1980.* Berkeley: University of California Press.

Harries, Karsten. 1975 "The Infinite Sphere: Comments on the History of a Metaphor." *Journal of the History of Philosophy* 13:5–15.

Havell, B. 1933 *Benares.* Calcutta: Thacker Spink.

Hein, Norvin 1972 *The Miracle Plays of Mathura.* New Haven: Yale University Press.

Henry, Edward O. 1988 *Chant the Names of God: Music and Culture in Bhojpuri-Speaking India.* San Diego: San Diego State University.

Hess, Linda 1983 ''*Ram Lila:* The Audience Experience." Pp. 171–94 in Monika Thiel-Horstmann (ed.), *Bhakti in Current Research, 1979–1982.* Berlin: Dietrich Reimer.

Hill, W.D.P. (trans.) 1952 *The Holy Lake of the Acts of Rama.* A translation of Tulsidas's *Ramcharitmanas.* Bombay: Oxford University Press.

Imperial Gazetteer. 1908 *Imperial Gazetteer—Varanasi.* Vol. 7. Oxford: Clarendon Press.

Inden, Ronald. 1978 "Ritual, Authority, and Cyclic Time in Hindu Kingship." Pp. 28–73 in J.F. Richards (ed.), *Kingship and Authority in South Asia.* Madison: University of Wisconsin Press. Publication Series No. 3.

Juyal, B. N. 1970 "Communal Riot and Communal Politics: Case Study of a Town." In M. Rafiq Khan (ed.), *National Integration—Its Meaning and Relevance.* Varanasi: Navachetna Prakashan for Gandhian Institute of Studies.

Kakar, S. 1980 "The Ties That Bind: Family Relationships in the Mythology of Hindi Cinema." *India International Quarterly* 8:11–12.

_____. 1982 *Shamans, Mystics and Doctors.* New York: Alfred Knopf.

Khan, M. Rafiq, and S. Mittal. 1984 "The Hindu Muslim Riot in Vanarasi and the Role of the Police." In A. Engineer (ed.), *Communal Riots in Post-Independence India.* Bombay: Orient Longman.

Kinsley, David 1987 *Hindu Goddesses.* Delhi: Motilal Banarsidass.

Kumar, Nita 1984 "Popular Culture in Urban India: The Artisans of Banaras, c.1884–1984." Ph.D. dissertation, University of Chicago.

_____. 1985 "Mud, Water, and *Gumchha:* The Dying World of Banaras Akhardas." *India Magazine* 5:33–37.

_____. 1986 "Open Space and Free Time: Pleasure for the People of Banaras." *Contributions to Indian Sociology* (n.s.) 20:41–60.

_____. 1988 *The Artisans of Banaras: Popular Culture and Identity, 1880–1986.* Princeton: Princeton University Press.

Kumar, Savitri V. 1983 *The Pauranic Lore of Holy Waterplaces.* New Delhi: Munshiram Manoharlal Publishers.

Levi-Strauss, C. 1966 *The Savage Mind.* Chicago: Chicago University Press.

Lutgendorf, Philip. 1987 "The Life of a Text: Tulsidas' *Ramcaritmanas* in Performance." Ph.D. dissertation, University of Chicago.

_____. 1989a "The View from the Ghats: Traditional Exegesis of a Hindu epic." *Journal of Asian Studies* 48:272–88.

_____. 1989b "Ram's Story in Shiva's City: Public Arenas and Private Patronage." Pp. 34–61 in Sandria B. Freitag (ed.), *Culture and Power in Banaras: Community, Performance, and Environment, 1800–1980.* Berkeley: University of California Press.

_____. 1991 *The Life of a Text: Performing the Ramcaritmanas of Tulsidas.* Berkeley: University of California Press.

Mani, Vettam. 1984 *Puranic Encyclopedia.* Delhi: Motilal Banarsidass.

Mathur, Poonam. 1978 "Notes on Banaras: Ramalila." *N.K. Bose Memorial Foundation Newsletter* 1: 30–40.

Mirzapur Municipal Board. 1972 *Mirzapur Nagarpilika ke Ek Sau Panch Varsh.* Mirzapur: Municipal Board.

Mishra, Vibhuti Bhushan. 1973 *Religious Beliefs and Practices of North India during the Early Mediaeval Period.* Leiden: E. J. Brill.

Mishra, Vishvanath Prasad. (ed.) 1962 *Ramcaritmanas.* Ramnagar, Varanasi: All-India Kashiraj Trust.

Morinis, E. Alan. 1984 *Pilgrimage in the Hindu Tradition: A Case Stude of West Bengal.* Bombay: Oxford University Press.

Murdoch, John. 1904 *The Religious Sects of the Hindus, Based on ''Sketch'' by H. H. Wilson.* London: Christian Literature Society for India.

Nanda, Serena. 1990 *Neither Man nor Woman: The Hijras of India.* Belmont, Calif.: Wadsworth.

Narain Singh, P. N. 1978 Interviews conducted by Richard Schechner and Linda Hess in Ramnagar.

Narain Singh, Vibhuti (Maharaja of Banaras). 1978 Interviews conducted by Richard Schechner and Linda Hess in Ramnagar.

Nomani, Abdus Salaam. 1963 *Tarikh Asar-i Banaras.* Banaras: Maktabah Nadvatulma, 'arif.

Noorani, A. G. 1989 "The Babri Masjid-Ram Janmabhoomi Question." *Economic and Political Weekly,* November 4–11.

Obeyesekere, G. 1976 "The Impact of Ayurvedic Ideas on the Culture of the Individual in Sri Lanka." Pp. 201–26 in C. Leslie (ed.), *Asian Medical Systems.* Berkeley: University of California Press.

_____. 1981 *Medusa's Hair: An Essay on Personal Symbols and Religious Experience.* Chicago: University of Chicago Press.

O'Flaherty, Wendy Doniger. 1973 *Asceticism and Eroticism in the Mythology of Siva.* London: Oxford University Press.

_____. 1978 *Hindu Myths.* New York: Penguin Books.

_____. 1980 "Inside and Outside the Mouth of God: The Boundary between Myth and Reality." *Daedalus* 109:93–125.

_____. 1984 *Dreams, Illusions, and Other Realities.* Chicago: University of Chicago Press.

Oman, John Campbell. 1905 *Mystics, Ascetics, and Saints of India*. London: Unwin.

Organ, Troy Wilson. 1974 *Hinduism: Its Historical Development*. Woodbury, N.Y.: Barron's Educational Series.

Ostor, A. 1980 *The Play of the Gods: Locality, Ideology, Structure, and Time in the Festivals of a Bengali Town*. Chicago: University of Chicago Press.

––––––. 1984 *Culture and Power—Legend, Ritual, Bazaar and Rebellion in Bengal Society*. New Delhi: Sage.

Parry, Jonathan P. 1980 "Ghosts, Greed and Sin: The Occupational Identity of the Banares Funeral Priests." *Man* (n.s.) 15:88–111.

––––––. 1981 "Death and Cosmogony in Kashi." *Contributions to Indian Sociology* (n.s.) 15:337–65.

––––––. 1982a "Sacrificial Death and the Necrophagous Ascetic." Pp. 74–110 in M. Bloch and Jonathan Parry (eds.), *Death and the Regeneration of Life*. Cambridge: Cambridge University Press.

––––––. 1982b "Death and Cosmogony in Kashi." Pp. 337–65 in T.N. Madan (ed.), *Way of Life: King, Householder and Renouncer*. New Delhi: Vikas.

Pattanayak, D.P. 1981 *Multilingualism and Mother-Tongue Education*. Delhi: Oxford Press.

Poplack, Shana. 1988 "Contrasting Patterns of Code-switching in Two Communities. Pp. 215-44 in Monica Heller (ed.), *Codeswitching*. Berlin: Mouton de Gruyter.

Ramanujan, A.K. (trans.). 1981 *Hymns for the Drowning: Poems for Visnu by Nammalvar*. Princeton: Princeton University Press.

Rangoonwalla, F. 1975 *Seventy-five Years of Indian Cinema*. New Delhi: Indian Book Company.

Romaine, Suzanne. 1989 *Bilingualism*. Oxford: Basil Blackwell.

Rudolph, L., and S. Rudolph. 1987 *In Pursuit of Lakshmi*. Chicago: University of Chicago Press.

Ryder, Arthur (trans.). 1960 *The Ten Princes*. Chicago: University of Chicago Press (3rd impression).

Sandelvi, Chaudhuri Nabi Ahmed. 1939 *Murukhai Banaras*. Nazirabad, Lucknow: Sultania Barti Press.

Sankalia, H. D. 1973 *Ramayana—Myth or Reality?*. New Delhi: People's Publishing House.

Saraswati, Baidyanath. 1975 *Kashi: Myth and Reality of a Classical Cultural Tradition.* Simla: Institute of Advanced Study.

_____. 1983 *Traditions of Tirthas in India: The Anthropology of Hindu Pilgrimage.* Varanasi: N.K. Bose Memorial Foundation.

Sarkar, J. N. 1912 *History of Aurangzeb.* Vols. 1–3. Calcutta: M. C. Sarkar & Sons.

Sax, William. 1982 "The Ramnagar of Ramlila." unpublished ms.

Schechner, Richard (ed.) 1985 *Between Theater and Anthropology.* Philadelphia: University of Pennsylvania Press.

Schechner, Richard, and Linda Hess. 1977 "The *Ramlila* of Ramnagar." *The Drama Review* 21:51–82.

_____. 1985 "The *Ramlila* of Ramnagar." Pp. 151–211 in Richard Schechner (ed.), *Between Theater and Anthropology.* Philadelphia: University of Pennsylvania Press.

Schechner, Richard, and Mady Schuman (eds.). 1976 *Ritual, Play, and Performance: Readings in the Social Sciences/Theatre.* New York: Seabury Press.

Schwerin, R. G. 1981 "Saint Worship in Indian Islam: the Legend of the Martyr Salar Mahmud Ghazi." In Ahmed, I. (ed.), *Ritual and Religion among Muslims in India.* Delhi: Manohar.

Scotton, Carol Myers. 1988 "Codeswitching as Indexical of Social Negotiations." In Monica Heller (ed.), *Codeswitching.* Berlin: Mouton de Gruyter.

Seymour, Susan. 1980 *The Transformation of a Sacred Town: Bhubaneswar, India.* Boulder, Colo.: Westview Press.

Sharma, Bhumika. n.d. *Mallayudha athwa Akhara Gyan.* Delhi: Dehati Pustak Bhandar.

Shastri, S. 1986 *Hanuman Upasna.* Delhi: Sadhana Pocket Books.

Sherring, M. A. 1975 *Benares, the Sacred City.* Delhi: B. R. Publishing Corporation (First pub. 1868).

Shukla, Ramchandra. 1968 *Hindi Sahitya ka Ithihas.* Varanasi: Nagari Pracharini Sabha (first published 1929).

Simon, Beth Lee. 1986 "Bilingualism and Language Maintenance in Banaras." Ph.D. thesis, University of Michigan microfilm.

Singh, Chandramani. 1979 *Marriage Songs from Bhojpuri Region.* Jaipur: Champa Lal Ranka.

Singh, H.B. n.d. "Editorial." *Akharden ki Or* 1:3–4.

Living Banaras

Singh, K.P. 1972a "Mallavidhya aur Sarkar." *Bhartiya Kushti* 10 (nos. 1, 2, 3): 47.

————. 1972b "Pehlwani aur Vyaktitwa." *Bhartiya Kushti* 9 (nos. 10, 11, 12): 21–25.

————. 1972–1973 "Saccha pehlwan vah ho jo dusron ko pehlwan banawen." *Bhartiya Kushti* 10 (nos. 4, 5, 6): 11–16.

Singh, Maan. 1979 *Subhandu and Dandin.* New Delhi: Moharchand Lacchmandas Publications.

Singh, Ram Bachan. 1973 *Varanasi ek paramparagat nagar.* Varanasi: Bharatiya Vidya Prakashan.

Sinha, Surajit, and Baidyanath Saraswati. 1978 *The Ascetics of Kashi: An Anthropological Exploration.* Varanasi: N.K. Bose Memorial Foundation.

Sitapati, P. 1973 (ed., trans.), *Enugula Veeraswamy's Journal.* Hyderabad: Andra Pradesh State Archives.

Skanda Mahapurana. 1987 *Skanda Mahapurana (Caturtha Bhag).* Delhi: Nag Publishers.

Smith, Jonathan Z. 1982 *Imagining Religion: From Babylon to Jonestown.* Chicago: University of Chicago Press.

————. 1987 *To Take Place: Toward Theory in Ritual.* Chicago: University of Chicago Press.

Sukul, Kubernath. 1977 *Varanasi Vaibhava.* Patna: Bihar Rashtrabhasha Parishad.

Suthankar, V.S. 1933 (Ed.) *Mahabharata.* Poona: Bhandarkar Oriental Research Institute.

Tiwari, J.N. 1985 *Goddess Cults in Ancient India.* Delhi: Sundeep Prakashan.

Tripathi, B.D. 1978 *Sadhus of India.* Bombay: Popular Prakashan.

Tuck, Donald R. 1986 *The Concept of Maya in Samkara and Radhakrishnan.* Columbia, Mo.: South Asia Books.

Upadhyaya, Baldev. 1972 *Kashi ki Panditya Parampara.* Varanasi: Skanda Samsthan.

Uttar Pradesh Board. 1984 *Hamara Itihasa* Bk. 2. Lucknow: Rajakiya Publishers.

Van der Veer, Peter. 1988 *Gods on Earth.* London: Athlone Press.

Van Gennep, Arnold. 1960 *The Rites of Passage,* translated by Monika B. Vizedom and Gabrielle L. Caffee. Chicago: University of Chicago Press (first published 1908).

Varadaraja. 1960 *Girvanapadamanjari,* edited by V.P. Shah. Baroda: University of Baroda, Oriental Series No. 4.

Varma, Bal Mukund. 1932 *Kashi ya Banaras*. Bulla Nala: Varma Press.

Vaudeville, C. 1984 "Krishna Gopala, Radha, and The Great Goddess." Pp. 1–12 in J.S. Hawley and D.M. Wulff (eds.), *The Divine Consort*. Banaras: Motilal Banarsidass.

Verma, Manindra K. 1968 "Some Aspects of Interaction between Standard and 'Non-Standard' Languages." *Pakha Sanjam* 1:73–76.

Vidyarthi, L.P. 1961 *The Sacred Complex in Hindu Gaya*. Delhi: Concept Publishing Company.

Vidyarthi, L.P., B.N. Saraswati, and Makan Jha. 1979 *The Sacred Complex of Kashi*. Delhi: Concept Publishing Company.

Wadley, Susan. 1975 *Shakti: Power in the Conceptual Structure of Karimpur*. University of Chicago Studies in Anthropology No. 2. Chicago: University of Chicago Press.

White, H. 1973 *Metahistory: The Historical Imagination in Nineteenth Century Europe*. Baltimore, Md.: Johns Hopkins.

Wolcott, Leonard. 1978 "Hanuman: the Power-Dispensing Monkey in North Indian Folk Religion." *Journal of Asian Studies* 37:653–61.

Zaehner, R. C. 1966 *Hindu Scriptures*. London: J. M. Dent.

Zimmer, Heinrich. 1946 *Myths and Symbols in Indian Art and Civilization*. New York: Pantheon (Bollingen Series, 6).

Contributors

Joseph Alter, an anthropologist who completed his graduate training at the University of California at Berkeley in 1989, was born and raised in India, where he has conducted research on the cultural economy of dairying in the Himalayas and on wrestling in Banaras. He is the author of a recent book, *The Wrestler's Body: Identity and Ideology in North India*, published by the University of California Press. He lives in Kalamazoo, Michigan and has taught at Goshen College, Western Michigan University, and Kalamazoo College.

Bradley Hertel is a sociologist specializing in the relationship between religion and social structure in the United States and among Hindus in north India. He is currently studying the variety of religious functionaries among Hindus, with emphasis on non-Brahmins and women, and the social structure and other patterns evident in the temporal and spatial dimensions of Hindu ritual practices. His recent studies in the United States have focused on gender, marital, and racial differences in the impact of work force participation on attendance of religious services. He teaches courses in sociology of religion, minority group relations, and research methods at Virginia Polytechnic Institute and State University.

Linda Hess is a student of *bhakti* literature and religion in North India. Most of her publications are related to the works of two great Hindi devotional poets who lived in Banaras in the fifteenth and sixteenth centuries: Kabir and Tulsidas. She is author and co-translator of *The Bijak of Kabir* (San Francisco: North Point Press, 1983) and has published numerous articles on the Tulsi *Ramayana* and on the annual Ramlila performance at Ramnagar. Her current book in progress, *Ramayana in Mind and Body*, is on the ways in which the Tulsi *Ramayana* enters people's lives on all levels, from the personal and spiritual to the social and political. She teaches Hindi literature, Indian civilization, and cross-cultural theory in the Department of South and Southeast Asian Studies, University of California, Berkeley.

Cynthia Humes is a historian of religions specializing in the life of Sanskrit religious texts in modern India. Her current book in progress, *The Glory of the Great Goddess: The Life of the Devi-Mahatmya*, examines the various approaches Hindus have had to this famous

Sanskrit text in the past, and traces some of the changes in its use and interpretation in North India due to social and technological change. Among her research interests are the intersection of religion, economics, and politics; cross-cultural comparisons of goddess worship; issues of gender in world religions (particularly Hinduism), and new Asian religious movements in the Americas. She teaches at Claremont McKenna College and Claremont Graduate School.

Thomas Parkhill completed both of his graduate degrees in Religious Studies at McMaster University. One of his chief research interests is how sacred texts find expression in lived religions. Besides a long-standing interest in the Hindu epics, he studies Native American religions, particularly the Micmac and Maliset religions. He now lives in Fredericton, New Brunswick where he teaches at St. Thomas University and keeps—among other things—a few bees.

Ratnesh Pathak was born and raised in a rigorously religious Hindu family living in the building immediately adjacent to Lolark Kund in Banaras, India. He received his bachelor's degree in Social Studies, History, and Public Administration from Banaras Hindu University, and his M. A. in Sociology from Kashi Vidyapith. Throughout his college studies, he worked as a research assistant for numerous foreign scholars coming to study Hindu religion in Banaras, and it is now a senior executive in a New Delhi export business.

Dana W. Sawyer is a historian of Asian religions and teaches in the B. F. A. program at the Portland School of Art. He also teaches a required Master's of Divinity course in World Religions at Bangor Theological Seminary. His research interests include the history and practices of India's Dandi Sannyasins, the Divine Life Society of Swami Shivananda, and the general increase of Asian religious practices in the United States today. He is currently finishing *Taoism, Zen, and the Maine Woods* for Walker and Co. Publishers of New York.

Richard Schechner is Professor of Performance Studies at the Tisch School of the Arts at New York University. He has written extensively on the Ramnagar *Ramlila* and his recent publications include *The Future of Ritual* published by Rutledge Press. During the summer of 1992, he became the first person to direct an African-American play in South Africa.

Mary Searle-Chatterjee studied philosophy and anthropology at the University of Nottingham and Manchester in the United Kingdom, and in 1963 went as a Commonwealth Scholar to study at Banaras Hindu University where she was awarded an M. A. in Indian Philosophy and Religion and, later, a Ph.D. in Sociology. She subsequently lectured at Banaras Hindu University for three years, spending, in all, nine years in that city. She has since taught at the universities of Bristol and Manchester and is now based at Manchester Polytechnic. Her publications include *Reversible Sex Roles—the Special Case of Banaras Sweepers* for Pargamon Press and articles and book chapters on caste and religion in India. Her current research interest, one reflected in her contribution to this volume, is ethnicity and religious sectarianism.

Beth Lee Simon specializes in the fields of South Asia Studies and socio-linguistics. She is engaged in a number of research projects in socio-linguistics and dialects within the Department of English at the University of Wisconsin, Madison, specifically pertaining to code-switching and discourse analysis. She also teaches at Edgewood College.

Index

Aditya: in battle with Shiva, 209-210; pilgrimage of the twelve in Banaras, 14, 206-207. *See also* Lolark; Surya

Advaita philosophy: and Dandi monasticism, 11, 164; influence on *Ramcharitmanas*, 84; and *maya*, 85; and Shaktism, 182

Aghori Tantra, 238-240

Akbar, 153-54

Akhara: description of, 129-31; photo 130. *See also* Hanuman; Wrestling

Annakut, 187, 189, 199

Antargriha, 7

Arati: and neighborhood *Ramlilas*, 109, 112, 113; and Ramnagar *Ramlila*, 48, 59, photo 60, 61, 63, 65, 66, 69, 93, 95, 96

Arka Vinayaka, 215

Ashvamedha Yajna: 46, 47

Asi *Ramlila*, 74

Asi River: and the *aditya* Lolark, 205, 210-11, 240

Asisangameshvara, 207, 240

Astrology, 148, 235, 247

Aurangzeb: destroyed Akbar's building, 153-54; symbolic narratives on, 10, 11, 146, 149, 151-55, 157

Avimukta: 1, *kosha* of Banaras, 7

Baburi Mosque, 156

Bahri Alang, 127, 143

Banaras: as archetypical Hindu Place, 2, 3, 7; *bahri alang*, 127, 143; beauty and holiness of, 1, 55, 205, 211, 240; as center of earth, 143; as City of Light, 1, 4, 205, 211; as City of Shiva, 121, 206, 211, 238; as City of Vishnu, 210; duplication of, 2; as goddess, 1, 207, 211; illness and death defeated in, 247; includes all *tirthas*, 2, 7, 181; mythical identity with, 2; sacred geography of, 1, 19; as Shiva's cremation ground, 3; as *tirtha* of the gods, 1, 181, 184, 186, 188, 189, 190, 201. *See also* Banarsi Culture

Banaras, Maharajas (kings) of: legitimizing rule through *Ramlila* ritual, 5-6, 23-24, 44, 46-47, 65-67; patronage of *Ramlila*, 22, 24, 37, 44-47, 48, 51, 52, 61, 65-67, 74, 90, 112, 219; patronage of temples, 184, 215, 217-19, 220, 225, 239; and *Ramlila*, 37, photo 40, 41, 74, 113; as representative of Shiva, 61

Banarsi Boli: and "Banarsi" identity, 15-16, 255-57, 261-62; definition of, 248; and gender, 250-51; and Hindu identity 15-16, 247-49, 262; and language status, 16, 250; Muslims and, 251-52; as unifier of Hindu and Muslim Banarsis, 15-16, 246. *See also* Language

Banarsi Culture: in battle for self-preservation, 127-28, 135, 136, 137, 143; diversity of, 245-46; as Hindu ideal, 3, 9-10, 17, 127-28; language use and linguistic diversity, 15-16, 245-46, 255-57, 261-62. *See also* "Disco"

Banarsis, *Pakka*: 190–91, 238–39, 247; and Muslims, 251–52

Bateson, Gregory, 88–90

Bathing: and astrology, 235; in Banaras, 3, 16, 127, 205; and devotees' marriage to Shiva, 212, 225–26, photo 227; in Ganges, 147, 162, 232–34; at Lolark Kund, 14, 211, 215, 230, 232–34; and purity, 117, 205; and Sun worship, 205–206

Bhaddar. See Religious Functionaries

Bhakti: and Hanuman in wrestling, 138, 139–41; and *Ramcharitmanas*, 78, 83, 85; and Shiva, 208, 209–11, 212; theological interpretation of, 92; and goddess, 194

Bharat Milap: of Nati Imli *Ramlila*, 48; of Ramnagar *Ramlila*, 23 29, 57, photo 58, 65

Bhojpuri, 248, 249–50

Brahmacharya (celibacy): of Ghazi Miyan, 157; and Hanuman, 138, 140–41, 142; initiation period of, 162; and wrestling, 134, 138, 140–41, 142

Brahman, 85

British: and communal division, 154; and *Ramlila*, 64; and Ramraj imagery 49

Buddhism, Buddhist: monasticism, 176; temple ruins, 154

caste: 194; and divisions among ascetics, 11, 162–63, 166, 179n.14, 180n.20; non-*Brahminical* rituals, 212, 219, 223, 226; specific worship patterns, 13, 189, 193, 198–201

Chaitganj *Ramlila*, 107–108

Chathi, 190. See also *Lalahi Chath*; *Lolark Chath*

Chitrakut *Ramlila*, 107 111, 115

Code-switching, 16; Banarsi identity and marked, 257–62; Banarsi identity and unmarked, 255;

definition of intersentential, 257; definition of unmarked and marked, 254

Communal violence: 10; and the British, 154; dispute over Jnan Vapi, 149, 151, 152, 153–54, 156; and *Ramlila*, 8, 117–120

Cremation grounds: Banaras as "Great Cremation Ground," 3; Burning ghats, 2

Dandi Monasteries (*maths*): appendix of those surveyed, 177–78; and gender, 162, 166, 178n.3; ideal and real structures of, 163–66; and lay disciples, 166, 170

Dandi Sannyasins: and caste, 11, 159, 162–63, 166, 176, 179n.14, 180n.20; deity worship and, 163; founding of, 159; and gender, 11, 162, 166, 176, 178n.3; internal division of, 171, 173, 174–75; photos, 160, 161, 168, 169; significance of Banaras for, 159, 175

Dante, 76

Darshan, 200; of Banaras as that of all the Hindu world, 3; of goddess mask, 186, 235, photo 237; of gurus, 167; at neighborhood *Ramlilas*, 111, 115; at Ramnagar *Ramlila*, 59, 61, 65, 66, 90, 92, 95–96

Dashahara: and Ramnagar *Ramlila*, 37, 46–48; photos, 38, 39, 40, 42

Dasnami Sadhus, 162, 164–65

Death: in Banaras, liberation by 3; and burning ghats, 2

Devi Bhagavata Purana, 231

Devotionalism. See *Bhakti*

Dham: 55, 234; Banaras contains all four, 2

Diglossia, 252–53

Digvijaya, 46–47

"Disco" 8, 9–10, 110–11, 115, 128, 135, 137, 142

Divodasa, 211
Dumont, Louis, 7
Durga, 13, 46–47, 184–86, 188, 200, 205. *See also* Vindhyavasini
Durga Kund Temple, 118, 184–86, 188
Durgapuja: and Ramnagar *Ramlila*, 46–47. *See also* Navratra
Durga Saptashati, 195, 199

Eck, Diana, 2, 185, 240
Economics: and change at goddess temples, 188, 190, 191–92; and change at Ramnagar *Ramlila*, 41, photo 42, 48, 51; and integration with Hindu "religion," 4, 24; of pilgrimage for Banaras, 246; system at Lolark Kund, 219–230, 235; and temple building or adding icons, 12, 13–14, 15, 190, 196, 197, 235, 238
Encompassment: 6–8; of all tirthas or worlds through Ramnagar *Ramlila*, 20–21, 41, 52–53, 67; of five *koshas* of Banaras, 8; and Hinduism, 7, 10; of language categories, 16; of many cultures in Ramnagar *Ramlila*, 63–64; of varying meanings and experiences in the *Ramlila*, 49

Film posters, 140
Fire-water Symbolism, 205–206, 212, 232–34
Folksinging: 230, Bhajan, 104, 113, 114, 127; Jagrata, 197–99; Kajali, 238; Kirtan, 22, 53, 92; Mata Git, 238; Qawwali, 150, 239; Sohar, 225, 238
Frame(s): demonstrative of *maya* and *lila*, 6, 84, 86, 87–97; as "ghats" of *Manas* Lake, 77; God's body as ultimate, 83; of the *Ramcharitmanas*, diagrams 76 and 77; and Ramnagar *Ramlila*, 91, 96

Gahadavalas, 217
Gandhi, Mahatma, 49, 265n.14
Ganesh, 212, temple photo 214, 215, photo 216
Ganges: and *aditya* Lolark, 205, 212; burning ghats on, 2; fertility rituals and, 233–34; icons found in, 192, 194–95; purificatory rituals and, 3, 136–37, 147 162; Ramnagar *Ramlila* and, 19, 41, 44, photo 45, 49, 53, photo 54, 55, 71n.6, 90–91, 96, 103
Gayatri Mantra, 206, 230
Gender: and *Dandi* monasticism, 11, 162, 166, 176, 178n.3; literacy and language use, 199, 250–51, 253–54, 266–67n.22, 267n.24; and *Ramlila*, 8, 10. *See also* Women
Ghazi Miyan: cult of, 150–52; as first Muslim Banarsi, 147; symbolic narratives on, 10–11, 146–50; 157; worshiped by both Hindus and Muslims, 150
Ghaznavi, Mahmud: symbolic narratives on, 146–47, 149
Goddess, Great Goddess: 181–82, 183–84. *See also* Shaktism
Goffman, Erving, 87–88, 90
Guruism, 12, 162, 166
Gurus: rivalry among, 174

Hanuman: and *bhakti*, 138, 139–41; and *Brahmacharya*, 138, 140–41, 142; and ethical nationalism, 8, 10, 141–43; as icon, 137–41; wrestlers' worship of, 131, 139; Sankat Mochan Temple, 59, 74; and *shakti*, 138–41; temples in Banaras, 137–38
Hess, Linda, 52, 67, 69
Hijras: at Lolark Kund, 223, 225, 228, 239–40; in *Ramlila*, 109, 113, 114, 121
Hindi: and Banarsi Boli, 15–16; and Hindu identity, 247–49. *See also* Banarsi Boli; Language

Hindu Crusaders: Shivaji and
Marathas, 11, 154 155; and
wrestling, 135–36
Hindu Nationalism, 10, 120, 134–37,
141–43, 239
Hinduism: varied meanings of
term, 7; as integrative way of life,
3–4, 7
Hindu Trinity: and Surya, 206, 208
Hofstadter, Douglas, 82
Holkar, Queen Ahalya Bai, 217
Human sacrifice, 148, 151

Innovation: in *Ramlila*, 8, 9, 10, 64,
104, 107 109, 111, 112, 114, 115,
121; in Ramnagar *Ramlila*, 24, 26,
32, 90, 112

James, William, 87–88
Jhanki: in *Ramlila*, photo 60, 61, 93,
94, 113
Jihad, 156
Jnan Vapi, 149, 151, 152, 153–54, 156
Jyotirlinga, 2

Karahiya, 228, photos 218 and 222
Karinda. See Religious Functionaries
Karpatri (Swami Hariharananda
Saraswati): 170–71, 173; photo of
Dharma Sangh monastery of, 161
Kashi: as outermost *kosha*, 7
Kashi Khand: and Lolark Kund, 205,
207, 208, 211, 221, 230, 234, 240;
used to glorify Vindhyavasini
temples, 13, 184–86, 187, 188,
193–94, 201
Kathavachak, 74
Kedar Nath Temple: 152, and
Vindhyavasini, 186–87
Khatri caste, 13, 198–201
Khojwan *Ramlila*, 107, 108, 109, 112,
115
Kinaram, Baba, 238–240

Koshas: pilgrimage of the five, 7
Kot Vidai: 66–67
Krishna: and Vindhyavasini, 182–83,
189–90, 197
Kumar, Nita, 128, 143

Lalahi Chath, 230–31, 232
Lallapur *Ramlila*, 117–19, photos,
105 and 106
Language: and gender, 199, 250–51,
253–54, 266n.22, 267n.24; and
religion, 4, 16, 150, 251–52; as
symbols of social norms, 257,
261–62. See also Banarsi Boli
Lat Bhairav: *Ramlila*, 108, 119–20;
Temple, 152
Lila: Vaishnava theological views of,
84–85; multivalency of *Ramlila* as,
67
Lingam of Light, 2–3, 208
Lingam of Shiva, 59, 208, 210, 226,
234, 235, photo 236, 238
Lolark: as devotee of goddess
Kashi, 211; in *Kashi Khand*, 205,
207, 208, 211, 221, 230, 234, 240;
as "Lola [Lulad] Ravi," 209, 210,
211, 212, 240; protecting Banaras
tirthas, 205, 211; significance of
the name, 210–11, 212, 241n.2
Lolark Baba, 208, 226, 235, 238
Lolark Chath Mela, 14, 208, 212,
photo 213, 228
Lolarkeshvara, "Lord of Lolark": 14,
208; devotees' marriage to, 14,
212, 225–26, photo 227, 232–34;
and fusion with Surya-Agni, 14,
208, 212; as "Lolark Baba," 208,
226, 235, 238; overpowering Vedic
sacrifice, 209–11. See also Shiva
Lolark Kund: 14–15, description,
212–19; fertility rituals at, 14
221–28, 233–34, 235, 239; healing
waters of, 215, 221, 230, 234;
photos, 213, 214, 216, 218, 222,
224, 227 229, 236, 237; ritual life

of, 219–230, 235. See also *Lalahi Chath Mela; Lolark Chath Mela; Lolarkeshvara; Lolark Mayee; Shiva*
Lolark Mayee, 235, 238; photo, 237
Lutgendorf, Philip, 75–76, 115, 116, 117

Madhyameshvara, 7
Mahabharata, 47, 231, 232
Maharishi Mahesh Yogi, 167, 170–71, 180n.20
Mahatmya: "glorifications" used to establish Hindu Place, 12–14, 184–85, 186, 188, 191–92, 193–94, 197, 201, 211
Mahishasura, 46–47
Mahishasuramardini, 217, 219
Mallah. See Religious Functionaries
Margashirsha: astral myth of, 209; and bathing at Lolark, 211, 230, 233
Matri Kund *Ramlila*, 118
Maunji *Ramlila*, 108
Maya: and *Lila*, 84–85; multivalency of *Ramlila* as, 67; in theological context of *Ramcharitmanas*, 6, 81–90
Mirapur *Ramlila*, 108, 109 110, 113
Miyan, Ghazi. See Ghazi Miyan
Mobius effect: applied to Hindu concepts, 82, 83, 86–87, 92–93
Modernization: 8–9, 238; and *Ramlila*, 41, 51; and wrestling, 141, 143. See also "Disco"; Economics
Moksha: granted by Shiva in Banaras, 3
Mundan: at Lolark Kund, 15, 228, photo 229, 230; at Vindhyachal, 184
Muslim(s): and Banarsi identity, 8, 251–52, 124n.27, 156, 245–46, 251–52, 258–62; and Hindu encounters, 49–50, 117–120, 145–58; iconoclasm, 148, 152; language choice, 15–16, 150, 251–52;

and *Ramlila*, 49–50, 64, 117–20; worship of Ghazi, Miyan, 150

Nationalism: 239, and wrestling, 10, 127, 137, 141–43
Natyashastra, 50–51
Nau. See Religious Functionaries
Navratra, 46–47, 183, 186, 187, 199–200, 217. See also *Dashahara*
Nemi, 5, 53, 66, 69
Nirguna Philosophy: and *Ramcharitmanas*, 78, 83–85. See also Vaishnava Theism

O'Flaherty, Wendy Doniger: and Mobius Effect, 82, 86–87; and Shiva-Surya, 205, 208–9

"*Pakka*" Banarsis: 190–91, 238–39, 247; and Muslims, 251–52
Panchakroshi Pilgrimage, 8, 151
Panchatirtha Pilgrimage, 207
Panchayatana Puja, 206
Panda. See Religious Functionaries
Participant-pilgrims, 5, 55–59 91
Patronage by Royalty: at Lolark Kund, 215, 217–19, 220, 225; and *Ramlila*, 22, 24, 37 44–47, 48, 51, 52, 61, 65–67, 74, 90, 112; and Vindhyavasini, 184
Pilgrimage; from Banaras to Vindhyachal, 191, 198–99; *Chaurasi Kroshi Parikrama*, 184; of five *koshas* in Banaras, 7; of gods to Banaras, 1, 181, 184, 186, 189, 193, 201; multiple motives for, 53, 67, 191; *Panchakroshi*, 8, 151; *Panchatirtha*, 207; process, 14, 189, 191, 192, 196, 197, 200, 240; and Ramnagar *Ramlila*, 21, 29 48, 53, 55; and tourism, 191; of twelve *adityas* in Banaras, 14, 206–207

Place: use of *Ramlila* ritual to establish, 8, 52, 53, 64, 116, 118–21; use of texts to establish, 12–13, 157, 184–85, 186, 188, 193–94, 201

Politics. *See* Banaras, Maharajas (kings) of

Possession: by the goddess, 195, 196–97, 253

Prinsep, James, 42

Ram: and devotees, 41, 85, 94; and movement, 5–6, 19–21, 24, 46–48, 52, 55–56, 61, 63, 64, 67, 69–70n.1; and relation to Shiva (Shankara), 49; as transcendent yet incarnate, 78, 82–83, 84–86, 89–90

Ram, Mansa, 44

Ramayana: Indo-European nature of, 20–21; significance of title of, 20; spread through Sanskritization, 63; varieties of, 64

Ramcharitmanas: and Advaita, 84; and *Bhakti*, 78, 83; Encapsulation of, 272–78; fixity of, 115; framing of, 6, 75ff; and paradox, 82; popularity of, 4, 22; and *Qawwali*, 239; and *Ramlila*, 4, 47, 74, 91; significance of title of, 77, 84, 91; Tulsidas within the, 80

Ramlila: of Asighat, 74; and Banaras, 74, 104, 115, 247; *Bharat Milap* in, 23, 29, 48, 57, photo 58, 65; of Chaitganj, 107–108; of Chitrakut, 107, 111, 115; and "disco", 8, 9–10, 110–11, 115; innovation and traditionalism in, 64, 104, 107, 109, 111, 112, 114, 115, 121; of Khojwan, 107, 108, 109, 112, 115; of Lallapur, photo 105, photo 106, 117–19; of Lat Bhairav, 108, 119–20; and literary and performative texts, 21–22, 50–51; m(t)aking Hindu Place by, 8, 52, 53, 64, 116, 118–21; of Matri

Kund, 118; of Maunji, 108; of Mirapur, 108, 109, 110, 113; and Muslims, 44, 49–50, 117–20; of Nati Imli, 48; overturning ideas of times and space, 74, 91–92; of Ramnagar, *see* Ramnagar *Ramlila*; as ritual or sacrifice, 111, 112, 115, 116, 120–21; sacred geography of, 20, 118; theological interpretation of, 5–6, 20–21, 55–56, 91; of Tulsighat, 111; of Varunapul, 108, 109, 112, 113; and verisimilitude, 35, 52, 92; and Westernization, 121; and wrestlers, 9, 10, 120

Ramnagar *Ramlila*: as commentary on *Ramcharitmanas*, 74, 91; economics and change at, 41, photo 42, 48, 51; experience for participants, 5, 6, 29, 48, 49, 52–53, 55–59, 91, 94–96; founding of, 5–6, 44, 46–47; and India's *tirthas*, 20–21, 41, 52–53, 55, 57, 67; and Muslims, 44, 49–50, 64; photos, 25, 26, 27, 28, 30, 31, 33, 34, 36, 38, 39, 40, 42, 43, 45, 54, 56, 58, 60, 62, 68; as prototype, 6, 48, 107, 111, 112, 113–14, 115; as ritual or sacrifice, 4, 50–51, 63; theatrical structure and symbolic geography of, 23–44, 50–51, 64, 67; theatrical structure as demonstrating *maya* and *lila*, 90–97; theatrical structure as model of *Ramcharitmanas*, 29; theological interpretation of, 5, 21, 41, 48, 52, 55–56, 61, 63, 64; Thirty-One Day Program of the, 269–72

Ramraj, 21, 23, 24, 49–50

Religion: definitions of, 7

Religious functionaries: at Banaras Vindhyavasini temples, 183, 185, 186, 188, 191, 192, 194, 196–97; at Lolark Kund, 15, 219–30

Ritual: *Annakut*, 187, 189, 199; *Ashvameda*, 46, 47; Death, 2, 3; *Digvijaya*, 46–47; fertility, 14, 221–28, 233–34, 239; healing, 13, 14, 196–97, 200, 215, 221, 230, 234: human sacrifice, 148, 151; *Karahiya*, 228, photos 218, 222; marriage to Shiva, 14, 212, 225–26, photo 227, 232–34; non-Brahminical, 212, 219, 223, 226; purification, 3, 117, 136–37, 147, 162, 205; *Mundan*: 15, 184, 228, photo 229, 230; *Panchayatana Puja*, 206; *Ramlila* as, 4, 50–51, 63, 111, 112, 115, 116, 120–21; thanksgiving, 226, 228; and theater, 51; *Totaka*, 212, 223, 225–26; as unifier and divider, 8; weapons worship, 6, 46–47. *See also Arati*; Bathing; *Darshan*; *Navratra*

Sacred: 116–17; city 1, 55; definition of, 4; and wrestlers, 120
Sadhus: 74, 104, 107, 110, 154; and Ramnagar *Ramlila*, 48–49, 55, 61, photo 62, 69, photo, 94, 95. See also *Dandi Sannyasins*
Saguna philosophy: and *Ramcharitmanas*, 78, 83–86, 89–90
Sai Baba, 167
Samvad: fluidity of, 114; as frames of *Ramcharitmanas*, 75; of Ramnagar *Ramlila*, 22, 24
Sandhya Puja, 53, 59, 92
Sankat Mochan Temple, 59, 74
Sannyasins: See *Dandi Sannyasins*; *sadhus*
Sanskritization: and spread of *Ramayana*, 63
Sanskrit Texts: in translation, 199; used to establish Hindu Place, 12–14, 184–85, 186, 188, 193–94, 201, 211
Sax, William S., 46–47, 55
Schechner, Richard, 90
Shaiva Ascetics, 162–65. See also *Dandi Sannyasins*

Shaiva Worship. *See* Shiva
Shakti: 32; and Hanuman, 138–41
Shaktism: 181–82, 195, 238
Shankara (philosopher): 151, and Advaita, 85, 182; and *Dandi sannyasins*, 11–12, 159, 164–65; and guruism, 175–77; and *panchayatana puja*, 206
Shankaracharyas, 12, 159, 164, 165, 170–71, 173, 175–76
Shashti Devi, 230–31, 232
Shitala Temple: and connections to Lolark Kund, 221; and Vindhyavasini, 194–96
Shiva: Banaras king as his representative, 61; grants *moksha* in Banaras, 3; and, Ganges River, 234; *lingam* worship, 59, 208, 234, 235, photo 236, 238; as "navel of Kashi," 7; and Somnath, 145, 147, 148, 149; as Vishvanath, 145, 152–58. *See also* Lolarkeshvara
Shivaji, 11, 154
Shivananda, Swami, 167
Shruti, 175
Singh, Balwant, 24, 44
Singh, C. P. N. Narain, 32
Singh, Ishvari Prasad Narain, 24
Singh, Vibhuti Narain, 24, 26, 32, photo 43, 67, 69, 122–23n.15
Sita, 35, 61, 63
Skanda: at Lolark Kund, 232–34; and wife Shashti Devi, 231
Smith, Jonathon, Z., 116–17
Smriti, 175
Somnath (also Someshvara), 145, 147, 148, 149, 151, 157
Sun. See *Aditya*; Lolark; Surya
Surya: and the Hindu Trinity, 206, 207; relation to Shiva, 206–211; solar worship, 14, 205–208
Svarup: theological interpretations of the *Ramlila* actors as, 48, 59, photo 60, 61, 66–67, 90, 94–95, 104, photo 105, photo 106, 112, 115–16, 117, 119, 120
Svayambhu icons, 3, 186, 188, 193, 198

Tantric, 239, 243n.15, 253
Tapasya: 48, and Shiva, 208
Temples: building or adding icons
  at, 12, 13–14, 15, 190, 196, 197,
  235, 238; and caste, 13, 189, 193,
  198–201; "regional," in Banaras, 2;
  and spatial organization, 13–14,
  189, 191. See also Economics
Theater: as worship, 4, 50–51, 63.
  See also Ramlila; Ramnagar
  Ramlila
Tirtha(s): Banaras as most sacred,
  181, 184; Banaras as prototype, 2,
  3, 6, 7; Banaras contains all, 2;
  Lolark protects purity of Banaras,
  205, 211
Totaka, 212, 223, 225–26
Tulsidas, 4, 80
Tulsidas Temple, 73, 207
Tulsighat Ramlila, 111
Twain, Mark, 172

Upanishads, 175

Vaishnava theism, 84–86, 89–90
Vamana Purana, 208–211
Varanasi: as kosha, 7
Varunapul Ramlila, 108, 109, 112, 113
Vijayadashami. See Dashahara
Vinayakas: worship of the, 56, 215
Vindhyavasini: appearing to
  devotees, 183, 192, 193–94, 196,
  197, 200, 201; birthday of, 187,
  189–90, 195; at Durga Kund
  Temple, 184–86; and Kashi Khand,

13, 184–86, 187, 188, 193–94, 201;
  at Kashipura Temple, 192–94; at
  Kedar Nath Temple, 186–87; and
  Krishna, 182–83, 197; at Inglishiya
  Line Temple, 196–200; and
  "pakka" Banarsis, 190–91; as a
  pilgrim in Banaras, 181, 184, 186,
  189, 193, 201; near Sankata
  Temple, 188–92; and Sharada,
  190, 191; at Shitala Temple,
  194–96
Vindhyeshvari Chalisa, 186, 190, 195
Vishnu: and expansion of space
  and time, 5–6, 19–20, 46–47, 52,
  67, 69–70n.1. See also Mobius
  Effects; Vaishnava Theism
Vishvanath: 7, 145, as innermost
  kosha of Banaras, 7; Temple, 55,
  152–58
Vyas, 66, 108

Weapons worship, 6, 46–47
Women: and religion, 10, 11,
  109–110, 157, 162, 166, 178n.3,
  196–200, 220, 235,238
Wrestling: and Brahmacharya, 134,
  138, 140–41, 142; and crusading
  Hindu Nationalism, 10, 120,
  134–37, 141–43; daily regimen of,
  131–34; as devotional worship, 4,
  138, 139–41; ideology of, 127–28,
  141; and Ramlila, 9, 10, 120; and
  shakti, 138–41

Yuga, 69